[*Yale Studies in English, Vol. 69*]

SBN: 208 00765 2
Library of Congress Catalog Card Number: 69-15688
Printed in the United States of America

THE LIFE AND PO
NICHOLAS GRIM

BY

L. R. MERRILL

ARCHON BOOKS
1969

PREFACE

TO-DAY the name of Nicholas Grimald is almost unknown even to the students of sixteenth-century literature: Warton's *History of English Poetry* devotes but seven pages to an account of his work, and these are filled for the most part with quotations from it; while Courthope's *History of English Poetry,* and the *Cambridge History of English Literature,* give much less space to him. Even less is known about his life than his work. Edward Arber, in the preface to his edition of *Tottel's Miscellany,* makes a mistake as to the identity of the poet; while the brief account of him given in the *Dictionary of National Biography* is not altogether correct in regard to the facts of his life. Although Grimald has become but a mere name, or, at most, but a shadowy figure, on the pages of literary history, he is a personage of real consequence, a very vital force, not only in English literary history, but in that of the Continent as well. As teacher, poet, translator, preacher, and dramatist, he made his mark, a mark that has endured; and although his work is well-nigh forgotten, it is of no less significance.

In his day Grimald was regarded as the foremost alumnus of Cambridge, and one of the greatest scholars in England. Next to Sir Thomas Wyatt and Henry Howard, Earl of Surrey, he was the principal contributor to the first printed anthology of English poetry, then known as *Songes and Sonettes,* now known as *Tottel's Miscellany,* the first and by far the most popular of the early anthologies. The sonnets which he and other poets contributed to this volume were the first published compositions of this sort in the English language, while his two poems in blank verse, included in the book, were possibly the first ever seen in England. As a contributor to this volume, and as a teacher of rhetoric in Christ Church, Oxford, he probably did more to influence the new movement in poetry, and to popularize the new verse-forms which came from the Continent, than did any other poet of his time. As an avowed apostle of humanism, he did a great service to the English people in his translations from the Classics, especially by his English version of Cicero's *De Officiis,* which was long the standard translation in England. His Latin tragedy, *Archipropheta,* one of the first tragedies known to have been written by an Englishman, far surpasses any previous effort in the field of English drama; while his Latin tragi-comedy, *Christus Redivivus,* has had an influence lasting almost down to our own time, since it was the principal source of the oldest known version of the Oberammergau Passion Play.

It has been the object of this dissertation to present a life of Grimald, the facts of which have not been known; to reproduce the text of his two Latin dramas, *Christus Redivivus* and *Archipropheta,* the latter of which has been inaccessible to students of early sixteenth-century drama; and to present both of these plays in translation.

Many thanks for advice and assistance are due to Professor John M. Berdan, under whose guidance this dissertation has been written, and also to Professors Albert S. Cook, George L. Hendrickson, C. F. Tucker Brooke, Messrs. William A. Speck and Hoyt H. Hudson, and the Reverend William M. Noble.

CONTENTS

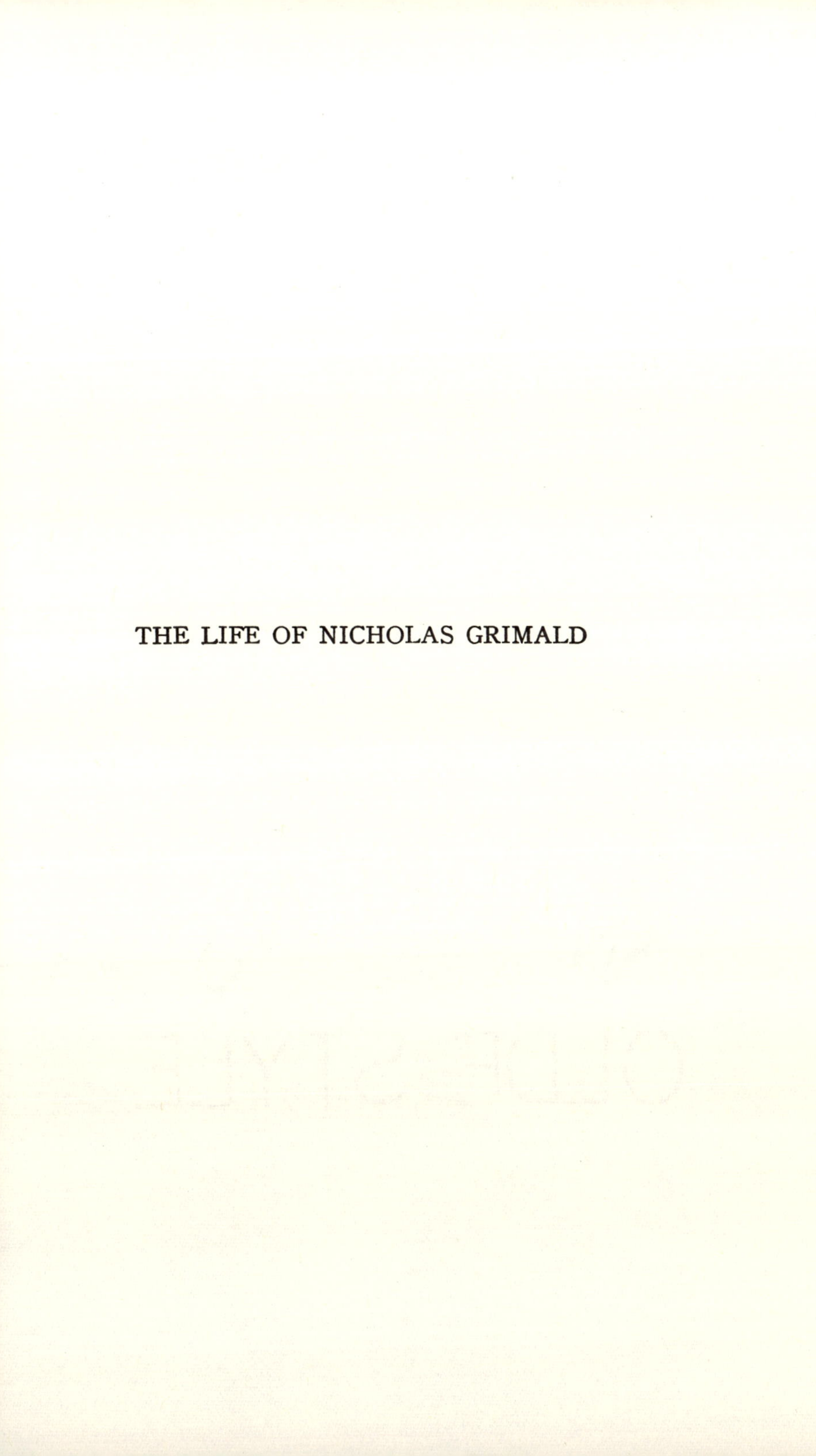

THE LIFE OF NICHOLAS GRIMALD

THE LIFE OF NICHOLAS GRIMALD

The latter part of the reign of Henry VII of England was a very peaceful one, for he was on friendly terms with his neighbors. Since he was no longer harassed with wars, he gave full vent to his passion for money-getting, and indulged it to such an extent that by the end of his reign he had accumulated an enormous fortune. His chief instruments in the collection of this hoard were Sir Richard Empson and Edmond Dudley, who caused wealthy subjects to be accused of violation of the laws. These victims, who were discovered by a sort of accuser, called a promoter, were brought before Empson and Dudley, whom the King had made his 'masters and surveyors of forfeits.' Their method was to compel the accused to present himself before them, not in a public court, but in one held in their own homes, where they dealt with him summarily, and extorted from him great fines. In their eagerness to find victims, they revived long-forgotten laws, for the breaking of which they spared no one.

When Henry VIII came to the throne, there was so great an outcry against these men that he published a proclamation stating that if any man could prove himself to have been wrongly deprived of his goods, he should present his complaints; he also granted letters patent of general pardon,[1] excepting from it, however, a number of persons to whom he did not dare to extend his clemency. Among these were Empson, Dudley, and one of their promoters, John Baptista Grimaldi. So great a number of complaints were made that the council thought it best to quiet the people by committing Empson and Dudley to the Tower.

Henry VIII was loth to bring to justice these two serv-

[1] *Letters and Papers, Foreign and Domestic, of the Reign of Henry VIII,* 1509-1514, I. 5 [sec. 12].

ants, who had been so diligent in amassing the fortune which he enjoyed spending. The strict execution of laws, however obsolete, could not be imputed to these men as a crime sufficient to be visited with the death-penalty; so, to gratify the people, they were arrested on the charge that, on the death of the late king, they had entered into a conspiracy to seize the government. They were tried, found guilty, and again committed to the Tower. But King Henry, 'riding in his progress for his disport,' was obliged to hear more and more complaints; so, driven by force of public opinion, he sent writs to the Sheriff of London to put the two men to death.

In the meantime, the promoters were treated with no less severity, and with much more indignity, for they were ridden about the city 'with their faces to the horses' tails, and a paper on their heads,' and, after they had been set on a pillory, were brought to Newgate, where they died, as Lord Herbert says,[2] 'all within seven days after for verie shame,' except one, John Baptista Grimaldi, called by Stow 'the most cruel wretch of all,' who, foreseeing the storm, fled to Westminster, and, taking sanctuary there, escaped the penalty for his wrong-doing. Although Grimaldi was excepted from the general pardon, and was the most cruel of all the accusers, King Henry, on February 2, 1510, issued a warrant for his pardon.[3]

Of such a father, the poet, Nicholas Grimald, is said[4] to have been begotten; and, considering the conduct of his life, he might well have come of such stock; however, no records of the time can be found to substantiate this asser-

[2] White Kennett. *A Complete History of England;* Edward, Lord Herbert of Cherbury, *Henry VIII*, London, 1706, 2. 3.

[3] *Letters and Papers, Foreign and Domestic, of the Reign of Henry VIII*, 1509-1514, 1. 129 [sec. 848].

[4] *Dictionary of National Biography*, London, 1890, 23.249; Lewis Einstein, *The Italian Renaissance in England*, London, 1903, pp. 264, 331; Frederick S. Boas, *University Drama in the Tudor Age*, Oxford, 1914, p. 26.

tion, and it does not seem probable. The records of Christ's College, Cambridge, the first college which he attended, are deficient in information regarding his parentage and birthplace, since the entries in the Admission Book of that college concerning those matters do not appear until 1622. The only records of that sort which exist are those of Merton College,[5] Oxford, in which he is described as 'of the diocese of Lincoln,' and those of Christ Church,[6] Oxford, according to which his 'patria' was Huntingdonshire, at that time in the diocese of Lincoln. According to Grimald's own statement in his poem, *A funerall song, upon the death of Annes his moother,*[7] his home was at Brownshold. The sixteenth-century maps of Huntingdonshire, which are most complete, show no such place or estate as Brownshold. There was, however, and still is, a place called Leighton-Bromswold, a few miles northeast of the city of Huntingdon, which can with reasonable certainty be identified with the Brownshold of the poem; and the two different names, Brownshold and Bromswold, may be regarded as variants of many possible ways in which the name may have been spelled in sixteenth-century times, when names seem to have been spelled in every possible way. Leighton-Bromswold is now a small village, of only a very few hundred inhabitants, and of much less importance than it was in the sixteenth century. Its chief claim to literary interest now lies in the fact that George Herbert, the poet, spent the early days of his priesthood there, and the village has a very fine church erected in memory of him.

Unfortunately, no parish registers of so early a date exist in Leighton-Bromswold, for these were not generally kept

[5] Merton College Register, f. 287, Merton College Archives, Oxford.

[6] MS. Wood f. 28, f. 172, also MS. Wood C. 8, Bodleian Library.

[7] Henry Howard, Earl of Surrey, Sir Thomas Wyatt the Elder, Nicholas Grimald, and Uncertain Authors, *Songes and Sonettes,* Arber, London, 1870, p. 115.

throughout the kingdom until 1538, when Cromwell, the Vicar General of Henry VIII, published a royal injunction ordering the clergy to keep registers of all christenings, burials, and weddings. But various legal records that exist of the affairs and transactions in that neighborhood show that the Grimald family had lived there since the days of Henry I,[8] about four hundred years before the days of John Baptista Grimaldi. During these years, the records show many variations in the spelling of the family name, a thing not uncommon in those times. Through these centuries it appears in parish registers and various legal documents, when there can be little doubt that the same family is referred to, as Grymbaud, Grymbold, Grymbolde, Grimbold, Grimald, Grimbald, and Grymbalde. From these records it appears that the Grimalds were a yeoman family, of moderate means, who were engaged in farming. Their name, though of some local consequence, does not appear in any records of the gentry of the county. That this family had any connection with John Baptista Grimaldi, who is said to have been a son of Giovanni Grimaldi of Genoa, a merchant who was made a citizen of England[9] in 1485, does not seem probable.

The only records which give any information as to the date of the poet's birth are those of Christ Church,[10] Oxford, in which he is enrolled in 1547, at the age of twenty-eight. According to this, he was born in 1519-20, the year of the famous Field of the Cloth of Gold. No information in regard to his parentage appears in any of the college records, nor are there any parish registers which chronicle his birth. The only account of his own immediate family is that which appears in the poem on the death of his mother, Annes, who possibly is the Agnes Grymbold whose death

[8] Cotton MS. Faustina C. 1, f. 12. b, Cartulary of the Priory of St. Mary, Huntingdon.

[9] *Calendar of the Patent Rolls, Henry VII,* 2 [1476-85]. 496.

[10] MS. Wood C. 8, Bodleian Library.

was recorded in 1555 in the parish register of Winwick, Huntingdonshire, a little village where the Grimald family flourished. This village is not far from Leighton-Bromswold, and lies on the same ridge of low hills on which Leighton lies. The name of Grimald in all its variant spellings is so common in the early records of Ellington, Old Weston, and Barham, near-by hamlets, that it does not seem necessary to ascribe to it an Italian origin.

The sole account that we have of the poet's youthful days is to be found in the following lines, quoted from the poem mentioned above, *A funerall song, upon the death of Annes his moother:*

> Should I not expresse my inward wo,
> When you, most lovyng dam, so soon hence go.
> I, in your frutefull woomb conceyved, born was,
> Whyle wanderyng moon ten months did overpasse.
> Mee, brought to light, your tender arms sustaynd:
> And, with my lips, your milky paps I straynd.
> You mee embraced, in bosom soft you mee
> Cherished, as I your onely chylde had bee.
> Of yssue fayr with noombers were you blest:
> Yet I, the bestbeloved of all the rest.
> Good luck, certayn, forereadyng moothers have,
> And you of mee a speciall judgement gave.
> Then, when firm pase I fixed on the ground:
> When toung gan cease to break the lispyng sound:
> You mee streightway did too the Muses send,
> Ne suffered long a loyteryng lyfe to spend,
> What gayn the wooll, what gayn the wed had braught,
> It was his meed, that me there dayly taught.
> When with Minerve I had acquaintance woon:
> And Phebus seemd to love mee, as his soon:
> Browns hold I had at parents hest, farewell:
> And gladly there in schools I gan to dwell:
> Where Granta gives the ladies nyne such place,
> That they rejoyse to see theyr blissful case.
> With joyes at hert, in this pernasse I bode,
> Whyle, through his signes, five tymes great Titan glode:
> And twyse as long, by that fayr foord, whereas

Swanfeeder Temms no furder course can passe.
O, what desire had you, therwhile, of mee?
Mid doutfull dreeds, what joyes were wont to bee?
Now linnen clothes, wrought with those fyngers fyne,
Now other thynges of yours dyd you make myne:
Tyll your last thredes gan Clotho to untwyne,
And of your dayes the date extreem assygne.
Hearyng the chaunce, your neybours made much mone:
A dearworth dame, they thought theyr comfort gone.
Kinswoomen wept: your charge, the maydens wept:
Your daughters wept, whom you so well had kept.
But my good syre gave, with soft woords, releef:
And clokes, with outward chere, his inward greef:
Leste by his care, your sickness should augment,
And on his case your thoughtful hert be bent.
You, not forgetting yet a moothers mood,
When at the dore dartthirling death there stood,
Did saye: Adeew, dear spouse, my race is roon:
Wher so he bee, I have left you a soon,
And Nicolas you naamd, and naamd agayn:
With other speech, aspiring heavenly raign:
When into ayre your sprite departed fled,
And left the corps a cold in lukewarm bed.
Ah, could you thus, deare mother, leave us all?
Now, should you live: that yet, before you fall,
My songs you might have soong, have heard my voyce,
And in commodities of your own rejoyce:
My sisters yet unwedded who shall guide?
With whose good lessons shall they bee applyed?
Have, mother, monuments of our sore smart:
No costly tomb, areard with curious art:
Nor Mausolean masse, hoong in the ayre:
Nor loftie steeples, that will once appayre:
But waylful verse, and doolful song accept.

In the poem quoted above, Grimald devotes but a few lines to his father, but in these he gives a picture of a loving and devoted husband. That he was a farmer and a raiser of sheep is evident, since the poet says:

What gayn the wooll, what gayn the wed had braught,
It was his meed, that me there taught.

As to his mother, he leaves the reader in no doubt in regard to her splendid character, and as to his parents' love and devotion to one another. He says that he was the best beloved of all the children. Probably this was, as he intimates, because he was the only son among a large family of girls. His mother fancied that he would have a brilliant future, and so, at an early age, at a time when most children were at play, she set him at his studies. As soon as he showed signs of poetic talent, she sent him to Cambridge, though at the cost of much anguish to herself at the separation from her only boy, who was at this time fifteen years old.

At Cambridge he remained 'whyle, through his signes, five tymes great Titan glode,' and was graduated from Christ's College with the degree of B.A. in 1539-40. The College's books show no record of him or of his work other than his having paid for his commons,[11] of money being allowed in lieu of commons that he could not eat when he was ill,[12] of his petition having been granted for admission to the final examination for the degree of B.A.,[13] and of the degree having been granted.[14]

The following year he went to Oxford. This he did at the earnest request of Gilbert Smith, 'clerc prebendarye[15] of the prebend of Leighton-Bromswold, within the cathedral church of Lincoln in the county of Huntingdon,' to whom he says he owed his food, books,[16] in short everything need-

11 Mary Bateson, *Grace Book B, containing the Records of the University of Cambridge for the Years 1539-1540*, 2.225.

12 John Peile, *Biographical Register of Christ's College, Cambridge, 1505-1905*, 1.23.

13 W. G. Searle, *Grace Book T, containing the Records of the University of Cambridge for the Years 1501-1542*, p. 342.

14 John Venn, *Grace Book Δ, containing the Records of Cambridge University for the Years 1542-1589*, p. 12.

15 Andrew Clark, *Lincoln Diocese Documents, 1450-1544*, London, 1914, p. 236.

16 Nicholas Grimald, *Christus Redivivus*, Epistola Nuncupatoria, A 3, Cologne, 1543.

ful for his studies. Smith, who was prebendary of Leighton-Bromswold from February 1506-7 to February 1548-9,[17] and who continued to reside there after he rose to the rank of archdeacon,[18] must have known Grimald from earliest boyhood, and have been sufficiently impressed with his abilities to send him to Oxford. For the first month or two while in Oxford, Grimald stayed at Brasenose College, whose first principal had been Matthew Smith,[19] a relative of his benefactor. He was hampered for some weeks in his work, and was unable to continue his course of reading because of the non-arrival of his books. To make up for his interrupted studies he decided to write a drama, which he had had for some time so well in mind that he found the notes he had made for the work were not necessary. In doing so, he got a great deal of encouragement from the president of the college, from some of the teachers, and from the students, who were eager to enter the field of the drama; so, not only in order that he might be busy, but that he might stimulate the minds of the students, and give to the citizens of Oxford some representation of life, he pushed his work on to a conclusion, and completed the play, which was to have no little force and influence upon the drama. This was the Latin resurrection-play, *Christus Redivivus, The Resurrection of Christ,* which he dedicated to his friend and patron, Gilbert Smith, Archdeacon of Peterborough. It is not unlikely that the play was written for presentation at Easter-time; at any rate, the composition of it took place during the winter, for, in his dedicatory epistle to the play, he complains of the difficulty of composition, because of the severity of the winter's cold.

This epistle is rather interesting, not only because he gives in it the foregoing facts in regard to the conditions under

[17] John Le Neve, *Fasti Ecclesiæ Anglicanæ,* 1854, p. 177.

[18] *Valor Ecclesiasticus,* 1821, 27 Henry VIII, p. 257.

[19] Nicholas Grimald, *Christus Redivivus,* Epistola Nuncupatoria, A 4, Cologne, 1543.

which the play was written, but because he sets down a good many of his observations in regard to dramatic art. Although a classical scholar, he commends many things quite distinctive of the romantic drama. He approves of the mixture of elements, the high and the low, the incredible and the probable, the joyous and the sad; in fact, he calls his play a tragi-comedy. He commends a variation in diction to suit the various types of characters, and to suit the situations. He approves of unity of place, because the scenes can then be reduced to one stage-setting. On the other hand, he defends violations of the unity of time, and also the mixture of tragic and comic elements, by quoting classical precedents. No records have been discovered of the production of this play at Oxford, but records of its performance exist in Germany, where it was published at Cologne in 1543, two years later, and apparently widely circulated, since numerous copies exist in the various libraries there. A pirated edition of the play was also brought out at Augsburg, where the play was given in 1556. Not only do the city archives of Augsburg contain an expense-account of the production,[20] but there is a copy of the pirated edition of the play in the Hof-und-Staats Bibliothek in Munich, which has a cast of the persons who appeared in the performance at Augsburg. This is written on the flyleaves of the book, and there is also written in German a synopsis of each act, which synopsis was evidently intended to be recited by *Chorus,* so that those whose knowledge of Latin was imperfect or lacking might more fully understand the contents of the play.

Grimald did not remain longer at Brasenose College than to see his play produced in the spring. Just what his connection with Brasenose was, is not evident; as his name does not appear on the College's books, he could not have been

[20] A further account of the Augsburg production of *Christus Redivivus* will be found in the preface to the translation of that play.

a member of that College, but was probably merely a lodger there, for in those days, if a college had rooms to spare, it let them to any university men.

In April of that year (1542), when he was twenty-three years old, he obtained the degree of B.A. at Oxford,[21] a degree that was necessary if he wished to enter Merton College, which was evidently his intention; for on May 5, 1542, he was chosen probationer-fellow[22] of that College. In 1544 he received his degree of M.A.[23] at Merton, and the same year returned to Cambridge, where he also received the degree of M.A.[24] at Christ's College.

How Grimald spent the next two or three years after taking his degree at Cambridge is not known, but it is likely that he returned soon after to Oxford, since he entered that University in 1541, and probably left it when he was licensed to preach in January 1551-2;[25] for having remained in all ten years, as he says, 'by that fayr foord," his stay there must have been practically continuous. On his return to Oxford, he doubtless busied himself with his literary work, particularly with the composition of his Latin tragedy, *Archipropheta,* which he presented to Dr. Richard Cox, the newly chosen dean of Christ Church, as evidence of his ability when he applied for a fellowship in that institution, which had been refounded in November, 1546, and was to be reopened in January of 1546-7.

His efforts were attended with success, for he was entered there 'as a senior or theologist,' and, as Wood says,[26] 'read lectures on rhetoric in the refectory there.' This ap-

[21] *Oxford University Register,* Oxford Historical Society, I. 203.

[22] *Merton College Register,* f. 287, Merton College Archives, Oxford.

[23] *Oxford University Register,* Oxford Historical Society, I. 203.

[24] John Venn, *Grace Book Δ, containing the Records of Cambridge University for the Years 1542-1589,* Cambridge, 1910, p. 12.

[25] John Strype, *Ecclesiastical Memorials,* Oxford, 1822, 4. 2. 269.

[26] MS. Wood C. 8, f. I. v, Bodleian Library.

pointment was no small tribute to his attainments as a scholar, for Richard Cox admitted as members of the new college only those whose attainments would add distinction to it, rather than receive distinction from it. Among the manuscripts in the Bodleian Library in Oxford there is a receipt and note in Grimald's own hand, dated October 3, 1550, for salary received for lectures.[27]

If one may judge from the long list of translations and commentaries given by John Bale[28] as Grimald's work, these lectures probably covered a wide range of classical literature, both Greek and Latin, including Virgil's *Georgics* and *Eclogues,* Cicero's *Epistles, Partitiones,* and *De Officiis,* Horace's *Epistles,* the works of Xenophon and of Hesiod, the *Andria* of Terence, the Psalms of David, and the disputed passages in the Scriptures.

While at Christ Church, Grimald published his Latin tragedy, *Archipropheta.* Both his *Christus Redivivus* and his *Archipropheta* were published at Cologne by Martin Gymnicus, the first in 1543, and the second in 1548. It does not seem unlikely that their publication may have been arranged for by Grimald's friend, John Bale, who spent the years from 1540 to 1547 in Germany, and whose printer was also Martin Gymnicus. *Archipropheta,* a tragedy dealing with the life and death of the arch-prophet, John the Baptist, is a remarkable piece of work, in that it is one of the first tragedies known to have been written by an Englishman. It is dedicated to Richard Cox, the President of Christ Church. This Latin tragedy was written at least three years before the first performance of *Ferrex and Porrex,* or, *The Tragedie of Gorboduc,* the earliest tragedy written in the English tongue.

During the years that Grimald taught at Christ Church,

27 Index Codicum MSS. Thomæ Tanneri 4. 944, Bodleian Library.

28 John Bale, *Scriptorum Illustrium Maioris Brytanniæ . . . Catalogus,* Basle, 1557, p. 701.

he must have given no slight evidences of his ability as a preacher, and of that 'eloquence in both English and Latin' for which Bishop Ridley praised him,[29] for on January 2, 1551-2, Grimald was licensed by Richard Sampson,[30] Bishop of Lichfield, to preach at Eccles, an appointment which was by no means an unimportant one, as the church there, one of the earliest in that part of England, was one of the most prominent in the large see of Lichfield, although to-day Eccles is but a suburb of the city of Manchester. Unfortunately, the records of the early days of the church at Eccles are incomplete, and date back only to 1563; so no account of Grimald's incumbency remains. His stay was of no great length, for the following year he received a position in London, as chaplain to Nicholas Ridley, Bishop of London. Here he must have given evidence of being something more than a popular preacher, for in 1553 he was chosen by Ridley to deliver an address[31] before the bishops assembled in public synod. In this speech, made in Latin, Grimald spoke very boldly and pointedly to the clergy on the subject of their shortcomings.

The years from 1543, the first known date of any of his publications, until 1555, must have been very busy for Grimald, for, besides being engaged in teaching and preaching, he did no small amount of literary work. John Bale, churchman, dramatist, and England's first writer of literary history, gives in Latin a sketch of Grimald and his work in his *Scriptorum Illustrium Maioris Britanniæ . . . Catalogus,*[32] which is somewhat supplemented by his voluminous

[29] *The Works of Bishop Ridley D.D.: The Letters of Bishop Ridley,* Parker Society Publications, Cambridge, 1843, p. 361.

[30] John Strype, *Ecclesiastical Memorials,* Oxford, 1822, 4. 2. 269.

[31] Nicholas Grimald, *Oratio ad Pontifices, Londini in Aede Paulina, A. D. 1553,* London, 1583.

[32] *John Bale, Scriptorum Illustrium Maioris Britanniæ . . . Catalogus,* Basle, 1557, p. 701.

notebook, *Index Britanniæ Scriptorum,*[33] on which the former book is based.

It is unfortunate that Bale has given in Latin the following account of Grimald's life and works, and that he has not commented more fully on his works. Consequently, it is not possible in many cases to determine whether or not they were written in Latin or in English; since many of his works are no longer extant, and there is no contemporary account of them other than Bale's. Possibly many of these works were never published, but existed only in manuscript form.

NICOLAUS GRIMOALDUS

Nicolaus Grimoaldus, scholasticorum sui temporis non infimum decus, & Cantabrigiensis academiæ primum alumnus, ex Christi collegio, quod condidit olim Margarita Henrici septimi regis mater, artium professione donatus, prodijt. Maximam a bonis literis & utriusque linguæ cognitione hic laudem sibi peperit, & partam adeo auxit, in Oxoniensi gymnasio rhetoricæ lector publicus, ac progymnasmatum seu præexercita mentorum eius artis interpres, ut ornamentum plane eximium et illic haberetur. Tanta certe eloquentia Marci Tullij Ciceronis Partitiones oratorias, Epistolas familiares, & ad Octavium de Republica, homo disertus publicavit, tantaque gratia Publij Vergilij Maronis Georgica atque primam eius Eglogam exposuit, ut admirationi quam multis esset. Animum insuper ad rem vere Christianam applicans, tam scriptis quam viva voce, salutem in unico servatore Iesu sitam esse, ferventer & ostendit & docuit, suæ non, sed divinæ tandem gloriæ studiosus. Quæ liberalitas maior, aut largitio liberior esse potest, quam quæ magno sumptu ac labore didicimus, gratis imperitiri cæteris?

[33] John Bale, *Index Britanniæ Scriptorum,* Reginald Lane Poole and Mary Bateson, Oxford, 1902, pp. 302-4.

quemadmodum hic noster Grimoaldus fecit. Qui, ut nostri operis scopum attingam, scripsit super clarissimi ducis Somersetensis Edvuardi Semerij restitutione,

Congratulatorium carmen,	*Lib. 1. Qui comples hu- (milem cœlesti.*
Archiprophetæ tragœdiam,	*Lib. 1. Postquam hoc a me (poema tra.*
In Georgica Vergilij,	*Lib. 4. Quæ de agricul- (tura, Mecænas.*
In Eglogam primam eiusdem,	*Lib. 1.*
Ad amicum Ioan. Baleum,	*Lib. 1. Labores tuos, op- (time atq; eru.*
Famæ comœdiam,	*Lib. 1. Illustrissimo atq; (optimo prin.*
Vocem populi,	*Lib. 1. Universi qui curam (animarum.*
Christum nascentem,	*Lib. 1.*
Christum redivivum,	*Lib. 1.*
Protomartyrem,	*Lib. 1.*
Athanasium, seu infamiam,	*Lib. 1.*
De controversis scripturæ locis,	*Lib. 1.*
Epistolarum familiarum,	*Lib. 1.*
Carminum & epigrammatum,	*Lib. 2.*
Declamationum & orationum,	*Lib. 1.*
In Partitiones Tullij,	*Lib. 1.*
In eundem ad Octavium,	*Lib. 1.*
In quasdam eius epistolas,	*Lib. 1.*
In Andriam Terentianam.	*Lib. 1.*
In Epistolas Horatij,	*Lib. 1.*
In Officia Ciceronis,	*Lib. 1.*
Explicationes psalmorum,	*Lib. 1.*
Conciones aliquot,	*Lib. 2.*
Troilum ex Chaucero, comœdiam,	*Lib. 1.*
Rhetoricam in usum Brytannorum,	*Lib. 1.*
Cantiones rhythmicas,	*Lib. 1.*

E Græco Transtulit

Xenophontem de disciplina Cyri,	*Lib. 8.*
Hesiodum Ascræum,	*Lib. 2.*
Chiliades Erasmi transt.	*Lib. 1.*

Matthæi Vindocinensis Tobiam emendavit, & Iosephi Devonij sex libros de bello Troiano, aliaq; multa fecit, carmine ac prosa celeberrimus. Claret in Anglia, hoc anno a communis nostræ Salutis origine 1556, quo hæc scripsimus, magno Antichristo per fœminam illic regnante, ac sese sanctissimorum martyrum sanguine ingurgitantem.

Nicholas Grimald

Nicholas Grimald, not the least illustrious of the scholars of his time, was first of all an alumnus of Cambridge. Devoted to the profession of the arts, he was graduated from Christ College, which Margaret, the mother of Henry the Seventh, founded some time ago. Here he gained for himself great praise for his skilful writing, and for his knowledge of both tongues; and what he had, he so increased as public lecturer in rhetoric in Oxford, and as skilled interpreter of the preparatory exercises and practice of this art, that he was very highly distinguished there also. Certainly, with so great eloquence did this learned man publish the *Partitiones Oratoriæ*, the *Epistolæ Familiares*, and the *Ad Octavium de Republica* of Marcus Tullius Cicero, and so acceptably did he expound the *Georgics* of Publius Vergilius Maro and his first *Eclogue*, that he was an object of admiration to a great many. Moreover, applying his mind to the truth of Christianity as much in writing as in speaking, he fervently showed and taught that our salvation is alone in Jesus the Saviour, and that he himself was intent not on his own, but on the divine glory. What liberality can be greater, what generosity can be broader, than to impart to others free of charge what we have learned at great expense and with labor, as our friend Grimald did? To come to the purpose of this work, I will say that he has written on the restoration of Edward Seymour, the illustrious Duke of Somerset:

(1) *Congratulatorium carmen—A Song of Congratulations,*[34] 1 vol. "Qui comples humilem cœlesti" . . .
(2) *Archiprophetæ tragœdia—The Tragedy of the Archprophet,* 1 vol. 'Postquam hoc a me poema tra.' . . .
(3) *In Georgica Vergilij—On the Georgics of Virgil,* 4 vols. 'Quæ de agricultura, Mæcenas' . . .
(4) *In Eglogam primam eiusdem—On the First Eclogue of Vergil,* 1 vol.
(5) *Ad amicum Joan. Baleum—To my Friend John Bale,* 1 vol. 'Labores tuos, optime & eru.' . . .
(6) *Famæ comedia—A Comedy of Reputation.* 1 vol. 'Illustrissimo et optimo prin.' . . .
(7) *Vox populi—The Voice of the People.* 1 vol. 'Universi qui curam animarum' . . .
(8) *Christus nascens—The Birth of Christ,* 1 vol.
(9) *Christus Redivivus—The Resurrection of Christ,* 1 vol.
(10) *Protomartyr—The First Martyr.* 1 vol.
(11) *Athanasius, seu infamia—Athanasius, or Disgrace.* 1 vol.
(12) *De controversis scripturæ locis—On Disputed Passages of the Scriptures.* 1 vol.
(13) *Epistolares familiares—Letters to Friends.* 1 vol.
(14) *Carmina et epigrammata—Songs and Epigrams.* 2 vols.
(15) *Declamationes et orationes—Declamations and Orations.* 1 vol.
(16) *In Partitiones Tullii—On Cicero's Divisions of Oratory.* 1 vol.

[34] Owing to the fact that Bale seldom tells us whether or not Grimald's works are in Latin or in English, that he gives their titles in Latin, and that these are given in the accusative case rather than in the nominative, both the Latin and the English titles are here given. For the sake of convenience in reference they have been numbered.

(17) *In eundem ad Octavium—On Cicero's Letter to Octavius.* 1 vol.

(18) *In quasdam eius epistolas—On Certain Letters of Cicero.* 1 vol.

(19) *In Andriam Terentianam—On Terence's Andria.* 1 vol.

(20) *In Epistolas Horatii—On Horace's Letters.* 1 vol.

(21) *In Officia Ciceronis—On Cicero's Duties.* 1 vol.

(22) *Explicationes psalmorum—Explanations of the Psalms.* 1 vol.

(23) *Conciones aliquot—Some Orations.* 2 vols.

(24) *Troilus ex Chaucero, comœdiam—Troilus, a comedy based on Chaucer's tale.* 1 vol.

(25) *Rhetoricam in usum Brytannorum—A Rhetoric for the Use of the British.* 1 vol.

(26) *Cantiones rythmicæ—Metrical Songs.* 1 vol.

He translated from the Greek:

(27) *Xenophon de disciplina Cyri—Xenophon on the Education of Cyrus—The Cyropedia.* 8 vols.

(28) *Hesiodum Ascræum—Hesiod of Ascræa.* 2 vols.

(29) He translated the *Chiliades* of Erasmus, 1 vol.

(30) He emended Matthew of Vendome's *Tobias,* and

(31) Joseph of Exeter's six books on the Trojan war; and many other things he did, being most famous in verse and prose, and renowned in England in this year of our common salvation 1556, in which we have written these things, while the great Antichrist reigns in the form of a woman,[35] glutting herself with the blood of the holy martyrs.[36]

Besides the works cited above, Bale, in his *Index,* enumerates several others, under the following entries:

Nicolaus Grimoaldus scripsit—Nicholas Grimald wrote [p. 303]:

[35] Mary.

[36] Cranmer, Latimer, and Ridley.

(32) *Epistole Ciceronis ad P. Lentulum tertie, et ad C. Marcellum prime, artificiosam expositionem,* li. I.

Epistole Ciceronis ad P. Lentulum tertie, et ad C. Marcellum prime, artificiosa expositio, li. I.

A Technical Exposition of Cicero's Third Letter to Publius Lentulus, and of his First Letter to Caius Marcellus. I vol.

(33) *In Georgica Vergilij annotationes, li. iiij.—Notes on the Georgics of Virgil.* 4 vols.

(34) *Platonis Critonem, seu de re agenda dialogus,* li. I.

Platonis Crito, seu de re agenda dialogus, li. I.—*The Crito of Plato, or the Dialogue on what should be done.* I vol.

(35) [p. 304] *Cantiones rythmis inclusas que sparsim in utroque dei testamento leguntur,* li. I.—*The Metrical Songs which are to be read here and there in the Old and New Testament.* I vol.

Nicolaus Grimoaldus, scripsit Anglice—Nicholas Grimald wrote in English:

(36) *De puerorum in musicis institutione,* comœ. I.—*On the Instruction of Boys in Music,* a comedy. I vol.

(37) *Georgica Vergilij in rythmis Brytannicis,* li. iiij.—*The Georgics of Virgil in English Metres.* 4 vols.

(38) *Restitutionem psalmorum Thome Viati libraris corruptorum cum prefatione ad Marchionem,* li. i.—*A Restoration of the Psalms of Thomas Wyatt, corrupted by copyists, with a preface to the Marquis.* I vol.

(39) *Psalmos Davidis aliquot rythmis explicatos,* li. I.—*Some Psalms of David metrically rendered.* I vol.

It is to be regretted that Bale's information in regard to Grimald's works is so hazy. Much of it is not based on accurate first-hand knowledge, but upon hearsay, and is quite misleading: for instance, the title, *In Georgica Vergilii—On the Georgics of Vergil,* would lead one to anticipate a commentary or a critical essay on the *Georgics;*

whereas the book is a paraphrase of them, rendered in Latin. The title, *In Officia Ciceronis,* also leads one to expect a commentary or essay on Cicero's *De Officiis,* or a paraphrase of it in Latin, as in the case of the *Georgics;* whereas it is neither, but an English translation of Cicero's *De Officiis.* Possibly Bale actually saw those books from which he quotes the first lines, but of the others his exact knowledge is doubtful. In his *Index* he several times mentions the same book twice, and some books mentioned in the *Index* are not recorded in his *Catalogus.* Why they are omitted is not quite clear. Possibly they were inadvertently left out, or he thought their existence doubtful, or they had been wrongly ascribed to Grimald. In consequence of the defects of Bale's sketch, a discussion of the works of Grimald is given. The order in which Bale has given them is not preserved, but the poems, dramas, etc., have been grouped. For convenience of reference to Bale's list the various works have been numbered.

Poetry

(1) *Congratulatorium carmen,* lib. 1. 'Qui comples humilem cœlesti'—*A Song of Congratulations,* 1 vol. 'Thou who fillest the lowly (earth) with thy celestial (power).'

In the *Index* (p. 302), the title and the first line of this volume are given at greater length. They read: *Gratulationem factam sub nomine clarissimi viri Edwardi Seymeri ducis Somersetensis iam suis restituti,* li. 1. 'Qui comples humilem cœlesti numine mundum'—*A thanksgiving addressed to that most distinguished man, Edward Seymour, Duke of Somerset, on his restoration to his friends,* 'Thou who,' etc. This volume of poems must have been written shortly after April, 1551, when the Duke of Somerset, who had been Regent of England during the childhood of Edward VI, was released from the Tower, into which he had been thrown on the charge of having attempted to seize the throne. The *Index* further states that there were one hundred and fifty-five poems in the volume—'Carmina sunt C. lv.' One hundred and fifty-five poems on such a subject seems to be a very great many, but perhaps not for an age of hungry, subservient scholars. Bale cites as his authority in regard to this work one Joannes Pullanus, now unknown. No copies of this work are known to be extant.

(5) *Ad amicum Joan. Baleum,* lib. 1. 'Labores tuos, optime & eru.'—*To my Friend John Bale,* 1 vol. 'Your labors, most worthy and most learned (Bale).'

The *Index* (p. 302) mentions this same volume as *Epistolas quasdam ad Baleum*—*Some Letters to Bale,* and gives the first line quoted as, 'Labores tuos, optime atque eruditissime Balee.' In the *Index,* Bale cites as his authority for his statement in regard to this volume: 'Ex quadam epistola eiusdem Grimoaldi'—'From a letter of this same Grimald.' No copies are known to be extant.

(14) *Carmina et Epigrammata,* lib. 2.—*Songs and Epigrams,* 2 vols.

No copies of this work are known.

(35) *Cantiones rythmicæ,* lib. 1.—*Rhythmical Songs,* 1 vol.

This work is probably spoken of in the *Index* (p. 304) as *Cantiones rythmis inclusas que sparsim in utroque dei testamento leguntur,* li. i.—*The Metrical Songs which are to be read here and there in the Old and the New Testament,* 1 vol. This collection of Biblical lyrics is not now known.

(37) *Georgica Vergilij in rythmis Brytannicis,* li. iiij.—*The Georgics of Vergil in English Metres,* 4 vols.

It is to this book[37] that Googe probably referred in his *Epytaphe of Maister Thomas Phayre:*

[37] Barnabe Googe, *Eglogs, Epytaphes, and Sonettes,* Arber, London, 1871, pp. 73-4.

The Noble H. Hawarde once,
  that raught eternall fame
With mighty Style, did bryng a pece
  Of Virgils worke in frame,
And Grimaold gaue the lyke attempt,
  and Douglas wan the Ball,
Whose famouse wyt in Scottysh ryme
  had made an ende of all.

No copies of this translation of the *Georgics* into verse are known.

(39) *Psalmi Davidis aliquot rythmis explicati,* li. 1.—*Some Psalms of David metrically rendered,* 1 vol.

This volume is not mentioned in the *Catalogus;* the entry in regard to it is to be found on p. 304 of the *Index,* where it is recorded as an English composition. In regard to this work Bale cites as his authority: 'Ex suo museo'—'From Grimald's own study.'

Forty poems by Grimald appeared June 5, 1557, in a volume entitled *Songes and Sonettes,* published by Richard Tottel, London. Eight weeks later, on July 31, another edition of this book was issued, but of the forty poems by Grimald thirty-one were omitted. Subsequent editions from Tottel's press appeared in 1558, 1565, 1567, 1574, 1585, and 1587. Sewell, Park, and Hazelwood issued an edition in 1717, Anderson in 1795, Percy and Stevens in 1807, Chalmers in 1810, John Nott in 1812, and Bell in 1854. In 1870 Edward Arber issued his first edition of *Tottel's Miscellany,* which is a combination of the edition of June 5, 1557, and July 31, 1557—the first and the second editions. Of the first edition only one copy is known, Malone's, which is now in the Bodleian Library, Oxford; of the second edition two copies are extant; these are to be found in the Library of the British Museum, London, and in the Capeli Collection, Trinity College, Cambridge. It is not possible to identify the forty poems of Grimald, which appeared in the first edition of *Songes and Sonettes,* with either the *Carmina et*

Epigrammata (14) or with the *Cantiones Rythmicæ* (26) mentioned by Bale. Bale's account of Grimald was written in 1556, while *Songes and Sonettes* did not appear until 1557. However, Grimald's lyrics that appear in *Songes and Sonettes* may have been selected from either or both of these volumes. Grimald's poems which appear in *Songes and Sonettes* are discussed in a subsequent section, which deals with Grimald's shorter poems.

Prefatory to William Turner, Dean of Wells', *A Preservative or Tryacle agaynst the Poyson of Pelagius, lately revived and styrred up agayne, by the furious secte of the Annabaptistes,* London, 1551, there are to be found four poems, three in Latin and one in English, by Grimald. The first, addressed to Hugh Latimer, to whom the volume is dedicated, is entitled *D. Hugoni Latimero, Nicolaus Grimoaldus S.;* the second, to the author, *Ad Guilielmum Turnerum;* the third is *Ad Catabaptistam;* and the fourth, in English, is *To the reder.* Copies of this book are to be found in the Bodleian Library, Oxford, in the University Library, Cambridge, and in the British Museum, London. In the latter part of this volume, devoted to Grimald's shorter poems, these three poems may be found. They are not mentioned by Bale.

Plays

(2) *Archiprophetæ tragœdia,* lib. I. 'Posteaquam hoc a me poema tra.'—*The Tragedy of the Archprophet,* I vol.

The title of this play is here incorrectly given; it is *Archipropheta.* This is a Latin tragedy, based on the life and death of the arch-prophet, John the Baptist. Printed by Martin Gymnicus, Cologne, 1548. For a more detailed account of this play, see the preface to the translation of it. Copies of this edition of the play are to be found in the National Library of Wolfenbüttel, Germany; in the Council-School Library of Zwickau; in the Royal Library, Copenhagen; in the National Library, Paris; in the library of Jesus College, Oxford; and in the British Museum Library. Bale frequently cites his authority for the existence of the works he mentions. Of this volume he says, 'Ex officina Edwardi Braynwode,' which might be variously interpreted. If he means that the volume was from the press of Edward Braynwode, he cites an edition of the play not now known.

(6) *Famæ Comedia,* lib. I. 'Illustrissimo atq; optimo prin.'—*Fame, a comedy,* I vol. 'To the most famous and most worthy Prince.'

The *Index* (p. 302) records this as a tragi-comedy. No copies of this play are known, though Anthony à Wood speaks of having seen the book.[38]

(11) *Athanasius, seu infamia,* lib. I—*Athanasius, or Disgrace,* I vol.

This composition, *Infamia,* might readily be supposed to be a companion play to *Fama,* the play listed above, though the title rather suggests a theological discussion. If a play, it must have dealt with the life of Athanasius (293-373), who became Bishop of Alexandria in 326 A.D., an office that he held forty-seven years. In the great theological struggle which led up to the Council of Nicæa, he appeared as an opponent of the presbyter Arius. His life is intimately connected with the progress of the Arian controversy, and he was by far the most formidable antagonist of the doctrine that, although the Son was of like substance with the Father, He was the first of creation, and more than man. Athanasius maintained that the Son of God is of the same essence or substance with the Father.

(7) *Christus nascens,* lib. I—*The Birth of Christ,* I vol.

The *Index* (p. 302) mentions this as a comedy. Probably

[38] *Athenæ Oxonienses* I. 407.

it was a nativity play, written to be acted by the students of Oxford at Christmas time. No copies are known to be extant.

(9) *Christus Redivivus,* lib. 1—*The Resurrection of Christ,* 1 vol.

This is a Latin resurrection-play, probably written for performance at Easter-time. Printed by Martin Gymnicus at Cologne, 1543. The *Index* (p. 302) mentions it as a tragi-comedy. For a more detailed account of this play, see the preface to the translation of it. Copies are to be found in the University Library of Heidelberg, of Königsberg, of Leipsic, in the National Library of Dresden, of Rudolstadt, and of Wolfenbüttel, in the State Library of Berlin, the Town Library of Trier, the Council-School Library of Zwickau—all in Germany. There are copies also in the British Museum Library, in the Library of Lincoln Cathedral, England, and in the Library of Cornell University, New York. In the Royal Library in Munich, and also in the University Library there, there are copies of another edition, printed by Philippus Ulhardus, Augsburg, 1556. In 1899, Professor J. M. Hart, of Cornell University, reprinted the play, using the Cologne version of 1543. This reprint appeared in 1899 in the *Publications of the Modern Language Association of America* 14. 271-448.

(10) *Protomartyr,* lib. 1—*The First Martyr,* 1 vol.

According to the *Index* (p. 302), this is a tragedy. Probably it was a play based on the life and martyrdom of Saint Stephen. No copies are known.

(24) *Troilus ex Chaucero, comœdia,* lib. 1.—*Troilus, a comedy, founded on Chaucer's tale of Troilus.* 1 vol.

No copies are known.

(36) *De puerorum in musicis institutione,* comœ. 1—*On the Instruction of Boys in Music,* a comedy, 1 vol.

That this is not the exact title of the comedy seems evident; it is probably merely the subject of the comedy, which is mentioned only in the *Index* (p. 304).

Works on the Reformation

(7) *Vox populi,* lib. 1. 'Universi qui curam animarum habent.'—*The Voice of the People,* 1 vol. 'All those who have the care of souls.'

The *Index* has a more extended account of this volume: 'Anglice scripsit, Vocem populi, ad eos rectores, vicarios, archdiaconos, decanos, prebendarios, etc., qui procul a suis gregibus vitam degunt, aut non prestant officia sua. Item ac eos laicos indoctos qui avide arripiunt et inique sibi retinent decimam et sacerdotia, unde vivere oporteret concionatores et ministros sacrarum rerum'—'He wrote in English *The Voice of the People* to those rectors, vicars, archdeacons, deans, prebendaries, etc., who spend their lives far from their flocks, or do not perform their sacred duties. Also to those unlearned laymen who greedily seize and wrongly retain for themselves the tithes and sacred offerings which ought to provide a livelihood for the preachers and ministers of religion.' This work is not to be mistaken for the anonymous poem entitled *Vox Populi, Vox Dei,* sometimes attributed to Skelton.

The *Index* quotes as the authority for the existence of this volume 'Ex eiusdem Grimaldi museo'—'From the study of this same Grimald.' Anthony à Wood, in his *Athenæ Oxonienses,* includes this among the works of Grimald that he has seen, and gives as the date of its publication London, October, 1549. No copies of this work are known to be extant.

Oratio ad Pontifices—A Sermon before the Bishops.

This sermon, unknown to Bale, is a Latin sermon that

was delivered before the bishops assembled in public synod in Saint Paul's Cathedral, London, April, 1553. It was not published until 1583, twenty years after Grimald's death, the publisher being Henry Binneman, London. The subject-matter is so similar to that of the *Voice of the People,* mentioned above, that it may have been a Latin version of it, or *vice versa.* Copies of this work are to be found in the Bodleian Library, and in the Library of the University of Cambridge.

Translations

(13) *Epistolæ familiares,* lib. I.—*Letters to Friends,* I vol.

Bale, in his sketch of Grimald in the *Catalogus,* mentions these letters as those of Cicero. As he does not group them with those writings which he says Grimald expounded or explained, it seems likely that this is a translation of Cicero's letters to his friends. No copies are known.

(21) *In Officia Ciceronis,* lib. I.—*On the 'De Officiis' of Cicero,* I vol.

The actual title of this work is, *Marcus Tullius Ciceroes thre bokes of duties to Marcus his sonne, turned out of Latine into English by Nicolas Grimalde,* London, 1556. This English translation of Cicero's *Duties* ran through the following editions: 1553 (?), 1556, 1558, 1568, 1574, 1583, 1595, 1600. Many copies of this work are extant. Among the Douce fragments, f. 25 (2) in the Bodleian Library, there is the introduction of what is thought may be a 1553 edition of this work. No title-page and no date appear. This library also possesses the 1574 edition of Tottel, London. The Cambridge University Library has the following editions: 1558, 1568, 1574, 1583, Tottel, London, and also the 1596 edition of Thomas Este, London. Christ's College, Cambridge, has the edition of 1568, Tottel, London. Merton College, Oxford, has the editions of 1558 and 1583, Tottel, London; the British Museum, the editions of 1556, 1568, 1574, 1583, Tottel, London, and that of 1600, Thomas Este, London. The Mazarin Library, Paris, has a copy of the edition of 1558, Tottel, London. The Public Library of Boston, Massachusetts, has copies of the editions of 1558 and 1583, Tottel, London; the Yale University Library, New Haven, the edition of 1556, Tottel, London; the Newberry Library of Chicago, the editions of 1596 and 1600, Thomas Este, London; and the Library of Henry E. Huntington, San Gabriel, California, the editions of 1556, 1558, 1568, Tottel, London, and 1596, Thomas Este, London.

The following extract from Grimald's preface to his translation of *De Officiis* shows him as a protagonist in the cause of humanism:

> This boke playnly is the myrrour of wisdom, the fortress of justice, the master of manlinesse. the schoole of temperance, the jewell of comelinesse: I wished many mo to be partneres of such sweetnesse, as I had partly felt myself: and to declare: I laied to my helping hand, endevoring by translation, to do likewise for my contrimene as Italians, Frenchmen, Spaniardes, Dutchmen, and other foreins have liberally done for theyrs. So, chiefly for our unlatined people I have made this latine writer english, have now brought into light that from them so longe was hidden: have caused an auncient wryting to become, in a manner new agayne: and a boke used but of fewe to wax common to a great meany: so that our men, understanding what a treasure is among them, for the fashioning of their life: and beeing by nature most of all nations given to civilitie and humanitie, when they shall be aided and directed by these perfite precepts may in all pointes of good demeanour become people perelesse.

(28) *Hesiod of Ascræa,* 2 vols.

According to the *Index,* he translated Hesiod's *Works and Days* from the Greek into the Latin. No copies of this work are known to be extant.

(27) The *Cyropedia,* 8 vols.

The *Index* says that he published this work, yet no copies of it are known. It also says 'Latinos fecit,' that is, he translated it into Latin; but this comment was deleted, and 'publicavit' substituted. Presumably he published a Greek edition or an English translation, as he did of the other Greek classics.

(34) *Crito Platonis, seu de re agenda,* li. 1. *The Crito of Plato, or Concerning What Should Be Done,* 1 vol.

The *Index* makes no comments on this work. No copies of it are known. It is not possible to determine whether it was translated into Latin or into English.

A Briefe and Learned Treatise, containing a true description of the Anti-Christ who was foretold by the Prophets and Apostles, and an Evident Proofe that the same agreeth unto the Pope. Written in Latin by M. George Sohn, Doctor of Divinitie and Publike Professor thereof at Heidelberg, and translated into English. Printed at Cambridge by John Legate, 1592. The English translation of this work, published thirty years after Grimald's death, has been ascribed to him, since the dedicatory epistle to Catherine, Countess of Huntingdon, is signed *N. G.* According to the *Allgemeine Deutsche Biographie,* George Sohn was born December 31, 1551. At the time of Grimald's death in 1562-3, he was but eleven years old. It follows that Grimald could not possibly have been the translator of this work. Copies are to be found in the Library of the British Museum, in the Library of the University of Cambridge, and in the Bodleian Library.

Translations or Commentaries

(19) *In Andriam Terentianam,* lib. 1.—On Terence's *Andria,* 1 vol.

There are no comments on this work in Bale's *Index,* and no copies of it are known to be extant. It seems probable that it was either a translation of the play, or a commentary on it.

(20) *In Epistolas Horatii,* lib. 2.—*On Horace's Letters,* 2 vols.

There are no copies of this work known to be extant, and there are no further comments than that above. It seems probable that this, too, was a translation or a commentary.

Paraphrase

(3) *In Georgica Vergilii,* lib. 4. 'Quæ de agricultura Mæcenas.'—*On the Georgics of Virgil,* 4 vols. 'Quæ de agricultura, Mæcenas.'

The actual title of this work is *In P. V. Maronis quattuor libros Georgicum in oratione soluta Paraphrasis elegantissima.* This is a Latin paraphrase of four books of Virgil's *Georgics.* .It was printed by George Bishop and Radulph Newberry, London, 1591, thirty years after Grimald's death. It is not unlikely that this paraphrase was a result of Grimald's labors in teaching rhetoric. Copies of this book exist in the Library of Lambeth Palace, London; of Sion College, London; the British Museum; Christ's College Library, Cambridge; the University Library, Cambridge; the Mazarin Library, Paris; the Bibliothèque Nationale, Paris; and in the Newberry Library, Chicago.

(16) *In Partitiones Tullii,* lib. 1—*On Cicero's Partitiones Oratoriæ,* 1 vol.

According to Bale's *Index* (p. 303), this is a paraphrase of and a commentary on Cicero's *Divisions of Oratory.* No copies of it are known.

Abstract, Paraphrase, Commentary, and Explanation

(4) *In Eglogam eiusdem primam,* lib. 1—*On the First Eclogue of Virgil,* 1 vol.

Bale's *Index* (p. 303) says that this was an abstract, a paraphrase, a commentary, and an explanation of Virgil's *Eclogue.* No copies are known.

(17) *In eundem ad Octavium,* lib. 1.—*On Cicero's Letter to Octavius concerning the Republic,* 1 vol.

The *Index* (p. 303) says that this was a fourfold exposition of Cicero's letter to Octavius (pseudo-Ciceronian), and consisted of an abstract of it, a paraphrase, a commentary, and an explanation. It is not unlikely that it was altogether in Latin. No copies of it are known.

Commentaries

(22) *Explicationes psalmorum,* lib. 1—*Commentaries on the Psalms,* 1 vol.

According to Bale's *Index* (p. 304), these psalms are those of David. No copies are known.

(33) *In Georgica Vergilii annotationes,* li. iiij.—*Notes on the Georgics of Virgil,* 4 vols.

This work is mentioned only in the *Index.* No copies are known.

(32) *Epistola Ciceronis ad P. Lentulum tertia, et ad C. Marcellum prima, artificiosa expositio,* li. 1.—*A Technical Exposition of Cicero's Third Letter to Publius Lentulus, and of his first Letter to Caius Marcellus,* 1 vol.

This volume is mentioned only in the *Index.* No copies of it are known.

Emendations

(30) *Matthei Vindociniensis Tobias,* li. 1—*The Tobias of Matthew of Vendôme,* 1 vol.

No copies of this work are known.

(31) Josephi Devonii *de bello Trojano,* li. vj.—*Joseph of Devon's De Bello Trojano,* 6 vols.

This work is not known to be extant. 'Joseph of Exeter (d. c. 1210), a brother of Theobald, Archbishop of Canterbury, is the only Latin epic poet claimed by England. He is described as 'a miracle of this age in classical composition.' He produced (with the aid of Dares, and in the style of Ovid, Statius and Claudian) a poem *De Bello Trojano,* which is still extant.'

—J. E. Sandys, *History of Classical Scholarship,* Cambridge, 1903, I. 526.

(38) *Restitutio psalmorum Thome Viati librarijs corruptorum cum prefatione ad Marchionem,* li. I.—*A Restoration of the Psalms of Thomas Wyatt, corrupted by copyists, with a Preface to the Marquis,* I vol.

These are the penitential psalms, rendered into English verse by Sir Thomas Wyatt. No copies are known of Grimald's emendation.

(12) *De controversis scripturæ locis,* lib. I—*On the Disputed Passages in the Scriptures,* I vol.

It is likely that this work was a discussion of the disputed passages of the Scriptures, with a comparison of the Greek and Latin texts. This work is not known to be extant.

Technical Works

(25) *Rhetorica in usum Britannorum,* lib. I—*A Rhetoric for the Use of the British,* I vol.

No copies of this work are known.

This account of Grimald by Bale is the first and only contemporary biographical sketch that we have of him. All too meagre, it is probably more accurate than most of Bale's literary history; for, although Bale's prolonged absence from England, caused by the religious struggle going on, prevented any continuous intimacy between the two men, nevertheless they were on most friendly terms. Very possibly their friendship began through the fact that they were both Cambridge men. Among Grimald's work there is a volume entitled *Ad Amicum Joan. Baleum.* That Bale was intimate with Grimald is evident from his notebook, *Index Britanniæ Scriptorum.* In this he quotes Grimald freely as his authority in regard to various literary matters. Once he refers to a letter of Grimald[39] in regard to a certain author's works; again he speaks of a book as being in Grimald's study;[40] two others are in his library;[41] six are in his study;[42] and in regard to five others he cites Grimald as his authority.[43]

One wonders why it is, then, that a man who was once so highly rated is now quite forgotten. Many a man of letters who has been accounted great in his own time, and whose work has had no little influence on the world's literature, has ceased to be a person of any interest in later years, and his works are no longer read; but few such men have left so little record of themselves, or have inspired in these latter days of research so little interest, so little desire to make inquiry into their lives and personalities, as has Nicholas Grimald. Nevertheless, John Bale[44] tells how renowned he was in that day, and calls him 'not the least illustrious of his time.' Next to Sir Thomas Wyatt and Henry Howard, Earl of Surrey, he was the principal contributor to the first printed anthology of English poetry, then known as *Songes and Sonettes,* a book which enjoyed astonishing popularity. His name is here joined to those of two men who are still remembered. Another reason for the interest of posterity is that two of Grimald's poems in this volume, *The Death of Zoroas* and *Marcus Tullius Ciceroes Death,* were possibly the first compositions in blank verse to be published in the

[39] Anthony à Wood, *Athenæ Oxonienses* I. 302.

[40] *Op. cit.,* p. 311.

[41] *Op. cit.,* pp. 107, 462.

[42] *Op. cit.,* pp. 103, 144, 205, 216, 302, 304.

[43] *Op. cit.,* pp. 66, 276, 277, 432.

[44] John Bale, *Scriptorum Maioris Brytanniæ . . . Catalogus,* Basle, 1557, p. 701.

English language. The credit, to be sure, is commonly given to Surrey for having written the first blank verse, for, although the translation in that poetic form which he made of the second and fourth books of the *Aeneid* was published June 21, 1557, a little over two weeks later than *Songes and Sonettes,* it must have been written at least ten years before, as Surrey died in 1547. Nevertheless, it is not impossible that Grimald's compositions in blank verse were done even before Surrey's, for in 1547 he was appointed lecturer in rhetoric at Christ Church, Oxford. To hold such a position he must have been proficient in versification. Warton suggests[45] that Grimald's verses were 'prolusions or illustrative practical specimens' for our author's course of lectures in rhetoric, which were given there. As a teacher of rhetoric at Oxford, and as a contributor of two specimens of blank verse to a volume of which there were eight editions within thirty years, whereas Surrey's translation of Virgil had but two within that time, his influence on the production of poetry in that form must have been much farther-reaching than Surrey's. But these poems were not the first of the compositions from Grimald's pen, for he had been engaged in literary work for some years. His poetic drama, *Christus Redivivus,* which was published in 1543, was written about 1539, when, as he says in its dedicatory epistle, he was about twenty. In 1548 he published his *Archipropheta,* which shows him to be a master of a great variety of verse-forms.

As a dramatist, Grimald's work was also of no little consequence. His *Archipropheta,* a Latin play based on the life of John the Baptist, is one of the first tragedies known to have been written by an Englishman; again, the influence of his tragi-comedy, *Christus Redivivus,* can scarcely be ignored, since it is one of the plays on which the original Passion Play of Oberammergau was based.

[45] T. Warton, *History of English Poetry,* 1840, 3. 69.

Grimald was also widely known as a commentator and translator: his translation of Cicero's *De Officiis* alone ran through ten editions in fifty-seven years, and he enjoyed an enviable reputation in his generation as a teacher and apostle of humanism.

Why is it, then, one asks, that the memory of the man has passed away, and that even his name was removed from the second edition of *Songes and Sonettes,* which appeared less than two months after the first editions? What makes the case still more peculiar, of the forty poems by Grimald which appeared in the first edition, thirty-one—those in which the personal element was prominent—were suppressed, and the nine which were retained appear with merely the initials *N. G.* The answer may perhaps be found in the questionable character of the man.

There is no cloud upon Grimald's reputation, however, in the testimony by his contemporary, John Bale, who pays him the following tribute: "Moreover, applying his mind to the truth of Christianity as much in writing as in speaking, he fervently showed and taught that our salvation is alone in Jesus the Saviour, and that he himself was intent not on his own but on the divine glory." During the critical period of Grimald's life, Bale was absent from England, since he was sent to Ireland as Bishop of Ossory in 1553; and, on the accession of Mary, when Roman Catholic opposition to him became too strong, he fled to the Continent, where he remained until 1559, so that the absence of unflattering comment is possibly due to his ignorance of the character of his friend, which was brought out during the Reformation. At this time Grimald was nothing more than a timeserver, shifting from the Roman Catholic faith, and then back again, recanting secretly, and betraying his friends, as was necessary to save his life.

In the manuscript of Duke Humphrey[46] in the Bodleian

[46] Bodleian MS. Duke Humphrey b. 1., f. 186.

Library are the following anonymous verses, never before published, ironically called *Carmen in laudem Grimmoaldi,* which portray him as a self-seeker and a toady:

Carmen in laudem Grimmoaldi

Omnibus occurris per compita templa theatra,
Ut laudem captes o Grimmoalde brevem.
Laudasti paucos sed multos labe notasti,
Ut laudem captes o Grimmoalde brevem.
Quos modo vituperas nunc illos perfide laudas,
Ut laudem captes o Grimmoalde brevem.
Grammaticus rethor detractor præco poeta,
Ut laudem captes o Grimmoalde brevem.
Omnia cum facias periture laudis amore.
Dij tibi dent laudem sed Grimmoalde brevem.
Finis.

The following lines are a translation of the verses above:

You meet everybody at the cross-roads, the churches, the theatres,
That you may gain brief praise, O Grimald.
You have praised few, but many have you branded with infamy,
That you may gain brief praise, O Grimald.
Those whom you have just blamed you now praise, O deceiver!
That you may gain brief praise, O Grimald.
A grammarian, a rhetorician, a detractor, a crier, a poet,
That you may gain brief praise, O Grimald.
Since you do all things with a desire for transitory praise,
May the gods give you praise, but brief praise, O Grimald.

That Grimald may have been suspected and disliked, to the extent that he was *persona non grata* alike to both Roman Catholics and Protestants, and, in consequence, was so ignored by both that the memory of the man and his admirable work passed away, may be readily seen from the following series of letters which reveal the baseness of his character, and furnish almost positive evidence that he was the betrayer of the martyrs of the Reformation—Cranmer, Latimer, and Ridley.

These letters, assembled for the first time, have not attracted the attention of students of either literary, political, or ecclesiastical history. The complete text of all but one of these letters is accessible in Foxe's *Acts and Monuments,* Strype's works, or the Parker Society's publications; accordingly, from these only excerpts which refer to Grimald are here printed. The first letter, however, which exists only in the manuscript collection of the British Museum,[47] is here printed in full.

This letter, which is from Grimald to Sir William Cecil, presents Grimald as an ardent champion of the Reformation. It bears the address: 'To the ryght worshypfull and his especyall good maister M. Cicell at Savoy be thys D. D.' Another hand has added the endorsement: 'From Mr. Grymold the xiiij of May 1549. Upon Sir Wm. Cecyls desire to know how y[e] Students of Christs Church and others at Oxon were disposed as to the reformed Religion Hee relates y[t] a great part were idle & another part were such as had Livings abroad, and Lived at their ease there.'

The attitude of the members of the Universities toward the Reformation was at that time regarded as a matter of the utmost importance. In order 'that such statutes and ordinances as maintained Papistry, superstition, blindness, and ignorance might be abolished, and that such might be established as would further God's word and good learning,' a commission for the visitation of Cambridge and Oxford was issued[48] to John, Earl of Warwick, Thomas Goodrich, Bishop of Ely, Nicholas Ridley, Bishop of Rochester, and others, on May 8, 1549, about the time that this letter was probably written.

Sir William Cecil then held the office of 'Master of the Court of Requests' under Edward Seymour, Duke of Somerset, an office which the Lord Protector had created in order to escape the worry of looking over the too numerous petitions presented to him. At that time Somerset had but recently been released from the Tower, and had only in

[47] Lansdowne MS. 2, Art. 31.

[48] *Calendar of State Papers* 1547-1580, p. 15.

part recovered his former standing. Cecil, although apprehended at the same time as his master, was confined for a much shorter period. His star, however, was not in the descendant, as was his master's, for the following year, when Somerset was again sent to the Tower and then to the block, Cecil became Secretary of State.

At the time the letter was written, Grimald, avowedly the bitter enemy of the Papacy, was a lecturer on rhetoric at Christ Church, Oxford. In this letter we have the first indication of the poet's duplicity, for we find him serving as a spy for Sir William Cecil upon the Roman Catholic students at Oxford, and furnishing him a list of the names of those who would not conform to the Protestant religion:

A Letter from Nicholas Grimald to Sir William Cecil concerning the Students at Oxford

Utinam penes me esset tuæ (clarissime atque optime vir) benignitati aut gratiis agendis, aut præstandis officiis, aut ulla omnino ratione pro meo voto respondere. Effectum est enim tua et gratia, et humanitate, et opera id quod ego mihi vehementer gratulor: ut cum studiis meis non esset impetrata quies, in loco tum optatiss. tum literariæ progressioni accommodatissimo collocari possem. Fuit hoc liberalis profecto naturæ, nullo ut meo merito provocatus, sed tu apte sponte faceres. Fuit raræ cuiusdam facilitatis, ut primo quoque tempore aditum ad te dari permitteres. Fuit affabilitatis eximiæ, quod caussam meam omnem audire sustinueris. Fuit ingenii in bonarum artium studia propensissimi, quam primum mihi commodare et prodesse velle. Breviter quod tua de bonitate fama prædicat, quod utriusque nostrum animi affirmaverant, quod ipse habebam in spe & expectatione, quod erat hominis summa et elegantiss. doctrina informate & exculti: id omne sum expertus a te meam in gratiam atque utilitatem cum libenter, tum etiam diligenter esse perfectum. Me igitur non solum tanti beneficii memorem, tam salutaria tua monita observantem, gratum erga te talem patronum, tui denique amantissimum præstabo: sed præterea etiam cupidissimum doctrinæ, studiosisimum piorum, acerrimum contra Papatum, impigerrimum in in expromendo talento, paratissimum ad amplificandam & ornandam rem publicam Christianam esse promitto & spondeo. Eorum nomina (quem ad modum requirebas in discessu meo) qui nondum expuerent imbibitam animo malam opinionem de divinis rebus collegi, collecta in tabellam hanc, quam una tibi cum hisce literis mitto retuli. Sunt autem a me silentio prætermissi; qui, vel parum aut nihil possunt, sed tanquam ignavum pecus inane tempus apud nos terunt, vel pastorum munia & concionatorum functiones alibi nacti feriantur hic, *secumque* (ut dicitur) *vivunt.* Nam & ex illo genere non paucos & ex hoc vix credas quos multos fuisset in promptu recensere: qui nisi utrique profligentur, & hii (quod ist æquissimum) ad suos greges, illi (pro eo ac postulat cuiusque indoles) ad opus faciendum relegentur: bonis & studiosiss. adolescentibus nec honestæ quietis aut otii, nec iustii præmii aut emolumenti ulla aliquando spes affulgebit. Equidem nullius cuiusquam vel mediocre ingenium damno, dummodo quam debet diligentiam adhibeat: de inertibus loquor ad hoc tantum utilibus, ut consumant fruges, & præstantium loca virorum, freti amicorum vi occupent. De illis autem alteris, qui quid agant miseri homines quorum ex operis & impensis victitant adeo nihil pensi habent, ut ab iis procul secure degant, non possum non vehementer animo angi: tum quia nostros autoritate premunt, ludificantur dolis, persuasione decipiunt, quibus demum cumque rationibus queunt aut exagitant aut corrumpunt: tum quia suos quorum in se curam susceperunt, quos tueri, consolari, instituere deberent, pro quibus denique vitam cum morte commutare opporteret, neglectos, desertos, & fame propemodum enecatos esse patiuntur. Cave putes (prudentiss. Vir) hoc esse meum solius iudicium, sed commune omnium eorum, qui (quoniam syncerae castæque pietati propagandæ sedulo student) & hodie sentiunt & iamdiu senserunt istas pestes propter eam unam rem omnes crescentium ingeniorum bonorum conatus nimium (pro! dolor) nimium infestantes. Et quidem cum de cæteris utriusque sectæ hominibus nominatum a me facta mentio sit: de hiis quoque tot numero, improbitate tantis in universum dicere necesse videbatur. Tibi vero (humaniss. & opt. vir) libere & audacter in eius modi rebus animi sententiam exponere quid est quod dubitem? Ubi enim eloquar? Quem implorem? Cuius in sinum publicas querelas fundam, nisi eius qui & autoritate valet & veræ ac puræ religioni unice favet? Imo si non tu, D. Cicelle, tuique similes in id omni animo atque voluntate incumbatis, omnique studio & contentione in eo perficiendo elaboratis, ut honos alat artifices probos, ut cum dedecore arceantur a præsepibus fuci, ut otiosi & securi & verbo tenus pastores ab aulis revocentur ad caulas i. a collegiis nostris ad suam quisque provinciam: profecto non video quænam studiosiss. alacritas adferri, quæ honesta ætati teneræ proponi exempla, qui literarum fructus ad vulgus hominum prevenire possit: aut quibus tandem modis provideri & prospici queat, ne barbariem posteris, indiligentiæ nostræ testem relinquamus, & unacum barbarie perturbationem vitæ & summam confusionem quasi manu tradamus. Sed sane facere te quidem hac in parte quod tali viro dignum est & una voce testantur omnes quibuscumque notus es, & ipse tum ope mihi præstita, tum aliis nonnullis argumentis exploratum habeo ac penitus perspectum. Perge per Deum ita ut cœpisti, pergentem iuvabit omnium adiumentatorum author. Ego, quod mearum est partium, precibus apud eundem agam, ut ex incommoda valetudine nunc demum emergens ad rei totius publicæ utilitatem confirmato corpore prodire in publicum possis. Vale vir eruditiss. & intigerrime.

Oxonia. Ex æde Christi. 4 Idus Maij.
Nicolaus Grimoaldi tuus.

Oh, if it were only in my power, noblest and best of men, to respond to your kindness as I should like, either by thanking you, or by doing you a favor, or in any other way; for, through your favor, your kindness, and your efforts, you brought it about that when quiet for my studies was not to be had, I could be placed in a situation not only most desirable, but most advantageous for my literary progress—a thing on which I congratulate myself exceedingly! This was surely characteristic of a noble nature, for you were not incited by any merit of mine, since you did it of your own accord. It was a mark of rare courtesy that, even from the first, you permitted me to have access to you. It was indicative of the greatest kindness that you were willing to hear all my case. It was typical of a disposition most favorably inclined toward the study of the liberal arts to wish to be of service to me as soon as possible, and to aid me. In short, whatever report said of your kindness, whatever the friends of both of us affirmed, whatever I myself had in hope and expectation, whatever was characteristic of a man whose mind had been formed and perfected by the very finest kind of instruction, all this, done not only freely but even diligently, I have experienced at your hands, to my own profit and advantage. And so I shall not only show that I am mindful of this great kindness of yours, observant of your very wholesome advice, and grateful to such a patron as you, in short, devoted to you, but I pledge and promise besides that I will be most eager for learning, most studious of holy things, most bitter against the Papacy, most unwearied in displaying my talent, most ready to extend and adorn the Christian state. As you asked on my departure, I have collected the names of those who have not yet rejected the evil conceptions acquired on religious matters, and I have made them into a list, which I am sending you along with this letter. Those have been passed over in silence by me who can do very little or nothing, and who, as an ignoble herd, vainly waste their time with us; or, having got elsewhere the offices of pastors and the duties of lecturers, make holiday here and 'live,' as it is said, 'at their ease.' Not only are there not a few of the first kind, but of the second you would scarcely believe how many it would have been easy to count up; unless both of these classes be driven out, the latter sent to their flocks, as is most just, and the former put to doing the kind of work that the natural ability of each one requires, no hope of honest quiet and peace, nor of just reward and emoluments, will ever appear for good and studious youth. For my part, I condemn the ability of no one, however mediocre, as long as he shows the diligence that he ought; but I say this concerning the lazy, who serve only to consume food, and who, relying on the power of friends, seize upon the positions of worthy men. Concerning the others, moreover, who have so little regard for the fate of the wretched men from whose labor and at whose expense they live, that they dwell heedlessly far away from them, I cannot but be deeply distressed; first, because they not only oppress our people with their authority, cozen them with craft, and deceive them by persuasion, in short, either harry or corrupt them by whatever means they can; but also because they allow their own people to be neglected, deserted, and almost half dead from starvation, whom they ought to watch over, console, and instruct; in short, for whom they ought to exchange life for death. Most prudent man, beware of thinking that this is my opinion alone, for it is the common opinion of all those who, since they constantly desire to promote pure and simple piety, perceive not only to-day, but have seen for a long time, that these pests, on account of that one thing, are destroying all too much, alas and alack! the entire efforts of good characters in their course of development. And, indeed, since mention has been made by me of other men of both kinds, it seemed necessary for me to speak in general of these, too, who are so many in number, and so great in depravity. Why, indeed, O kindest and best of men, should I hesitate in matters of this sort to give you my opinion boldly and freely? Where then can I speak, whom can I implore, into whose bosom shall I pour the public complaint if not into his who has authority, and who especially favors 'pure religion and undefiled'? Nay, if you, Master Cecil, and all those like you, do not fall to, body and soul, and work with all zeal and rivalry to bring it about that honor may maintain upright workers, that drones may be kept in disgrace from the hives, that the idle, the negligent, the pastors in name only, shall be recalled from their halls to their sheepfolds, that is, from our colleges to their parishes, I do not see what zeal can be inspired in the studious, what honest examples can be set before tender age, what fruits of literature can come to the common people, or how we may look to it and prevent ourselves from leaving to posterity a heritage of barbarism, as a proof of our lack of diligence, and from handing down, as it were, perturbation of life and great confusion, along with savagery. But, truly, that you are, indeed, doing in that direction what is fitting for such a man as you to do, not only all to whomsoever you are known testify, but I myself feel sure and am thoroughly convinced of it, not only because of the aid you have given me, but for certain other reasons. With the grace of God, go on, as you have begun; the Author of all assistance will aid your progress. I, as far as I am able, will endeavor by my prayers to aid you as you go, so that you, now at length recovering from ill health, may, with strengthened body, come before the public, to the advantage of the whole state. Farewell, most learned and upright man.

Oxford, Christ Church, May 12.
Thy Nicholas Grimald.

The first of the following excerpts is from a letter under date of November 18, 1552, by the Protestant martyr, Nicholas Ridley, Bishop of London. It tells of Ridley's desire to have the chantership of St. Paul's cathedral conferred upon any one of four men, whom he praises highly. Grimald, who had only the year previous received his license to preach, was fortunate enough to get the appointment, and he became chaplain to Bishop Ridley, and his trusted friend as well:

If ye would know unto whom I would this dignity of our church, called the chantership, should be given, surely unto any one of these, either unto Mr. Bradford, whom in my conscience I judge more worthy to be a bishop, than many a one of us that be bishops already to be a parish priest; or unto Mr. Sampson, a preacher; or unto Mr. Harvey, a divine and preacher; or unto Mr. Grimbold, a preacher.[49]

[49] *The Works of Nicholas Ridley,* Parker Society Publications, Cambridge, 1843, p. 337.

During the two years that elapsed between the writing of this letter and the one which follows, Edward VI died, Mary came to the throne, and the Roman Church was reëstablished. Latimer, Cranmer, and Ridley were arrested, thrown into prison in London, and afterwards removed to a jail in Oxford, called the Bocardo. It was from the latter place that Ridley wrote the letter from which the following excerpt is given, to Austin Bernhere, a devoted servant and clerk of Latimer, who attended Latimer when imprisoned in the Tower of London, and who waited on him and the other bishops, Ridley and Cranmer, when all three were confined together in Oxford:

> But that at your last being here you cast cold water upon mine affection towards Grimbold, else methinks I could appoint wherein he might occupy himself to his own profit in learning which he liketh, and to no small profit which might ensue afterward to the Church of Christ in England: as, if he would take in hand and interpretate Laurentius Valla[50] (which, as he knoweth, is a man of singular eloquence), I say, his book, which he made and wrote against that false feigned fable, forged of Constantinus Magnus, and his donation and glorious exaltation of the see of Rome: and, when he hath done that, let him translate a work of Aeneas Sylvius, *De gestis Basiliensis Concilii.*[51] In the which, although there be many things that savoureth of the pan, and also he himself was after-

[50] Laurentius Valla (c. 1407-57), an Italian humanist of the Renaissance, who was a pioneer in the higher criticism in writing his comparison of the Vulgate New Testament with the Greek original. He wrote numerous tractates of a destructively critical character, and made himself especially obnoxious to the professors of the current theology by his *Annotationes in Novum Testamentum* (afterwards edited by Erasmus), in which he attacked with much acrimony the Vulgate translation of the Gospel. The work referred to by Bishop Ridley is Valla's *De Falso Credita et Ementita Constantini Donatione Declamatio* (1439), in which he attacked the claims of the Papacy to temporal dominion.

[51] Aeneas Sylvius Piccolomini, better known as Pope Pius II (1458-1464), who in his early years was a member of the Council of Basle, which declared for the supremacy of the Council over the Pope. In the work mentioned, Aeneas Sylvius upheld this opinion.

ward a bishop of Rome, yet I dare say, the papists would glory but a little to see such books go forth in English.[52]

From this letter it is evident that Bernhere had some suspicions of Grimald's loyalty to the Protestant cause, and that Ridley, too, was perhaps becoming a bit doubtful of his integrity.

After a time, Ridley was removed from the Bocardo, and imprisoned elsewhere in Oxford. From his place of confinement, he wrote late in December, 1554, to Latimer and Cranmer, in regard to the arrest and imprisonment of his brother-in-law, George Shipside, who had been sending copies of Ridley's writings, which had been done in prison, to Grimald, upon Grimald's request. Suspicion that Grimald was playing false was not lacking, but Ridley was loth to believe that Grimald could be unfaithful:

> The cause of my brother's imprisonment is this, so far as I can perceive. There is a young man called Mr. Grimbold, which was my chaplain, a preacher, and a man of much eloquence both in the English and also in the Latin. To this man, being desirous of all things which I had written and done since the beginning of mine imprisonment, my brother (as is said) hath sent copies, no more but of all things that I have done. First, a little treatise which Mr. Latimer and I wrote in the Tower; where there is before my sayings, *N. R.* and before Mr. Latimer, *H. L.* Also another draught which I drew out of the Evangelists and of St. Paul, that the words of the Lord's Supper are figuratively to be understood; alleging out of the doctors only six, three of the Greek Church, which are Origen, Chrysost. ad Cesa. monachum, and Theodoret; and three of the Latin church, Tertullian, Augustine, and Gelasius. He had of my brother also a copy of my *Three Positions to the Three Questions*[53]

In later years he formally retracted his defense of the Council of Basle.

[52] *The Writings of John Bradford,* Parker Society Publications, Cambridge, 1853, p. 160.

[53] *Disputation at Oxford between Dr. Smith with his other Colleagues and Doctors and Bishop Ridley, Works of Ridley,* Parker Society Publications, Cambridge, 1843, pp. 190-252. This disputation was in regard to the sacrament.

here propounded to us at Oxford. Then also a copy of my disputation in the Schools, as I wrote it myself after the disputation. Item the letter, *Ad fratres in diversis carceribus.* All these things they have gotten of Grimbold, as my brother doth suppose; not that Grimbold hath betrayed him, but (as is supposed) one which my brother trusted to carry his letters unto Grimbold; for it will not sink into my head to think that Grimbold would ever play me such a Judas's part.[54]

The following excerpt is from an unsigned letter which is attributed to Bishop Ridley, and is thought to have been written to John Bradford, who later suffered martyrdom. It doubtless refers to the arrest of Ridley's brother-in-law, George Shipside, for conveying the writings of Ridley to Grimald, and to the rumor of Grimald's treachery:

If I dared to send anything to my brother, who is now I think dragging out a wearisome existence in solitary confinement, I would indeed desire that he too should transcribe somewhat; but I greatly fear lest they should again surprise him in some incautious moment, and thence to take occasion to exercise still greater severities upon him. I pray you, bid him be of good courage, for there is nothing whatever for him to fear. If the rumor which they are now circulating concerning Grimbald be true, I grieve much for Grimbald's sake; for the rest, I know that it matters not one jot to the cause of my brother.[55]

Grimald himself, however false he may have been to the Protestant cause, did not escape suspicion on the part of some of the Roman Catholics, for he, too, was arrested. From the letter of Ridley to John Bradford, written in Oxford about January 18, 1555, we learn of Grimald's arrest and imprisonment in the Bocardo in Oxford, and of his subsequent release:

I have heard that Master Grimbold hath gotten his liberty; if without blemish of Christ's glory, I am right glad thereof. My brother-in-law is where he was, that is in Bocardo, the common gaol of the town.[56]

[54] *Op. cit.,* p. 361.
[55] *Op. cit.,* p. 537.
[56] *Op. cit.,* p. 371.

Ridley wrote to John Bradford of the rumor current that Grimald had been sentenced to death, and afterwards released:

> With us it is said that Master Grimbold was adjudged to be hanged, drawn and quartered; of whom we hear now, that he is at liberty.[57]

Grimald was possibly removed from the Bocardo in Oxford to the Marshalsea prison in London before he was released, for in the latter part of May, 1555, Ridley wrote to Edmund Grindall, who was in exile in Frankfurt:

> Many (as we hear) have suffered valiantly, confessing Christ's truth, and nothing yielding to the adversary, yea, not for the fear or pains of death. . . . Grimbold was caught by the heel and cast into the Marshalsea but now is at liberty again; but I fear he escaped not without some becking and bowing (alas) of his knee unto Baal.[58]

Laurence Saunders, one of the Protestant martyrs, in writing from the Marshalsea prison to a friend who had inquired as to what the Roman Catholic prelate, Doctor Weston, had accomplished in his visits to the Protestants in the prison, gave the following brief reply, in which one detects some misgivings in regard to Grimald's steadfastness:

> Master Weston came to confer with Master Grimoald. What he hath concluded I know not: I wish it may be to God's glory, Amen, Amen.[59]

It was this visit, in all probability, that brought about Grimald's complete turning from Protestantism to Catholicism, his 'becking and bowing the knee to Baal,' for John Bradford, giving an account of a visit which Doctor Weston paid him in prison, informs us that Weston endeavored to persuade him to recant by telling him how Grimald had secretly apostatized and so saved his life:

[57] *Op. cit.*, p. 379.

[58] *Op. cit.*, p. 388.

[59] John Foxe, *Acts and Monuments*, London, 1838, 6. 618.

And so when he Master Weston had overly read my arguments, and here and there spake little to the purpose for avoiding of them, (and therefore I eftsoons prayed him to give me in writing his answers;) he began to tell me how and what he had done for Grimbold, and how that I needed not to fear any reproach or slander I should sustain, belike meaning to have me secretly to have come to them, as Grimbold did; for he subscribed.[60]

Less than two years before, Grimald, in preaching before an assembly of bishops in St. Paul's, had dramatically declared: "Much better it is to be deprived of life for God's sake than to be deprived of God himself for the sake of life."[61]

In the following extracts from 'The Story of Laurence Saunders, Martyr,' in Foxe's *Acts and Monuments,* we have two scenes presented which show something of the undaunted courage of the martyrs, and the inconstancy, the self-acknowledged guilt, of the tricky Grimald, who betrayed the martyrs to their deaths.

The first of these pictures, which are highly suggestive of the dramatic events of the times, describes the coming of Bishop Bonner, the Roman Catholic Bishop of London, to the Marshalsea prison, for the ceremony of unfrocking Laurence Saunders, who had been imprisoned there for over a year at the order of Bonner, because of his preaching against the Roman Church; and we see the courage of Saunders in facing Bonner, who sought his death.

On the day following, a dramatic scene occurred at St. Albans, where the party conveying Saunders to Coventry to be burned stopped for the night. There Saunders received a visit from Grimald, whom he rebuked for his infidelity. Taking a cup in his hand, he asked Grimald if he would take a pledge to drain the cup of martyrdom that he himself was about to drink. Whereupon Grimald, more

[60] *The Writings of John Bradford,* Parker Society Publications, Cambridge, 1843, p. 548.

[61] Nicholas Grimald, *Oratio ad Pontifices,* London, 1583, p. 25.

anxious to save his life than his own soul, refused the cup, though he was willing enough to drink to the health of the man who was to suffer martyrdom on the morrow:

> The 4th day of February 1555 the bishop of London did come to the prison, where he [Laurence Saunders] was, to degrade him; which when he had done, Laurence Saunders said to him, 'I thank God, I am none of your church.' The day following in the morning, the sheriff of London delivered him to certain of the queen's guard, which were appointed to carry him to the city of Coventry, there to be burned. The first night they came to St. Albans, where Master Grimoald (a man who had more store of good gifts than of great constancy) did speak with him. After master Saunders had given him a lesson meet for his lightness, he took a cup in his hand, and asked if he would pledge him of that cup, of which he would begin to him. Grimoald, by his shrugging and shrinking showing what he was, said, 'Of that cup which is in your hand, I will pledge you: but of that other which you mean, I will not promise you.' 'Well,' said master Saunders, 'my dear Lord Jesus hath begun to me of a more bitter cup than mine shall be; and shall I not pledge my most sweet Saviour? Yes, I hope.'[62]

John Strype, in his *Ecclesiastical Memorials,* gives us his impression of Grimald's treacherous character, and an account of his betrayal of his friends, that he might escape being burned alive as they were:

> As they had these true friends, so they had false ones too, treacherous Judas's, that betrayed them; discovering to their enemies who their benefactors were, the relief they received, the letters they wrote, and such like. Of this sort was Grimbald: who this year being in the Marshalsea for religion, was persuaded to recant; and confessed and revealed everything he knew concerning the professors. Many writings of Ridley he got, and secretly put them into the hands of Popish superiors. But this recantation of his was kept secret from the prisoners, and they were not to know it, though they suspected him: and so remaining among them, he served as a spy upon them.[63]

Grimald not only came under the condemnation of the leaders of the Reformation in England, but under that of

[62] John Foxe, *Acts and Monuments,* London, 1838, 6. 627.

[63] John Strype, *Ecclesiastical Memorials,* Oxford, 1823, p. 229.

the Roman Catholic Church as well, for his writings are among those which are under the ban of the Church. The earliest record of their condemnation is to be found in the Vatican Library[64] under the date of 1564; but it is not unlikely that they were banned at an earlier date.

Little further is known of Grimald's career after these incidents of the Reformation. He seems to have dropped out of public life altogether. In 1556, three years after Mary's accession to the throne, and a year after Ridley's death, Tottel published a translation of Cicero's *De Officiis* by Nicolas Grimalde, dedicated to Thomas [Thirlby], Bishop of Ely. Edward Arber, the editor of the modern edition of *Songes and Sonettes,* called *Tottel's Miscellany,*[65] has argued that the Grimbold who was chaplain to the Protestant Bishop Ridley could not have been the Grimalde who was the translator of Cicero, and who dedicated it to a Roman Catholic bishop. The mere difference in the spelling of the two names is of no significance. The name Grimald, as has been previously shown, was spelled in every conceivable way in the county of Huntingdon, where the family flourished. In the Cambridge registers, or Grace Books, the poet's name appears as Grymold, Grymbold, Grinuuall, Grynwall, Grynwhall. In the Memorials of Merton College the name appears as Nicholas Grimoalde and Grymboldus. The register of Christ Church, Oxford, has it as Grimwald. That the alumnus of Cambridge, the fellow of Merton, and the instructor of Christ Church, were one and the same, there can be no doubt, as Grimald, in his preface to *Christus Redivivus,* which was written after his coming to Oxford, makes it quite clear that he had come from the University of Cambridge; further, the *Memorials of Merton College,*[66]

[64] Rossi, *Index Librorum Prohibiturum: cum regulis confectus per pp. a Tridentia synodo dilectus,* Bononiæ, ap. Rubrium, 1564.

[65] *Tottel's Miscellany,* Arber, London, 1870, pp. ix, xi.

[66] George C. Brodrick, *Memorials of Merton College,* Oxford Historical Society, Oxford, 1885, p. 259.

Oxford, state that he was of Christ College, Cambridge. That the grammarian, the rhetorician, and the poet were one, the verses from Duke Humphrey's MS. attest. That the translator of Cicero's *De Officiis,* who dedicated them to Thomas, Bishop of Ely, was the same man, there can be no doubt, for the list of the works of the poet, as given by Bale, includes that. In the various letters of the martyrs which have been previously quoted, in which Grimald is referred to, his name is variously spelled: Grimbald, Grimbold, Grimoald. That Ridley's chaplain was the commentator and translator is quite conclusive from the letter previously quoted, in which Ridley suggests that he might 'interpretate' Laurentius Valla's book on the 'false feigned fable forged of Constantinus Magnus, and his donation and the glorious exaltation of the see of Rome,' and translate Aeneas Sylvius' *De Gestis Basiliensis Concilii.* Arber assumes that Grimald was chaplain for Bishop Thirlby,[67] because Grimald signs the dedicatory epistle of the translation of Cicero's *De Officiis:* 'Your humble oratour, Nicolas Grimalde.' Because the man signed himself 'Your humble oratour,' it does not necessarily signify that he was Thirlby's chaplain. But even if he were—and of this there is no documentary proof—it would be but further evidence of the duplicity of Grimald's character, and of his seeking to curry favor with the great.

In the book entitled *Eglogs, Epytaphes, and Sonettes,*[68] *Newly written up by Barnabe Googe,* there appears *An Epytaphe on the Death of Nicholas Grimaold.* The death of the poet must have occurred before May, 1562, since at that time Googe left England for the Continent, leaving the manuscript of his book in the hands of a friend who sent it to the printer. In the winter of 1562-3 Googe returned from Spain, and was astonished to learn that his poems

[67] *Tottel's Miscellany,* Arber, 1870, Introduction, Sec. 1.

[68] Barnabe Googe, *Eglogs, Epytaphes, and Sonettes,* London, March 15, 1563. Reprinted by Edward Arber, London, 1871, p. 73.

were in the printer's hands, where they had been sent without his knowledge, but he consented to their appearance, since a considerable amount of money had been spent for paper for their issue. On March 15, 1563, his book appeared with the following verses:

An Epytaphe of the Death
of Nicolas Grimaold.

Beholde this fle-
tyng world how al things fade
Howe every thyng
doth passe and weare awaye,
Eche state of lyfe,
by comon course and trade,
Abydes no tyme,
but hath a passyng daye.
For looke as lyfe,
that pleasaunt Dame hath brought,
The pleasaunt yeares,
and dayes of lustynes,
So Death our Foe,
consumeth all to nought,
Envyeng these,
with Darte doth us oppresse,
And that whiche is,
the greatest gryfe of all,
The gredye Grype,
doth no estate respect,
But wher he comes,
he makes them down to fall,
Ne stayes he at,
the hie sharpe wytted sect.
For if that wytt,
or worthy Eloquens,
Or learnyng deape,
could move hym to forbeare,
O Grimaolde then,
thou hadste not yet gon hence
But heare hadest sene,
full many an aged yeare.
Ne had the Mu-

ses loste so fyne a Floure,
Nor had Miner-
va wept to leave the so,
If wysdome myght
have fled the fatall howre,
Thou hadste not yet
ben suffred for to go,
A thousande doltysh
Geese we myght have sparde,
A thousande wytles
heads, death might have found
And taken them,
for whom no man had carde,
And layde them lowe,
in deepe oblivious grounde,
But Fortune fav-
ours Fooles—as old men saye
And lets them lyve,
and take the wyse awaye.

CHRISTUS REDIVIVUS

PREFACE

THAT a tragi-comedy such as Grimald's *Christus Redivivus* should have come from the hands of a sixteenth-century college boy of twenty is nothing short of remarkable. This piece, as Grimald himself says in the dedicatory epistle of the play to Gilbert Smith,[1] Archdeacon of Peterborough, was written during the first weeks after his arrival in Oxford. Here he had come, after having just been graduated from Cambridge, with the intention of taking his Master's

[1] Very little is known of the career of Gilbert Smith, to whom Grimald dedicated his *Christus Redivivus.* It is probable that he is the Master Gilbert Smyth who incepted in Arts at Cambridge in 1501. This record does not appear in Cooper's *Athenæ Cantabrigienses,* but is included in Dr. J. A. Venn's *Alumni Cantabrigienses,* which is soon to be published. No record of Smith's ordination is known to exist. From June 28, 1498, until Feb. 22, 1506-7, he was prebendary of Gretton (John Le Neve, *Fasti Ecclesiæ Anglicanæ,* 1854, p. 153), from which he collated to the prebend of Leighton-Bromswold, the home of Nicholas Grimald, where he was prebendary until Feb. 25, 1548-9 (*op. cit.,* p. 177). On Aug. 26, 1506, he was installed as Archdeacon of Northampton, and held that position as long as Northampton remained a part of the diocese of Lincoln (Browne Willis, *A Survey of the Cathedrals of Lincoln, Ely, Oxford, and Peterborough,* 1730, p. 112). The value of this position was two hundred and nine pounds per year, while the prebend of Leighton-Bromswold brought him sixty-six pounds (*The Chapter Acts of the Cathedral Church of S. Mary of Lincoln,* Vol. 12). Upon the erection of the diocese of Peterborough in 1541, Smith was made first archdeacon of the new Cathedral of Peterborough. Records of 1536 show that the archdeacon was then a resident of Leighton-Bromswold (*Valor Ecclesiasticus,* 1821, p. 257). He manifested his interest in the village, and in the cause of education, by establishing a free school there (Browne Willis, *op. cit.,* p. 209). There he probably made the acquaintance of Nicholas Grimald, and was so impressed with his ability that he sent him to Oxford, if indeed he did not educate him at Cambridge as well.

degree at 'that other light of England.' The drama was composed at Brasenose College, Oxford, where he was probably but a mere lodger, rather than a member of that College, since his name does not appear on the college's rolls. Probably also this College had been recommended to him by Archdeacon Smith, inasmuch as Matthew Smith, a relative of the archdeacon, had been its first principal. Owing to the non-arrival in Oxford of the poet's books, his studies suffered considerable interruption; that he might not be idle, he went to work on the composition of a play.

As Grimald says in his preface to the play, it was noised abroad by some of the stage-struck youths of Brasenose who frequented his room that he was engaged in such a work, and they urged him to let them have the piece for performance. When Matthew Smith heard of it, he added his persuasions to their entreaties. So, too, did Robert Cauldwell, a man of distinction and learning, and so did Grimald's tutor, John Aerius, as well. When the news of the composition reached the ears of the Archdeacon of Peterborough, who was paying Grimald's way at Oxford, and who added his requests that the play might be put upon the boards, Grimald, who had been seemingly reluctant to have this done, could not but consent.

The piece was pushed to conclusion, though its composition was attended by some difficulty, because of the discomfort which attended the great severity of the winter's cold, and was probably given at Easter-time, since it is a resurrection-play. It was presented before not only the students of Oxford, but the citizens as well, since Grimald was anxious not only to stimulate the minds of the students, but to give a representation of the most important event in the life of the Saviour for the edification of the townsmen of Oxford.

Christus Redivivus is a poetic drama of a distinctly lyrical type. The play presents a wider departure from the classical model of the drama than one would expect from a student and a devotee of the humanities. Indeed, Grimald's play rather invites comparison with the popular, or Shakespearean, variety. Lack of unity of plot is at once apparent in glancing at the long list of the characters employed, for twenty principals are called for, and a large number of 'extra people' for the Chorus of Galileans, the Chorus of Disciples, and the Manes Piorum. Among the characters appear not only those of the Bible—Christ, Peter, John, Thomas, Nicodemus, Joseph of Arimathea, Mary Magdalene, and Caiaphas—but also four swaggering comic soldiers of the Miles Gloriosus type, Alecto the Fury, and a character, unnamed in the *dramatis personæ,* who, serving as Chorus, delivers the argument or prologue to each act.

In his dedicatory epistle of the drama, Grimald seeks to justify his departure from the classic type, not only by giving his own views upon the subject, but by quoting those of his tutor, John Aerius. He defends his varying diction by saying that the variety of characters demands a corresponding variety in the choice of words, and also that as the spirit of the various scenes changes, so should the metre, and he declares that the fulness of expression has arisen out of the fulness of the subject. He defends the interspersing of tragic and comic scenes by saying that Aerius had found no breach of good taste in this, and that he had cited the *Captivi* of Plautus as a precedent.

It is rather surprising that, in writing a Biblical drama, Grimald, who was a thorough student of the Bible, did not employ the language of the Vulgate, but that of Virgil, and that he has not merely largely adopted Virgilian diction, but has used phrases and even whole lines from the *Aeneid,* besides imitating the elaborate figures of speech of Virgil. The introduction of such a character from Grecian mythology as Alecto, and the use of such oaths as 'By Hercules!' and 'By Apollo!' are no less curious. Since classical treatment has been accorded to a Biblical subject, the translation of the play has been attended with some difficulties. These have been not only in the matter of diction; the punctuation has been an obstacle as well, since it is by no means modern. Question-marks were used after indirect questions, as well as after direct, and these marks are often so like exclamation points that they can scarcely be distinguished from the latter. Many sentences have no stops at all, and stops often appear where there should be none; so the punctuation is frequently more of a hindrance than a help in reading. The faulty punctuation, and the emendations of the text that have been found necessary, show that the printers' work was not at all carefully done, and that there could have been no preliminary typesetting and reading of proof. Inasmuch as Virgilian diction has been used, the elaborate figures of speech of Virgil imitated, and classical treatment accorded to a Biblical subject, the translation of the play necessarily presents to the modern ear, accustomed to the simplicity of Biblical English, what seems at first to be jargon. As Grimald's Latin is neither purely that of the Vulgate nor that of the *Aeneid,* so the English of the translation is neither that of the King James version of the Bible nor that of present-day English, but necessarily presents a mixture of elements as curious as the mixture of the Christian and the Pagan elements in the play.

The construction of the drama is hampered by its necessary dependence on the Bible, just as the English chronicle plays were by history; consequently it is much the same type of piece as John Bale's *King John* and Shakespeare's *Henry VI,* which are the versification of scene after scene in the life of the hero. Although the scenes in *Christus Redivivus* likewise could not be so planned and altered as to increase in interest, to rise to a climax, and reach a *dénouement,* nevertheless Grimald has succeeded in presenting a play of more dramatic value than any other drama that had up to this time been written. This success was no doubt due to the influence of humanism, whose apostle he was, as the preface to his translation of Cicero's *De Officiis* shows. That Grimald possessed a distinct sense of acting values is quite evident from his portrayal of the highly emotional rôle of Mary Magdalene, and the low-comedy parts of the soldiers. It is also remarkable that the play is divided into acts, a division that had not as yet become common in English drama, although his friend John Bale had already adopted it.[2]

It would be interesting to know something of the production of the play at Brasenose College, but no records in regard to its presentation have been preserved there. Its production in Germany, however, is much more fortunate in this respect, for records of its presentation, which were brought to light by Johannes Bolte,[3] still exist there. In 1543, two years after the play was written, and when Grimald had become a fellow of Merton College, Oxford, the play was revived through the insistence of Grimald's patron, the Archdeacon of Peterborough, and published by Martin Gymnicus at Cologne. That its circulation in Germany was large is attested by the existence of so many copies in German libraries to-day, ten being extant there, while there are only two in England, and one in America. There was not only the edition published in Cologne, but another, possibly unauthorized, which was published by Philippus Ulhardus in Augsburg in 1556. This differs from the Cologne edition only in the pagination and the title-page, which has an ornamental floral border. It is not unlikely that this edition was brought out to supply the demand for play-books at Saint Anna's Gymnasium, where the schoolmaster, Sixt Birk,[4] had introduced the performance of Latin school-

[2] John Bale, *God's Promises, John Baptist, The Temptation of Our Lord,* 1538.

[3] Johannes Bolte, 'Nicholas Grimald und das Oberammergauer Passionspiel,' *Archiv für das Studium der Neueren Sprachen* 105. 1.

[4] Sixt Birk (Lat. Xystus Betulius oder Betulejus), dramat. Dichter geb. 1501 in Augsburg, gest. daselbst 1554, studierte in Tübingen und Basel, wo er späterhin als Korrektor und seit 1530 als Schulmann tätig war. In 1536 wurde er als Rektor des Gymnasiums in seine Vaterstadt zurückberufen. Seine Dramen *Ezechias,*

comedies. In the Hof-und-Staatsbibliothek in Munich there is a copy of this edition which once belonged to Philip Rechlinger, one of the students at the Gymnasium, who played the part of Christus in the Augsburg production, and who, as the *Hochzeitbuch der Patrizier* shows, was at that time but fourteen years old.

On the flyleaves of the copy in the Hof-und-Staats Bibliothek there is written the following caste of persons who appeared in the play, as presented at St. Anne's Gymnasium in Augsburg in April, 1556:

Personæ

Magdalene	1. Jo: Sporerus
Cleophis	2. Jo: Schenckius
Salome	3. Laos Schidner
Josephus Arimathiensis	4. Dawerckh
Nicodemus	5. Hie: Krayer
Caiaphas	6. Th. Iecklinus
Annas	7. Nicholaus
Dromo	8. Leonhardus Curtius
Dorus	9. David Hoserus
Sangax	10.
Brumax	11. Georgius Kugelmannus
Cacodemon	12. M. Kintzius
Manes piorum	13.
Christus	14. Ph. Rechl(inger)
Petrus	15. Ca: Seylianus
Johannes	16. Jo: Georg Palderstain
Angelus 1	17. Maxus Sulzing
Angelus 2	18. Elias Meysenberg
Chorus Discipulorum	19.
Alecto	20. Georgius Celenius
Cleopas	21. Komel
Thomas Didymus	22. Georgius Ruch
Johanna	23. Seb. Volandt
Amaon	24. Hie Manlich
Chorus Galileidum	25.

Zorobabel, Judith, und *Tragödie wider die Abgötterei* stehen an Bedeutung zurück hinter seinen beiden Dramatisierungen der Geschichte Susanna, die wiederholt von spätern dramatischen Bear-

There are also the following verses written in German on the flyleaves; they were evidently intended to be spoken by Chorus to explain the action of the play to those whose knowledge of Latin was imperfect or lacking.

Act: I

Hert zu jr freindt vnd merckt vorab,
Es khumbt erstlih zu disem grab,
Ein weiblin Christo wol erkhant,
Maria Magdalena genant
Mit sampt auch anderen weiberen guett
Bewaÿnt vnd clagt mitt schwerem muet
Den todt Christi, den sÿ gedacht
Nun gantz erwirgt und umbegracht.
Und seins lebens sein beraubt
Das sÿ noch nit verstandt und glaubt
Dass in Got auferwecken wolt
Welchs sich doch balt erzaygen solt
Es sprücht sÿ Nicodemus an,
Desgleich Joseph ein reicher man,
Der Christum auch hat herzlich lieb,
Si bittendt sÿ dass nit betrieb,
Ir Hertz und allso heÿl undt wain,
Befelchs Gott und gang mit ins Haus,
Gedenck auch zu jrem trost hiebey
Dass er jetz ebig selig seÿ,
Bey Gott hab funden rechte Rhue,
Nun sucht mit ernst der handlung zu.

Actus II

Nun gat die an d handlung an,
Darin, vermerck mich jederman
Dritt brachtlich fur her Caiaphas
Der Christo auch zuwider was,
Freud sich seins totts, von hertzen hoch

beitern desselben Stoffes (z. B. P. Rebhun) benützt wurden. Seine deutsche *Susanna* erschien 1532 (Neudruck von Gessler, Zürich, 1891); die lateinische (1537) besser als die deutsche, voll trefflichen Charakterbildern (hrsg. von Bolte, Berl. 1893), wurde ins Räto-romanische und ins Dänische übersetzt.

—*Meyer's Konversations-Lexikon,* Leipzig, 1905.

Wie all sein andere feynnt och
Er sagt es sey sein rechter lon,
Man solts jm lengest han gethon
Es samlet sich dass gantz geschlecht
Der gleysner, pfaffen, templ khnecht,
Hatt dag und nacht khayn rast noch rhue
Lofft Pontio Pilato zue
Bit das er sey vor weytterer gfar
Dass Grab durch Kriegsleuth wol verwar
Verbit schier auch den stain voraus
Pilatus richts durch Annam aus
Derselb versieht al sachen wol,
Sagt jeden huetter das er soll
Wachen und halten vleysig huett
Erforderst wein und labe guett
Si sagent zu jrent hochsten vleys
Und wil ein jeder han den Breys,
Rumbt sich seiner sterck und manlichayt
Und mist im zu grossen dapferkhayt
Dass werdt jr jesund sehen fein
Ich bit jr solt aufmerckig seyn.

Actus III

Nun folgt wass sich verloffen hab
Mit Christo an dem dritten Tag
Gott der all jn henden hallt
Den ertboden erschutt mit gwalt
Zwen engl thont vom grab die thur
Christus gaet lebendig herfur,
Und weyl er hat verbracht als dass,
Im selber und uns zu wider wass
Und aufgehebt des tottes bein
Hayst er uns vorthin frolich sein
Als syt uns trosten seiner umsthent
So fern mir selig werden werdt
Die wechter all erschrecken sehr
Khayn understatt sich dass er wehr
Jr manlich hertz ist gar dahin
Und Khayner wil der hinderst sein
Maria khumbt am morgen frue
Sambt anderen dass sy ehr an thue
Dem herren Christō bringt herbey
Kostliche salb und spetzlerey

Die weyber sorgendt wehr den steyn
Von grab jnen hinweg wel thun
Und als sy noch hinzu sindt khumen
Habendt sy dass grab offen gfunden
Ein engel auf sitzen darbey
Der gsagt Christus erstanden sey.
Johanni sy zu wyssen thondt
Auch Petro wass sy gesechen handt
Die bayt sych machent gleich auf Ban
Wend aller ding ein wissen han
Ir jede d sach grundlich erferdt
Zum grab Maria wider khert
Die engel findt sy schon dar ston
Sieht Christum selbs zunechst bey jr stohn
Halt jn fur ein gartner, kent jn nit
Biss er sich selbs zerhennen bigt
Wie er den andern weybern guet
Sich auch hernach erzaygen thuet.
In dem Christus zur helle fert;
Dass der teufel erschreckt hert
Fleucht raus mit gschray wayst nit wo aus
Jedoch Christus sein ampt richt aus
Erloset aus der helle quall
Die auf in habendt gwartedt all,
Dass werdt jr

Actus IIII

Nun sindt al still und horent zue
Wass jetz undt weyter folgen thue.
Nach dem die weyber s grab verlandt
Die wechter jn sich selber gandt
Verwundern sich nach langer weyl
Loffendt zum priester hin in Eyl
Und brichtens aller sache woll
Khainer weiss was man drin halten sol.
Es sameldt sich der gantze Rhat
Nach langem es allso zuegat
Dass niemand wa auss wa an,
Auch khayn nichts gwisses erfahren khan
Das ist dem Theuyel glebt jm saus
Er schickt sein botten fraue auss
Ein hellisch weyb vol list und trug
Die fert mit freut hin ohn verzug
Und rhet den Briestern al gemain

Wie sy den sachen sollendt thain
Die wechter bstechen mit vil gelt
Damit es nit auskhumb jn d welt
Und dass jr jeder due sagen
Man habe Christum hingetragen
Als jr ein jeder gschlaffen hett
Mit freud folgen sy jrem Rhatt
Die wechter nement s geldt an
Und sagendt d luge jeder man

Actus V

Als Christus sich hat sehen lassen von Jungern
Die sich zamen gthan und Thoma nit ist gwest dabey
Hat er nicht globt dass allso sey
Ob sy jm schon anzayget klar
Noch hat ers nit ghalten fur war
So lang biss Christus selber khumbt
Thudt jm sein uhr stendt so als khundt
Sagt dass er mit den finger reg
D mal zaychen handt in d seyten leg
Den jungern gibt er bschayt zu handt
Wie solchs man sondt bekhant
Inn aller welt durch jre leer
Die Junge geben Gott die ehr
Lobendt seyn guet die er gwendt
An uns damit has als ein Endt

The city archives of Augsburg also have the following expense-accounts of the production, which show that the play was produced at Easter-time in April, 1556:

Apprillis

adi. 18. ditto ....

adi. —— ditto fl.36 kr.13 hlr.3, zt. und allerlei uncosten, sampt vererungen, so über die Comoedi, der Uffersteung Christi, zu Sannt Anna Kirchen gehalten worden, uffgeloffen und gegangen ist, thut alles. lt. 2. zell. —— —— so. 338 ff. 36 13 3

April

18—36 florins, 13 kreutzer, 3 heller, and sundry expenses including tips, which have accrued by the performance of the Comedy of the Resurrection of Christ at Saint Anna's Church according to the 2 bills enclosed, amount to —— —— according to folio 338 36 13 3

Philip Rechlinger's book was passed on to other hands, and the following year, 1557, it seems to have become the property of Johannes Wolmuet, and then of Carolus Hieber, and Hanns Manng von Rechlinger. Possibly these were schoolboys who played in revivals of the piece on subsequent Easters. No records of any such performances are to be found, but such records would not exist were there no expenses incurred. As the initial expenses had once been paid, possibly none further were necessary.

Whether or not more performances of the play were ever given, the influence of *Christus Redivivus* was not at an end. In 1566, ten years after the performance of Grimald's play in Augsburg, Sebastian Wild, an Augsburg tailor, schoolmaster, and *meistersinger,* published a volume[5] containing twelve plays, the third one of which, *Eine schöne Tragedi, aus der heyligen schrifft gezogen, Von den Leyden und Sterben auch die Aufferstehung unsers Herrn Jesu Christ,* was based upon Grimald's *Christus Redivivus.* The text of this German passion play shows that Wild translated and used Grimald's play with the greatest freedom, combining it with his own materials. That the schoolmaster, Wild, witnessed a performance of Grimald's play at Saint Anna's is probable; that he possessed a copy is a certainty, for the Latin play and the German play present points of similarity which are unmistakable.

Of all the countries in which plays based upon the passion of our Lord have flourished, Germany has been and still is preëminent; for even to-day all the world flocks to the little mountain village of Oberammergau to see the passion play given there. As far back as the twelfth century it is said that there was a passion play performed in that village, but, toward the close of the sixteenth century, the wars that wasted Germany left little or no inclination in those dwellers

[5] Sebastian Wild, *Schöner Comedien und Tragedien swölff: Aus Helliger Göttlicher schrift, und auch auss etlichen Historien gezogen,* Matthew Franck, Augsburg, 1566.

of the remote highlands for dramatic performances of this sort. As was usual, pestilence followed in the wake of the wars, and the Bavarians of southern Germany suffered greatly from a plague which resembled the Black Death. While village after village fell a prey to its ravages, Oberammergau remained untouched, because of the rigorous quarantine maintained by the villagers. At last one of the natives, overcome by a desire to see his wife and child, returned, and brought the plague with him. In two days he was dead, and the plague that he had brought spread so quickly that a terrible panic seized upon the villagers. They cried out to God in their agony, and vowed that, if they were delivered from the pestilence, they would perform a passion play every ten years. According to tradition, from that hour the plague was stayed; and the passion play became a fixed institution, having been performed, according to the vow, every decade, except for the interruptions occasioned in 1870 by the Franco-Prussian War, and in 1920 by the great World War.

The oldest known text of this play, written in 1662, is still extant. The original, which is in the possession of the firm Georg Lang sel. Erben of Oberammergau, was reprinted in 1880 by Dr. August Hartman,[6] who has made a thorough study of the text, and discovered that it was composed of two older plays—one of which was used in the fifteenth century in the cloister of St. Ulrich and Afra in Augsburg, while the other was Wild's play. The latter play appeared as the third in a volume of plays by Wild, entitled *Schöner Comedien und Tragedien zwölff: Aus heiliger Göttlicher schrift, und auch auss etlicher Historien Gezogen,* published by Matthew Franck, Augsburg, 1566. All these three plays —*Das Augsburger Passionsspiel aus St. Ulrich und Afra, Sebastian Wild's Passionsspiel,* and *Das Oberammergauer*

[6] *Das Oberammergauer Passionsspiel in seiner Altesten Gestalt,* Leipzig, 1880.

Passionsspiel vom Jahre 1662—have been included by Hartman in his volume cited above.

Johannes Bolte made a still further, though not exhaustive, study of these plays, and discovered that Wild had made as free use of Grimald's *Christus Redivivus* in writing his play as the unknown author of the passion play of 1662 had of Wild's play. Although the scenes of these two plays must necessarily be much alike, since they are founded upon the Scriptures, yet it will be found that the scenes cited to show Wild's dependence upon Grimald's are a much closer rendering of Grimald's play than they are of the Bible.

The following lines of Wild's prologue closely follow the first eight lines of Grimald's:

Der HEROLDT geht ein und spricht.

Heyl und genad von Gott allein
Sey euch, so hie versamblet sein!
Lieben Herren und Christenleüt,
Wir haben uns für gnommen heüt,
Ein schöne Tragedj zu halten
Zum ebenbild Jungen und Allten.
Der grund und das gantz fundament
Ist ausz dem newen Testament
Gezogen und zusam gericht.

—*Sebastian Wild's Passionsspiel* 1-18.
Hartman, *op. cit.,* p. 103.

As Wild's play begins with the episode of Judas' bargain to betray his Master for thirty pieces of silver, and covers a period not included in Grimald's play, which begins with the visit of Mary Magdalene to Christ's tomb, no further similarities are to be noted between the two plays until that point in the action is reached. Here we find Wild utilizing the material in the Magdalene's soliloquy, which comprises the entire first scene of Grimald's first act, which he puts into the mouths of Maria Magdalena, Maria Jacobin, and Maria Salome.

MARIA MAGDALENA spricht

O jr schnöden Juden verwegen,
Was noht hat euch gegangen an,
Das jr also ein ghrechten than,
Der nyemand schädlich ist gewesen,
Sonder vil Armer thet erlösen
Von grosser noth und schwerer sucht!
O du heylig Göttliche frucht,
Solt du nun ligen in der Erden?
Wie möcht ich ye betrübter werden?
Ach, Fraw Maria Salome,
Ist mir in mein hertzen so wee!
Ich kan und weiss nit mer zuleben.

MARIA SALOME

Ach Gott! also ist mir auch eben,
Mein allerliebste Schwester, nun.
Er war ye warer Gottes Son,
Gerecht und fromb in allen Dingen.
Wasz man jm fur kranchleüt thet bringen.
Die macht er alle sampt gesundt
Mit eim wort, das kein Artzet kundt.
Und dise böse art unrein
Solt jn in solche schnach und pein
Bringen ohn alle schuld und not!
Ach, Jesu, wer ich für dich todt!
So müszt mir ye besser sein eben,
Dann ohn dich hinfür mehr zu leben.
Ach, Maria Magdalena
Und Maria Jacobin, wa
Wölln wir unser zuflucht hin haben,
So unser Meyster ist begraben?
Ach, Gott und Herr, lasz dichs erbarmen!
Wie wirt hinfür geschehen uns armen?
Wie trostlosz werden wir nun sein!

MARIA JACOBIN spricht

O allerliebste Schwester mein,
Er möcht noch ein trews hertz erbarmen
Er hieng da mit auszgspannen armen
An einem hohen Creütz erhaben,
An beyd hend und füszen durch graben,

Das von jm flosz das rote blut.
Noch fienge also an der gut,
Bat Gott seinen Vatter für die
In martern theten, das er sie
Nicht entgelten liesz diser that.
Also war sein herz frü und spat
Zu barmhersigkeit geneyget,
Nicht rach umb rach begeren thet.
O herr Jesu, du höchster hort,
Het ich dasz gmerkt auff deine wort,
Weyl du bey uns warst in dem leben!
Ob ich yetzt gern thet achtung geben,
So kan ich dich nun nymmer hören.
Ach! wasz möcht mein herz basz beschweren
Als es vorhin beschweret ist?
O du mein Herr und Jesu Christ,
Wie wirt ich dein wider ergetzt?
Wol bin ich in trawren gesetzt,
Das mir nun nymmer mag vergahn,
Die weyl ich hie mein leben han.
O mein hertz bricht mir gleich dahin.

MARIA MAGDALENA

Ach, Fraw Maria Jacobin,
Hie ligt all unser trost und leben.
Wie mag ich nun hinfüran eben
Getröstet und gebessert werden?
Ich komm dann auch unter die Erden,
Sonst hat mein trawren nymmer end.
O jr falschen Juden verblend,
Wol habt jr ein joch auff euch gladen,
Wol müszt jrs so mit so grossem schaden
Büssen und all ewre Kinder.
Ewr wirt hinfür geachtet minder,
Dann eines todten Hunds ellendt,
Das jr so wenig habt erkendt
Die gnedig heimsuchung des Herren.

MARIA SALOME

Ja, der nye kein Mensch thet beschweren,
Sonder mitleydig ist gewesen,
Wie vil thet er vom tod erlösen,

Die mit tödtlicher Kranckheit eben
Beladen waren und umbgeben,
Ja auch etliche gar vom todt
Erweckt: noch hat er diser rott
In keiner sach recht mögen than.

—*Sebastian Wild's Passionsspiel* 979-1059.

The scene between Joseph of Arimathea, Nicodemus, and the women at Christ's tomb in Wild's play is a condensation of Act I, Scene II, pp. 18-24, in Grimald's play:

Joseph unnd Nicodemus gehen ein. JOSEPH spricht

Jr Frawen, seyt jr noch beym Grab?
Was hilfft ewer wainen und klagen?

MARIA MAGDALENA

Ach, mein Herr Joseph, was thust sagen?
Solt ich dann nicht klagen, der mir
So grosse trew bewise, jr?
Wist jr? vil Teuffel mich besassen,
Der er mich entledigt dermassen,
Die mich sonst Ewig hetten quelt,
Und nyemand war in diser Wellt
Der mir ye helffen kund dann er,
Und sonst vilen jr kranckheit schwer
Vertryben hat eynig allein,
Sollt diser nit zu klagen sein,
Der auch mein Bruder Lazarum
Vom tod erwecket widerum
Und ander mehr, wie jr wol wist?
O du mein Herr und Jesu Christ,
Das ich für dich gestorben wer!

NICODEMUS

Es mag euch doch nit helffen mehr.
Es ist uns auch sehr leyd von herzen
So wol als jr tragt grossen schmerzen
Umb jn. doch künden wir jn nit
Wider lebendig machem mit
Unserem wainen und beklagen.

Doch dencken wir, wie thet sagen,
Er wolt in dreyen tagen eben
Widerumb aufferstehen und leben.
Das ist unser hoffnung und trost.

MARIA SALOME

O dadurch wirt mein Hertz erlost
Wo solliches geschehe, wie
Du sagest, aber warlich die
Hoffnung ist klein und ungewisz.

MARIA JACOBIN

Ach Gott! wie möcht geschehen disz?
Wiewol er den Lazarum eben
Und der Wittfrawen Son das leben
Widerumb gab, aber das sein
Zunemen ist die hoffnung klein,
Wiewol er das gesaget hat.

JOSEPH

Ir Frawen, kommet! es ist spät.
Der Sabath ist gebrochen an.
Wann dann der Sabath thut vergahn,
Möcht jr weyter beklagen jn.

MARIA MAGDALENA

Ach, wie soll ich mein trawren hin
Legen? das mag in Ewigkeit
Nymmermehr nit geschehen, seit
Mir mein Herr so unschuldigklich
An dem Creütz ist ermördet, ich
Sech in dann wider in seim leben.

NICODEMUS

Ich hoff, es soll geschehen eben
Nach seinem wort. kommet herein!

MARIA MAGDALENA

Ach allerliebster Herre mein,
Soll ich dich nun im Grab verlassen:

Und du thetest mir nit solcher massen
An meinem Bruder Lazarum,
Dem du halffst auff frey widerum;
Aber ich musz dich ligen lahn!
O hertz, wie kanst das oberstahn?

Sie thut, sam woll sie fallen,
JOSEPH nimbt sie bey den armen
und spricht

Ey, Maria, nun sey getröst!
Ich hoff, wir werden bald erlöst.

Gehen darmit trawrig ab.

—*Sebastian Wild's Passionsspiel* 1062-1121.

In Act III of Wild's play there is a scene between Annas, Cayphas, and the soldiers who have been engaged to guard the tomb of Christ, and who swagger and brag about what they will do if Christ's disciples come to take away Christ's body. This is very similar in tone, though not in the actual lines, to the corresponding scene, Act II, Scene III, in Grimald's play. The names of Grimald's soldiers, Brumax, Dromo, Dorus, and Sangax, Wild changes to Prunax, Troma, Romox, and Marcurinux.

CAYPHAS spricht

Lieben Kriegsleüt, mercket mich eben,
Was ich fur euch befelch will geben!
Hie ligt der verführer begraben,
Welchen wir gecreütziget haben,
Der sich vil mal hett mercken lahn,
Er wöll wider vom tod erstahn.
Darummen thun wir euch bestellen
Und euch gar wol besolden wöllen,
Das jr dessen Grab heüt die nacht
Verhüttet und mit fleysz verwacht,
Auff dasz nit seine Junger eben
Kommen, Stehlen jn und fürgeben
Er sey erstanden von dem todt.

PRUNAX

Herr, derhalben habt nur kein noht!
Wir wöllen das Grab wol verhüten
Nach ewrem befelch und gebieten
Das er uns nymmer ausz dem Grab
Kommet, weil ich mein leben hab.
Uns soll sein leychnam nyemand nemen.

Marcurinux

O das seine Junger her kemen,
Und theten uns hochmut zufügen!
Jr freuel soll sie wol betriegen.
Dann ich hab ohn das noch ein grollen
Zu dem allten glatzeten dollen,
Welcher ewr Ehrwürt Knecht Malchus
Ein Ohr abschlug im Garten dusz.
Es soll jm werden vergolten.

ROMOX

O kemen sie! ich mein, sie solten
Von uns werden empfangen hie,
Und werden jr noch zwölff wie sie,
Keiner solt uns den leib wegtragen.

Troma

Ich allein wölt sie all zwölff schlagen.
Mein Herr, schlafft nur ohn sorg die nacht!
Das Grab sollt wol werden verwacht,
Das er uns nit sollt aufferstahn
Noch gestohlen. ich als ein Man
Wolt das Grab noch allein versehen.

Marcurinux

Herr, also soll mir auch geschehen.

Annas

Wolan, lieben trewen Kriegesknecht,
Wir wöllen euch befolden recht.
Was wöllt jr, Taller oder Goldt?

Prunax

Ehrwürdiger Herr, was jr wolt.
Es ist uns alles sampt gut Gellt,
Wans nur allein dem Würt gesellt,
Wir wollen es nit graben ein.

Cayphas

Secht! da hat ein yeglicher sein
Gebürend Gellt, lauter gut Taller.
Es fehlt ewr keinem umb kein haller.

Troma

Ho! ho! so ich nur einmal Gellt han
Ich wolt den Teüffel hütten than
Das er nit wurd hinwegk getragen.

Romox

Herr, thut die nacht mit friden schlaffen!
Wir thun, wie jr uns thut verschaffen.

Marcurinux

Herr, schlaffend bisz an liechstem Morgen
Dise Nacht und lassend mich sorgen!

Troma

Herr, seit die Nacht in sicherer rhu!
Nyemand soll uns leyd fügen zu.

Annas

Wolan, so habt gut fleysz und acht!
Drauff wünsch ich euch gute nacht.

Cayphas

Halt! ich musz vor das Grab verriglen
Die Thür mit dem Secret versiglen.

CAYPHAS versigelts Grab, spricht weyter

Nun seyt frölich in diser sachen
Thu einer dem andern dweyl kurz machen!

Prunax

Ja, lieben Herrn, ziecht frolich hin!
Der Tod soll wol bleyben hie in.

Annas und Cayphas gehen ab.

—*Sebastian Wild's Passionsspiel* 1145-1212.

Two other old German passion plays, the second *Sterzinger Passion* and the third *Pfarrkircher Passion*,[7] also show the influence of Grimald in their use of the comic soldiers; the lines of these plays do not, however, show marked resemblances to those of Grimald.

A part of Christ's soliloquy after the resurrection, Act III, Scene II, p. 37, 1. 9-16, has been freely rendered by Wild.

CHRISTUS ersteht und spricht

Nun hab ich den Tod uberwunden,
Im sein spitzigen stachel unden
Zerbrochen und gar stumpff gemacht,
Mit dem er vil mord hat verbracht.
Sein bogen hab ich jm darbey
Gerissen in mitten entzwey.
Nun ist jm sein macht alle sand
Genommen, das er mag nyemand
Kein schaden zu fügen fürthin.
Nun will ich hinab faren in
Die Hell, dieselbig auch zerreissen,
Den Teufel umb die ohren schmeissen.

—*Sebastian Wild's Passionsspiel* 1328-1349.

The awakening from their stupor of the soldiers in Wild's play is also a free rendering of Act IV, Scene I, in Grimald's play:

[7] J. E. Wackerell, *Altdeutsche Passionsspiele aus Tirol*, Graz, 1897, pp. 77-177, 185-253.

PRUNAX richt sich auf und spricht

Ich hab ein guts schläflein verbracht
West ich nur, wies wer in der nacht,
Ob es auch mein stund her geschlagen,
Das ich dem Romox thet anfangen!

Er steht auff, sicht das Grab offen, spricht weyter

Ach Jupiter! wie wirts mir gahn?
Der ist, dieweyl ich geschlaffen han,
Gestigen ausz dem Grab herfür.
Prunax, Marcurinux, O jr
Lieben Gsellen, nun thut auffstahn!
O wie thut es so ubel gahn!

Die zwen richten sich auff.
PRUNAX rüfft auch den Troma

Troma! Troma! ach wach doch auff!

TROMA bleybt ligen. ROMOX spricht

Was? seind die Junger da mit Hauff?

PRUNAX

Ach! der ist ausz dem Grab dahin.

Romox und Marcurinux stehn auff.
MARCURINUX spricht

Das wer der Teuffel! wie hast jn
Ubersehen? hast etwa gschlaffen?
Oder thetst sonst hin und her gsffen?

ROMOX weckt den Troma und spricht

Troma! Troma! kreüch doch herfür!

TROMA richt auff und spricht

Was? ist die wach yetzund an mir?

ROMOX

Ey! der ist ausz dem Grab schon hin.

TROMA

Wo wöll wir wider finden jn?

ROMOX

Ja, er wirt dir sitzen daher!
In das Grab bringst du jn nicht mehr.
Ist er wider lebendig worden,
So ist er schon an andern orthen.

TROMA

An welchem war die stund zu wachen?

MARCURINUX

Prunax sach so fein zu den sachen.

TROMA

Solt du uns in solliche noht
Setzten, in Ewig schand und spott,
Dienest all mal also deim Herren?
Ich glaub, du wölst uns allsand geren
Mit dir hin bringen an den Galgen.
Komb her und thu dich mit mir balgen!
Ich will dir deines wachens geben.

PRUNAX

Acht, du werst mich des uberheben;
Hast gleich so wol gschlaffen als ich.

TROMA

Warumb hast nit gewecket mich,
Da du ye nit hast wachen wöllen,
Oder thetst den Romox auffstennen?
Bist ein Lantzknecht, so wehr dich mein!

PRUNAX

Nur her, weyls nit anders mag sein!

Sie schlagen ein streich oder zwen zusammen.

ROMOX spricht

Ey, haltend frid sollicher sach!
Es gebürt sich nit auff der wach
Zu balgen, es ist doch schon gschehen.

Sie stecken ein. TROMA spricht
Ich kund jm das nit ubersehen;
Ist ein allter gstandner Kriegsman,
Und soll uns solche schmach anthan?

PRUNAX

Ir habt doch auch gnommen das Gellt,
Laget dannoch schlaffen im Feldt,
Als wer das grosz schnarchen ein kunst.

MARCURINUX

Du hasts verspilt, wir hetten sunst
Nit also gschlaffen, lasz dir sagen!

ROMOX

Und wann wir lang einander schlagen,
So ist doch der schad schon geschehen.
Wir müssen umb ein ausred sehen.

TROMA

Ach! werden wir so übel bstahn,
Hetten wir sonst ein todten Mann
An sein statt zu legen hie her!

MARCURINUX

Prunax, wie ist entrunnen er?

PRUNAX

Ich kan euch gar nichts sagen von.
Der schlaff thet mich hart ubergohn.
Ish steüret mich ein wenig nider
Gedacht bald zu erwachen wider.
Ich lag gleich als in trawmes qual,
Sam höret ich ein donner knall,
Das sich das Erdterich erschüt.
Da erwachet ich gleich darmit,
Schawet umb mich, fand das Grab offen;
Da ward er schon herausz geschloffen.
Ich stund da in angst, noht und zwang,
Der Schweysz mir allenthalb ausztrang;
War auch mit grosser forcht umgeben,
Sah auch ein glastigs liecht darneben.
Da war ich gleich sam wer ich todt.

ROMOX

Fürwar solliche pein und noht
Hett mich gleich also auch gefangen.

MARCURINUX

Mit dem traum bin ich auch umbangen,
Wie du mich auff thest wecken eben.

TROMA

Ja, darmit thet ich auch fast streben.
Ich war gantz kranck und kraftlosz;
Da lag ich wie ein todtes Rosz.

ROMOX

Wie wöllen wir jm aber than?

PRUNAX

Wir wöllens also zeygen an
Und, ob sie gleich ein wenig schelten,
So wirt es doch kaum henckens gelten.
Mir können wider Gott nit streben.
Ist er Gott, wie er sich ausz geben
Hat, wie die Schrifftgelehrten sagen
Und also fast uber jn klagen
Das er sich selbst genennet hab,
Und ich auch selbst kan nemen ab,
So müssens wol zufriden sein.

ROMOX

Also ist auch die meynung mein.

MARCURINUX

So kompt her! wir wöllen den allten
Dise handlung also für halten.

Gehn darmit ab.

The arrival of the three Maries at the tomb in the German play is almost identical with that of Magdalene, Cleophis, and the women of Galilee in the Latin drama, Act III, Scene V, p. 42, 1. 8-15.

Die drey Maria gehn ein, tregt yede ein Buchszen mit salben. MARIA JACOBIN spricht

Ach Maria, yetzt felt mit ein:
Wer wirt uns wegk welten den stein
Von dem Grab? er ist grosz und schwer.

MARIA SALOME

Maria, mich gedüncket, der
Stein sey schon von desz Grabes thür.

MARIA MAGDALENA

Ja, er ist wegk, nun wöllen wir
Hinein gehn und den Herren salben.

Sie gehn zum Grab und sehen nyemand.

MARIA spricht weyter

Ach Gott! in dem Grab allenthalben
Find ich kein toden Leychnam mehr.
Ach Herr Gott! wie geht das Zu? wer
Hat mir mein Herren wegk getragen?

—*Sebastian Wild's Passionsspiel* 1476-1486.

The scene of the arrival of Peter and John at the tomb in Wild's play is somewhat similar to the same scene in Grimald's play, Act III, Scene IV, p. 43, I. 7-20, though it does not follow the Latin play closely:

JOHANNES eylt vor zum Grab und spricht

O Petre, wie die Frawen sagen,
So ist Jesus hinweg getragen.
Da sich ich weder flaisch noch bein.

PETRUS spricht

Ich will gar steigen hinein.

PETRUS steygt ins Grab, zeygt die Leynwat und spricht weyter

Ach! da ist kein Herr in dem Grab.
Die schwaiszthuch ich wol funden hab,
In die er gewichlet war hie.

Nimb sie zu dir, auff das wir sie
Unseren Brüdern zeygen eben,
Auff das sie uns gelauben geben,
Das er in dem Grab sey nicht mehr!

JOHANNES

O Petre, so komb eylends her!
Dann ich förcht mich wol also hart.

PETRUS

Gang hin! ich auch nit lenger wart.

Gehn darmit ab.

—*Sebastian Wild's Passionsspiel* 1524-37.

Mary Magdalene's scene with the angels, and with Christ at the tomb, is similar in the German drama to the corresponding scene, Act III, Scene V, p. 44, 1. 10-28, in the Latin drama:

ZWEN ENGEL steygen wider ausz dem Grab;

DER ANDER spricht

Weyb, warumb wainest du also?

MARIA MAGDALENA

Ach! man hat mir mein Herren do
Gestohlen ausz des Grabes theich.

DER ENGEL

Es ist doch vor gesaget euch,
Er sey erstanden, er werd da
Euch vorgehn in Gallilea.

Die Engel gehen ab. Die Frawen wenden sich auch vom Grab.

JESUS geht gegen jnen als ein Gärtner und spricht Weyb, warumb wainest du so fast?

MARIA MAGDALENA

Ach, mein Gärtner, sag mir an: hast
Du mein Herren hinwegk getragen?
Wo hast jn hin glegt? thu mirs sagen!

JESUS

Maria, nach wem fragst du mich?

MARIA MAGDALENA

Rabi, bist du es, so nenn dich!

—*Sebastiàn Wild's Passionsspiel* 1542-1553.

The bribery scene between Caiaphas and the soldiers in *Christus Redivivus,* Act IV, Scene VI, p. 61, I. 16 et seq., pp. 62, 63-4, I. 1-12, has not been closely followed by Wild, but has been imitated:

PRUNAX

Kein Mensch, er ist selbert erstanden
Ausz eygner krafft von todes banden,
Dieweyl wir da lagen erschlagen.

CAYPHAS

Bey leib thut solches nyemandt sagen!
Zeygt uns die rechte warheit an,
Wie sich all ding verloffen han!
Haben jn sein Junger vertragen,
So thut uns den rechten grund sagen!
Oder jr solt des todes sterben.

ROMOX

Ob jr uns gleich all thet verderben,
So künden wir doch nichts darfür.
Er ist erstanden, müssen wir
Bekennen; dann sein Gottlich krafft,
Mit der allzeyt war behafft,
Hat uns zur Erd geschlagen nider.

ANNAS

Seyt jr auch Christen worden sider
Necht, da wir theten von euch gahn

Und jr uns thet geloben an
Bey ewrem Leyb und leben fest
In zu bewaren auff das best?
Wie? wann jr jn selbst het wegk tragen?

MARCURINUX

Herr, solliches solt jr nit sagen!
Er ist selbst erstanden vom todt,
Wie ein sigreicher Gott.

CAYPHAS spricht

Habt jr die wach versehen recht?

PRUNAX

Ja, wer ein gantz Regiment Knecht
Beym Grab gewest, wir hetten jn
Nit behalten; er ist schon hin.

Cayphas erschrickt hart. ANNAS spricht

Wie? ist er ausz desz grabes banden?

PRUNAX

Ja, Herr, er ist mit gwalt erstanden.

CAYPHAS

Solten ewr so vil starcker Mann
Ein eynigen lassen darvon,
Warumb gaben wir euch das Gellt?

PRUNAX

O Herr, es het nit fast vil gfelt,
Wur weren all kommen umbs leben.
Ein harter schlaff thet uns umb geben.
Etwa nach Mitternach da kam
Gar ein glentziger flam
Und auch ein Erdtbietem darmit
Das sich das gantz Erdtrich erschüt.
Uns thet ein solche forcht umbgeben,
Das keiner bey seim leib und leben
Nit kundt auff seinen füssen stohn.
In diser zeyt ist er darvon,
Dieweyl wir als halb tod da legen.

ANNAS

Wer hat jn euch hinweg tragen?

CAYPHAS

Und wann er gleich erstanden wer,
Ward jr all nit so starck als er,
Das hr jn wider hett erschlagen
So wol als vor den zweyen tagen,
Da jr jn an dem Creütz thet todten?

TROMA

Yetzund aber thet er uns nötten
Mit seinen kräfften, das wir all
Lagen als todt in gleichem fall.
Sein krafft ist unmenschlicher art.
Jr habt doch sein Grab selbst bewardt
Und auff das aller best verrigelt,
Mit ewr eygnem Secret versigelt
Und habt jn kendt, auch gewist nun,
Das er ware ein Gottes Sun!
Ich acht, jr habt uns nur darumb
Zum Grab gstelt, dasz er uns all umb
Das leben soll bringen, von wegen
Das wir hand an jn theten legen,
Da er ans Creütz geschlagen wardt.
Welliches doch ewr böse art
Mit gantzem gwalt hat haben wöllen
Yetzt wolt jr uns jn für dar stellen,
Ey, lieben Herrn, bedenckt euch recht!
Ob wir schon seind arme Landesknecht,
So wöll wir doch der warheit bstehn
Und mit euch für Pilato gehn
Und uns versprechen vor sein gnaden.
Wir uns dann von jm straff auffgladen,
So wöllen wir die willig tragen.

CAYPHAS

Lieben Kriegsleut, ich will euch sagen:
Ob wir schon für Pilato kemen,
So müst jr euch ewer hut schemen,
Nun sag ich euch: weyl er ye ist
Ausz dem Grab hinweg zu der frist,

Damit wir abe diser sachen
Und wir kein grosz gschrey daraus machen.
Sonder das es bleib in der still,
So were dises unser will,
Das wir euch behielten bey ehren:
Sprecht vor jederman, knechtund Herren,
In haben seine Junger ungschaffen
Gestohlen, wie jr habt geschlaffen!
So kompt jr mit ehren darvon
Und wir auch mit ehren bestohn
Vor der Gmain, die vil auff jn helt;
So wöllen wir euch geben Gelt.
Sagt nur nit, das er sey erstanden!

ROMOX

Ja, Herr, hie und in allen Landen
Sollen wir nimmer anders reden.

Hannas.

Wo wir anders erfaren theten,
Dann wie wir euch yetzt under sagen,
So wöllen wir euch all verklagen
Vor Pilato; der soll euch schlecht
Darummen thon ewere recht.
Desz solt jr eben versehen!

MARCURINUX

Ja, Herr, anderst soll nit geschehen!
Von wem jr anderst thut erfahren,
An dem solt jr die straff nit sparen!

PRUNAX

Laszt sehen, Herr, thut uns Gelt zeygen!
Wir künden gar wol darzu schweygen.
Wir wöllen sagen unverholen,
Seine Junger haben jn gstohlen,
Und nyemand soll uns widerstahn.

ANNAS

Send! da habt jr Gellts gnug zu lahn,
Und globet an, solches zuhalten!

PRUNAX

Herr, mein trew soll sich gar nit spalten.

Sie globen all an. TROMA spricht

Lieben Herren, seyt nur ohn sorgen!
Die sach soll wol bleyben verborgen.

CAYPHAS

Wolan, so schawt, das jr es halt!

ROMOX

Herr, seyt sicher aller gestalt!

Die Hohenpriester gehen ab.

—*Sebastian Wild's Passionsspiel* 1628-1743.

Wild developed as dialogue the recital of the events of the journey to Emmaus, and the first appearance of Christ after his resurrection to the disciples, both of which are given by Grimald as bits of narrative related by his characters. The most striking mark of similarity between the passages relating to these events is the mention of Moses' lifting up of the brazen serpent on the cross, which is not mentioned in Luke, chap. 24, which gives the account of the journey to Emmaus:

Quid loquor, aut suspensum a duce colubrum aeneum,
Quo, serpentum afflatu prostrata corpora
Per campum surgebant sanata et integra:

—*Christus Redivivus,* p. 71, l. 10-12.

Auch zeugt die schrifft von mir dermassen;
Das ich den tod solt leyden nur,
Desz habt jr ein klare figur.
Wie nun Mose die erin Schlangen
Auffricht und an ein Creütz thet hangen,
Also must auch desz Menschen Sun
An ein Creütz werden gschlagen nun.

—*Sebastian Wild's Passionsspiel* 1943-1949.

Since the text of the Oberammergau passion play, which was a compound of Sebastian Wild's play and the play from the convent of St. Ulrich and St. Afra, remained in use until 1740, Grimald's influence in Germany for two centuries is easily apparent.

CHRISTVS REDIVIVVS, COMOEDIA

Tragica, ſacra & noua.

Authore Nicolao Grimoaldo.

Coloniae Ioan. Gymnicus excudebat.
Anno M. D. XLIII.

The Resurrection of Christ

A new sacred tragi-comedy

by

Nicholas Grimald.

Martin Gymnicus,
Cologne,
1543

OPTIMO ET HONO-

ratissimo uiro Gilberto Smitho, Ar-

chidiacono Petroburgensi, Nicolaus

Grimoaldus à Christo domino

S. D.

Vtrùm audacius, aut durius esset committere, ut opus recèns confe ctũ, per quorumuis manus *&* ora, ueluti securum uagaretur, an tuis ut creberrimis postulationibus ob sisterem, saepè, doctissime uir, ac multùm *&* à repræhensione mihi cauens, *&* morem tibi gestum cupiens, apud me cogita-[1] ri. Nonnihil equidem uerebar, ne forsan hæc subita iuuenilis inuenti peruulgatio, penitus immatura, *&* an te diem properata, doctis ac prudentibus uiris existimari posset. Namq; si uel inter clarissimos scriptores memorantur, qui suas commentationes per multos annos sibi diligentur euoluendas, *&* frequenti studio reco lendas putauerunt, donec quod desideraretur, supplerent, quod abundaret ac effflueret, quasi luxuriantem segetem paulatim depascerent: quam confidentiam ego prodidisse uideri potero, qui cùm eosdẽ sequi fortasse, nunquam adsequi, *&* de illis iudicium facere, nũquam efficere similia queo: tamẽ quod propter inclementiam brumalis frigoris haud sine difficultate, proq; ratione temporis magna cum festinatione parturiebã, tam ci tò, tamq; nullo ad retractandũ sumpto spacio, párere nõ dubitauerim? Ac sanè, si repetenti mihi, measq; aut

[1] Emendation:
cauens, *&* morem tibi gestum cupiens, apud me *cogitaui.*

To Gilbert Smith,
Archdeacon of Peterborough,
A man of the greatest excellence and highest distinction,
Greetings in Christ our Lord
from
Nicholas Grimald.

Learned sir, in my desire both to avoid censure for myself and to gratify you, I have reflected earnestly and often whether it be a bolder and ruder thing to trust a work recently finished to pass through the hands and lips of any one, as if its future were secure, than it is to resist your oft-repeated requests. I have, indeed, been somewhat afraid that this hasty publication of a youthful fancy might by good judges be regarded as immature in thought, and premature in presentation. For if even among the most celebrated authors it is recorded of some that they thought their dissertations must be diligently developed for many years, and improved by uninterrupted study, until they added what was wanting, and gradually pruned down, as an over-fruitful crop, what was abundant and superfluous; what self-confidence shall I seem to have displayed, who, although I can emulate these same men, can never equal them, and though I can pass an opinion on them, can never produce similar works? Nevertheless, without taking time for revision, a task which was difficult on account of the severity of the winter's cold, and also because of the shortness of time, should I not have hesitated to bring forth the offspring of my travail?

If, indeed, on going back, and reviewing my plays, fiction,

fabulosas, aut fictitias, aut ueras exercitationes, quas non ita pridem chartis mandabam, recognoscenti, uete res usq; adeò labores displicent, ut in illis ipsis uix memet agnoscam, & quodammodò pœniteat operæ collocatæ: quid scis, nuḿ nam idem posthac etiam usu mihi ueniat, uti meipsum ultrò castigās, istis, quæ nunc præ cipito ueriûs quàm scribo, magìs elaborata & perpolita uellem sufficere? Metuebam prætereà, ne fortè quis me parùm nauiter humeros explorasse, ac meam facultatem consuluisse censeat: quandoquidem ineptum uiribus meis onus, atq; argumentum grauius & maius uidear suscipere, quàm quod ab homine adolescentulo tractari uel possit, uel debeat. Etenim cùm multæ res in sacra Philosophia, nequaquam facilè cognoscũtur, nisi quis Græcam simul & Hebræam linguam tenue rit, nisi quis in ea perdiu uersatus fuerit, & singula inter se loca studiosè contulerit: tum de Christi à mor tuis exurrectione, quam sic antè constituere, quasi si res iam ageretur, contendo, haud paucis difficultatibus, inuoluta historia est. Neq; uerò desunt, qui imber bem adhuc & crescentem cum consilio ætatem, aut à sa crarum lectione literarum omnino arceri uolunt, aut si admittunt aliquando, ut auscultricem quidem accede re patiuntur, ut interpretem autem nullo modo. Tum demum, haud mediocriter illud pertimescebam, futuros, qui nimiùm iustè conquerantur: me rem gestam ri tè digerere, ac talem tantamq́; materiam digna oratione uestire non posse. Nimirum, tanquam in communi hominum uita & moribus, arduum in primis habetur, in unaquaq; re decorũ perspicere & obseruare, de quo sapienter à Philosophis in Ethica disciplina præcipitur: sic in poëmatis, consentaneam rebus & personis orationem adfingere, hominem peracuto ingenio, lima to iudicio, singulari diligentia, summoq́; ocio abundan-

or serious compositions, which I committed to manuscript not so long ago, I am so dissatisfied with my previous work that I can scarcely recognize myself in those very productions, and, in a certain way, regret the pains spent, how do you know but hereafter it may be beneficial for me to take to censuring myself of my own accord, and to desire to substitute works of greater polish and refinement for those which I now throw off rather than write? Furthermore, I feared that some one might perchance think that with too little zeal I had examined my capacity to bear the burden, and had taken counsel of my ability, since I am apparently undertaking a task incompatible with my talents, and a theme too weighty and too great to be treated with skill and propriety by a youth. For, as there are many things in the philosophy of the Bible that are by no means easily understood unless a man has mastered the Greek as well as the Hebrew tongue, and has been for a long time engaged in the study of the Bible, and has zealously compared various passages one with the other, so the account of the resurrection of Christ, which I am trying to set before you as if it were now taking place, involves a great many difficulties. Indeed, there are some who desire either that young people, while they are still in the callow years of undeveloped judgment, should be entirely restrained from reading the sacred Scriptures, or, if it be permitted them at times, that they should approach as listeners, but in no wise as expounders. Then, finally, I feared in no small degree that there would be those who would very justly complain that I could not set forth this event properly, and clothe so great a theme in appropriate diction. I know, of course, that, as in everyday life and conduct, it is considered especially difficult to perceive and note in each instance what is proper—a subject that is learnedly treated by philosophers in their ethical teachings—so in poetical compositions, to fashion diction in harmony with the matter and characters demands a man of keen insight, of refined judgment, unusual diligence, and

tem requirit. Certum est enim, nec locupletem & tenuem fortunam, nec simplicem narrationem & iactationem Thrasonicam, nec blandam consolationem & querimoniam, nec cœlestem uocem & tartareos clamo res, unum atq; idem postulare dictionis genus. Proinde, perfici oportere, ut pro rerum natura, uarietate & modo, nunc Oratoriorum luminum & conformationum ueluti parcus, humili passu repat uersus, interdum uerò, uolubiliùs ac profluentiûs excursitet, sæpè autem numero uerborum agmen instar hybernarum niuium ingruat, & plenis habenis prorumpens oratio, campum, in quo exultare possit, obtineat. Adhæc, dum lêgi carminis inseruitur, operosam quandam rem, ac propè desperatam esse, ita postrema uerba cum insequentibus primis copulare, ut neq; iunctura uocalium hiulcas, neq; consonantium concursus uoces efficiat asperas: itaq; compræhensionis cuiusq; ambitum exple re, ut aureis teretes & religiosæ, neq; mutila & quasi decurtata sentiant, neq; superuacanea & redundantia. In primis igitur, quod ad huiusce libri êditionem attinet, uideor mihi uidere quosdam, me ut nimis ac nimis temerarium arguenteis: qui cùm tutiùs in umbratili Philosophorum schola, nŏ secus ac in aliquo nido pos sem delitescere: tamen multo meo cum periculo implumis euolare gestiam. Qui si nullum aliud à me responsum auferrent, nisi quòd roganti Gilberto Smitho mo rigerari uolui, esset fortassis honesta ratio: cùm præsertim & de me quàm optimè promerito, & bonarum literarum amantissimo uiro, & recta, & suo quodam iure poscenti, deesse nolui. Sed enim ut paulò altiùs hu iusce facti consilium repetam, cùm è Cantabrigiensi

blessed with great leisure. For it is certain that one and the same sort of style is not called for in the case of a rich man as of a poor one; in plain, straightforward narrative as in thrasonical boasting; in soothing consolation as in complaint; in a voice from heaven as in the wailings that arise from hell. Consequently, the work ought to be done so in accordance with the nature, the change, and the manner of the action, that at one time the verse may creep along in an unpretentious measure, shunning, as it were, the adornments and forms of oratory, whereas at other times it may speed along in a fuller and more precipitous course. Often, however, with marshaled words in battle array, it makes an onset like the snowstorms of winter, and its eloquence bursts forth unchecked, and gains the fields in which it can revel. Moreover, while attention is being paid to the laws of versification, I will remark that it is a troublesome and almost impossible business so to join the ends of words with the beginnings of following words that a union of vowels may not produce a hiatus, or the joining of consonants a harsh pronunciation; and to bring the period of each idea to a close in such a way that ears which are sensitive and overscrupulous may not perceive things mutilated and curtailed, or superfluous and redundant. Above all, then, so far as the publication of this book is concerned, I seem to see certain persons accusing me of excessive rashness, when I could hide away in the shady school of the philosophers, as securely as in some nest; nevertheless, I am desirous of flying forth, unfledged, with the greatest danger to myself. If they received no other answer from me save that I wished to gratify the desire of Gilbert Smith, my reason would perchance be a proper one; especially since I did not wish to fail in my duty toward a man from whom I have enjoyed such excellent favors, a man fond of good literature, who makes a just request in his own right. But, to go a little further back in explaining my decision, I will say that when, on

Academia decedens, uehementer hortante te & pecu nias ultrò suppeditante, uenissem ad alterum Angliæ lumen Oxonian, nec eò libri mei per hebdomadas aliquot essent adlati: hanc sum ingressus prouinciam, & quia intermissum legendi cursum, fructuoso aliquo com mentandi genere pensare concupiui, & quia res ipsa sic inhærebat animo meo, ut ex memoriæ thesauro tan quam de scripto promere liceret singula. Postea uero quàm uersatus in Collegio doctorum, quod ab Aeneo naso nomen inuenit, per mensem unum & item alterum istam pro mea uirili Spartam ornauerã, ac fortè for tuna ita, ut fiebat, arderet pubes domestica theatrum conscendere, quô & suos excitarent animos, & civibus imaginem quandam uitæ spectandam exhiberent: continuò ex paucis, qui meum cubiculum frequentabant, cœpit multis innotescere, quid molirer, quidq́; in manibus haberem. Egit itaq; mecum Matthæus Smithus Collegij præses & consanguineus tuus, homo mirifica modestia, liberalitate & sanctimonia præditus: egit Robertus Cauduuellus, uir perhonestus, & insigni-

my departure from Cambridge University, I had come to that other light of England, Oxford, at your earnest request, accompanied by your present of money, inasmuch as my books were not brought there for several weeks, I undertook this new task, both because I was eager to make up for the interrupted course of reading with some fruitful sort of study, and because the subject so clung to my mind that it was possible to produce the details from the storehouse of my memory, as if they were written before me. But, when, living in the learned college which takes its name from the brass nose,[1] I had adorned that Sparta[2] to the best of my abilities for one or two months, it happened by chance that the youths of the community were eager to enter the field of the drama, that they might stimulate their minds, and that they might give some representation of life to the citizens. Immediately what I was undertaking, and what I had on my hands, began to be made known to many by the few who frequented my room. And so Matthew Smith,[3] the principal of the college, who is also your relative, a man of surprising modesty, and gifted with a broad mind and devout heart, together with Robert Caldwell,[4] a man

[1] Brasenose College, Oxford.

[2] Quoted, among others, by Cicero, *Ad Att.* I. 20, from a fragment of Euripides' lost play, *Telephus; cf.* King, *Classical and Foreign Quotations,* 3d ed., 2605; Euripides, ed. Nauck, Fr. 722 (3. 195).

[3] Smith (Mathew) Smygth, B.A. 30 June 1505, Fellow of Oriel College 27 April 1506, first principal Brasenose Coll., 1510, M.A. supd. 24 Feb., 1513-14, B.D. disp. 20 Oct., 1519, D.D. supd. 1519, canon of Lincoln, 1508, buried in St. Mary's Church, Oxford.

—Joseph Foster, *Alumni Oxonienses,* Oxford, 1892.

[4] The name of Robert Caldwell does not appear on the records of Brasenose College, nor on those of the University of Oxford. This may be a misprint for Richard Caldwell, whose record is here given: Caldwell (Cauldwell, Caldwall, Calwale), Richard (Staffs.). B.A. 20 July 1533; M.A. 12 Mar. 1538-9; Fellow (Founders); Senior Bursar 1540-2; Senior Student of Christ Church c. 1547;

ter doctus: egerunt lectissimi atq; optimæ spei adolescenteis, ut meam sibi fœturā, in Scenam producendam concrederem, in eaq́; re, meam illis operam dicarem ac deuouerem. Quoniam autem negare eis tum præclara petentibus, tum indole sua digna cupientibus, difficile mihi uisum fuit: permisi sanè, ut eorum auspicijs, hæc ista Comœdia etiam in eruditissimorum uirorum coro na publicitus ageretur. Quod simul ut fama uoce loquaci perstrepens, in aureis tuas effuderat: me non solùm per diligentissimum institutorem meum Iohannem Aërium admonere, sed & ipse tu iterum atq; iterum huius poëmatis êditionem rogare comiter sustinuisti. Atque adeò, quoties egomet admiratione & pudore propè confusus, ad caussas ingeniosus extiti: dicebamq́; non posse non in adolescente uiginti plus minus annos nato, undiq; apparere inscientiæ uestigia, habebamq́; in obiectis omnia, quæ sunt à me superiùs adducta: toties præceptor ille meus (quæ sua fuit & tibi obsequendi, & prouocandi mei sedulitas) instabat, & exemplis cùm recentiorum, tum etiam ueterum utebatur, quorum extarent monumenta, id ætatis, haud sine summa laude conscripta. Neq; mihi magnoperè sequendam esse aie-

of distinction and remarkable learning, and many excellent young men of very great promise urged me to entrust to them my production for presentation on the stage, and to dedicate and devote my exertions to them for this purpose. As it seemed hard for me to deny them, since they were making so excellent a request for things worthy of their talents, I gave my full consent to have this comedy performed publicly, and that, too, in a circle of the most learned men. As soon as Rumor,[5] making a great din with its chattering tongue, had poured this information into your ears, you courteously persisted not only in advising me through my devoted teacher, Johannes Aerius,[6] but also in begging me yourself, again and again, for the publication of this poem. So, whenever in surprise and embarrassment I resorted to ingenious excuses, and kept saying that in a youth about twenty years old it was impossible for signs of ignorance not to be evident in all his work, and added to my objections all the points already brought forward, my teacher pressed me (such was his eagerness to obey you and to urge me), and made use of illustrations not only of modern but of ancient writers, whose works, written at this age, have survived to win the highest praise. He said that I should pay no great attention to the maxim of Horace[7]

B. Med. 9 Mar. 1554-5; D. Med. 29 July 1555; F.R.C.P. 1559; PRCP. 1570; died 1584.

—*Brasenose College Register, 1509-1909.*
Oxford Historical Society, 1910.

[5] Cf. *Aeneid* 5. 174-188.

[6] This is probably a Latin version of an English name. No other name on the University records seems to resemble it other than that of John Harreys, or Harreis, who was admitted fellow of Merton College, Oxford, in 1512, and who may have been Grimald's tutor there.

[7] . . . Si quid tamen olim
Scripseris, in Maeci descendat judicis aures

bat uocem illă Horatianam, quæ nonum in annum premi iubet opusculum: quin potiùs, quô tibi extrema iam ætate confecto (dùm licet) gratum facerem, festinădum, agendum' que in tantis meis occupationibus domesticis cum uiro aliquo exquisitè docto, ut & legere librum & inter legendum uultus inimicos induere uelit. Neq; si grauioribus deinceps annis, grauius industriæ speci men édere me posse confidam: continuò, ab hoc proposito desistendum. Vt enim (exempli gratia) M. Tullij Rhetoricis ad Quintum fratrem aduentante senectute cōscriptis, omnem admirationem tribui uidemus: ita & libris de Rhetorica inuentione, quos adolescens composuit, suam esse laudem & commendationem. Non P. Vergilium detinuisse à scribendo Culicem aut Aeclogas, rei rusticæ describendæ speratam gloriam: non eam cum Hesiodo contentionem, magni Homeri æmulationem restinxisse. Itemq́; non Maronianum Aeneam, primis tantùm in cursu, uerùm & secundis, & etiă infra secŭdos quibusdam, certa elargitum esse præmia. Iam uerò, illud peropportunè cecidisse confirmabat, quòd in argumentum adsumerem non leuiuscula Epigrammata, non amatorios iocos, non morias, non mimos, non postremorum hominum colloquia, non Atel

which decrees that a production should be suppressed for nine years; but rather that, in order to please you, advanced in years as you are, I ought to hurry, and in spite of my own many preoccupations, work with some man of fine scholarship, who would read my book, and assume a critical attitude. Nor, even though confident that I can produce a weightier example of my industry in more advanced years hereafter, ought I to abandon this theme immediately; as, for example, not only do we see great admiration bestowed on Cicero's *Rhetoric,* written in his later years to his brother Quintus, but also the books entitled *De Rhetorica Inventione,* which he wrote in his youth, have their own praise and commendation. Virgil did not refrain from writing the *Culex,* or *Eclogues,* because of his hope of renown from the *Georgics;* the rivalry of Hesiod did not quench the emulation of great Homer. And, again, Æneas in Virgil's poem bestowed fixed prizes not only on the first in the race,[8] but on the second, and even on some below the second. Indeed, my teacher asserted that it was commendably fitting that I had incorporated in the play no frivolous epigrams, no jokes about love, no silly talk, no mimes, no dialogue of the lowest

Et patris et nostras, nonum que prematur in annum,
Membranis intus positis. Delere licebit
Quod non edideris; nescit vox missa reverti.

Horace, *Ars Poetica* 386-390.

But if at some chance hour you aught compose,
See 't is correct ere to the world it goes;
Submit it to Tarpa's critic ears,
Your sire's, and mine; and keep your piece nine years.
What is not published you can blot or burn;
But words, once uttered, never can return.

—Translation by Francis Howes, in Cook, *The Art of Poetry,* Boston, 1892.

[8] Tum pater Aeneas 'Vestra' inquit 'munera vobis
Certa manent, pueri, el palmam movet ordine nemo;'

Aeneid 5. 348-9. Add *Aeneid* 5. 249-267.

lanam Comœdiam, nō Tabernariam, aut si qua sunt Ethnicarum fabularum portenta, quæ nihil ad morum conformationem, nihil ad solidam eruditionem, ni hil ad diuinæ laudis amplificationem adferunt emolumenti: sed quòd pro creaturis, creatorem, pro perditis & execrandis redemptorem & conseruatorem, pro hu mana ostentatione, cœlestis gloriæ propagationem, denique ipsum autorem carminis Iesum Christum, in materiam carminis accepissem. Omninoq; rem digniorē aut magìs diuinam, ex omnibus omnium scriptis, de ligi nunquam potuisse. Quippè quæ totius nostræ salutis quasi tabula sit, & uiuida repræsentatio. Nam qui reducem à morte Christum, ac pro suo scelere satis ab eo factum planè sentit, eiusdemq; spiritu sanctiorem ad uitam renouatur: eum inconcussa & efficaci fiducia uictorum, nihil sibi uel à prauarum adfectionum pulsionibus, uel à mortis periculo timentem, quin uiciorum colluulem strenuè fortiterq; pugnando dies in singulos repressurum, ut & ipse cum Christo suo mortuus peccatis, uiuat uni Deo. Vnde pronunciare Petrum, bonæ conscientæ fœdus erga Deum constare, per exur rectionē Iesu Christi à mortuis, qui patris ad dexteram considet. Cùm etenim diuinæ gratiæ non nisi per fidem in Christum participes fieri possumus: nūquam eò niti ualere persuasionem nostram, si non mortem illo uindice uictam iacere, si non illum genitori cœlesti adsidentem regnare, si deniq; nō omnibus antepositum & prælatum certò crediderimus. Si quidem, ut subeun dum ipsi letum fuisse, quô indignationem Dei, quam so lus Adamus contraxerat, solus Messias tolleret, inq; nobismetipsis peccata perimeret: sic uitæ restitui oportuisse, ut ad eius ipsius imaginem & formam suo spiritu perpetuò refingeremur, utq; suo munere iusti

types of men, no Atellan comedy, no tavern-plays, none of the strange tales of heathen dramas, which contribute nothing of profit toward the formation of character, to sound learning, or to the extension of divine praise. On the other hand, I had taken for the subject of my poem a Creator, instead of creatures; instead of lost and deplorable human beings, a Saviour and Redeemer; instead of human display, the furtherance of divine glory; in short, the very author of song, Jesus Christ: and that in general a worthier or a more uplifting topic could never have been chosen from all the writings of all people, inasmuch as this is, as it were, the picture and living portrayal of our whole salvation. For he who clearly perceives that Christ is brought back from death, and for our sins has made atonement, and who by the spirit of this same Christ is renewed to a holier life, he shall live in unshaken and powerful faith, fearing nothing for himself, either from the assaults of base desires, or from the peril of death; nay, struggling earnestly and bravely day by day, he shall even suppress his vile mass of faults, so that he himself, done with sin, may live with his Christ for God alone. My teacher further declared that for this reason Peter announced that the covenant of a good conscience toward God[9] is established by the resurrection of Christ, who is seated on the right hand of the Father. For as we cannot become partakers of divine grace except through faith in Christ, our conviction is never able to rely on Him if we have no firm belief that death lies vanquished, and that He is our liberator, that He reigns, seated at the right hand of His heavenly Father; finally, that He has been exalted and placed above all. The Messiah Himself had to submit to death, in order that He alone might take away the wrath of God, which Adam brought upon himself, and that He might destroy sin in ourselves; so it became Him to be restored to life, in order that we, by His own Spirit, might be continually refashioned according to His own image and

[9] 1 Pet. 3. 18-31.

redderemur. Idcircò, ualdè probandam operam meam in hoc negocio constantissimè adseuerauit, quoniam, cu ius fidem ipse Christus tam diligenter astruebat, & qua una in re spes atq; opes humanæ omneis collocari debent, perfeci, non solùm ut auditione accipi, sed etiam coram oculis proponi & statui queat. Semper inculca ri, semper mente & cogitatione reponi, semper fidelissima persuasione retineri, triumphum hunc Seruatoris nostri de peccato & morte, summè necessarium fore: tum quòd humana ratio & intelligentia uix ualet eum compræhendere: tum quòd improba suasio maligni dæ monis in hoc nos maximè remorari solet, in quo nouit salutem nostram totam esse positam. Itaq; non modò flo res ex oratione lectorem decerpturum: uerum etiam ex ipsa re fructus percepturum uberrimos. Quod autem ad uireis meas, & ætatis rationem attineret, nihil uide re se dictitabat, uel impudens, uel indecorum. Primùm enim non id me suscipere atq; profiteri, ut reuelem abdita mysteria: sed ut nudam ac ueram historiam enarrem, & modo quodam Poëtico, hoc est, claro & illustri spectaculo patefaciam. Nec sibi dubium esse, quin eam ad rem præter linguarum atq; librorum adminicula, & diligentem meditationem, & assiduam precati onem adhibuerim. Hac scilicet ratione & uia infanteis, paruulos ac pusillos regni Dei, citius ad germanam ac diuini eloquij scientiam atq; intellectum peruenire: quàm Cicerones, Aristoteles, Galenos, aut quoscun que etiam alios, qui suo ipsorum acumine, proprio inge nio, & humana sapientia nitũtur. Deinde, illud maxi mè decere & cõuenire, ut in Christiana Ecclesia mem brum nullum ocio desidiaq́; torpescat: sed, qua potest parte, uniuerso corpori famuletur & inseruiat. Atq; ijs, qui tãtarum rerum explicationem committi nolunt adolescentibus, cogitandum esse, quid' nam de Timo-

likeness, and that we might be made perfect by His gift. Therefore my teacher constantly asserted that my labor in this task was praiseworthy, because the doctrine, for faith in which Christ so earnestly builded, and on which all hope of human power ought to be founded, was not only audible, but even visible, in my work; saying, furthermore, that it would be necessary above all things that this triumph of our Saviour over sin and death be always impressed, be always stored up in the mind and thought, be always retained with most faithful conviction; on the one hand, because human reason and intelligence is hardly able to understand it; on the other, because the impious persuasion of the evil spirit is wont to hinder us especially in this matter, in which he knows our whole salvation is placed. Therefore the reader would not only pluck flowers from the language, but would indeed gather the richest fruits from the subject-matter. He kept saying that, as far as consideration of my abilities and my age was concerned, he saw nothing either shameful or indecorous. For, first of all, I did not attempt or profess to reveal hidden mysteries, but to tell a plain, unadorned tale, and to set it forth in a certain poetical manner, so to speak, that is, by a bright and glorious spectacle. And he had no doubt that, in addition to the aid derived from language and literature, I had added earnest reflection and unremitting prayer, and that by this method infants, little children, and the weaklings of God's kingdom sooner arrive at a true knowledge and understanding of divine eloquence than the Ciceros, the Aristotles, the Galens, or any others whatsoever who rely on their own keenness, personal genius, and human wisdom. Then, too, the thought is especially fitting and proper that no member of the Christian church should grow listless through want of work and activity, but that, with the ability at his command, he should be a servant, and of use to the whole body of the church. Also, that the people who do not wish to have young men entrusted with the teaching of so great truths ought to reflect what the

thei iuuentute senserit Paulus Apostolus: istis uerò, qui ne legēdi quidem uerbum illud salutiferum, Deiq; placita potestatem faciunt, D. Erasmi paraclesin pro-[2] ponendam esse, & quid Christianæ professionis intersit, etiam atq; etiam considerandum. Postremò, quod spectat ad huius Tragicæ Comœdiæ tractationem, suo quæq; loco ritè disponi, decorum custodiri, è rerum copia nasci uerborum copiam, numeros Comicos & fe rè Terentianos obseruari iudicabat. Bellè uidelicet, me temporum ordine ad finem decurrisse: & magna paruis, læta tristibus, obscura dilucidis, incredibilia probabilibus intexuisse. Quemadmodum enim quò res ipsa nomen tueatur suum, primum Actum Tragico mœrori cedere, quintum uerò & ultimum iucunditatibus adcommodari & gaudijs: ita quô uarietas satietati occurrat, cæteris omnibus intermedijs, nunc lugu bria, nunc festiua interseri. Etiam nihil ineptum, nihil indecorum, nihil quod aut personæ, aut rei, aut tempo ri, aut loco minùs quadret, inueniri posse arbitrabatur. Nam quis, inquit, Oratoriæ facultatis expertus, non rem gestam indicātibus & subitò colloquentibus, tenuem, pressum, & familiarem sermonem: non consolatoribus, læticiæ nūcijs, atq; plaudētibus, tractam, suauem & uenustam dictionem: non gloriosis, exultabundis, & indignantibus, acrem, ardentem, & grandiloquam orationē attribuerit? Loca item, haud usque eò discriminari censebat: quin unum in proscenium, facilè & citra negocium conduci queant. Ac si quis miretur, uel quòd plurium dierum historiam atque diuersa tempora, in unam & eandem actionem coëgerim, uel

[2] Emendation:
placita potestatem faciunt, D. Erasmi *paraphrasin* pro-

apostle Paul thought about the youth of Timothy;[10] but those who do not permit even the reading of the healing word and decrees of God ought to set before themselves the Paraphrase[11] of Erasmus, and ought to consider time and again what is of importance to the Christian profession. Finally, as far as the treatment of this tragi-comedy is concerned, he judged that each thing was duly assigned to its proper place, that propriety was observed, that the fulness of expression sprang from the fulness of the subject, that the metre of comedy, almost that of Terence, was preserved, that the play had been brought becomingly to a close in chronological arrangement; and that great things had been interwoven with the small, joyous with sad, obscure with manifest, incredible with probable. Moreover, just as the first act yields to tragic sorrow, in order that the subject-matter may keep its title, so the fifth and last adapts itself to delight and joy; likewise, in order that variety may be opposed to satiety, in all the other intermediate acts sad and cheerful incidents are inserted in turn. He thought also that it was not possible to find a breach of good taste, of decorum, anything out of harmony with character, theme, time, or place. 'For who,' he said, 'experienced in the art of oratory, does not give a meagre, terse, and colloquial diction to characters who report an occurrence, and who speak in rapid dialogue, to those bringing consolation, or good news; to those who applaud, a fluent, pleasant, graceful style; and to the vainglorious, the boasting, the indignant, a keen, ardent, grandiloquent speech?' Likewise, he concluded that the scenes were not so far apart but they could easily, and without trouble, be reduced to one stage-setting; and that, if any one is surprised, either because I have united in one and the same action a story covering several days, and different periods of time, or because such a pleasing

10 2 Timothy 1. 1-15; 2. 1-2.

11 Erasmus' Paraphrase of the New Testament.

quòd funestum & perluctuosum principium, tam plausibilem sortiatur exitum: eum intelligere debere, me autorem sequi M. Actium Plautum, cuius præter alias Capteiuei & compluribus interiectis diebus agi fingūtur, & ex initio mœsto in lætum etiā finem trans eunt. Deniq; certa spacia, numeratos pedes, atque circumscriptos ueluti cancellos in uersibus scrupulosè sa tis retinuisse me adserebat: etiamsi non Christianæ libertatis hominibus, sed ijs, qui se superstitiosis & anxijs profanorum authorum legibus illigarēt, scripsis sem. Et tamen, metri seruitutem, nunquam uim uerbis auferre, aut quasi natiuam lucem & gratiam eripere sentiebat. Ego uerò, hæc omnia, & alia permulta in eandem sentētiam ab eodem instructore meo perorata: partim eius erga me beneuolentiæ, partim animi tui explendi desiderio tribuenda existimabam. Sed enim, quomodocunq; se res habet, testificor me tuis mandatis impulsum, & penè inuitum hanc uel Comœdiam, uel Tragœdiam, uel etiam utramq; publicare esse ausum. Mâlo etenim dum uoluntati tuæ sim obsecutus, desiderari à te prudentiam meam, quàm si non sim obsecutus, animi propensionem atq; parendi studium. Nam quæ tandem esset inhumanitas, illi, cui uictū, cui libros, cui demum omnia præsidia studiorum meorū debeam, qualemcunq; saltem tam collati beneficij sui, quàm relati officij mei fructum flagitanti abnuere? Nunc ergò, quemadmodum antiquitatis obseruatione à priscis usque seculis ac hominum ætatibus ducta, & diuturni tate temporis confirmata, receptum est: hasce primitias ingenioli mei secundùm gratiæ modum acceptum à Domino, tibi, perillustris Archidiacone, nuncupo, consecro, & uelut in clientelam trado, ut patrocinio tuo defensæ, tum in Dei Opt. Max. gloriam & honorem, tum in Christianæ iuuentutis usum & emolumentum

close is given to such a mournful and lamentable beginning, he ought to understand that I follow Plautus, whose play, the *Captivi,* above all, is represented as taking place during an interval of several days, and passes moreover from a sad beginning to a happy ending. Finally, he asserted that I had as scrupulously retained definite quantities and measured feet, limited boundaries, as it were, in my verses, as if I had not written for people of Christian liberty, but for those who bound themselves to the too exact and nice tenets of pagan writers. Nevertheless, he felt that my observance of the metre nowhere deprived the words of their force, or destroyed, as it were, their natural color and charm. I, however, considered that all these words, and a great many other expressions, spoken to the same effect by this same master, must be ascribed partly to his good will toward me, partly to his desire of gratifying your wish. But however this may be, I bear witness that, induced by your exhortations, and almost against my will, I have dared to publish this play, be it comedy, or tragedy, or even both; for I would rather have you find me wanting in discretion in complying with your wish than have you miss my inclination and eager obedience in my failure to comply. For what an act of unkindness it would be to refuse the man to whom I owe my food, my books, in short everything needful for my studies, when he entreats me for their fruit, which, of whatever quality it be, is at least as much the result of his beneficence as of my corresponding duty? Now then, according to the custom of ancient days, which dates back to the very earliest generations and ages of mankind, and which is strengthened by time-honored observation, I dedicate and consecrate to you, most illustrious archdeacon, these first fruits of my feeble intellect, according to the measure of grace received from the Lord; and I consign them, as it were, to your protection, that they may go forth safeguarded by your patronage, both for the honor and the glory of God all good and all powerful, and for the enjoyment and edifi-

exire possint. Bene ualeas, & gratia Domini nostri Iesu Christi te regat, foueat, conseruet.

Oxoniæ. è Collegio Martonensi. Anno M.[3] D. XLIII.

PERSONAE

Magdalene.
Cleophis.
Chorus Galileidum.
Iosephus Arimathiensis.
Nicodemus.
Caïaphas.
Annas.
Dromo.
Dorus.
Sangax.
Brumax.
Cacodæmon.
Manes piorum.
Christus.
Petrus.
Iohannes.
Angelus primus.
Angelus secundus.
Chorus discipulorum.
Alecto.
Cleophas.
Amaon.
Thomas Didymus.

[3] Emendation:
Oxoniæ. è Collegio *Mertonensi.* Anno M.

cation of Christian youth. Farewell, and may the grace of our Lord Jesus Christ guide, cherish, and keep you.

Merton College, Oxford, 1543.

THE CHARACTERS OF THE DRAMA

Magdalene
Cleophis
Chorus of Galilean Women
Joseph of Arimathea
Nicodemus
Caiaphas
Annas
Dromo
Dorus
Sangax
Brumax
Cacodemon
Spirits of the Blessed
Christ
Peter
John
First Angel
Second Angel
Chorus of the Disciples
Alecto
Cleophas
Amaon
Thomas Didymus

PROLOGVS.

Iambici Trimetri uel senarij.

Gratia uobis & pax adsit, uiri optimi à
Summo Deo: factoq́; iam silentio, huc
Aureis, oculos, mentemq́; uestram intendite:
Vti, qua uenistis caussa, expeditiùs
Intelligatis, hoc quid sit spectaculi.
Christum rediuiuum, comœdiam sacram,
Diui quam suppetunt Euangeliographi,
Vobis præbemus intuendam singulis.
Et id quidem non externis tantummodo
Luminibus, intimo sed & haustu pectoris.
Est absq; ulla dubitatione, eiusmodi
Res, quæ ob oculos frequens uersari debeat.
Monstratur enim, sub aspectumq́; ponitur,
Summum Dei Opt. Max. & amplissimum
Beneficium. Quia in Christo, superûm pater
Penitus expressit, quo scilicet modo
Erga genus humanum animatus extitit.
Is enim (quæ sua fuit Patrisq́; charitas)
Pro scelere nostro fecit abundè satis:
Intimum amorem suo testatus sanguine.
Ac ne quis precium non solutum adhuc putet,
Noluit mortis detineri carcere:
Quin hac, & peccato uictis atq́; obrutis
Erupit, & sanctorum regna repetijt.
Hinc spiritus locuples in orbem effunditur,
Dominantis iam Christi donum optatissimum:
Nos qui suos uera sic instruit fide,
Vt & Dei factam per Christum gratiam
Nobis persuadeat, & efficaciter
Sese ipsa per amorem uehementem exprimat.
Iam Christus noster est, & nos Christi sumus,
Ac ipse Christus corporis est nostri caput, &

PROLOGUE

Grace and peace from God on high be with you, most worthy men! Now that silence has been obtained, hither turn your ears, your eyes, and your minds, that you may understand more readily what this spectacle is which is the cause of your assembling. *The Resurrection of Christ,* a sacred comedy, the subject-matter for which the divine evangelists present, we show for each of you to watch; and that not only with the outward eye, but with the heart, drinking it in deep. It is, without doubt, a play of such a kind as ought frequently to move before the eyes, because here is shown and set before your view the highest and greatest service of the all-good and all-powerful God; for in Christ the heavenly Father expressed fully how He was minded toward the human race, since He (such was His and His Father's love) was the propitiation for our sins, bearing witness with His own blood to His deep love. And that none should think that the price is still unpaid, He refused to be held in the prison-house of death. Nay, from death, and from men subdued and overcome with sin, He broke forth, and returned to the realms of the saints. Hence upon the world His rich spirit is poured forth, the most precious gift of Christ, who now rules, who so instructs us, His people, in the true faith, that He may convince us that not only did the grace of God come through Christ, but that it effectually manifests itself in ardent love. Now Christ is ours, and we are Christ's, and Christ Himself is the head

Se nobis reddidit undequaq; similem.
Vtq́; ille recepta mole reuixit carnea:
Sic *&* nos (eius qui quasi membra existimus)
In rediuiuo mortalitatis unicam
Spem Christo figere, par est *&* consonum.
Nunc autem, ea in re, qua fit illustrissimum
Salutis æternæ summam consistere:
Quàm mirificè domini gratuita bonitas
Cum incredulitate suorum certauerit,
In hac tota historia licebit cernere?
Quum ne Angelis quidem eius alumni crederent,
Eum pòst organa resumpsisse corporis,
Quàm uis Iudaica sibi uitam exhauserat:
Semet uiuum coràm exhibuit, *&* sæpiùs
Manifestis declarauit testimonijs.
Nam præter mutua hinc indè habita colloquia,
Panem suo quodam more in parteis tribuit,
Oppessulatis foribus introijt domum,
Comedit unà, tangendum se præbuit,
Omisit nihil, hæc uitæ recuperatio
Nobis, ut omnibus esset persuasissima.
Si ergò hîc Dei tanta elucet benignitas,
Quantam non cuncta opera ostentant cætera:
Certè nullum spectrum uberiore gaudio
Christiadum poterit pertentare pectora.

ARGVMENTVM ACTVS I.

Nvnc uestra ne fallatur expectatio,
Sic accipitote, quod primum in scenam uenit.
Christus in eo iacet sepulchro conditus:
Quem Magdalis cum cæteris mulieribus,
Quæ à Galilæa Iesum sequutæ uenerant,
Flet à Iudæis interemptum atrociter.
Ast *&* Nicodemus, *&* Iosephus illicò hàc

of our body, and has made Himself in all ways like unto us. As He lived again after taking the burden of flesh, so, too, it is meet and fit that we, who are, as it were, members of Him, should fix in Christ's resurrection the only hope of our mortality. Now, moreover, in that matter, in which it becomes most manifest that the principle of our eternal welfare rests, it will be permitted us to see, in all this story, how marvelously the free goodness of the Lord strove with the unbelief of His people. Since his disciples did not believe even the angels, that He had resumed the organs of the body after Jewish violence had taken away His life, He showed Himself alive before all, and very often made it known by evident signs. Besides mutual exchange of speech, He divided bread into portions according to His custom, He entered the house when the doors were barred, He ate with others, He offered Himself to their touch, He left nothing undone that this recovery of life might be most convincing to us all. If, therefore, the loving kindness of God shines forth more brightly here than it does in all His other works, surely no sight can pervade the hearts of the sons of Christ with more abundant joy than this.

ARGUMENT OF ACT I.

Now, that your expectation be not disappointed, hear what comes first upon the stage. Christ lies buried in that sepulchre; the Magdalene, with the other women, who, following Jesus, came from Galilee, bewails his savage slaughter by the Jews. Both Nicodemus and Joseph will wend their

Viam carpent. qui cùm spe animos erigent,
Tum uerò etiam secum illas deducent domum. &
Actum istum, nox interuentu claudet suo.
Ego uobiscum unà spectator ero fabulæ.

ACTVS I. SCENA I.

Magdalene. Cleophis. Chorus Galileïdum.
Octonarij.

O vos iniqui Iudæi, ô scelere inflămati acerrimo,
O uos feri, ô uiolenti, ô & multò crudelissimi:
Dicite, qua tandĕ cote hanc insignĕ uestră inuidientiam
Plus plusq; sic exacuitis? Dicite, quá nam è fornace tot
Spirant irarum æstus uobis, ac tanta ruunt incendia?
Credo equidĕ, uos omneis immanitate q̃ teterrimos,
Rabiem satiauisse uestram, in hoc neci iam dedito.
Scelerosa Solyma, scelerosa Iudæa propagatio
Ac soboles, integris bonis & sanctis plerisq; omnibus,
Heu nimium pertinaciter infensa & inimica uatibus,
Quid est quod tantopere bilem concitauerat tuam?
In hunc spectatum hominem, quid? hominem dico? imò sanè (quidem
Diuinum & cœlestem prophetam appellarem ueraciùs.
Vt qui stupenda potentia miserrimis mortalibus
Opem & auxilium ferens: hæc (etsi ualdè ingrata immania
Ac turbida) lustrare loca minimè recusauerit.
Hic pro sua mera bonitate, alijs posthabitis gentibus,
Tete sibimet unam præter cæteras delegerat:
Quă signis, quă meritis, quă admirădis rerŭ miraculis
Ad ipsum cœlum usq; efferret & eueheret, quam demum
Beneficijs & rebus gestis, æqualem olympo redderet. (suis
Ergò, hunc tam præclarè & magnificè de te promeriuirum,
His cumulas egregijs donis? ergò isti, quem præstabilis
Honestas exculpauerat, hæc (tanquă præmia uidelicet)

way to this very place. They will rouse the women's spirits with hope, and will lead them home. Nightfall will close this act. I shall be a spectator of the play with you.

ACT I, SCENE I.

Magdalene, Cleophis, Chorus of Galilean Women.

Mag. O unjust Jews, inflamed with most bitter wickedness, savage, violent, and of surpassing cruelty, say then on what whetstone you sharpen more and more the edge of your great hatred. Tell me from what furnace the heat of your wrath breathes, and the great flames belch forth. I believe, indeed, that you all, most hideous in your cruelty, have now vented your wrath on Him whom you have given over to slaughter. O guilty Jerusalem, guilty Jewish race, and guilty Jewish progeny, all too obstinately hostile to many upright, good, and holy men, and to all prophets! What is it that has so greatly stirred your wrath against this man of tried worth? What! 'Man,' do I say? Nay, verily, I should more truly call Him divine and heavenly prophet, who, with marvelous power, bringing help to wretched mortals, did not refuse to visit this most ungrateful, monstrous, and disordered land. Esteeming other nations less, He, in His sheer goodness, chose thee alone for Himself, that by signs, benefits, and wondrous miracles, He might bear thee away, and at length by His favors and deeds exalt thee to heaven itself. Dost thou then heap up these fine gifts on Him who has done thee such splendid and glorious services, on Him whom pre-eminent virtue rendered blameless?

Animum induxti, hospitia digna referre & rependere?
Hæc' cine tecta? hasce sedes? hosce constituisti toros?
Hunc' cine honorē addidisti? ô horrĕdŭ atq; nefariŭ scelus.
O facinus nulla cuiusquă lingua oĭno excusabile.
Non tot uatum uoces, nŏ tam clarissima Iamb.
Stupendaq́; prodigia, non te deniq; Trimet.
Tam præsens numen potuit unquam inflectere?
Tu istam sciens uolensq́; peregisti necem.
Tu uulnificis, heu, sertis inflictum caput,
Tu palmas traiectas acuta cuspide,
Tu clauis confossos pedes,
Alta in pinu ac tristi pendenteis machina:
Tu, tu, dico, exultans respexti hostiliter.
Scribe hunc tibi de Christo triumphum, si uoles:
Habe hanc laudem, ut de cæde bonorum gaudeas.
Erit, erit dies, qua te mirum in modum
Pœniteat perpetrasse tam indignum nefas.
Verùm ista dolorem auget commemoratio.
Attamen ego meis unà cum sororibus
Lachrymas gemitusq́; fundens & suspiria,
Si non (mi Christe) illud corpusculum tuum, at
Saxum, quo tègeris, tamen amplexa suauiter,
Lubens officium tibi nunc persoluam ultimum.
Valeto dulce decus meum, decus meum[4]
Valeto ad tempus, ast' non æternùm quidem.
Neq; enim tu iam planè atq; omnino extingueris:
Sed astra leuem partem, terrestrem humus tenet,
Sese tandem aliquando uisuram denuò.
Viuent, uiuent, quæ fingimus ossa mortua.
Intereà, hîc molliter quiescas, Christe mi:
Intereà mi Christe, quiescas hîc molliter.

[4] O et præsidium et dulce decus meum, Horace, Ode I. 1. 2.

Didst thou, as a reward, bring thyself to return and to repay this worthy hospitality? Is this the dwelling, this the abode, this the couch thou didst prepare, this the honor thou didst give? O horrible and impious guilt! O crime utterly inexcusable by the tongues of any! Could not the voices of so many prophets, such clear and marvelous portents, could not Deity in person ever sway thee? Thou, thou, I say, exulting in enmity, didst gaze on that head smitten and wounded with the crown of thorns, on the palms pierced with the sharp nails, on the feet of Him, transfixed by spikes, who hung from the lofty tree, the cruel cross. Ascribe to thyself this triumph over Christ, if thou wilt. Have this praise, that thou rejoicest in the slaughter of good men. A day will come, when, in a wondrous manner, thou wilt repent of having committed so shameful a sin. But these remembrances increase my sorrow. Nevertheless, I, together with my sisters, shedding many tears, groaning and sighing, will gladly pay Thee now the last rites, gently embracing the stone by which Thou art covered, if not Thy body, O my Christ. Farewell, my Glory dearly cherished, farewell for a time, but not for eternity. Thou art not now wholly destroyed, but the stars possess Thy heavenly part, the ground Thy earthly part, which will at last see itself renewed. They shall live; the bones which we imagine dead shall live. Meanwhile, mayest thou rest gently here, O my Christ, mayest Thou rest here gently!

ACTVS I. SCENA II.

Iosephus Arimathæus. Nicodemus. Magdalis.
Salóme. Cleoph. Iohann.

Amabò te, mi Nicodeme, animum attendito, ut
Fœmineo plangore hortus totus personat? Trimet.
Sedet Magdalis in medio posita marmore
Capillis dilaceratis, ore pallido.
Nec iam uocem ullam ualet ampliùs emittere.
Sed magnis exanimata cruciatibus,
Lapidi adhæret, non secus ac esset mortua.
Aliæ, non modò non hanc à mœstitia uocant:
Verùm etiam profusis indulgent fletibus,
Pugnisq́; frequentibus concutiunt pectora.
Breuiter, omnes omnia replent luctu loca.
Nic. Iosephe, mihi mediusfidius morsu quasi
Quodam, sensum planè peracerbum inferunt.
Atq; adeò incredibili iam ipse dolori meo
Vel mœrori potiùs, quem è tam diro exitu
Optimi hominis accepi, uix queo resistere:
Sed imperabo tamen meis adfectibus,
Quin adgredimur propiùs ut flenteis fœminas
(Quoad à nobis fieri & præstari potest)
Leuemus, atq; spem illis præbeamus aliquam.
Quomq́; umbra terræ iam solis opacat iubar,
Ne fortè meticulosis incommodet,
Atq; noceat nocturna concursatio:
Exanguem in tecta reportemus Magdalim,
Easq́; singulas abducamus domum.
Ios. Satis admodum tu commodè mones. nam id &
Ratio temporis, & rerum postulat status.
Agè festinanter, compellemus alacriter.
Nic. Quousq; tandem Galilææ lachrymabitis?
Aut quàm diu ad hanc petram querulæ manebitis?
Quem ad finem in squalore iacebitis & sordibus?

ACT I, SCENE II.

Joseph of Arimathea, Nicodemus, Mary Magdalene, Salome, Cleophis,[12] Johannes.

Jos. I pray thee, my Nicodemus, take note how all the garden resounds with women's wailing. Within the marble tomb sits Magdalene, her hair torn, her face pallid. She is no longer able to utter a word, but, exhausted by her great agony, she clings to the stone as if she were dead. The others not only do not rouse her from her sorrow, but they, too, indulge in profuse weeping. With clenched hands they frequently beat upon their breasts, and fill the whole place with their lamentations.

Nic. By heavens, they distress me greatly, with a gnawing pain, as it were, and now I myself can scarcely withstand my own great sorrow, or rather grief, which I have suffered from the dreadful end of that most worthy man. Nevertheless, I will command my feelings. Why do we not approach and console the weeping women as best we may, and afford them some consolation? Since the shadow of the earth now obscures the brightness of the sun, and lest by chance the timid women be troubled and hurt by going to and fro in the night, let us carry the lifeless Magdalene back to her dwelling, and lead the others home, one by one.

Jos. You give good, fitting advice; for both consideration of the time and the state of affairs demand this. Hasten, let us speak to them quickly.

Nic. How long, Galilean women, will you continue weeping, how long will you remain by this stone lamenting, and to what end will you lie in the dust and the dirt?

[12] The name Cleophis does not appear in the Bible. The character is undoubtedly intended for Mary, the wife of Cleophas, described by John as standing by the cross of Jesus in company with his mother and Mary Magdalene (John 19. 25). By some commentators she is thought to have been the mother of Joses, Jude, Simon, and James the Little (*Cyclopædia of Biblical and Ecclesiastical Literature,* New York, 1873). In Act III, Scene III, p. 39, Cleophis mentions these, her children.

Ios. Hoc non fit sanè sine diuino numine:
Vos parcitote lachrymosis questibus.
Et iam nox ruit, ac somnum hortantur sydera.[5]
Vos ploratu finem atq; modum imponite:
Sedatè oportet tolerari, quod ferre necessitas iubet. Octona.
Vos eiulatum ergò deponite, & iam conticescite.
Mag. Heû me quid obsecro misera, misera,
Quid agam tandem aliud misera, misera,
Quàm quod furtim erepta sibi querens pignora,
Philomela & noctu factitat & interdiu?
Turpe profectò mihi duco, post hunc mori
Non posse me, uel sola mœroris face.
Nic. Maria, caue Maria, ne insanis clamoribus
Cœlestis patris iras aduersùm te incites.
Mag. Eheu, mihi cur, cur non licuerit mihi,
Christum extinctum saltem lamentari meum?
Nic. Non est, mihi crede, non est extinctus tuus
Christus: sed potiùs exemptus iam uinculis
Corporeis, æthereo fruiscitur polo.
Non est amissus, sed præmissus ad Deum.
Nec sibi finem uitæ, sed initium quidem
Aeternitatis morte consequutus est.
Nec perijt, sed à nobis discedens & migrans,
Ad societatem abijt superum immortalium.
Vbi pro seruitute uitam liberam,
Pro umbris lucem, pro rerum incertitudine
Securitatem, pro labore præmium est
Adeptus, nullo intermoriturum seculo.
Mag. In hoc equidem tibi facilè adsentior,
Quòd quemadmodum eius ossa sepulchro dormiant:
Ita mens cum Deo & reliquis uiuat pijs.
Sed ut suam sortem non omnino fleam:
Propria damna tamen, atq; incommoda publica,

5 . . . Et iam nox umida cælo
Præcipitat, suadentque cadentia sidera somnos.
Aeneid 2. 8-9.

Jos. Surely this did not happen without the divine will; you must spare your tearful plaints. Now night falls, and the stars urge sleep. Put an end to your wailing. We must endure calmly what necessity bids us bear; therefore cease your lamentations, and be silent now.

Mag. Alas, wretched woman that I am! I beseech you what else can I do than does Philomela, who day and night perpetually bewails her children, snatched from her by stealth? I count it base indeed that I cannot follow Him in death, with the torch of grief alone as my guide.

Nic. Mary, Mary, beware, lest with thy wild cries thou rouse against thee the heavenly Father's wrath.

Mag. Alas, why am I not permitted at least to mourn my dead Christ?

Nic. Believe me, He is not destroyed; but, released now from the fetters of the body, He enjoys the ethereal heaven. He is not lost, but sent before to God: this is not the end of life that He has won by His death, but the very beginning of eternity. He has not perished, but has left us, and, passing over, He has gone away to the fellowship of the immortals above, where He has gained a reward: in place of slavery, free life; of shadows, light; of uncertainty, security; and, in place of toil, a reward that shall in no age pass away.

Mag. In this, indeed, I readily agree with you, that, like as His bones sleep in the tomb, so His spirit lives with God and the saints: but, though I should not bewail His lot at all, still my own loss and the general misfortune bid me weep

Diuinum hominem deplorare ereptum iubent.
Nam qui mihi meisq; semper extitit
Præsens perfugium, portus, & opitulatio,
Qui me torquenteis effugabat dæmonas.
Qui Lazarum ad uitæ reuocabat munera.
Quo præsente mea plaudebat Bethania:
Eheu, mihi cur, cur non licuerit mihi,
Eundem ademptum saltem lamentarier?
Nic. Quibus te simul & nos exornauit bonis,
Horum fructus nobiscum perpetuò manent.
Quàm sit iniquum autem optare, hanc uitam ut uiueret,
Potiùs quàm ubi nunc est, ipsa per te cogites.
Tellure indignus, cœlo collocatus est.
Mundus eum respuit, exceperunt cælites.
Quapropter neq; te destitutam dixeris:
Et eius conditioni gratulabere.
Mag. O Nicodeme, lubens agnosco illud equidem,
Me sic ipsius cumulatam esse munere,
Vt omnem in uitam sim futura melior.
Verùm, quoties tenax repetit memoria,
Punctum corolla spinifera sinciput
Manus adfixas, ferrò contrusos pedes,
Turpatos crineis, barbam cretam sanguine,
Illusum, pulsatum, ignominiosè pendulum,
Vnà cum pessimæ notæ latronibus,
Deiectos oculos, ora morientia,
Et etiam hastam cruore intepuisse lateris:
Toties, eheu, cur non licitum erit mihi,
Sic cæsum insontem, saltem lamentarier?
Nic. Sanè multas perdis lachrymas, ô Magdalis,
Ad rem amissam recuperandam faciunt nihil.
Imò magìs nostrum dolorem exasperant,
Quàm tibi quid consolationis adferunt.
Sed qui ex usu rei totius publicæ
Tot supra hominem res ărduas olim êdidit:

for the divine Man who has been torn from us. For He who put to flight the demons that tormented me, who recalled Lazarus to the duties of life, at whose presence Bethany applauded, has ever been a present refuge, a haven, a help to me and mine. Alas, why should I not, why should I not, be permitted to lament Him who has been taken from me?

Nic. The fruits of the blessings with which He adorned thee and me will remain with us for ever. Do thou reflect in thine own mind how unjust it is, moreover, to wish that He should live in this life rather than where He now is. Accounted unworthy on earth, He has been deemed worthy of a place in heaven; the world rejected Him, the dwellers in heaven welcomed Him; wherefore do not call thyself forsaken, but rejoice in His condition.

Mag. O Nicodemus, of a surety I gladly acknowledge that I am so enriched by His gift that all my life I shall be the better. But as often as memory recalls the head pierced by the crown of thorns, the hands nailed to the cross, the feet fastened together with iron, locks befouled, beard clotted with blood—Him mocked, beaten, hanging in dishonor, together with robbers of most evil repute, eyes cast down, dying lips, and the spear, too, warm with the blood from His side, why should I not be permitted at least to lament the innocent thus slain?

Nic. Thou dost waste many tears indeed, O Magdalene, but they avail thee naught in recovering what thou hast lost; nay, they rather provoke our grief than bring thee aught of consolation. Doubt not that He who for the sake of the whole commonweal once performed so many arduous tasks

Is (ne dubites) haud absq; nostris omnium
Vtilitatibus, uolens efflauit spiritum.
Ac sanè nescio quid istiusmodi
Futurum, mihi præsignificabat: etenim
Quom multa nocte, à Iudæis metuens mihi,
Eum consulerem, memini dicere solitum,
Quòd ut in agris atq; desertis locis,
Mose serpens erectus quondam fuit:
Ita oporteret seseipsum exaltarier.
Quanquàm quid sibi uoluit, non planè intelligo.
Potuisset letum subterfugere, sat scio,
Modò uoluisset: at sponte ipse sese dedit
Violentis inimicorum armis obuium.
Quid quòd summus parens iussis haud mollibus
Vrgebat: cuius cùm reliquis in omnibus,
Tum uerò istac in re standum est arbitrio.
Si ergò rectum iudicium, si modestiam
Retinere dignam forti fœmina uoles.
Si eius uoluntati conspirabit tua,
Si parebis Dei ipsius prudentiæ:
Non erit ullo pacto, non tibi licitum erit,
Christum occisum tam acerbè lamentarier.
Ios. Surgas nunc Magdalis, Maria consurgito:
Abundè suus à te tumulo datus est honos.
Mag. Adsurgam ego? me nullus ab hoc marmoreo
Antro diuellet, anima dum exuperabo mea.
Salo. Imò surge, & senis dicto sis audiens
O Maria. nam, quod ipsa tu nosti probè,
Cras festa pro recepta consuetudine
Nobis quidem celebranda sunt solennia.
Pòst reuenienteis, modò sic stat sententia,
Huic aromata precioso corpori,
Bene olentia & amœna comparabimus.
Agédum, Arimathæe, istanc ab humo subleua.
Mag. Ah, quamuis ægrè mihi discedendum siet,
Tamen amicis adquiescam hortatibus.

beyond human power, willingly breathed out His spirit, not without advantage to us all. Indeed, that something of this nature would come to pass He foretold to me. Moreover, when, for fear of the Jews, I used to consult Him late at night, I remember that He was wont to say that just as in the fields and desert places Moses' serpent was once lifted up, so it was necessary for Him to be lifted up. Although I do not clearly understand what He meant, I well know that He could have avoided death, had He only willed: but of His own accord He exposed Himself to the weapons of His violent enemies. What of the fact that the Father on high, He whose decision we must abide in this as in all else, with no mild bidding urged this? If, then, thou wilt maintain right judgment, and the modesty worthy of a brave woman, if thy will be in harmony with His, if thou wilt yield to the wisdom of God Himself, thou wilt in no way permit thyself so bitterly to lament Christ slain.

Jos. Arise now, Magdalene; Mary, arise with her; honor enough has been abundantly paid by thee unto the tomb.

Mag. Shall I arise? No one shall tear me from this marble sepulchre while I have the breath of life.

Salo. Nay, arise, Mary, and listen to the words of the old man; for to-morrow, as thou thyself knowest, according to the established custom, we must celebrate a solemn festival. Afterwards, on our return, if our intention still remains, we will prepare sweet-smelling spices for this precious body. Come, Arimatheus, raise her from the ground.

Mag. Although with reluctance I must depart, yet I will assent to your friendly counsel. Most devout matrons, after

Facite igitur matronæ religiosissimæ, ut
Sabbaticæ requietis transacto curriculo,
Huc simul ut ortus uicerit noctem dies,
Myrrham, costum, spicæq́; Cilissæ acerrimæ,
Et summæ suauitatis unguenta, ueluti
Suprema sacro sepulchro addentes munera,
Celerem quàm primùm referamus pariter pedem.
Sal. O fiat per Deum immortalem, quod petis.
Nil etenim nos (ut pro istis quoq; respondeam) in
Votis habemus, aut in optatis prius.
Nunc neq; lux prona celebrare inferias sinit,
Et hoc ipsum prohibet crastina uacatio.
Quare, mora nulla, primo quoq; tempore
Perendinæ lucis ad hortum hunc properabitur,
Vt monuisti. Locum ritè notauimus.
Ios. Bene habet. restat, uos ut duos, inanibus
Remotis cruciamentis, consequamini.
Sal. Nobis pérplacet. Mag. Ac mihi certè nō displicet.

ARGVMENTVM ACTVS II.

Caïaphas de Christi obitu quodammodò
Triumphat. Eidem obiecta recenset crimina.
Expectat socius, Pilatum qui adiêre, uti[6]
Sepulchrum huius multo seruetur milite.
Custodes adducens, responsa præsidis
Refert Annas. Vallant locum armata manu.
Abeunt. Speluncæ autem tutores illicò
Sese quàm ipsum Herculem plus posse iactitant.
Tum spiritus defuncti ad manes deuolat,
Quæ animæ piorum læti' accipiunt plausibus.[7]

[6] Emendation:
Expectat *socios,* Pilatum qui adiere, uti

[7] Emendation:
Quem animæ piorum læti' accipiunt plausibus.

the time of the Sabbath rest is over, and the rising sun has vanquished night, let us all return hither as quickly as we may, bringing myrrh, aloes, pungent spikenard, and ointments of great sweetness, as last gifts unto the holy sepulchre.

Sal. May what you ask be granted by the eternal God! For there is nothing (I answer for these here as for myself) which we put before that in our prayers or in our wishes. Now the fading light does not suffer us to celebrate the last rites, and to-morrow's rest forbids it also; wherefore, with no delay, at the dawn of the morrow, we will hasten to this garden, as you have suggested. The place we have duly noted.

Jos. It is well. Now that your vain anguish has been laid aside, it remains that ye follow us two.

Sal. It pleases us so to do.

Mag. Of a surety it does not displease me.

ARGUMENT OF ACT II.

Caiphas triumphs in a certain fashion in the death of Christ. He also enumerates the charges against Him. He awaits his companions, who have besought Pilate that Christ's tomb may be guarded by many soldiers. Annas, leading the guards, brings back the governor's answer. They surround the place with an armed band, and depart. Now the guardians of the cave boast on the spot that they can do more than Hercules himself, while the spirit of the dead Christ descends to the shades below, where the souls of the blest receive Him with a joyful noise. He, the

Ille, illas promissum ad polum uictor uehit.

ACTUS II. SCENA I.

Caïaphas.

Secunda quidem sors est, & ad nostram fluens Trimet.
Voluntatem, qua hunc authorem discordiæ,
Antequàm adesset dies ista celeberrima,
Se ualdè digna occisione occidimus.
Qui se passim omnium regem esse gentium, ac
Prolem Iehoua, garrire nunquam destitit.
Qui summi rectoris dominiq́; numina
Sibi adsumens, errata confitentibus
Impunitatem est solitus & ueniam dare.
Qui ubi mortale corpus elanguesceret,
Volaretq́; à membrorum mens compagibus,
Ademit penitus omnem pœnarum metum,
Infernaq́; tormenta suos ridere docuit.
Qui uetera retractans iura (si dijs placet)
Nouas quasdam lêges, nouas ceremonias,
Decreta noua, ritus nouos, sacra noua,
Noua & inuisa & inaudita plurima,
Per uniuersam constituit Rempublicam.
Eisq́; dolis Iudæam sic plebeculam,
Et imperitam undiq; sic multitudinem
Deceperat, fefellerat, induxerat,
Huius ut unius obseruarent uestigia, &
Tanquam cælesti missum ab arce colerent.
At enimuerò scelus ille suum pectore
Fallaci dissimulare nequibat diu,
Quin familias frequentaret sæpè impias,
Ac se prohibitis consotiationibus
Etiam admonitus neutiquam subduceret.
Tum festis quoq; diebus, queis fas est nihil
Exercere, ipse, ut erat rebelli' & pertinax,
Quoscunq; morbos profligauit sedulò.

Conqueror, bears them to the promised heaven.

ACT II, SCENE I.

Caiphas.

Cai. Chance, indeed, has been favorable, and has accorded with our desires, whereby, before the festive day approached, we have slain with fitting slaughter this author of discord, who never ceased to boast that he was king of all nations far and wide, and that he was the son of God, and who, assuming to himself the divinity of the supreme Lord and Ruler, was wont to grant impunity and pardon to those who confessed their sins; and who, when his mortal body was languishing, and his soul taking its flight from the framework of the limbs, banished utterly all fear of penalties, and taught his followers to laugh at the torments of hell, who, annulling ancient laws—good heavens!—set up throughout the whole state certain new laws, new ceremonies, new decrees, new rules, new sacred rites, new things in abundance, both hateful and unheard of, and by these devices so deceived, cheated, and misled the Jewish rabble and the ignorant multitudes everywhere, that they watched the footsteps of him alone, and worshiped him as if he had been sent from the heights of heaven. But he, with his deceitful heart, could not long dissemble, for he often resorted to godless households, and, though warned, did in no wise withdraw himself from forbidden associations. Then, too, on feast-days, on which it is the law to do no work, he, rebellious and obstinate as he was, zealously cast out all manner of diseases. Why should I recall how, unpunished,

Quid referam, ut illius consorteis publicè
Illicitis uescebantur impunè cibis?
Atq; ut præter morem illotis manibus etiam, &
Contactu spurco fœdarent obsonia.
Quasi uerò Pater omnipotens, nunc denique
Tot sæcula placitas reuocet ceremonias,
Ac mentem nutans peruertat sententia.
Quin etiam (quis probus inultum hoc relinqueret?)
Minitabatur se aras destructurum sacras.
Quod omen in ipsum iustus contorsit Deus.
Sed & in templa erecta à nostris maioribus,
Magnificis ac penè infinitis sumptibus,
Voluerat nefarias faces intendere. Ac
Dudum molitus est tenebras offundere
Phœbo, reliquorum moderatori luminum.
Tam adhæc ridiculè stulta erat fiducia, ut
Socijs mœrentibus, ad lumina uitalia
Rediturum sese coràm promitteret.
Sed nimirum, opportunè nos huic malo
Remedium adhibuimus quàm præsentissimum.
Confluxêre ad Pilatum templi præsides,
Mystarum cœtus, turba sanctorum senum,
Pharisæi, Iuris prudentes, qui à satrapa, ad
Vnum omneis contendunt, ut armatos uiros
Det, bustum defensuros noctes ac dies.
Atqui, dum redeant, sedes hæc esto mea.

ACTVS II. SCENA II.

Annas. Caïaphas. Dromo. Dorus. Sangax.
Brumax.

Hoc in loco iamdudum nos Caïaphas
Amicus noster, unà expectat cum suis:
Dummodò statutum ei pactum non excidit.

he fed his comrades publicly on unlawful food, and how, contrary to custom, with unwashen hands and unclean touch they defiled their food, as if the omnipotent Father were now revoking at last the ceremonies acceptable to him through so many ages, and, wavering in mind, were changing his opinions? Nay, indeed—what good man could leave this unavenged?—he used to threaten to destroy the sacred altars, a threat which a just God turned against him. He wished to apply impious torches even to the temple erected by our ancestors with lavish, almost infinite, expenditure. And not long ago he tried to spread darkness over the sun, the ruler of the world of light. Moreover, so ridiculously foolish was his confidence that he promised his sorrowing companions that he would return to the light of life, and appear before them. But methinks we have fitly applied a most powerful remedy to this evil. The rulers of the temple have flocked to Pilate, a company of the priests of the mysteries, a crowd of holy elders, Pharisees, lawyers, who all with one voice demand of the governor that he give armed men to guard the tomb night and day. Until they return, let this be my seat.

ACT II, SCENE II.

Annas, Caiphas, Dromo, Dorus, Sangax, Brumax.

Ann. In this place, our own friend, Caiphas, together with his men, has long been awaiting us, provided the agreement made has not fallen through. Behold him sitting alone.

Ellùm sedentem solum. Caï. Ecce autem quem uolo,
Stipatus aduentat militibus quatuor.
Ann. Miror quòd nullus ei adiungitur comes.
Caï. Cur unus adest, satis exputare non queo.
Adsurgam equidem. An. Adibo iamiam, & colloquar.
Caï. Nunc addiscam, acta quæ sunt in prætorio.
An. Hem noster: Deus hunc tibi solem det prosperum. Caï. (Et
Tu etiam atq; etiam aueto præsul dignissime. At
Vbinam sunt reliqui? An. confecto negocio,
Penates rursus quisq; petebat suos.
Caï. Bellè factum illud est. pulchrè se res habet.
Sed dicito, quod Romanus responsum dedit?
An. Illum, simul ac ad eius uentum est atria,
Conuenimus, & apud eum ista perorauimus.
Aduerti Ponti, imisq́; repone sensibus,
(Nec enim est leuicula res aut parui ponderis)
Quid Ψeudoprophetes uiuus adhuc uulgauerit.
Ego (inquit) post triduum è mortis faucibus
Eaudam: & ab Orco uicto me reducem dabo, ac
Rediuiuus emergam. Ideò Romulidûm optime,
Forteis & fidos ne molestum sit tibi
Tradere, qui sarcophagi tueantur ostia,
Vsque dum tantillum temporis effluxerit.
Nam eius forsan comites cadauer clepere, &
Noctu sepultum auferre furto cogitant,
Ac postea totam urbem falsis rumoribus
Implere: qui nusquam est, usuram luminis
Huius recepisse, & communem spiritum.
Vt igitur ignis tenuis tenui de fomite
Primùm exilit, mox auctus per totam domum
Furit, & flamma lambit extructas trabes,
Ruinamq́; patitur ædes diram & flebilem:
Ita primo rumore, qui percrebuit
De illius ostentis ac de uirtutibus,
Opinionem istam sequens insania

Cai. Here is the man I want. He is approaching, surrounded by four soldiers.

Ann. I am surprised that no companion is at his side.

Cai. I cannot quite understand why he is here alone. At all events I shall rise.

Ann. I shall approach and speak.

Cai. Now I shall learn what has been done in the palace.

Ann. Well, friend, God prosper you this day!

Cai. And hail to thee again and again, most worthy prefect! But where are the rest?

Ann. When the business was finished, each one again sought his own hearth.

Cai. That was well done. The affair is going well. But tell me, what answer did the Roman give?

Ann. As soon as we reached his hall, we accosted him, and pleaded at length with him thus: 'Observe, Pontius, and store away in thy inmost thoughts, what the false prophet spread abroad while he was yet alive; for the matter is not trifling or of little weight. He said: "After three days I shall escape from the jaws of death, and, returning from vanquished hell, I shall show myself again in the flesh." Therefore, most worthy of the sons of Romulus, take it not ill, but give us brave and trusty men to guard the mouth of the sepulchre until a little time has passed; for his followers, perchance, are thinking of stealing his body, and of carrying it away to bury, and afterwards filling the whole city with false rumors that he, who is not, again enjoys the light of day and the common breath of life. Therefore, as a slight fire from a bit of tinder leaps forth, but, soon increasing, rages through the whole house, licking with its flames the lofty beams, and the building suffers dire and lamentable ruin, so madness at the first rumor of his miracles and

Multo maiore periculo grassabitur.
Plebes leuis est, & inconstans & mobilis,
Plebs aucupatur stultorum rumusculos:
Apud plebem ualebunt plus deterrima
Quæuis, quàm si uel optima inculcabimus.
Ergò, donec licet, prinçipij' occurrito, &
Insidias pelle præses prudentissime.
Nobisq́; potestatem facias, ut undiq;
Spelæa circum hastatos sistamus uiros.
Siquidem nauiter & cautè prospici
A nobis debet, ut uafri hominis asseclas,
Nostro consilio, spe sua frustrarier,
Planè apparere possit. Atq; hæc hactenus.
Tum Pilatus: Quod uoltis Hebræi, annuo.
Annuo uobis uigilias & custodias,
Annuo sepulchri tutores, qui ad crastinum
Vsque diem perpetuas excubias agant.
Sub hæc sigillum, quo hunc locum obsignem dedit,
Cum hisce unà spectatis bellatoribus.
Deinde uiri Solymi, quisq; ad suos lares
Abeunt simul, ouanteis & uoti compotes.
Ego, quoniam huc me uenturum ad te receperam,
Memet sponte obtuli, solus qui hos dirigerem.
Idcirco uirilem operam nauate fortitèr.
Tu Dromo, latus dextrum occupato. tu Dore
Quò te proripis? Ad cornu fac sinistrum eas.
Illic Sangax, istic Brumax consistito.
Si quis furtum facturus huc accesserit,
Vos post suum Christum hunc ad manes mittite.
Nam præter umbram quod timeatis, est nihil.
Quid multa? magnanimis dictum satis puto.
Quid multa? magnanimis dictum satis puto. Drom. hàc
Quisquis uenerit, experietur mehercule̊,
Quàm aptas Dromo uireis ad uindictam gerat.
Dor. Et in me reperiet cor dignum milite.
Sang. Quicunq; Sangacem uel procul adspexerit,

virtues, following that belief, will rage with far greater danger. The common people are light-headed, fickle, easily moved, and are eager to catch the idle gossip of fools. With the multitude, all that is the very worst will prevail more than the very best that we could inculcate. Therefore, most prudent governor, while it may yet be done, oppose it in the beginning, and foil the plot. Give us authority that we may place armed men on every side around the cave, since we ought diligently and carefully to use foresight, that it may plainly appear that by our counsel the rogue's followers are disappointed in their hope.' So much for this. Then Pilate spoke: 'Hebrews, I grant what you wish; I grant you watchmen and guards, keepers of the tomb, who shall hold unbroken watch until to-morrow.' Thereupon he gave me this seal, with which I am to close up the place of burial, and also gave me these tried warriors. Then the men of Jerusalem departed at once, each to his own home, rejoicing at having gained their wish. Since I had promised to come hither to you, I willingly offered myself alone to direct these soldiers. Therefore, as men, do your duty bravely. Dromo, you take the right; and you, Dorus, whither are you hurrying? Go to the left wing. Sangax, take your stand here, and Brumax there. If any one comes hither to commit theft, send him after his Christ to the world below. There is nothing for you to fear but a shadow. What need is there of many words? To men of spirit, I think that enough has been said.

Drom. By Hercules, whoever comes here shall find out what strength fit to give punishment Dromo wields.

Dor. And in me he shall find a heart worthy of a soldier.

Sang. Flight alone will avail to make him safe, whoso-

Eum sola poterit fuga tutum reddere.
An. Quid tu uerò Brumax? Bru. Quid? per caput hoc,
Iuare ausim, quòd si quis fortè obuenerit, (tibi
Aut ego eum occidero, aut is me fugauerit.
An. Quod posterius dixti, credo futurum priùs.
Bru. Imò cognoscito clarissime uir, tam & cordatos
Et etiã oculatos, ut nec ire gygas nec muscula (esse nos
Præteruolare per nos impunè queat.
Caï. Quando igitur unusquisq; suum tenet ordinem,
Nos lætum hunc atq; hilarem traducenteis diem,
Expectemu' huius fabulæ catastrophen.

ACTVS II. SCENA III.

Dromo. Dorus. Sangax. Brumax.

Haud frustrà, mento bene barbato ætas mea Trimet.
Voltum ornauit, præsertim cùm mihi mascula
Corda nequaquam desint. Quid est quod ego tremam?
Ecquis tam à uero exorbitabit, ut putet
Muliebrem animum habitare in isto corpore?
O quot ego labores exantlaui bellicos?
Non me durissima fregerunt prælia.
Neque belligerandi disciplina me latet.
Nec à pueris modò, sed ab ipsis cunabulis
Sum armatus feliciter; ac Mauorti meum
Ingenium finxit naturæ benignitas,
Meamq; genesin Mars influxit ferox.
In me cum lacte materno iuraueris
Esse imbibitam bellatricem iracundiam.
Et hunc formidarem proiectum uermibus?
Quem uicimus, quem uictum ex orbe fugauimus.
Dor. Mihi uerò quanquam in cœlum non prominet
Bicorpor atq; gygantea granditas:
Tamen animum altum, excelsum, generosum, nobilem,

ever beholds Sangax even from a distance.

Ann. What do you say, Brumax?

Bru. What do I say? By my head, I would dare swear to you that if any one by chance should cross my path, I will either slay him or he shall put me to flight.

Ann. What you said last I think will happen first.

Bru. Well, know then, most noble sir, that we have such courageous hearts and such sharp eyes that neither a giant can pass, nor a fly flit by us, without danger.

Cai. Since then each one keeps his own post, let us spend this glad and joyous day awaiting the outcome of this play.

ACT II, SCENE III.

Dromo, Dorus, Sangax, Brumax.

Dro. Time has not adorned my face with a well-bearded chin to no purpose, especially since I do not lack a manly heart. Why should I tremble? Is there any one who will so depart from the truth as to think that a woman's spirit dwells in this body? How many toils of war have I endured! The hardest battles did not subdue me. The teachings of warfare are not hidden from me. Not only from boyhood, but from the very cradle, I have borne arms successfully; the kindness of Nature fashioned my genius for war; fierce Mars influenced my birth. You could have sworn that in me a passion for war was imbibed with my mother's milk. And should I fear this prey of worms whom we conquered, and drove from the world?

Dor. In my case, indeed, there does not stretch aloft to heaven the lofty stature and the huge body of a giant: but it is soul, high, lofty, generous, and noble, not bulk of body,

Non uastam, & prodigiosam corpulentiam
Iustus rerum æstimator in quoquam exigit.
Nam mutis pecudibus adsimilantur corpora:
Animis æquamur superis immortalibus.
Animisq́; sumus apti sydera transcendere.
Quanta est uis animo, tanti corpus æstimo.
Neq; enim ego magnitudine & ueluti gradibus,
Sed potiùs conditione metior uirum.
Virtutem non præstat figura uel statua:
Sed omnis in corde residet uirilitas.
Omninoq́; uirum fortis animus efficit.
Neq; uerò sumus nos ipsi corpora.
Neq; etiam ego hæc apud uos uerba faciens,
Corporibus iam uestris loquor, sed animis.
Est uerum, quod circunfertur prouerbio,
Non mercabor hominem in ulna atq; in pollice,
Ast in precio solus habetur animi uigor.
Quid quòd maiora patent uulneribus corpora?
Quid quòd moles ingens agilitatem impedit?
Quid quòd crassa caro animi uim sepelit & obruit?
Exiguæ corporaturæ, nunc si placet,
Vnum ante oculos uestros exemplum ponite.
Minutu' accipiter uos magna docere poterit.
Superant profectò fidem, quæ audet auis tantula.
Obsecro, quàm longum collum, quàm largos pedes,
Quàm acutum rostrum, quàm amplas alas ardea
Possidet? Attamen à dominis cùm dimittitur,
Sinistra hic ales & in sublime uolitat: eam
Adoritur atque insequitur strenuissimè.
Ac motis pendenteis tibijs campanulæ
Tubæ sonitum supplent, crescat ut audacitas.
Iamq́; pugnæ huius finem attendite. Vincit minor
Maiorem auis, atq; rapinam apprensam unguibus
Curuis crebro rotundat orbe uolubilem. at
Quid aureis hisce uestras exemplis moror?
Ne dubitetis, quin modicus ego maxima

that a just appraiser demands in each; for our bodies are like those of dumb beasts; it is with our minds that we match the immortal gods; our minds fit us to rise above the stars. I value the body according to the strength of the mind, nor do I, indeed, measure a man by his size, and, as it were, by inches, but rather by his nature. A figure or a statue shows no valor; but all manliness dwells in the heart, and a brave soul always makes the man. Nor truly are we ourselves only bodies; nor, indeed, do I, speaking these words, address your bodies, but your minds. The current proverb: 'I shall not buy a man by inch and ell,'[13] is true; for, in estimation of him, vigor of mind alone is the thing that counts. What about the fact that large bodies are the more exposed to wounds, that vast bulk impedes agile movements, and that gross flesh overwhelms and buries vigor of mind? Now, if you please, place before your eyes a single example of a tiny body. The little falcon can teach you a great lesson. Verily, it surpasses belief what so small a bird dares to do. Mark, I pray you, how long a neck, what large feet, how sharp a beak, what broad wings, the heron possesses. Yet, when the hawk is sent forth by its masters, it flies aloft on the left, and attacks the heron most vigorously; and, as its legs move, the hanging bells give forth the sound of a trumpet, so that the bird's daring may increase. Now observe the end of this battle. The smaller bird conquers the larger. Wheeling about in many a circle, it surrounds its prey, and seizes it in its curved talons. But why do I trouble your ears with these examples? Do not doubt that a middle-sized man like myself can subdue one

[13] 'God does not measure men by inches.'—Old Scotch Proverb.

Subdere ualeam, si res & caussa postulat.
Sum equidem nunc iam seu uiuere præsto seu mori.
Sang. Si quis nimium nimiumq́; temerarius
Iter hàc nobis fucum factum susceperit:
Se cognoscat summo esse periculo proximum.
Nam qui sentit Sangacis quid possint manus,
Nisi me communis philautia decepit,
Se rursum infantem cupiet maximoperè
Inter genetricis adhuc latentem uiscera.
Equidem haud uerear cum Sampsone congredi.
Quid in hoc corpore desideretur? siue quis
Proceritatem siue magnitudinem,
Siue optime compacta membra expenderit.
Arma illorum, quos exteri celebres habent,
Puto Cyclôpum esse fabricata manibus.
Ita non ad infligendos sunt tantummodò,
Sed ad declinandos ictus habilia.
Num uoltus, in quo cuiusque uelut indoles
Relucet ac uoluntas, me planissumè
Inuictum bello, & armis terribilem indicat?
Ac de hisce externis fari plura supersedeo.
Hîc, hîc uiget uis quædam innata & insita,
Quæ nil non audet, quod ferro est penetrabile.
Quomq́; ars, quod inchoat natura, perficit:
Quid in re militari est, quod scientiam
Fugit meam? Quis me uno bellicosior?
En uobis quæ' nam à prælij' & conflictibus
Animosè pugnans, uolnera reportauerim.
Non' ne in bellando mira mihi felicitas
Data est? quando uirus toties euaserim?
Quamobrem, si molientem imposturas modò
Quenquam deprendero, in quem peccarit, sciat.
Bru. Qui me irritans, potis est dextram hanc euadere,
Hic deinceps lucro, quos aget, annos deputet.
Adesdum, qui uitæ capiens tædium, ad
Horæ fatalis punctum cursitare uis.

of the greatest strength, if occasion and cause demand it. At this very moment I am ready to live or to die.

Sang. If any one too, too rash, try to make his way here to trick us, let him learn that he is very near the greatest danger. For he who feels what the hands of Sangax can do, unless common self-love has deceived me, will wish very much that he were an infant again, still hidden in his mother's womb. As for me, I should not fear to fight with Samson. What is lacking in this body, whether one considers height, or size, or limbs well set up? The arms of those whom foreigners consider famous were, I think, made by the hands of the Cyclops.[14] So they were adapted not only for inflicting blows, but for turning them aside. Does not the countenance, in which, as it were, the nature and the will of each shines forth, plainly show that I am invincible in war, and terrible in arms? But I forbear to speak more of these external things. Here, here, there thrives a certain innate, inborn force which dares attack anything that steel can penetrate. And, since art perfects what nature begins, what is there in military affairs which has escaped my knowledge? Who is more warlike than I? Lo, look at the wounds that I, bravely fighting, have brought back from battles and conflicts. Has not wonderful success in making war been given me? How many times I have escaped poison! Wherefore, if I catch any man contriving trickery now, he may know against whom he has sinned.

Bru. He who is able to escape this right hand, on provoking me, let him count those years as gained that he passes thereafter. Approach, you, who conceiving a dislike for life, wish to run upon the point of the fatal hour, and we

[14] *Aeneid* 8. 416-438.

Ac stabimus hîc socij, hîc unà pugnabimus.
Si quando fuerit opus, si este caput exeret
Præstigiator, reuicturum quem somniant
Quidam, disseminante' ineptas fabulas,
Perinde quasi posset uel magus Aegyptius
Tam magna operari post mortem miracula. Hoc
Pol mihi nemo persuadebit mortalium.
Nec aureis adhibebo magistris mendacibus.
Ecquando à corporeis functionibus
Qui deficiuntur semel, ab irremeabili, &
Clauso barathro suum reducent halitum?
Quid? num uitam retinere facilius fuit,
Quàm nunc restituere amissam atq; perditam?
Verùm illud cùm nequijt, neq; hoc faciet quidem.
Sed quid speremus facturum hunc ueneficum,
Quod nec fuit, nec extat, nec fieri potest?
Ideoq́;, sodales, si comitum manipulus
Hunc suffurari clanculum conabitur:
Armati nudos, strenui infirmo' ac debiles,
Incautos, ita parati persequamur, ut
Nullam esse testentur pedibus podagram suis.
Nemo igitur definitum egrediatur locum.
Det alteri quisque animos, terrorem hostibus
Horrificum incutiamus, & etiam exitiabilem.

ACTVS II. SCENA IIII.

Cacodæmon.

O ô cælum, ô tellus, prata ô Neptunia,
Vos Plutonem recipite, quem tartarus euomit.
Date locum, in quem me liceat abstrudere:
Donec lux tanta, meis resedit sedibus.
Manes. Quàm tu expectatus aduenis clarissime
Olympi honos? Nos quàm replesti gaudio?
Venisti nanq; uenisti, humanum ut genus
A regnis umbrosis & sole carentibus,

will stand here, comrades, here together we will fight, if there be need, if that juggler stick out his head, he of whom some dream, and tell foolish tales that he will live again. As if even an Egyptian sorcerer could work such great miracles after death! By Pollux, no mortal will persuade me to believe this, nor shall I give ear to lying teachers. Shall they whose bodily functions have once ceased ever bring back their breath from the closed pit from which there is no returning? What, was it not easier to keep life than it is to restore it now, when lost and destroyed? But as he could not do that, neither will he do this. Why should we expect that this sorcerer will do this, which neither was, nor is, nor can be done? Therefore, comrades, if a band of his followers try to steal him away secretly, let us, armed against the unarmed, vigorous against the weak and feeble, prepared against the unwary, so pursue them that they may bear witness that there is no gout in their feet. Let no one then go beyond his appointed place. Let each give courage to the other, and strike terror, deadly terror, into the hearts of the enemy.

ACT II, SCENE IV.

Cacodemon, Spirits.

Cacod. O heaven, O earth, O meadows of Neptune, receive Pluto, whom Tartarus spews forth. Give me a place in which I may hide myself as long as so great a light remains in my abode.

Spirits. Ornament of heaven, how gloriously thou comest to us who await thee! How thou hast filled us with joy! Thou hast come, ay, come to lead forth the human race from the realms of shade, that lack the sun, and to bear them to

Educens, stellanti cælo sic inferas.
Cacod. Oh, iam splendet nouis aër fulgoribus.
Oh, uolitant agminatim ad cælum cælites.
Nunc uisam apud nos commotas tragœdias.

ARGVMENTVM ACTVS III.

Audistis binorum gesta dierum omnia:
Sequitur lux tertia. Terræ fit agitatio.
Metu fracti tumuli statores concidunt.
Iesus Christus consurgit rursum è funere.
Mariæ uerò cum emptis noctu odoribus,
Valde mâne cauernam adeunt Galileïdes,
Perungant ut corpus telluri creditum.
De Christo multa suo per agros uerba faciunt.
Cùm ad bustum acceditur, & de saxo quæritur
Seponendo, insperatis atque subitis
Ab angelis monumentum recluditur.
Hæc Iohanni renunciantur & Petro.
Citi adcurrunt, uera experiuntur. Petrus
Animum huc illuc alternans regreditur:
Iohanne' herum resurrexisse indicat.
Pòst Magdaléne sola eò reuertitur.
Compellat nuncios, astat forma Deus
Agricolæ, illiq; se prodit uoce solita.
Ad eumq; modum fit & reliquis mulierculis.
Illæ discipulis, hæc narrant incredulis.

ACTVS III. SCENA I.

Dromo. Dorus. Sangax. Brumax.

Deum immortalem, ubinam gentium sumus? Trimet.
Commilitones, quid' nam hoc esse creditis?
Vt omnia confusa ac turbata cernimus?

the starry heavens.

Cacod. Oh, now the air gleams with unwonted brightness; oh, the inhabitants of heaven are flying in their ranks upward to the sky! Now I behold the disaster that has come upon us.

ARGUMENT OF ACT III.

You have heard all the events of the two days; the third day dawns. An earthquake takes place. Overcome by fear, the guardians of the tomb fall down. Jesus Christ rises from the dead. Now, as it begins to dawn, the Galilean women, bringing the perfumes that Mary had bought by night, approach the cave, that they may anoint the body that was committed to the earth. They talk much of their Christ as they come through the fields. As they approach the tomb and inquire of one another how the stone is to be rolled away, suddenly and unexpectedly the sepulchre is opened by angels. This is reported to John and Peter. They run there quickly, and find the report to be true. Wavering between this and that belief, Peter returns. John declares that the Master has risen. Afterwards Magdalene returns thither alone. She speaks to the heavenly messengers; her Lord stands near by in the form of a gardener, and reveals Himself to her by His familiar voice. So it is with the rest of the women also, who tell the tale to the doubting disciples.

ACT III, SCENE I.

Dromo, Dorus, Sangax, Brumax.

Dro. By the immortal God, where in the world are we? Fellow soldiers, what do you suppose this is? How confused and disordered is everything that we see! What a

Vt auræ ruptæ colluctantur in auribus?
Fragore ut ingenti conuulsa uox sonat?
Qui terrarum motus ueniunt in prœlia? Vt
Tellus mugit, mouetur, concutitur, fremit?
Credo ego non illam uno duntaxat in loco,
Sed omnibus horrendum tremiscere partibus.
Dor. Bone Deus, è cauea quantá nam exit fulgu- Octona.
(ratio? Iambic.
Non armis, consodaleis, hîc est utendum, sed cruribus.
En ipsemet in fuga sum. Sang. Et me fugæ dabo.
Bru. Me item in fugă confero. Dro. Postremus nŏ ero.
Quis post terga sequatur, non curabo quidem,
Si mihi semel dabitur cunctos præcedere.
Sed ô Deus bone, tuam fidem obsecro.
Quid hoc? Heî nullus sum. Do. Perij. Sang. Interij.
(Brumax. Occidi.

ACTVS III. SCENA II.

Christus.

Ergò, sunt rata de me uatum præsagia, Trimet.
Finemq́; suum propè adepta sunt ac terminum.
Ergò, quod dissolubile modò corpu' extitit,
Quod conditionem habuit, ut posset mori,
Aeternitate iam imbutum, renascitur.
Et omni cum immortalitate æquabitur.
Tuq́; adeò Mors, quæ cæteris hominibus
Nunquam non impendes, ut quod certissimum.
Abiecta protinus hasta, uictorem agnoscito.
In me posthac tantum tibi posse negabitur.
Atque ecce tibi felix & faustum nuncium,
Quisquis es ô homo. Nam ut omittam tyrannidem Octo. 2.
Peccati, mortis & inferni, à queis liber iam factus es,
Ego duræ lêgis austeritati pro te feci satis.

noise the struggling and wrestling winds make in our ears! How strangely one's voice sounds, shaken by the mighty din! What earthquakes come to battle! How the earth bellows, how it is moved and shaken, and how it roars! I believe that it trembles horribly not only in one place, but everywhere.

Dor. Good God! What great flashes of lightning come from the cave! Comrades, here we must use not our arms, but our legs; here I take to flight.

Sang. I, too, will flee.

Bru. And I likewise will flee.

Dro. I shall not be the last. I do not care who follows at my back, as long as I outstrip them all. But, O good God, I implore Thy protection! What is this? Alas, I am no more!

Dor. I am undone!

Sang. I am lost!

Bru. I am slain!

ACT III, SCENE II.

Christus

So the predictions of the prophets concerning me have been fulfilled, and have almost reached their end and goal. This body, which but a while ago was subject to dissolution, and was of such a nature that it could die, is now born again, imbued with life eternal; and it shall be made the peer of everything immortal. And thou, too, O Death, who, as the greatest certainty, dost ever threaten the rest of mankind, do thou straightway cast aside thy spear, and acknowledge thy conqueror. Whosoever thou art, O man, here are glad tidings for thee: I say naught of the tyranny of sin, of death, and of hell, from which thou art now made free, for I have given satisfaction in thy behalf to the severity of the harsh

Si qua igitur tanti tangit amoris gratia:
Confide, tuam caussam sanguis aget meus.

ACTVS III. SCENA III.

Magdaléne. Cleophis. Chorus Galileïdum.

Bono animo este sorores, magnam partem uiæ Trimet.
Superauimus, & multum æquoris confecimus.
Ast, quomodo nunc tecum Cleophis agitur?
Equidem te non tam fessam esse de uia,
Quàm sollicitudine fatigatam arbitror.
Cleop. Vix credas quoties inter eundum mihi
Veniebant in mentem huius ardua facinora.
Etenim memoria repetebam ultima
Tempus, quo Chanan urbem unà cum parentibus,
A ueteri quodam amico accitis, uenerat.
Qui adolescenti cupido, in matrimonium
Locabat filiolam castam & nubilem.
Et quum iam epulis optimis pulsa fuit fames,
Atque coronari uina potissimùm oportuit,
Ministrorum murmur cæpit consurgere,
Vacuis cadis Lyæi nihil esse reliquum.
Tum difficultateis miserata domesticas
Pia parens, & secum uoluens incommoda:
Nato confestim significabat suo,
Omnem domum absumpto Baccho tristarier.
Simul & famulos perbenigna monuit,
Vt quod mandaret eis, obirent sedulò.
Is etsi commotus, primùm caussatus est
Non aduenisse, quæ expectaret tempora:
Tandem tamen sex impleri à famulis iubet
Fontanis & puris undis carchesia.
Quæ simul ut heros aspexerat: ecce omnibus
Humor cernebatur subitò rubescere.

law. If, then, any gratitude for my great love touch thy heart, be assured that my blood shall plead thy cause.

ACT III, SCENE III.

Magdalene, Cleophis, Chorus of Galilean Women.

Mag. Be of good courage, sisters, we have completed a great part of the journey, and passed over much of the plain. How dost thou fare now, Cleophis? Indeed, I think thee not so much wearied from the journey as worn out with anxiety.

Cleop. Thou wouldst scarcely believe how often His mighty deeds came into my mind while walking; for I was recalling, in my earliest recollections, the time when He came to the city of Cana, together with His parents, who were invited by a certain old friend who was giving in marriage his dear daughter, a virgin, to a loving youth. And now when hunger had been banished by a most excellent feast, and it was most fitting for the wine-cups to be crowned, a murmur began to arise among the servants that there was no wine left, and that the jars were quite empty. Then the good mother, noting their embarrassment, and pitying the difficulties of the house, at once pointed out to her son that all the house was saddened by the lack of wine; and at the same time she most kindly advised the servants to do diligently what He commanded them. He, though moved, at first gave the excuse that the time He was awaiting had not yet come; but at length He ordered six waterpots to be filled by the servants with pure spring water. As soon as the Lord looked upon them, the liquid was seen

Sentit aqua uireis insuetas, & induit
Nouum quendam saporem alieno ex munere.
Hoc nesciens quidam è numero primarius,
Sponsum appellans, me magna (ait) admiratio tam diu
Tenet, quid sit, quòd præter morem
Liquorem ambrosiæ similem conseruaueris.
Itaq; stupefacti omnes, priùs incognita
Vehementer admirantur Christi numina.
Suamq; in eum comites conijciunt fidem.
Fama quoq; fuit, illum super alta maria
Et illæsum ambulasse, & summo in gurgite haud
Pedeis tinxisse. audieram & eius ipsius
Dicto, compesci agitationes fluctuum:
Et quamlibet proteruos austri spiritus,
Ac uenti flamina uim suam deponere.
Sunt plurima, quæ sæpè Iosephus mihi
Et Iudas, & Simon, & Iacobus, mea
Dulcissima narrare solebant pignora.
Mag. Imò si animo tuo iam compræhenderes,
Mihi, quæ nota sunt, magìs obstupesceres.
Nec ad stuporem modò res miras êdidit:
(Quod aliqui aliquando fortè præstiterint magi)
Verùm ad salutem operabatur uir inclytus.
Nam si uellem enumerare, haud uerbis consequi
Quot ægris, adflictis, atq; laborantibus,
Quot hominum damnis ac incommoditatibus
Curationem atq; medicamentum attulit:
Non promptiorem haberet finem oratio,
Quàm si cuperem hac dictione persequi
In Lybico quanta iaceat arena littore: aut
Quot orbem stelligerum distinguant sydera.
Nam quos malè Erynnis uexabat pessuma,
Quos æstus ac febris iactabat ignea,
Quos profusis tumens hydrops humoribus
Aut quicunq; etiam alius torquebat dolor,

suddenly to grow red; the water experienced an unwonted strength, and took on a new flavor by another's gift. Not knowing this, the ruler of the feast called the bridegroom, and said: 'I marvel much how it is, that, contrary to the custom, thou hast kept back so long a liquor that is like ambrosia.' And so all in amazement marveled greatly at the power of Christ, which none knew before; and His followers put their faith in Him. There was a story, too, that He walked unharmed upon the deep sea, upon the surface of the waters, yet did not wet His feet. I have heard also that at His very word the tossing of the waves was stilled, and that the breath of the south wind and its blasts, however boisterous, ceased their violence. There are very many things, too, which my dearest children, Joses, Jude, Simon, and James, were wont often to tell me.

Mag. Nay, if indeed thou couldst comprehend the things that are known to me, thou wouldst be more astonished. Nor did He do miracles only to amaze, a thing which, perchance, sorcerers may at some time have done; but the glorious Man performed them for salvation's sake. If I wished to count over, and not express in words, to how many sick, afflicted, and suffering, and to how many men's losses and damages, He brought a cure and remedy, my speech could have no speedier end than if I sought to tell you how much sand there lies on the Libyan shore, or how many constellations adorn the starry heavens. For He restored to their former health those whom a most evil Fury tormented to their hurt, those whom the heat and fire of fever tossed, those whom swelling dropsy with its excessive humors, or other ailment whatsoever, tortured. Need I tell

Ad sanitatem restituebat pristinam.
Quid memorem? numerosam turbam concurrere,
Tam à disiunctissimis quibusq; partibus,
Vidisses quàm à patriæ propinquis finibus.
Cæcosq́; tum & claudos, mutosq́; cerneres,
Lucem oculis debitam, pedibusq́; uim suam,
Et eloquendi facultatem recipere.
At illud est in primis commemorabile,
Quod erga fœminam miserandam præstitit.
Ea cùm laxis uenis annos duodecim
Flumen fuisset passa impuri sanguinis,
Etsi iam adficeretur morbi doloribus,
Et succo membris exhaustis pallesceret:
Tamen exanguis tantam concepit spem suæ
Salutis apud Christum obtinendæ, ut protinus
Vel multitudine compressa sequentium,
Ad eum ipsum pleno cursu contenderet,
Quò saltem posset amictum contingere.
Vt ergò illum iuxta defessa steterat, &
Manum exporgens uestem extremam apprehĕderat:
Vim quandam toti subitò infusam corpori
Persentiscit, uenasq́; patenteis claudier.
Mulier Iesum latuisse facinus hoc putans,
Se cogitabat clanculùm subducere.
Verùm fugientem scius ille reuocat,
Coràm in medio ut factum fateretur lubens.
Eamq́; subtrepidam ac timidiusculam,
Sui colloquij suauitate recreat.
Quid, quòd & ab inferis quosdam excitauerit
Morte oppressa? Cùm enim ab ora Sydonia
Veniens, Naymam adijt suis comitantibus:
Ecce, puelli egregij corpus miserabile
Feretro impositum, & uita defunctum conspicit.
Genetrix mœsto complens ululatu uiam,
Filiolum immaturo flet raptum funere.

the story? You might have seen large crowds come together no less from the most distant parts than from the near-by sections of the country, and then you might have seen the blind, the lame, and the dumb receive the light due their eyes, strength for their feet, and the power of speech. That deed is particularly worthy of mention which He performed in behalf of a wretched woman. Although for twelve years she had suffered from an issue of impure blood, and though she was visited with the pain attending her malady, and had grown pallid because her limbs were drained of the vital sap; nevertheless, bloodless as she was, she had conceived so great a hope of obtaining her health at Christ's hands that, though hindered by the multitude of His followers, she pressed straight to Him, that she might at least touch His garment. When the exhausted woman took her stand close by Him, and stretched forth her hand, touching the hem of His garment, she straightway felt a certain vigor spread throughout her body, and the open veins close. The woman, thinking that her deed had escaped the notice of Jesus, was considering how to withdraw secretly; but He, knowing this, called her back as she was hastening away, that she might freely confess before them all what she had done. With the gentleness of His speech He reassured the woman, who was somewhat frightened and timid. Need I speak of some whom He recalled from the dead, thus overcoming death? When, coming with His disciples from the coast of Sidon, He approached the city of Nain, lo, He beheld the pitiful sight of the body of a fine lad dead upon a bier. His mother, filling the street with her lamentations, wept for her dear son carried away by premature death. When

Hanc Iesus noster ut uidit, mox parcere
Querelis iubet: & imperat corpusculo, ac
Denuò gelidis membris insinuatur anima.
Ipse uelut expleto somno, surgens puer:
Aperto se capulo (cunctis mirabile)
Viuum extollit, & exiliens matrem amplectitur.
Nec ita multò pòst, idem ille uirginem,
Quæ naturæ uitam reddiderat, cui calor
E pectore, & omnis dilapsus erat spiritus:
Amisso iterum isthoc donauit lumine.
Sed enim nunc tandem ad tumulatum uenimus.
Hîc si uidetur, ponamus uestigia.
Vos facitote, è gremijs ne quid odorum excidat.
At, quiś nam hæc à clauso sepulchro grandia
Saxa euoluet, sepulchralia nos debita ut
Possimus hîc persoluere? Dimet.
Circunspicite, si propè quisquam auxiliariu' est.
Hui, quid hos est? Atat, os monumenti patet.
Intremus. hem, perij: nihil hîc relinquitur.
Quàm uereor, ne quis etiam in extinctum sæuiat.
Quò properem? ubi quæram? quos uestigem? nescio.
Est animus tamen adire cum primis Petrum,
Eumq́; hac de re certiorem reddere.
Cleo. Quæso matres, ut ab hoc loco terroribus
Pleno, uelitis mecum unà secedere.
Vix mente consto, & cor extra se ponitur.
Nuper latratu reboabat tellus, ita ut
Nubes refracto responderet aëre.
Nunc quid sibi tumulus inanis uelit, & pate=
Factum claustrum coniectura non adsequor.

ACTVS III. SCENA IIII.

Iohannes. Petrus.

our Jesus saw her, He at once bade her cease her weeping; He gave commands to the body, and straightway into the cold limbs the breath of life made its way. The boy himself, as if he had but finished sleeping, rose up living from the open bier, and, hastening to his mother, embraced her—a marvel to all. Not so long afterward, likewise to a maiden, who had given her life back to Nature, and from whose bosom the warmth and the breath of life had vanished, He gave again the light of day which had been lost. But now indeed we have at length come to the tomb. If it seem good to you, let us rest our steps here. Take care that no perfume fall from your bosoms. But who will roll away these great stones that close the sepulchre, that we may pay here the due rites of burial? Look about, and see if any one is near by to aid. Ha! What is this? Strange! The mouth of the tomb is open. Let us enter. Alas, I am undone! Nothing is left here. How I fear that some one is venting his wrath even on the dead! Whither shall I hasten? Where shall I look? Whom shall I trace? I know not. Yet I have a mind to go to Peter first of all, and to inform him of this thing.

Cleo. I beg you, mothers, that you will leave this place of terrors with me. I seem scarcely in my right mind. I am beside myself. The earth lately so re-echoed with roaring that the air was cleft, and the storm-clouds answered. Now what the empty tomb and the open door mean I do not understand.

ACT III, SCENE IV.

John, Peter.

Videlicet, certò sciebam iam antea Trimet.
Me facilè posse Petrum cursu præuertere, ac
Priusquam ille huc tardo gressu perrexerit,
Mihi licitum erit audita inuisere.
Papè, quid ego uideo? nil, nisi linteamina.
Sed iam accurrit senior, & crebro spirituum
Vireis uento restaurat. Petr. Quid, quid obsecro
Fit Iohannes? Verá ne mulier omnia
Rettulerat? Ioh. omnia Simon uerissima.
Pet. Ingressus es? Iohan. Nequaquă, at conspexi tamen
Humi positum & iacentem pannum linteum.
Omnino, sese nusquam humatus obtulit.
Pet. Introëamus, & exploretur meliusculè
Cauerna. bone Deus: ecce uestem linteam,
En qua caput inuoluebatur, calanticam.
Nihil estptereà, ne trahamus hîc moram.
Huì profectò res mihi magna uidetur ac mirabilis. Octona.
Equidem hercle operam dabo, ut unde & quorsum hæc fiant,
(intelligam. Octona.
Abeamus. Ioan. Sine dubio meliora dabit Deus.
Quid ni reuixisse putem? Etenim eum si quis hinc
Furatus esset, non quæq; locasset ordine:
Sed uestes arripuisset cum corpore.

ACTVS III. SCENA V.

Magdaléne. Angelus. I. Ang. II. Christus.

Reuiso meæ portum atq; auram anxietudini.[8]
Nam iterum atq; iterū uel introspicere tumulū,
In quo membra Galilæi sunt recondita,
Meum dolorem non mediocriter leuat.
O utinam, utinam, hunc rursum erectum cernerem,

[8] Emendation:
Reuiso meae portum atq; *aram* anxietudini.
Vos eritis nostrae portus et ara fugae.
Ovid, *Ex Ponto* 2. 8. 68.

John. Of course, I knew for certain before this that I could easily outrun Peter. Before he with his slow pace gets here, I shall have a chance to look into these things of which I have heard. How strange! What do I see? Nothing but the linen clothes. But now the old man comes running, and with rapid panting recovers his wind and strength.

Pet. What, what, I pray, is happening, John? Was all that the woman reported true?

John. All most true, Simon.

Pet. Hast thou entered the tomb?

John. Not at all; yet I saw that the linen garments had been laid aside, and were lying on the ground, but the buried man has appeared nowhere.

Pet. Let us enter, and let the cavern be searched a little better. Good God! Behold the linen clothes, and the napkin in which His head was wrapped! There is nothing else to delay us longer here. Oh, verily, the thing seems great and wonderful to me. By Hercules, I will try to learn from what sources, and to what end, these things happen. Let us depart.

John. Without doubt God will give us better things. Why should I not believe that He has come to life? For if any one had stolen Him away, he would not have placed His garments in order, but would have taken them, together with the body.

ACT III, SCENE V.

Magdalene, First Angel, Second Angel, Christ.

Mag. Again I seek this place of refuge, and sanctuary for my anxiety. For even to look again and again into the tomb in which the body of the Galilean was laid away lightens my grief in no small measure. Oh, oh, that I could

Vt pridem germanum intuebar, qui incubans
Telluris gremio, iacuerat quatriduum.
Hei mihi, quòd precio, quòd precibus, quòd lachrymis
Obruta duro fato uita redimi nequit.
Ang. I. Quã tu ô fœmina uoce & querelis indicas
Tristiciam? Ang. II. Expedias matrona integerrima
Quid sit quòd êdere ploratum non desinis.
Mag. Eximij, pulchri & formosi adolescentuli, ex
Hoc monumento nescio quis herum abstulit meum.
Sed nec misera quonam deportatu' est, scio.
Væ mihi. Quid subitò obstupuistis perterriti?
Chr. Mea mulier, hoc unum mihi uelim edisseras
(Modò fides dignitasq́; patietur tua)
Quæ tantæ caussæ est lamentationis, aut
Quem uix orbe fugatis umbris iam quæritas?
Mag. Dabis hoc bone agricola uel facilitati tuæ,
Vel desiderio meo, ut si dum hortulo
Prospicis, ac metuis Iudæos, eum aliò
Detuleris mihi significes, ubinam nunc siet.
Tutò & honorificè illum terræ mandauero.
Quin certum est, quare stupefiebant iuuenes,
Ab his cognoscere.
Chr. Maria. Magda. hem, mi magister? Chr. optuma Mag-
(dalis

see Him risen again, just as I formerly beheld my brother,[15] who, resting in the bosom of the earth, had lain there for four days. Woe is me that a life, overcome by stern death, cannot be redeemed by price, by prayers, or by tears.

First Ang. O woman, what grief is this which thou declarest by thy voice and complaints?

Second Ang. Explain, most virtuous matron, why it is that thou dost not cease to wail.

Mag. Excellent, fair, and comely youths, some one has taken away my Lord from this tomb, nor do I, unhappy woman that I am, know where they have laid Him. Woe is me! Why do ye suddenly stand aghast with terror?

Christ. My good woman, I wish that thou wouldst tell me this one thing, if only thy confidence and thy dignity will permit it—why weepest thou so sorely, and whom seekest thou, when the shadows have scarcely been put to flight from the world?

Mag. Good gardener, yield either to thine own kindly nature or to my longing, and if, fearing the Jews and caring for thy garden, thou hast borne Him hence, show me where He now is, and I will safely and honorably commit Him to the earth. Nay, it is quite clear why these youths are amazed; Thou art recognized by them.

Christ. Mary.

Mary. O my master!

Christ. Most worthy Magdalene, do not show thyself so

[15] Mary Magdalene. In the New Testament Mary Magdalene is mentioned among the women who accompanied Christ and ministered to Him (Luke 8.2-3), where it is also said that seven devils had been cast out of her (Mark 16.19). She is next named as standing at the foot of the cross (Mark 15.40; Matt. 27.56; John 19.25; Luke 23.49). She saw Christ laid in the tomb, and she was the first recorded witness of the resurrection. The Greek fathers, as a whole, distinguish the three persons: the sinner of Luke 7.36-50; the sister of Martha and Lazarus, Luke 10.38-42 and John 11; and Mary Magdalene. On the other hand, most of the Latins hold that these three were one and the same.—*Catholic Encyclopædia* 9.761.

Noli adeò elata lætitijs incedere, & exultare de carnis præ-
Nihil intereà de me sublime cogites. (sentia, ut
Caue putes, te intueri morti obnoxium
Hominem, ut priùs, aut ea necessitudine
Vobis coniunctum: sed supremo cum patre
Ipso in cælo regnaturum perenniter.
Animum erigito, mente alta & insuperabili
Feraris ad cælestia. Dimet.
Quin uade, rei tantæ ut fias prænuncia,
Eisq;, quos fraterno amore prosequor,
Quorumq; naturam induere mihi placuit,
Dic me dein cælestem occupaturum thronum,
Cum nostro unà parente indulgentissimo.

ACTUS III. SCENA VI.

Cleophis. Chorus Galileïdum. Angel. I. Ang. II. Christus.

Huc huc nosmet referamus, & experiamur an Trimet.
Reuersio spem deturbatam reintegret.
Sed nunc memini, ut non solùm animo commota eram
Dudum, sed & corpore toto perhorrui.
Ang. I. Quid uos horretis ô matres? omittite
Metum & formidinem, nam isti iure optimo, ex=[9]
Animantur consideratissimi homines.
Vestram nihilominus mœsticiam dehinc noua, &
Aeternùm perfruenda uincant gaudia.
Quandoquidem quem uos hinc ademptum plangitis,
Debellato Erebi rêge, imis ex manibus,
Rursum has in lucis oras uictor prodijt.
Non est quòd eum existimetis mortuum.
Aethereis iam uescentem auris, & integrum.
Imò uobi' in mentem uenire debuit,

[9] Emendation:
Metum & formidinem, nam *istis* iure optimo, ex =

elated with joy, and exult so over my presence in the flesh, that thou wilt entertain no lofty thought of me. Beware lest thou think thou seest in me one subject to death, a man as before, joined to thee by that mortal tie, but rather one who with the Father on high shall reign in heaven itself for ever. Lift up thy heart, and with lofty and unconquerable soul be borne to heaven. Nay, go, that thou mayest first announce this great thing to those whom I honor with a brother's love, and whose nature it has pleased me to put on. Tell my brethren that henceforth I shall sit upon the throne of heaven with my loving Father.

ACT III, SCENE VI.

Cleophis, Chorus of Galilean Women, First Angel, Second Angel, Christ.

Cleop. Hither, hither let us betake ourselves, and let us see whether our return will not renew our downcast hopes. But now I remember that a while ago I was shaken, not in mind alone, but also my whole body shuddered.

First Ang. Why do ye tremble, O mothers? Lay aside your fear and dread, though the most circumspect are very right to be overcome by these feelings. Nevertheless, let new joys, ever to be experienced, master your grief, since He whom you bewail as carried hence has vanquished the king of hell, and as a conqueror has come forth from the shades below into the realms of light. There is no reason to think Him dead; He is unharmed, and enjoying the light of heaven. Nay, verily, there should have occurred to your

Quod adhuc in Galilæa uersatus dixerat,
Oportere satum uirgine incidere in manus
Sceleratorum hominum, & figi funestæ trabi,
Quô cunctorum suapte sponte crimina
Deleret, & cum sole rediret tertio.
Ang. II. Nazarenum uos uelle non sum nescius,
Qui superiore die animam efflarit cruce.
A iure mortis exemit se, & uinculis
Expedijt, hinc uicturus æuo perpete.
Quod cum terna luce renasci promiserat,
Reuera & facto nunc fidelis præstitit.
Accedite, adsistite, oculis omnem locum
Perlustratote, qui uacuus cadauere,
Signum etiamdum effigiemq́; sepulti corporis
Retinet. Et exuuias, quibus implicatus est.
Si non facilè adduci potestis, ut mihi
Credatis, nec persuadeat oratio mea,
Vobis præsentia præsentem hæc facient fidem.
Quare hisce uestris officijs opus haud erit,
Quin hinc potiùs uos nulla interposita mora
Recipite & istam rem mox reliquis ostendite.
Sui ducis & capitis qui deplorant necem:
Sed seniori Petro in primis, cui scilicet
Ter abnegatus herus gemitum conduplicat.
Cuius conspectum si cupiscunt, conferant
Iter ad Galilæam, ubi eundem uiuum uiderint,
Per hæc quem collugent tempora demortuum.
Dixi. Cleo. Videam. Ecastòr, ita sese res habet.
Eamus, nunciemus discipuli' omnia.
Chr. Saluere uos iubeo Mariæ Galileïdes.
Abijcite pauores ex animo, qui expectorant
Intelligentiam, & intrepidè me attendite,
Ne non sanum sit attonitis in sensibus
Iudicium, surgite, & his osculationibus
Finem facite, & hinc celeriter nunc uadite,
Meisq́; uisa monstratote fratribus,

minds that which He said when He was yet in Galilee: that the son of the Virgin must be delivered into the hands of sinful men, and be fastened to the deadly tree, that of His own accord He might blot out the sins of all, and rise again on the third day.

Second Ang. I well know that it is the Nazarene thou meanest, who on a former day breathed forth His spirit on the cross. From the law of death He freed Himself, and escaped from its bonds to live in eternal life. As to His promise that He would rise again on the third day, He has fulfilled it in word and deed. Come near, see all the place, which, though empty, still retains the marks and traces of the buried body. Behold the cloths in which He was wrapped. If ye cannot easily be led to believe me, and my speech does not convince you, these, the present sights, will give you ready faith. Wherefore there will be no need of your services, but rather go quickly and tell the others, who bewail the death of their Lord and Master. But first of all go to the old man, Peter, for whom the threefold denial of his Master makes double sorrow. If they wish to behold Him, let them go into Galilee, and there they shall see Him living, Him whom at this time they lament together as dead. I have spoken.

Cleop. I may see Him. By my faith, it is even so. Let us go, let us tell all to the disciples.

Christ. Daughters of Galilee, I bid you hail. Cast out from your hearts the fear which banishes understanding, and fearlessly give heed to me, lest in your astonishment your judgment be unsettled. Arise, and to these kisses put an end; go quickly now, and make known to my brethren

Vt in Galilæam post me proficisci queant.

ARGVMENTVM ACTVS IIII.

Egressis fœminis, ad sese milites
Redeunt, & uisa sacerdotibus indicant.
Interea, quæ iussit Christus Galileïdes,
Discipuli' exponunt. Sed pharisæorum quidem
Posteaquam in parteis distractum contraria', &
Nil certo statuens concilium dimittitur:
Delegatur Alecto statim à cacodæmone,
Quæ aurum singulis præberi militibus monet,
Orationem ut commutent, & falsa pro
Veris fidenter in apertum proferant.
Hij, sicut erant edocti, faciunt sedulò:
Ac inficias eunt Christum esse superstitem.
Itaq; & custodes, acceptis pecunijs
Lætantur, & recedens quoq; Caïaphas
Elatus insolenti exultat gaudio,
Quia res processum habet ex sua sententia.

ACTVS IIII. SCENA I.

Brumax. Sangax. Dorus. Dromo.

Equidem animi pendeo hoc quid sit negocij, Trimet
Quorsum hic stupor alienatioq; sensuum.
Ego sic timeo ut rerum nullam quodammodò
Perceptionem habeam, socij uerò mei
Timore stupidi obmutuerunt, strenuus modò
Ipse mihi uidebar, sed quò confidentia
Quò nunc animi uis, quò pristina generositas
Recessit? hei iacet sepultum in pectore
Omne meum robur, & omnis abest audacia.
Tentabo tamen si qua spes adfulgeat
In socijs. Tu Sangax, tu, inquam, Sangax age,

what ye have seen, that they may set out after me into Galilee.

ARGUMENT OF ACT IV.

After the women have departed, the soldiers come to themselves, and declare to the priests the things they have seen. Meanwhile, the women of Galilee make known to the disciples the things which Christ has commanded. After the council of the Pharisees has been divided into opposing parties, and no decision has been arrived at, it is broken up. Alecto is sent at once by Cacodemon to Caiaphas, whom she advises to give money to each of the soldiers, in order that they change their story, and boldly give out a false tale as true. They diligently do as they have been told, and deny that Christ survives. And so not only do the guards rejoice over the money that they have received, but Caiaphas, also, elated with immoderate joy, exults as he departs, because things are going according to his liking.

ACT IV, SCENE I.

Brumax, Sangax, Dorus, Dromo.

Bru. I am at a loss to know what this business is, and where this stupor and loss of reason came from. I am so frightened that, in a way, I have no idea of things. Moreover, my companions, bewildered with fear, have become dumb. I lately thought myself strong and vigorous, but where now have my courage of mind and my former noble spirit gone? Alas, all my strength lies buried in my breast; all my daring has departed. I will try, however, to find if there is any gleam of hope in my companions. You, Sangax, you, I say, Sangax, come, get up. Do not be afraid, every-

Surgito, ne paueas, in tuto sunt omnia.
Sang. Abierunt' ne igitur, abierunt fœmina, aut
Furiæ potiùs & flammis corusci dæmones?
Bru. Abiêre mihi crede. Excitemus nunc Dorum.
Heus heus Dore: Ocyus ô Dore expergiscere.
Expergiscere Dore. Iam nihil est periculi.
Dor. Exurgo, modò non sit quidquam discriminis.
Ah, uix apud me sum, tremor ita me occupat.
Bru. Quam tandem hanc esse metamorφωsin autumas?
Tam' ne citò accipitris dedidicisti audaciam?
Sed, ut uidetur, Dromo nec haurit anhelitum,
Nec spiritum ullum êdit. Dromo. Dromo. Dromo.
Quid, humi prostratus, longus ut es, Dromo iaces?
Atat, auras incassum stultus diuerbero,
Surdisq; auriculis me præconem præbeo.
Obsecro uos, uos aureis implete flatibus.
Sang. Dromo. Do. Dromo. Sang. Dromo. Do. Dromo.
San. Dromo. Do. Dromo.
Bru. Hem salua res est, nobis Deus hodie fauet.
Anhelat nunc breui subinde spiritu.
Quid agitur Dromo? Agedùm temet iam collige.
Reuocato animum. Trepidandi causa euanuit.
Dro. Quis Dromonẽ appellat? Bru. fortunæ particeps
Tuæ Brumax. Age surge, ego te fulciam.
Tenebo labentem, & corruere non sinam.
Dro. Heu uireis deficiunt. Bru. brachia exporgito.
Dro. Quis me, quis appræhendit? Brumax. Brumax dico
Consocius. Surge, surge. Dro. animo malè est meo. (tuus
Cor contrahitur, debilitatur, tremit.
Mirè uexatur caput, & sensuum organa

thing is safe.

Sang. Have they gone, then, have the women gone, or rather the furies and demons gleaming with flames?

Bru. They have gone, believe me. Let us now rouse Dorus. Ho there! Dorus, O Dorus! Wake up! Quick! Wake up! Dorus! There is no danger now.

Dor. I will get up now, if there is no danger. Ah, I have scarcely come to myself, trembling seized upon me so.

Bru. What do you say about this change? Have you so quickly unlearnt the boldness of the falcon? But, Dromo, as it seems, is neither drawing his breath, nor sending any forth. Dromo! Dromo! Dromo! Why do you lie with your long length flat on the ground? Oh, fool that I am to split the air in vain, and to make myself a herald to deaf ears. I beg you to fill his ears with your shouts.

Sang. Dromo!

Dor. Dromo!

Sang. Dromo!

Dor. Dromo!

Sang. Dromo!

Dor. Dromo!

Bru. Ha, we are safe; the gods favor us to-day. He is getting a little breath now. What is the matter, Dromo? Come, pull yourself together. Recall your courage. The cause for fear has vanished.

Dro. Who calls Dromo?

Bru. The partner of your fortune, Brumax. Come, get up, I will support you. I will hold you, since you are unsteady, and not let you fall.

Dro. Ah, my strength is gone.

Bru. Put out your arms.

Dro. Who, who is it that lays hold of me?

Bru. I tell you that it is Brumax, your comrade. Get up, get up.

Dro. I am troubled in mind. My heart is throbbing, it is weak, and it trembles. My head is strangely distressed,

Vix functiones præstant etiamdum suas.
Incredibiliter mihi metus ossa concutit.
Horrorq́; occupat extremas parteis corporis.
Verùm sinite me respirare paululum.
Bru. Tandem, ô, tandem nobiscum abige formidinem.
Tenuit & hic nos pallor crepitusq́; dentium,
Euasit homo cum suis fallacijs,
Ac præstigijs, neq; nos terrebit amplius.
Atqui quod facto confestim nunc est opus,
Faciam, hæc ut cognoscant sacerdotum duces.
Addito te Sangax adsectatorem mihi,
Tu uerò te Dore Dromoni adiungito.
Dor. Vos non ita longo interuallo comitabimur.
Quid nunc mi homo, reuixisti' ne bone Dromo?
Quomodo uiget robur uetus in corpore?
Dro. Bene iam, sed longè melius opinor foret
Mecum, si quàm primùm locum hunc relinquerem.
Dor. Fiat, sequamur præeuntes boni' auibus.

ACTVS IIII. SCENA II.

Petrus. Magdaléne. Chorus discipulorum.
Cleophis. Chorus Galileïdum.

Qvid narras Magdaléne? certá ne prædicas? Trimet.
Mag. Certissima. Pet. Sic scilicet ut dicam tibi.
Equidem tuos pauitanti' oculos existimo,
Vana quadam ac falsa lusos imagine.
Nam ueluti per quietem sepenumerò
Facit in se reflexa cogitatio,
Eorum uultus & simulachra cernere,
Quos maximè desideramu' interdiu,
Sic uel metum, uel amorem uel utrunq; te
Aut rapuisse, aut coniecisse reor in extasin,
Ita ut non secus ac mentiens quidam sopor
Sensus inanis præstringens fefellerit.

and the organs of my senses hardly do their work as yet. Fear shakes my bones in an incredible way, and I am trembling to my finger-tips. Just let me breathe a little.

Bru. O now, now, with us banish your fear. This paleness and this chattering of teeth seized us, too. The man, through his tricks and illusions, has escaped, and he will not frighten us any more. But I will let the leaders of the priests know of these things; it must be done at once. Sangax, join me as an attendant. But you, Dorus, join Dromo.

Dor. We will follow you at no great distance. What now, my man! Have you recovered, good Dromo? How is the old strength in your body?

Dro. Well, now. But I think that it would be far better for me if I were to leave this place as soon as possible.

Dor. So be it. Let us follow them, and may we have good luck.

ACT IV, SCENE II.

Peter, Magdalene, Chorus of Disciples, Cleophis, Chorus of Galilean Women.

Pet. What story is this that thou art telling, Magdalene? Are the things true that thou hast told?

Mag. Most true.

Pet. As true as I shall tell thee. Indeed, I think that, in thy fear, thine eyes were deluded by a certain false, deceptive phantom; for just as very often in sleep, thought, turning back upon itself, makes us see the faces and forms of those whom we especially long for by day; just so either fear, or love, or both, I think, carried thee away, or threw thee into transports, and nothing other than a sort of lying, deceiving stupor tricked thy dead senses.

Cho. Disc. Quid' nă hoc tandĕ est? Ain tu quæso? denuò
Nostrum uiuere dominum? Dic, age, dic bona
Nec aliena fide, ut sese tibi obtulit?
Longam (sîs) narrandi continuatio seriem.[10]
Et à capite ad calcem, iuxta prouerbium,
Singula diducito. De illo audire quidem iuuat:
Vtut, quod profers, parùm, sit probabile.
Mag. Quum de uacuo busto, tibi dixeram Petre:
Me recipiebam protinus eodèm loci.
Cumq; illò adueneram: eccè repentè mihi
Et nictu oculi, splendenteis albis uestibus
Apparent iuuenes. In uultu plurimus honos,
Et cœleste decus toto effulsit corpore.
Haud nostra stirpe, exortos esse dixeris:
Sed administros superûm speciosissimos.
Hij uerò à me caussas exquirunt questuum.
Sublati heri desiderio me confici
Respondeo. Quibus dictis à tergo stetit.
Tamen illum nesciebam: ut qui mihi se obuium
Dedit ignoti sub hortulani schemate.
Credo, ne si glorificam sumpsisset faciem:
Exanimasset me miseram præ formidine.
Cho. disc. Quî scis igitur, Christŭ esse, quĕ cŏspexeras?
Mag. Agnoui ex uoce. Nam cùm ab eo digressa sum:
Statim reuocata notum accipiebam sonum.
Quinetiam Mariæ me appellabat nomine.
Tunc ô tunc menti quæ infundebat gaudia?
Quæ tunc toto expellebat corde tristia?
Sic nube sub nigra quum deprensa est dies,
Quum cœlum squalet ac sol umbris conditur:
Aura exurgens sub Oceano, aut è montibus
Tenebras depellit, nubilaq; dissipat,
Lætamq; nitido faciem restiuit polo:
Omnino taleis sentiebam in pectore

[10] Emendation:
Longam (sis) narrandi *continuato* seriem.

Cho. Disc. Now what is this? Pray, sayest thou that our Master lives again? Tell us, come, tell us in all good faith how He presented Himself to thee. Tell us, please, without interruption, the long series of events, and, as the saying is, from first to last relate every detail. Even to hear of Him is a joy, although what thou revealest is all too little probable.

Mag. Peter, when I had told thee of the empty tomb, straightway I went to the same spot, and, when I had reached it, behold, suddenly, in the twinkling of an eye, young men clothed in shining white garments appeared unto me. There was great dignity in their countenances, and a celestial glory shone forth from their entire bodies. Thou wouldst have said that they had not sprung from our race, but that they were most splendid ministers of heaven. They, indeed, asked me the cause of my lamentations. I answered that I was worn out with grief for the Master whom they had taken from me. While these words were being spoken, He stood beside me; nevertheless I recognized Him not, since He appeared to me in the form of an unknown gardener. I believe that had He not taken on so glorious a countenance, I should have died of fright.

Cho. Disc. How knowest thou, then, that it was Christ whom thou didst behold?

Mag. I recognized Him by His voice, for when I was departing from Him, at once I heard the well-known sounds. Nay, indeed, He called me by the name of Mary. Then, oh then, what joys did He impart to my mind, what griefs did He drive from my sad heart! It was as when the light of day is caught under a black cloud, when the sky is overcast, and the sun is buried under shadows, a breeze, rising from the face of the sea or from the mountains, dispels the darkness, scatters the clouds, and to the shining heaven restores its glad aspect. Such a tumult, such a triumph I felt in my

Motus, taleis triumphos, tamq́; seriò
Tum gestiebam, ut iam nihil mirum mihi
Videatur, quod uix poteram olim credere,
Expirasse aliquos hilaritate nimia.
Et ille gaudium bene temperat meum,
Iubetq́; non tam corpus intuerier,
Quàm oculis animi diuinum honorem, & ipsius
Membra deinceps planè facta immortalia.
Demum superiora poli palatia, ad
Patrem se nostrum dixit uelle ascendere.
Ego uerò exprimere læticiam cogitans,
Ter sum conata loqui, ter eum affarier[11]
Incipiebam, solitasq́; uoces promere:
Sed mihi ter hæsit lingua prorsus mutilis,
Ter in summis labris mihi destitit sonus.
Dumq́; hæreo, quæ prima sumam exordia,
Nimis auidos reliquerat sensus meos.
Hæc summa est, hæc ut folia Sibyllæ credite.
Hæc uoluit, ego uobis ut prima panderem.
Cho. disc. Nimia mira, ô socij commemorat Magdalis.
Pet. Sunt incredibilia profectò, atq; ante hunc diem
Inaudita. At, quid hoc, quòd tam uelociter
Cleophis cum Galilæis huc aduolat?
Metuo ne quid eis obtigerit incommodi. At-
Tendamus. Ad nos rectà pergunt. Cleo. uidimus
Eia, eia uidimus (ô uiri) illum uidimus.
Pet. Quem̃ nam illum? Dic age. Cleo. Vidimus, inquam,
Illum ipsum Christum, quē putatis mortuum. (uidimus
Pet. Supreme Iehoua. Captum hæc superant meum.
Scio, esse uos nec mendaceis, nec perfidas:
Ipsa rei magnitudo tamen fidem negat.
Amabò, narra, quæ uidistis omnia.

[11]Ter conatus ibi collo dare brachia circum,
Ter frustra comprensa manus effugit imago,
Par levibus ventis volucrisque simillima somno.
Aeneid 6. 700-703.

heart, such great transports of happiness did I feel, that it does not now seem strange to me that some have died of excessive joy, a thing I once could have scarce believed. He well restrained my raptures, and bade me not to regard His body so much, but with the mind's eye to consider His divine glory, and after that the clear evidence of His immortal body. Lastly, He said that it was His will to ascend unto the lofty palace of heaven, to our Father. Thrice I tried to speak, thrice I began to address Him, to utter the usual words, but three times my tongue was utterly dumb; three times on my very lips sound failed me. But while I was at loss how to begin, He disappeared from my too eager senses. This is all. Credit these things as you do the Sibyl's leaves. These things He wished me to make known to you first.

Cho. Disc. O companions, the tale which Magdalene tells is marvelous beyond measure.

Pet. It is incredible, indeed, and unheard of until this day. But what does this mean, that Cleophis with the women of Galilee is running hither so swiftly? I fear that some disaster has befallen them. Let us wait. They are coming straight toward us.

Cleo. We have seen Him, oh, we have seen Him! Men, we have seen Him!

Pet. What him? Come, tell us.

Cleo. We have seen Him, Christ Himself, whom ye think dead.

Pet. Almighty Jehovah! These things are beyond my grasp. I know that thou art neither lying nor deceitful, yet the very greatness of the thing forbids belief. I beg of thee, tell all that thou hast seen, for long since we have

Nam ad audiendum animos iamdudum ereximus.
Cleo. Primùm omnium, ut illò accessimus, ut in limine
Sepulchri stetimus, ecce tibi, duo iuuenum
Pulcherrimorum corpora.
Quid quæris? omnia ex parte fuêre splendidi.[12]
Solantur. Quidq́; in Galilæa pollicitus est
Longè anteà Christus, reuocant in memoriam.
Nudum locum ostendunt, in eoq́; residuas
Exuuias. Atq́; nominatim te Petre
Voluêre Euangelio hoc per nos recrearier.
Hæc dixerant. Metum autem nostrum gaudia
Nunc uincunt, nunc eo mutuò uincuntur, *&*
Sese uicissim retrudunt pugnantia,
Atq; uiceis alternant spes *&* timor, usque dum
Nos ipse alacriter salutauerat herus,
Et aspectu ac sermone suo refecerat.
Qui se confirmabat, in ora Galileïde
A uobis omnibus uelle dein conspici.
Tum ab amplexu sistimus. Habetis ad omnia.
Pet. Multa audiui, multa inspexi, multa didici,
Multa memini: nihil post hominum memoriam
Tale accepi: nihil omni ætate huiusmodi
Cognoui: undè induci non queo, ut adsentiar.
Quoquomodo sit, nos nota adeamus loca.
Cho. disc. Eamus, *&* eas ueridicas faxit Deus.

ACTVS IIII. SCENA III.

Caïaphas.

Deum immortalem, quæ, quantaq́; miracula Trimet.
Modò mihi memorauit Brumax? quemadmodū
Imposita sigillisq́; obsignata adhuc petra:
Tamen erexit se tumulatus. Ac duo

[12] Emendation: Quid quæris? *omni* ex parte fuere splendidi.

roused our minds to listen.

Cleo. First of all, when we came there, and stood on the threshold of the sepulchre, look you, two young men most beautiful of form appeared. In a word, they were all glorious. They comforted us. They recalled to our memory whatsoever Christ had promised long before in Galilee. They showed us the empty place, and the clothes that were left behind. These things they said, and they named thee, Peter, whose spirit they wished to have renewed by these glad tidings. Now, our joys conquered our fears, and now, contending, they drove each other back; hope and fear came by turns until the Lord Himself eagerly hailed us, and by His looks and words revived our spirits. And He assured us that in Galilee He wished to be seen of you all. Then we ceased embracing Him. You have the whole story.

Pet. I have heard many stories, seen many sights, learned many things, and remember many, but I have never heard of anything like this within the memory of man; nothing like it in any age have I known; therefore I cannot be brought to regard these things as true. However it be, let us go to the well-known spot.

Cho. Disc. Let us go, and God grant that the women spoke truly.

ACT IV, SCENE III.

Caiaphas.

Cai. Immortal God! what great miracles Brumax has just now related to me: how, although the stone was laid and made fast with seals, nevertheless he arose, though entombed; and the two angels, more quickly than a word,

Lapidem dicto citius amôrunt angeli.
Vt antra sonabant occultis mugitibus,
Ventisq́; furebat solum pugnantibus.
Et eorum, quasi si occubuissent, iacentium:
Vt artus, intercepta anima, tenuit tremor.
Vt auram neq; dedit neq; suscepit Dromo: ut[13]
Vt sine colore, sine uoce, sine mente iacuit.
Quomodoq́; audierint alloquenteis fœminas,
Ministros angelicos, de cœli gente. Ita ut
Dubium non sit, uiuere Christum xylonicum.
Quid igitur? Quid nunc faciundum nobis erit?
Per urbeis ne hic rumor Palæstinas eat?
Nisi maturè uolgi sermoni occurrimus,
Ni astu famam premimus atq; extinguimus:
Actum de nobis est, sine controuersia.
Væ nostro tum ordini, uæ nostris mercibus.
Ibo, & cogam consilium in unum pectora, &
Legum, & religionis ritus callentia.

ACTVS IIII. SCENA IIII.

Cacodæmon. Alecto.[14]

Orcicolæ ô proceres, tartarei ô principes,
O Acherontæi magnates itinerum,
Voluntatum, sententiarum, facinorum,
Laborum, rerum deniq; nostrarum omnium
Socij perpetui, nullisq́; fatigabileis
Periculis, mementote, ut nos perpeti haud
Potuistis infandam conditionem, poli
Quando regnator nobis anteponeret
Hominum genus, ac nos deturbatos æthere,
Formidanda ui fulminis detruderet
In hæc loca tetra, horrenda, subterranea,

[13] Emendation:
Vt auram neq; dedit neq; suscepit Dromo: *et*

[14] See *Aeneid* 7. 324-347, 445-451.

moved away the stone; how the cave resounded with mysterious rumblings, and the ground raged beneath the battling winds; how the guards lay as if they had fallen in death, how trembling seized their limbs, and their breath was cut off, how Dromo neither gave forth breath nor drew it, but lay colorless, speechless, and senseless; and how they heard ministering angels, of heavenly race, consoling the women. And so there is no doubt that Christ, who died upon the tree, lives. What then? What must we do now, lest the rumor go forth through the cities of Palestine? Unless we quickly forestall common gossip, and with cunning suppress and stamp out the talk, without doubt it is all over with us. Woe then to our order, woe then to our fees! I will go, and I will assemble for consultation minds versed in both the law and the religious rites.

ACT IV, SCENE IV.

Cacodemon, Alecto.

Cacod. O ye who dwell in Orcus, chiefs and princes of Tartarus, great powers of Acheron, constant companions in our journeys, our wishes, opinions, deeds, and labors, in short, in all our affairs, and who are wearied by no perils, remember how we could not endure our hateful condition when the Ruler of heaven preferred the human race to us, and, driving us forth from heaven by the dread might of his thunderbolt, thrust us down into these realms beneath the

Terribilia, fœda, senta situ & squallida.
Probè hanc ulti estis luculentam iniuriam.
Nam horto Paradisiaco expulsum patrem,
Suamq́; sobolem eius contactam crimine,
Nobiscum ad sedes deuexistis infera', ac
Immani ditastis præda stygios lacus.
At enimuerò, humana sub nube & imagine
Deus occultatus, nuper hominum gratia, in
Terras descendit: illiusq́; spiritus
Apud nos hîc iamdudum, ut nostis, adfuit.
Quo præsente expauimus. Infernas hic domos
Reclusit. secum ingentem abduxit copiam.
Fuit, fuit tempestas, qua nostro iugo
Vel integrum terrarum orbem subiecimus.
Ast quæ nunc tanta nos tenet socordia?
Vbi nunc antiquæ uireis, arteis, machinæ,
Doli? Vbi nunc prisca imperij nostri gloria?
Sic' cine multis nobis regia spoliabitur?
Sic' cine rem prolabi patiemur desides?
Audite potiùs quæ mea sit sententia.
Christum interimebant Iudæi, hic se reddidit
Vitæ. Res iam multis Hierosolymarijs
Manifestior est, quàm ut dubitari queat.
Trepidant sacerdotes, semper amici fidissimi
Qui nobis extitêre: atq; hoc ne in publicum
Emanet, ponere student retinacula.
Id ad amplificandum nostrum regnum tam ualet
Quàm quod uel plurimùm. Hîc opibus uestris opus.
Viru' inspirate furtim animis mortalium, ut
Hæc tam mirabilia negent increduli.
Atqui (quod caput est) prodi, prodi mens mea,
Alecto prodi, cincta colubri & anguibus.[15]
Tibi mille nocendi arteis fœcundo in pectore.

[15] Emendation:
Alecto prodi, cincta *colubris* & anguibus

earth, terrible, unclean, and foul with mouldering filth. Ye have well avenged this serious affront, for with us ye carried down to the abodes below the father, banished from the garden of Paradise, and his offspring tainted with his sin; and with vast spoils ye have enriched the Stygian lake. But God, hidden under the disguise of human form, lately came down to earth for the sake of man; and His spirit not long ago was here amongst us, as ye know. We were terrified at His presence. He opened the infernal abodes, and led away with Him a vast number. Gone, gone is the time when we subdued to our yoke even the whole realm of the earth. But why does so great a sloth possess us now? Where are now our ancient powers, our arts, our devices and tricks? Where now is the former glory of our empire? Shall our royal palace be robbed of so many? Shall we thus idly suffer our state to fall? Hear rather what my judgment is. The Jews sought to slay Christ; He restored Himself to life. The thing is now too evident to many people of Jerusalem to be doubted. The priests, who have ever been our most faithful friends, are frightened; and, lest this rumor be spread abroad in public, they are eager to put a check on it. This is worth the very utmost to the increase of our dominion. Here there is need of your labor. Instil poison secretly into the minds of mortals, so that, incredulous, they may deny these great wonders. But, most important, go forth, Alecto, my soul; go forth girded with thy serpents. Thou hast a thousand hurtful arts in thy fertile

Tuum hoc erit munus, tuarum partium, ut
Mystas ancipites consilio iuues tuo.
Fac nummis obturetur os militibus, ut
Quidquid uiderunt, se uidisse pernegent.
Vadito, manibus pedibusq́; obnixè rem agito: nunc
Tentamentis peropus est, ac fallacijs.
Properato, horam utilem utiliter transmittito.
Alect. Citò imperata peragam adamussim tua.

ACTVS IIII. SCENA V.

Alecto. Caïaphas.

O mea quantum Adonij.
Penè apud omneis
Numina possunt?
Namq; ego semper
Ocyor euris,
Cursito nunc huc,
Nunc feror illuc.
Ac ea spargo
Dira uenena,
Quæ mihi cornu
Diuite, sæuus
Sufficit orcus.
Num tibi restim
Ipsa ferebam
Perdite Iuda?
Et tibi nummûm
Plena crumena
Est data, quorum
Sacra fames co-[16]
Egit herum te

[16] . . . Quid non mortalia pectora cogis
Auri sacra fames?
Aeneid 3. 56-7.

breast. This task shall be thine; it shall be thy part to aid the wavering priests with thy counsel. Make them close the soldiers' mouths with money, so that they will deny whatever they have seen. Go, and striving with hand and foot, do this thing. There is great need of proofs and deception. Hasten thou, and spend well a useful hour.

Alect. I will haste to fulfill thy commands.

ACT IV, SCENE V.

Alecto, Caiaphas.

Alect. Oh, how much my power can do with almost every one! For, ever swifter than the winds, I now run hither, am now borne thither; and I scatter these dire poisons which cruel hell supplies to me from the horn of riches. Lost Judas, did not I myself bring thee the rope? Was not a purse full of coins given thee, the accursed hunger for which compelled thee to betray thy righteous master? Now

Prodere iustum?
Sic similem rem,
Nunc faciam, quô
Qui modò uiuit,
Vsque putetur
Mortuus esse.

Euge, euge, eccum illum ipsum, quĕ uolo. Deus bone: ut
Ingreditur dubitabundus, & animum scindit in (Trimet.
Varias parteis? At paulisper ego tacita
Hîc auscultans, cautè obseruabo, quid nam agat.
Pòst, hominem adoriar, sicubi tempus monet.
Caïa. Non hoc mehercules mihi conuenticulum
Esse uidetur, hominum deliberantium:
Sed toto (ut aiunt) cœlo discrepantium,
Aut, quod ego uerè affirmem, delirantium.
Vnum aut altrum Annas sublimi è solio rogat,
Sententiam hac de re, ut pronunciet suam. Hic,
Quæcunq; uos, ait, iniungitis, ea perplacent.
Ille, in ponderosa, & seria & graui,
Certum spacium deliberandi postulat.
Alius, posse negat rem tantam occultarier.
Alius, ipsum Christum, iteratò occîdi uelit.
Reliqui nihil habuerunt, quod dicerent.
Sum itaq; multò incertior, ac dudum abiueram.
Alect. Hŭc ego tibi, si uis, bone uir scrupulŭ adimă: &
Paucis expediam, quid fieri oporteat.
Caïa. Quin immortali me tibi deuincies
Beneficio mortalem, si hoc effeceris,
Charissima domina. Alect. Pone metum, effectum dabo.
Inprimis, tumuli custodes argenteis
Fac superes muneribus, ut quæ uera sunt,
Nec proferant, nec diuulgent quouis modo.
Nummus rex, rex nummus, quid non facere potest,
In omnibus negocijs? Dimet.
Dicam, quod sentio, omnipotens pecunia,

I will do a like deed, whereby He who now lives may still be supposed dead. Good! Good! Behold the very man I want. Good God! He walks as though his mind were full of uncertainty, and rent in different directions! But, for a little while, I will silently observe here what he is about. Afterwards I will accost the man as occasion demands.

Cai. By heavens, this does not seem to me to be an assembly of counselors who merely disagree, but rather of men who, as they say, differ from one another by the whole width of heaven; or, as I may truly declare, an assembly of crazy men. Annas, from his high throne, asks one and another to give his opinion about this matter. This one says, 'Whatever you command quite pleases us.' That one demands a certain interval for deliberation on the affair, which is weighty, serious, and important. Another says that so great an event cannot be concealed. Another wishes Christ to be put to death a second time. The rest have nothing to say. I am therefore much more doubtful than when I departed a short time ago.

Alect. Good sir, if thou wilt, I will remove this difficulty from thee. In a few words I will explain what ought to be done.

Cai. Nay, dearest lady, thou wilt lay a mortal under an immortal obligation to thee if thou dost accomplish this.

Alect. Lay aside thy fear; I will bring it about. First of all, see that thou with gifts of money win over the guardians of the tomb, so that they neither tell the truth nor divulge it in any way. Money, the King, King Money, what can he not do in all affairs? I will tell you what I think: all-

Dat sola robur, uimq́; sola sufficit.
Quamobrem agitodum, & isthæc prædicta perfice,
Tibi quæ monstraui Furiarum ter maxima. Hîc
Scopus, hîc meorum uerborum meta est breuis.
Caïa. Quàm maximas habeo tibi diua gratias.
Nemo homo potuit melius consilium dare.
Geretur herclè mos tuis hortatibus.
Alect. Hei, nunc ergò nunc feci precium operæ, &
Nostro pergratum, perq́; iucundum gregi.
Multas regione' opplebit hæc opinio,
Quòd Christu' è mortuis non exurrexit.
Imò perficiam, ut apud mundi huius filios
Pium esse uideatur, eos occidere,
Quicunq; syncerè ipsius à morte reditum,
Et inde partam gratiam deprædicent.
Sed me, sat scio, Tartareus expectat chorus,
Re benè gesta, hinc memet recipio domum.

ACTVS IIII. SCENA VI.

Caïaphas. Dromo. Dorus. Sangax.
Brumax.

In hisce manibus est loculus pecunijs
Distentus & non pauco argento turgidus.
Intus latet, quod operatur miracula.
Intus latet, quod nil non cogit pectora.
Est intus, quod diuinam uirtutem exeret
Citò, atq; me magno exonerabit metu.
Nec dubito, quin hoc erit Annæ gratissimum.
Atq; etiam reliquis nostri ordinis hominibus.
Satius est unius obscurari gloriam,
Quàm tot nostrûm egregios honores eripi.
Ecce autem, commodum aduentare uideo
Dromonem & Sangacem, Brumacemq́; & Dorum,
Qui me leuabunt huius onere marsupij.

powerful wealth alone gives strength, and alone supplies power. Wherefore, bestir thyself now, and carry out these commands, which I, thrice greatest of the Furies, have made known unto thee. This is the aim, this is the brief intent of my words.

Cai. I feel the very greatest gratitude toward thee, goddess; no man could give better advice. By Hercules, I will comply with thy exhortations.

Alect. Ah now, now I have done what is worth while, and what is very acceptable and pleasant to our company. This belief, that Christ has not risen from the dead, will fill many regions. Nay, truly, I will bring it about that to the sons of this world it will seem righteous to slay those who in sincerity proclaim his return from death, and the grace gained thereby. But well I know the hosts of hell await me, and, since the deed has been well done, I will wend my way home.

ACT IV, SCENE VI.

Caiaphas, Dromo, Dorus, Sangax, Brumax.

Cai. In these hands is a purse filled with money, and bulging with no little silver. Within lies hidden what works miracles; within lies hidden what drives men's hearts to everything. Within is what will quickly show a divine quality, and relieve me from great fear. I do not doubt that this will be most pleasing to Annas, and also to the rest of the men of our order. It is better that the glory of one man be obscured than that so many of our high honors be taken away. But lo, I see opportunely approaching Dromo and Sangax, Brumax and Dorus, who shall relieve me of the burden of this pouch.

Dro. Salue pie præsul. Do. Salue antistes optime.
Sang. Sis saluos uir clarissime. Bru. Aue ipsa sanctitas.
Dro. Parmenoni seruo dedimu' obuiam tuo,
Qui te significauit, nos uelle colloqui.
Caïa. Volo certè quidem: quare animum aduortite.
Tu Dromo Christum esse rediuiuum non ambigis?
Dro. Equidem huius tibi rei argumenta protuli,
Neq; pauca, neq; parua. Nimis apertum illud est.
Caïa. Quid dicis Dore, sic' cine se res habet?
Dor. Ita factum prorsus est, ut te docuit Dromo.
Caïa. Adfirmaś ne tu Sangax hæc eadẽ? San. q̃dni ego
Adfirmem, qui unà cùm his in re præsenti fui?
Caïa. Quid tu aũt Brumax? Bru. Id quod socij dicitãt.
Caïa. Tacete, & mentem ad ea, quæ loquor, intendite.
Debetis nostra inuota condescendere,
Nisi exciderunt permulta in nos promerita.[17]
Dro. Quid est? quod pro te aut uestræ classis quopiam
Recusemus? Dor. Nil medius fidius, id nisi
Summo fiat nostro damno atque incommodo.
San. Dic egregie sacerdos, præstabimus,
Ne dubita. Bru. Si uereis requiras corporis,[18]
Faciemus, quod cordatos milites decet.
Dummodò non uersutis opponamuur magis.[19]
Sin animi uirtutem, constantiam, fidem,
Quis non sentierit quoduis cum tali duce?

[17] Emendation:
Nisi exciderunt permulta in *uos* promerita.
[18] Emendation:
Ne dubita. Bru. Si *uires* requiras corporis
[19] Emendation:
Dummodo non uersutis *opponamur* magis.

Dro. Hail, good leader.

Do. Hail, most worthy high-priest.

Sang. Heaven bless you, most noble sir.

Bru. Hail, holiness itself.

Dro. We met Parmeno, your servant, who told us that you wished to speak to us.

Cai. I do indeed wish it; therefore give me your attention. You, Dromo, do you doubt that Christ is living again?

Dro. For my part, I laid before you proofs of this thing which were neither few nor trifling. That is all too evident.

Cai. What do you say, Dorus? Is this thing true?

Dor. It happened just as Dromo told you.

Cai. Do you, Sangax, affirm the very same?

San. Why should I not affirm it, who together with these men was present at the time?

Cai. And what do you say, Brumax?

Bru. Just what my comrades say.

Cai. Keep silence, and put your minds on what I say. You ought to yield to our wishes, unless the many, many things that we have deserved at your hands have escaped your memory.

Dro. What is it that we would refuse to do for you, or any one of your class?

Dor. Nothing, by the god of truth; unless it be done with the greatest damage and trouble to us.

San. Tell us, worthy priest, and we will perform it. Do not doubt it.

Bru. If it requires strength of body, we will do what becomes prudent soldiers, provided that we are not matched against crafty enchanters. But if you want valor of spirit, steadfastness, and loyalty, who would not be filled with these qualities under such a leader?

Caïa. Statuunt primates uim certam pecuniæ
Vobis donare, ueruntamen hoc nomine,
Vt singulis quibusque interrogantibus,
Statim & semper respondeatis in hunc modum:
Quòd nocte intempesta, ut latrones perditi,
Corpus clàm fallaceis tulêre comites,
Ac furati sunt uobis dormientibus.
Quòd si commentum hoc ad uestri aureis præsidis
Delatum erit, nos illi persuadebimus,
Et nos tutos in portu collocabimus.[20]
Dro. Lubenter adsentimur. Do. Conditio placet.
San. Cur non authoritatem tantam imitabimur?
Bru. Sequimur decretum longè consultissimum.
Caïa. Accipite, unusquisq; thesauro ditabitur.
Agitote dum, eloquimini. quid dicitis?
Dromo, erexit' ne se Christu' ille à tumulo?
Dro. Non. Caïa. Quid' nam ergò? sepulchrum uacuum (fuit?
Dro. Nox erat, exanimum clepserunt corpus alumni.
Nostra quidem tum membra sopor Lethæus habebat.
Caïa. Dore, dic mihi bona & Iudaica fide,
Iesus in busto cur non repertus est?
Dor. Abstulit hũc furtiuũ agmen dominătibus umbris,
Cùm nostros oculos premeret mera mortis imago.
Caïa. Nuḿ nam & tu Sangax cantionem istam canis?
Dic quid habeas animi super hac re. dicito.
Sang. Funus iners noctu comites rapuêre dolosi,
Quando quies nostros nectebat languida sensus.
Caïa. Brumax tua superest unius adsentio.
Quomodo per omnia res acta est? edissere.
Bru. Surripitur gelidum media iam nocte cadauer,
Cùm nos fessa graui dederamus corpora somno.
Caïa. Laudo uos, quòd in ea diutius hæresi

[20] Emendation:
Et *uos* tutos in portu collocabimus.

Cai. The chief priests have decided to give you a certain amount of money, on this condition, however, that to every one who questions you, you answer at once, and always in this fashion, and say that in the dead of night his deceitful followers, like abandoned robbers, carried off the body, and stole it away as you slept. If this invention be brought to the governor's ears, we will convince him, and secure you from harm.

Dro. We gladly agree.

Do. The conditions are quite agreeable.

San. Why should we not comply with so great an authority?

Bru. We follow out a decision that is by far the most weighty.

Cai. Each one of you shall be enriched with treasure. Take it. Quick, now, speak. What do you say, Dromo? Did that Christ rise from the tomb?

Dro. No.

Cai. Well, what then? Was the sepulchre empty?

Dro. It was night; his disciples stole his lifeless body away while the deep sleep of Lethe held our bodies.

Cai. Dorus, tell me in good faith, Jewish faith, why Jesus was not found in the tomb.

Dor. A band of robbers carried him away while shadows had their sway, while the very likeness of death pressed heavily upon our eyes.

Cai. Now then, Sangax, do you, too, sing the same song? Tell what you have in mind about the thing. Speak.

San. His crafty followers carried off his lifeless corpse by night, when the dulness of sleep enthralled our senses.

Cai. Brumax, the assent of you alone is lacking. How, in all particulars, was the thing done? Explain.

Bru. The cold corpse was stolen away in the middle of the night, when we had given our weary bodies over to deep sleep.

Cai. I praise you because you will not persist longer in

Non perseuerabitis. istuc sapere quidem est.
Dro. Nemo tam nulla mente, uel tam nullius
Est consilij, qui respuat pecunias.
Dor. Conspiranteis animos, tam concinnat citò
Nihil, quàm hæc regina sacro sancta pecunia.
Sang. Quis est mortalium omnium, cui inest mica
Sani cerebri, qui hanc non ueneretur & colat?
Bru. O uos terq́; quaterq́; beatos, queis contigit
Tanta laborum merces, quantam uix tempore
Longo, aut talus nobis, aut alea dederit.
Dro. Valeto fortunarum nostrarum omnium
Auctor locupletissime. Dimeter.
Do. Deus te seruet nostri (ut res ipsa loquitur)
Thesauri supremum caput. Dimeter.
Sang. Tibi noster patrone beneficentissime
Dies agantur candidi. Dimeter.
Bru. Pro hisce opibus here Iehora summis tibi[21]
Opem sempiternam ferat Dimeter.
Caïa. Valete simul uiri fortissimi & optimi.
O faustam, ô niueam, ô peramœnam hanc istam diem.
Meoś ne labores operas atq; uigilias,
An prolixam diuæ bonitatem, an tempora
Vehementiùs extollam, planè nescio.
Quemadmodum etenim cùm sub nebuloso aëre
Et opaco cœlo sensus quodammodò
Hebescunt, & cuiq; suum corpus oneri est,
Tum si radios fortè Titan śplendidos
Fundens, fugam atris nubibus indixerit,
Mundoq́; arridens ore læto affulserit,
Quam mox erectam à corporeo pondere,
Animalem illam hominis partem spe ditissima
Pascit, quasiq́; consopitos spiritus
Permulcet, incitat, fouet, exuscitat:

[21] Emendation:
Bru. Pro hisce opibus here *Iehoua* summis tibi

this heresy. That is sense indeed.

Dro. No one is of so little understanding, or so lacking in sense, as to reject money.

Dor. Nothing so quickly joins together congenial souls as this most sacred Queen, money.

Sang. Who is there of all mortals, with a grain of sound sense in him, who does not honor her and worship her?

Bru. O thrice and four times happy are we to whom there has fallen so great a reward for our labors, such as neither the dice nor chance has given us for ages.

Dro. Fare thee well, richest author of all our good fortune.

Do. God preserve you, who, as the very deed speaks, are the supreme source of our treasure.

Sang. May bright days be spent by you, most generous patron.

Bru. For this great assistance may Jehovah give you everlasting aid.

Cai. Farewell to all of you, bravest and best of men. How fortunate and bright and lovely is this day! I do not know, indeed, whether I should more ardently extol my own exertions, labors, and vigils, or the abundant kindness of the goddess, or the times. For just as when, in a foggy atmosphere, and under a darkened sky, our senses are somehow blunted, and each one's body is a burden to him; then if perchance Titan, pouring forth his radiant beams, has ordered flight to the black clouds, and, smiling, has beamed with joyful face upon the world, how soon he feeds with richest hopes that living part of man, now lifted above bodily influence, and, as it were, soothes, supports, cherishes, and arouses our benumbed spirits, so, by heavens! through the

Ita mediusfidius, furiæ præclarissimæ
Beneficio, sum usq; eò exhileratus denuò, ut
Qui dudum adueniens, cogitabundum hunc animum
Omnei' in parteis dubitatione ueluti
Suspensus distribueram, nunc deniq;
Recedam, noua & insolita prorsus læticia,
Et alacritate perfusus mirabili.

ARGVMENTVM ACTVS V.

Qvoniam cùm Thomas Didymus aberat,
Intrans heros fenestris atq; foribus
Clausis, se discipulis ostentarat suis.
Illi reuerso uiuere conclamant herum.
Qui ut finem narrandi faciunt, ecce Cleopas
Alio loco, inquit, se conuenisse dominum,
Ad Emauntem dum iter castellum suscipit.
Quæ cùm cunctis uiderentur certissima,
Vnus Thomas se posse credere negat,
Tantisper dum improuisus adest iterum Deus,
Eiusq́; dubitatis confirmat fidem.
Pòst illos & dictis & factis instruit,
Quibus per populos dispergant noua gaudia.
Ad extremum autem undeni proceres admodum
De Christo rediuiuo plaudunt ad inuicem,
Salutem gratulanteis ac uitam sibi,
Deo reddenteis gloriam.

ACTVS V. SCENA I.

Thomas. Petrus. Cleopas. Amaon.
Chorus discipulorum.

O socij, neq; enim sumus antè malorum inscij,[22] Trimet.

[22] O socii—neque enim ignari sumus ante malorum—
Aeneid I. 198.

favor of the most famous of the Furies, I have been cheered to such an extent that I, who lately, on approaching, had pondered this way and that, as if held in suspense by doubt, will now at last withdraw, filled with a new and truly unaccustomed joy, and a wonderful ardor.

ARGUMENT OF ACT V.

Because when Thomas Didymus was absent the Lord entered, though the windows and doors were shut, and showed Himself to the disciples, together they cry out to Thomas on his return, 'The Lord liveth again!' As they conclude the story, lo, Cleophas says that in another place, while he was making his way to the citadel of Emmaus, he met the Master. And though these things seemed true to all, Thomas alone says that he cannot believe until the Lord comes again unforeseen, and changes his doubts to firm faith. Afterwards the Master instructs them by words and deeds, that they may spread new joy among the people. At last the eleven leaders, in turn, give praise that Christ lives again, rejoicing in salvation and life, and giving glory to God.

ACT V, SCENE I.

Thomas, Peter, Cleophas, Amaon, Chorus of Disciples

Tho. O comrades, not now nor aforetime are we ignorant

Vnde hic stupor, unde hoc mirum silentium?
Credo equidem ardentem & igne coruscum spiritum
E nube ruisse, & penetrasse hanc domum:
Ita statis trepidi, ita uos horror quatit.
Pet. Nullo pauore perculsi obstupescimus
Thoma frater: uerùm rei miraculo
Et nouitate attoniti ualdè reddimur.
Quam si plenè pernosceres, te, sat scio,
Velle lachrymas effundere præ gaudio.
Tho. Ne uiuam, si non quid sit acciperem lubens.
Pet. Lubentior ego rem omnem enarrauero.
Præsentem uidimus, loquentem audiuimus,
Ipsum Christum rediuiuum, quem nos modò
Multatum morte, & ademptum suspirauimus.
Tho. Quid prædicas? quæ uox aureis intrat meas?
Is per Deum, iam respirat' ne denuò?
An potiùs elusit simulachrum umbratile,
Et effigies quædam nobis apparuit?[23]
Pet. Thoma, Thoma, illŭ ipsum, haud incerta prædico,
Illa ipsa retinentem etiamdum uulnera
Aspeximus: ac membra palmis pertrectauimus.
Tho. Itá ne uerò? quæso expone seriem
Rei totius gestæ, atq; id bona fide.
Pet. Vespertinum tempus erat, occlusæ fores,
Occlusa fenestrarum etiam foramina.
Nos tenuibus escis & potionibus
Corpora refecimus & uireis reuocauimus,
Et ad unam cuncti mensam consedimus,
Quandò ille repentinò coràm in media domo
Diuino lumine circumseptus constitit.
Nos credenteis inanem adesse spiritum:
Primo aspectu tremebundi exhorrescere
Cœpimus, ac præ metu mensas relinquere.
Tum Christus, degenerem formidinem arguens,

[23] Emendation:
Et effigies quædam *uobis* apparuit?

of misfortune; why this bewilderment, why this strange silence? I think, indeed, that a spirit, blazing and glittering with fire, has rushed from a cloud and entered this house, ye stand so trembling, and terror shakes you so.

Pet. We are not panic-stricken and stupefied, brother Thomas, but we are indeed greatly astonished by the marvelousness and strangeness of the thing, and I well know that if thou wert to learn the whole story, thou wouldst shed tears for joy.

Tho. May I die if I would not gladly hear what it is!

Pet. The more gladly will I tell thee the story. We have seen Him present, we have heard Him speak, Christ Himself living again, whom we but now sighed for as punished with death, and taken away from us.

Tho. What sayest thou? What words are these that enter my ears? Does He now through God breathe anew, or rather has a shadowy phantom deceived you, and some ghost appeared to you?

Pet. Thomas, Thomas, I am telling thee nothing that is doubtful; we saw Him Himself still retaining those very wounds, and we touched His limbs with our hands.

Tho. Is it so indeed? I beg thee to set forth the entire story of the occurrence, and that in good faith.

Pet. It was in the evening; the doors were shut, shut too were the windows, with meagre food and drink we had refreshed our bodies and renewed our strength, and we were all seated at one table, when suddenly before us in the midst of the house He stood, surrounded by a divine light. We, thinking that an empty shade was present, and trembling at the first sight, began to shudder and to leave the table for fear. Then Christ, reproving our ignoble fear, said:

Quid, inquit, perturbato uersatis animo?
Cernite manus, latus, pedesq́; cernite,
Ego ipse sum: pacem unà coniunctissimi
Seruate, atq; trepidationem ponite.
Mox omnibus trectate dicit corpora.[24]
Hîc hîc uera ossa, & ueram carnem inueneritis,
Quorum nouistis exortem esse spiritum.
At nos cùm adhuc mirabunda perpendimus,
Nec herum nostrum esse illum nobis persuasimus:
Tum de assato pisce, & fauo apiario
Nobiscum edere non recusans, reppetit
Eum sermonem, in quo ante mortem plurimus
Fuit, quem si tenuissemus, meherculè
Ipsius abitum forti tulissemus animo.
Hæc ubi facta: is eadem uirtute subitò à
Nobis euanuit, qua intrarat lumina.
Tho. O Petre, Petre quid uerba frustrà funditas?
Quid surdo fabellam canis? Tam̃ ne stupidum
Tam absq́; ullo iudicio & sensu me uiuere
Putas, ut hisce fidem habeam ineptijs?
Nam hoc ex eo genere est, quod fieri non potest,
Vt sese à mortuis quisquam resuscitet.
Ec' quem è prophetis ec' quem è sanctis patribus
Commemorabis, qui tale quidquam fecerit?
Cho. disc. Sic & nos uix nobismetipsis credere
Primùm poteramus, nec satis habuimus
Loquentem audire semel, quin pacem sæpius
Nobis commendans, multa de fati sui
Necessitate, multa de nostri' omnium
Dicebat commodis. sic & Galileïdes,
Quæ primæ illum ipsum fœminæ conspexerant,
Tam nos tardos inuenêre ad habendam illis fidem,
Quàm tu iamdudum te præbes incredulum.
Quinimò Cleopæ non credidimus, & suo
Consocio, quibus ab urbe paulùm euntibus,

[24] Emendation:
Mox omnibus *tractare* dicit corpora.

'Why are ye troubled, and your minds confused? Behold my hands and my side, behold my feet. It is I myself. Together in closest union keep peace, and lay aside your fears.' Then to all He said: 'Handle my body. Here, here ye shall find real bones and real flesh, of which ye know a spirit has no share.' When we still pondered over these marvels, and could not persuade ourselves that He was our Lord, then, not refusing to eat with us of the broiled fish and the honeycomb, He renewed that discourse of which He was most full before His death, and to which if we had held fast, by heaven! we should have borne His departure with a brave spirit. When these things were done, He suddenly vanished from us by the same power as He had entered the light.

Tho. O Peter, Peter, why dost thou pour forth thy words in vain? Why dost thou preach to the deaf? Thou dost not think me to be so stupid, and so without judgment, as to have faith in this silly story, dost thou? For this is of the nature of the impossible, that any man should rouse himself from the dead. Canst thou recall any of the prophets or of the holy fathers who have done the like?

Cho. Disc. Just so we too at first were scarcely able to trust ourselves, nor did we consider it enough to hear Him speak once; but, commending peace to us again and again, He said many things about the necessity of His death, and many concerning the advantage of us all. So too the Galileans, the women who had been the first to behold Him, found us as slow to put faith in them as thou, who long hast shown thyself doubting. Nay, verily, we did not believe Cleophas and his companion, to whom He appeared as they were walking a little way out from the city, before He was

Antea quàm à nobis uisus est, apparuit.
Tho. De re tam inaudita, consensum tot hominum
Nusquam est reperire. Sed narra Cleopa omnia,
Nam te quoq; non minùs ac alios audiuero.
Cleop. Christum̃ met ipsum absq; ulla controversia,
Thoma, & ego & Amaon pariter aspeximus,
Et cum illo ultrò citròq; uerba fecimus.
Quandò etenim dirigeremus ad arcem Emauntem iter:
Tanquam peregrinus & hospes quidam barbarus
Et obscurus, nobiscum ingressus est uiam.
Quanquam nescio quid nostros præstrinxit oculos,
Quòd eum inter eundum minimè cognouimus.
At ille, qua de re, inquit, uos inter agitur?
Cur' nam uestros adfectus continere uix
Valetis, quô minùs erumpant in lachrymas?
Ego contrà: quid ais? num̃ nam tu solus es
Peregrinus hisce diebus in urbe Solyma, &
Nescis, quae dudum perpetrata fuerint?
Roganti quæ illá nam essent, responsum hoc dedi:
De Iesu Nazareno, qui uates fuit,
Qui rebus gestis atq; uerbis præpotens,
Tam apud ipsum Deum quàm apud homines fuit.
Et eum sacerdotum quo pacto principes,
Ac primates nostri cruci suffixerint.
Atq; ut nos omneis spes magna tenuit, eum
Redempturum Israël, ac meliorem exitum
Illi futurum, ut qui meliora meruerat.
Et quo modo post triduum Galileïdes,
Quæ uacuum se tumulum uidisse, & Angelos
Aiebant, qui affirmarent illum uiuere, ad
Stuporem usque admirari nos coëgerant,
Et quemadmodum quidam è nostro consortio,
Statim ad monumentum ipsum festinauerint,
Sintq; experti ueras fuisse fœminas,
Ipsum uerò Christum nùsquam repererint.
Tum ille: Eá ne uestros tandem animos incredulitas

seen of us.

Tho. The agreement of so many men on a matter so unheard of can be found nowhere; but, Cleophas, tell me all, for I will listen to thee no less than to the others.

Cleop. Thomas, both Amaon and I alike beheld Christ Himself, beyond all question, and with Him mutually talked. For when we were directing our way to the city of Emmaus, He, as if He were a foreigner and a stranger, unknown and of no note, went on the way with us; however, something, I know not what, bound our eyes, so that we did not recognize Him at all in that man. But He said to us, 'What manner of communication is this that ye have one with another, that ye can scarcely restrain your feelings from bursting into tears?' I replied, 'What sayest thou? Art thou, indeed, only a stranger in the city of Jerusalem these days, and hast not known the things that have lately come to pass?' When He asked what these things were, I gave Him this answer: 'Our talk was of Jesus of Nazareth, who was a prophet, and was mighty in deed and word before God and man'; and I told Him how the chief priests and our rulers had crucified Him; how we trusted that He would redeem Israel, and that there would be a better end for Him, as one who deserved better things; and how the Galilean women said that after three days they had seen the empty tomb and the angels, who declared that He was living, bringing us to the point of bewilderment, even to amazement; how certain of our company hastened at once to the tomb, and found it even as the women had said, but Him they found not. Then He replied: 'Has that unbelief, then, blinded your minds?

Excæcauit? Num uaticinationibus,
Num literis ac monumentis sunt tradita
Posteritati ducis uestri discrimina?
Nuḿ nam ille sic uos instruxit? Num deniq;
Istæc de se futura suis prædixerat?
Sic fatus, à Mose capiens exordium,
Obscura & inuoluta uatum oracula
Veterumq́; scripta Patrum de misericordia,
Et de sapientia Dei, & de criminum
Etiam expiatione nobi' euolere haud
Cessabat, ut omnia sibi crucem portenderent.
Quô uindicaret à tenebris hominum genus,
Quô peccatum, quô mortem, quô orcum uinceret.
Tum uerò, nos intrà motus quosdam nouos
Vterq; sentiebamus. Ita is animos
Dictis regebat, & mulcebat pectora.
Namq; memorabat, uti manuum laboribus,
Et seruitutis amaro depressos iugo,
Pharijs ab oris, ad proprios iterum Lareis,
Legumlator ciueis eduxerit suos.
Hinc Abrahamum iussis actum cœlestibus
Charissimum filiolum ense petentem Isacon,
Demissumq́; refert angelum ipso ab æthere:
Qui aliter suadet, ac pueri insontis loco
Litari arietem iuxtà pascentem iubet.
Hijs adiungit Iosephum, fratres inuidi
Quo funere, quibuś ue discerptum feris,
Patri falsò dixêre, cùm uenundarant
Illum exteris, propter descripta somnia.
Quid loquor, aut suspensum à duce colubrum æneum,
Quo, serpentum afflatu prostrata corpora
Per campum surgebant sanata & integra:
Aut, ut natasse quosdam homines narrauerit,
Inclusos machina, quum iam tellu' et mare
Nullo discrimine Monom.
Agerentur, & reliquos mortalei' unda raperet.

Were not the dangers of your leader handed down to posterity by prophecy, letters, and records? Did He not thus instruct you? In short, did He not show unto His disciples those things that should happen?' Having said this, beginning with Moses, He did not cease to unfold to us the obscure and involved predictions of the prophets, and the writings of the ancient fathers concerning the mercy and wisdom of God, and of the expiation of sin; how they all foretold the cross for Him, that He might deliver mankind from darkness, and that He might vanquish sin, death, and hell. Then truly we felt within us certain new emotions, to such an extent did He sway our hearts, and soothe our breasts, with His words. For He recalled to mind how the lawgiver led out from the land of Pharaoh his own countrymen, crushed by manual labor and the bitter yoke of slavery, to their own homes again. Next He reminded us of Abraham, driven by the commands of heaven to slay with a knife Isaac, his beloved son, and of the angel sent down from heaven itself, who persuaded him otherwise, and bade that a ram, feeding near by, should be sacrificed in place of the innocent boy. To these instances He added that of Joseph, whom his envious brothers falsely reported to their father as dead and rent in pieces by wild beasts, after they had sold him to strangers, because of the dreams that he related. Why should I speak either of the brazen serpent lifted up by the leader, whereby the bodies, laid low throughout the camp by the breath of the serpents, rose up, healed and sound; or how He told that certain men floated, shut up in an ark, when the earth and sea were stirred, there being no division between them, and that the deep swallowed up all

Omnia quæ quondam meditanda suis posteris
Prophetæ cecinerunt inflati numine,
Ille meminit, donec processit Hesperus
Olympo inuito, ut arbitror. Dimet.
Et peruentum à nobis est ab eundem locum,[25]
Quem suprà dixi. Sed quando ulteriùs iter
Habere se simularet, impetrauimus,
Vt idem nobiscum faceret hospitium.
Quod ipsum syderis alis superuolans,
Nox tacita suadebat. Mox diuersorium
Subit. Ad mensam nobiscum adcumbit pauperem.
Quàm primùm autem manu uidimus apprendere
Cererem, atq; modo peculiari frangere:
E uestigio mens nobis est reddita.
Agnoscimus & colimus aperta numina.
At ille in puncto ipso & momento temporis,
Abijt, & è conspectu se nostro abstulit.
Tho. Dixti pulchrè. Sed tam impossibile facinus,
Nemo homo quamuis uehemens, facundus, & eloquens,
Quamuis limatulè & politè pinxerit
Orationem, mihi persuadere poterit,
Eum ipsum his oculis nisi præsentem uidero,
Hijsq́; auribus nisi præsentis uocem hausero, &
Nisi hisce manibus uolnera præsentia
Reuera & indubitanter contrectauero.
Verùm, quid hic moramur? Repetamus domum,
Ne quis iudeat ex Iudæis primoribus.
Bene est, omneis iam nunc tuti consedimus.

ACTVS V. SCENA II.

Christus. Thomas. Chorus disc.

Sit pax uobis, fratres longè charissimi.

[25] Emendation:
Et pereuntem a nobis est *ad* eundem locum,

other mortals. He recalled all the things which once the prophets, inspired by divine power, had foretold, until the evening star appeared, against the will of heaven, as I think, and we drew nigh to the place of which I spoke before. But when He made as if He would go further, we entreated Him to abide with us, which night, flying above Him on the wings of the star, was silently urging. Soon He came to the inn. He reclined with us at the meagre table. But as soon as we saw Him take bread with His hand, and break it in His own way, instantly our eyes were opened. We recognized and worshiped the Deity disclosed. But at that very instant and moment of time He departed, and vanished out of our sight.

Tho. Thou hast told thy story beautifully. But no man, however forcible, fluent, and eloquent, however polished and elegant his portrayal, will be able to convince me of so impossible a thing, unless with these eyes I shall see Him Himself, unless in His presence with these ears I drink in His voice, and unless with these hands I really and undoubtedly touch His wounds. But why do we linger here? Let us return home, lest any of the leaders of the Jews see us. It is well; we are all now seated in safety.

ACT V, SCENE II.

Christ, Thomas, Chorus of Disciples.

Christ. Peace be unto you, most dearly beloved brethren.

Tu uerò age Didyme, huc huc manum admoueas,
Admoueas in latus meum, ne dubita, ego sum.
Tho. Mi domine, mi Deus, mea spes, uita mea,
Noli quæso hanc rebellionem, & pessimam
Incredulitatem posthac imputare mihi.
Næ inconsultus ego, atque excœcatus impia
Philautia fueram, qui proprio ingenio
Tantum attribuebam, ut rediuiuum credere
Te factum esse nequirem? quum & aderam & memini
Quandò alios quarta iam luce solo conditos,
Ad huius uitæ munia reuocaueris.
Nunc demum didici, quid sit à te deseri.
Nunc demum didici, ad præsidium unius tuum
Confugere, abiectis rebus illis omnibus,
Meo quæ animo uidentur plausibilia. Nunc
Demum, fiduciæ remoti' obstaculis,
Victoriæ mortis & inferni gustum habeo.
Mortem ô faustam, mortem quæ nostram interficit.
Modis ô omnibus utilissimam necem,
Quæ nos dehinc in uitam sempiternam asserit.
Quas tibi grateis agam pater opt. max.
Qui non uel unigeno parcebas filio in
Nostrûm miserorum alioqui hominum gratiam?
Ad quantas, quàm certasq; spes, nos anteà
Desperabundos erexisti? Ad quam gloriam
Ac dignitatem accersisti per filium?
Quum nos peccatorum grauitate & pondere,
Legisq; iudicio damnaremur miseri:
Tu clementissime & benignissime pater,
Quod nostra non potuit imbecillitas,
Effecisti, ut natus etiam tuus unicè
Tibi dilectus, pro nobis exolueret.
Quis autem, ô Christe, hominum uoluptas & quies,
Tam erit ingratus, ferreus, adamantinus,
Qui ad gratuitam tuam beneficentiam,
Non totus desiderio tui flagret?

But come thou, Didymus, reach hither, reach hither thy hand; thrust it into my side; doubt not; it is I.

Tho. My Lord and my God, my hope and my life! Do not, I pray Thee, hereafter ascribe to me this rebellion, this most wicked unbelief. Truly inconsiderate, and blinded by wicked self-love I have been, attributing so much to my own ability that I could not believe that Thou hadst been made alive again; although I was present and remember when Thou didst recall to life's duties those who had been buried for four days. Now at last I have learned what it is to be forsaken by Thee; now at last have I learned to fly for refuge to Thy protection alone. All those things have been cast away which seemed acceptable to me. Now at last, the obstacles to faith removed, I have a foretaste of victory over death and hell. O fortunate death, which slays our death! O slaughter in every way most useful, which claims us henceforth for eternal life. What thanks shall I give Thee, all-good and all-powerful Father, who didst not spare even Thine only-begotten Son for the sake of us otherwise miserable men? To what great and certain hopes didst Thou lift us, who were full of despair before? To what glory and dignity didst Thou call us through Thy Son, when we, wretched through the weight and burden of our sins, were condemned by the sentence of the law? Thou, most merciful and most loving Father, didst effect what our weakness could not, that even Thy only beloved Son should pay the penalty for us. But who, O Christ, Thou joy and peace of mankind, will be so ungrateful, iron-hearted, and adamantine, as in return for Thy free kindness not to burn wholly

Non totus amore tui inflammetur & ardeat?
Et, ut ad solem cera, liquescat medullitus?
Sed ego nescio qua corruptus dementia,
Vt limus ad phœbi radios durescere
Ni tua succurrisset præsentia, cœperam.
Quarè obsecro, facilis meam fidem adaugeas:
Vt mihi displiceam totus, uni tibi hæream, &
Vt, qui tua solius ope sic euaserim,
Per omnia semper te gratus deprædicem.
Christ. Post uisum ipsum corpus, & ipsissima uulnera
Tandem credis Thoma: sed felicissimos
Illos pronuncio, qui hoc persuadeant,
Etiamsi nunquam cernant. Verùm tu tamen
Rectè & facis, & loqueris. Morti caput obtuli
Pro multi' unus, meaq́; sponte, quô omnia
Quæ per Adamum à suo dilapsa erant statu,
Restituerem egomet maiori gloriæ.
Nunc igitur, quando me summus olympus manet,
Memori uos animo mea dicta recondite.
In omneis mundi regiones penetrabitis,
Et ubiq; gentium eritis rerum cœlestium
Nuncij: ut (si fieri possit) unusquilibet
Me mortuum sibi, me rediuiuum sibi putet.
Nihil opus erit, uetustas ceremonias,
Aut uictimas retinere, aut sacrificia.
Qui uiuida nixus fide, persuaserit
Sibi, quòd gratis una & sola morte mea,
Delicta & scelera remittuntur omnia,
Doniq́; signum huius aqua tinctus habuerit,
Et amori meo mutua responderit
Voluntate: is, quicunq; est, nil quidquam hæsitans,
Cœlum ut patriam nostro ex promisso uendicet.
Qui uerò isti non crediderit Euangelio,
Sed aud contemnit, aut uertit præposterè:
Nil hunc iuuabit lêgis obseruatio,
Nil philosophia, nil quæuis professio,

with desire for Thee, not wholly to be inflamed and glow with love of Thee, and, as wax before the sun, to melt in his inmost soul? But I, corrupted by some madness, had begun to grow hard, like mire in the sun's rays, when Thy presence rescued me. Wherefore, I pray Thee, graciously increase my faith, that I may be wholly displeasing to myself, and cling only to Thee; and, since by Thy aid alone I have escaped, that, ever grateful, I may proclaim Thee everywhere.

Christ. After the sight of the body itself and the very wounds, at length thou believest, Thomas. Yet I say, Most blessed are they that have not seen, and yet have believed. But nevertheless rightly thou dost speak and act. I alone, of my own accord, offered my life to death for many, that I myself might restore to greater glory all who through Adam had fallen from their estate. Now therefore, since highest heaven awaits me, do ye lay up my words in your memory. Go ye, therefore, unto all the regions of the world; everywhere shall ye be messengers of things celestial, so if it be that any one believe that I died for him, and lived again for him, there shall be no need of old-time ceremonies, or observing burnt offerings and sacrifices. He who, relying on a living faith, hath convinced himself that by my death alone all his sins are freely remitted, who, being bathed with water, has the sign of this gift, and has answered my love with mutual affection, let him, whosoever he is, from our promise claim heaven as his home, with no uncertainty. He that believeth not the Gospel, but either despiseth or distorteth it, neither the keeping of the law, nor philosophy,

Quô minùs æternis destinetur ignibus.
Vos, cùm res ipsa poscet, nostro nomine
Serpenteis profligabitis, ac dæmonia
Exterminabitis, & linguis etiam nouis,
Quasi si eas dedicissetis, loquimini.
Nec hausta nocebunt ueneni pocula.
Erga ægrotos nos ut medicos præbebitis.[26]
Et (quod maius quidem est) animi fœdissimos
Morbo', arrogantiam, acediam, lubidinem,
Ambitionem, odium, auaritiam, iram, abdomini
Deuotam gulam, & id genus innumeros propemodum
Diuina ui radicitus extirpabitis.
Nam paruo pòst tempore, uos æthereus pater
Cœlesti afflabit & inspirabit numine.
Quo profectò, pro me quid non audebitis?
Hoc duce, rêges & rerum dominos purpura
Et sceptro insignitos, nihil dubitabitis
Adire, & ueritatem condocefacere: haud
Longè petita erit uobis oratio,
Neq; loquendi tempus, neq; forma & modus:
Hîc spiritus præsens uestra ora diriget, ac
Dabit cuiq; uim uerborum & copiam.
Hunc, hunc animi' uestri' arrabonem accipite, quô
Vitæ illius uobis fiat certissima
Spes, cuius inæstimabilia gaudia
Sub cogitationem humanam non cadunt.
Cho. disc. Vicit iò, uicit leo de Iudæ sanguine.
Vicit iò, uicit almum Iessæi genus.
Quis non tam felici applaudat uictoriæ?
Hunc unum authorem & conseruatorem unicum
Agnoscat quilibet suum.
Qui nos fuso crouore, exemit crimine
Ab omni, & mortem morte deleuit sua
Nostram, ac uitam nobis rediuiuus attulit.

[26] Emendation:
Erga *ægrotis* uos ut medicos præbebitis.

nor any profession, shall profit aught to keep him from everlasting fire. When occasion demands, ye shall tread on serpents; and in my name shall ye cast out devils; and also in new tongues shall ye speak, as if ye had learnt them; nor, if ye drink any deadly thing, shall it hurt you. As physicians, ye shall lay hands upon the sick; and what is indeed greater, by divine power ye shall root out completely the foulest diseases of the mind—pride, sloth, lust, ambition, envy, covetousness, anger, the belly's accursed gluttony, and the like—diseases almost countless. Yet a little while, and the heavenly Father will breathe upon you, and inspire you with the Holy Ghost, whereby what indeed will ye not undertake in my behalf? Under its guidance, ye shall not hesitate to approach kings and the lords of the world, distinguished with purple and sceptre, and instruct them in the truth. Take no thought beforehand what ye shall speak, neither concerning time of utterance nor form and manner, for the Holy Ghost will guide your lips, and will give to each one power and abundance of words. Receive it in your hearts as a pledge, that to you may be given a certain hope of that life whose joys, beyond all price, are not within the range of human thought.

Cho. Disc. Lo, He has conquered! The Lion of the tribe of Judah has conquered! The gentle race of Jesse has conquered! Who would not applaud so happy a victory? Let every one acknowledge Him as the only Creator and sole Preserver, who by the shedding of His blood freed us from all guilt; and by His death delivered us from death; and, living again, brought life to us. So the gate of high

Adeò, quæ annorum tot clausa est recursibus,
Nunc sublimis olympi ianua recluditur.
Dies nunc est uatum promissa uocibus,
Vt monteis & colleis resultent læticia.
Nos autem, tantis iam cumulati gaudijs,
Solymæ simus, Deo canenteis gloriam.

Corônis.

Habetis rem totam, auditores optimi.
Quæ si uobis uisa est iucunda & amabilis,
Vt estis Christiani, uos de gloria
Christi rediuiui, deq́; uestris commodis
Iam seriò triumphanteis, plausum date.

Omnis uni Deo gratia
& gloria.

heaven, shut all those revolving years, is now open. This is the day promised in the words of the prophet[16] when the mountains and the hills shall leap for joy. Now, filled with these great joys, and singing the glory of God, let us return to Jerusalem.

The End.

Most worthy listeners, you have the whole play. If it seems pleasant and lovely to you, as you are Christians, rejoicing in the glory of Christ who liveth again, and in your own gain, give us your applause.

All thanks and glory be to the one God.

[16] Isa. 55. 12.

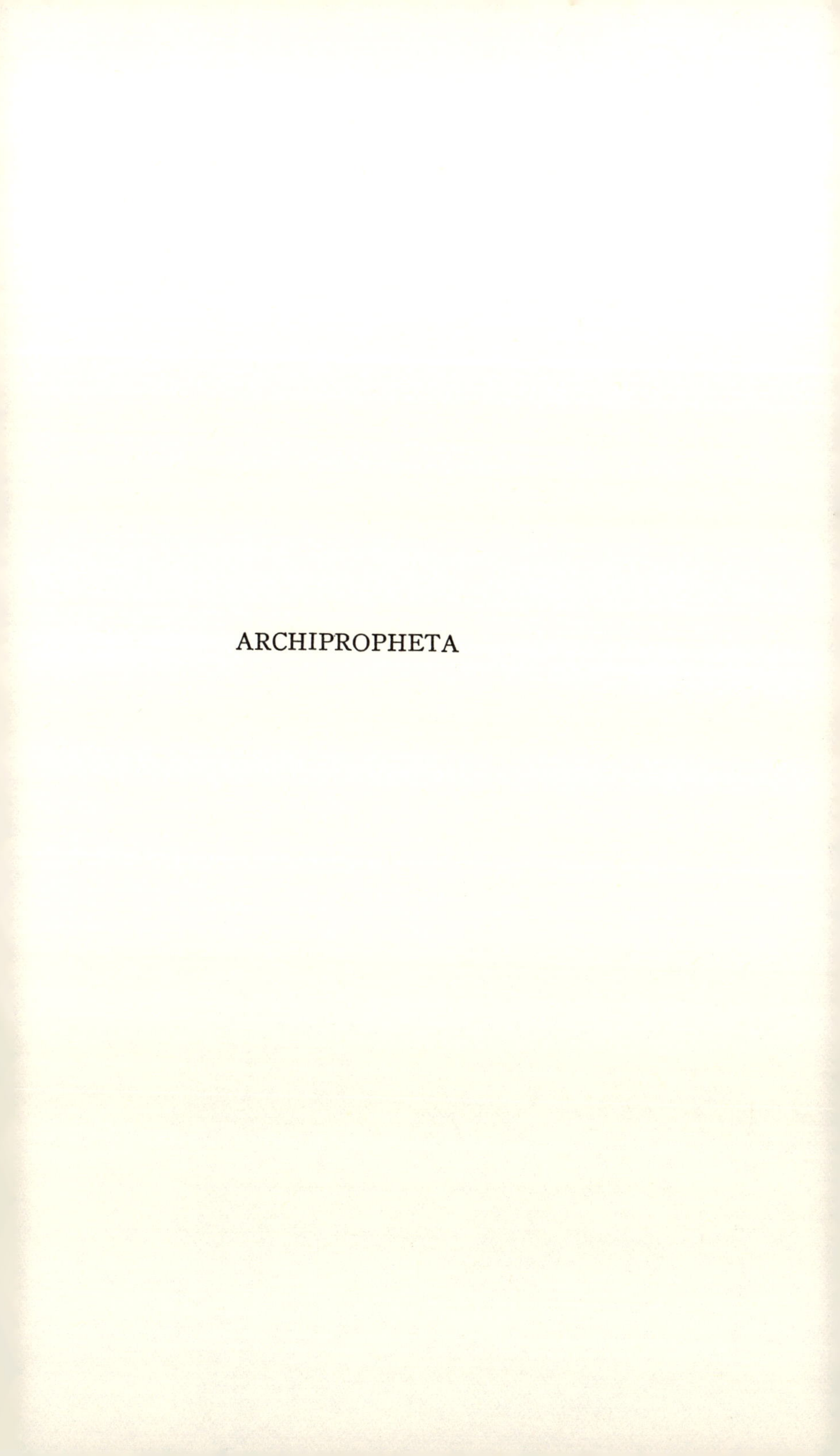

ARCHIPROPHETA

PREFACE

THE unusual character of Grimald's drama, *Archipropheta,* a Latin tragedy based upon the life of the archprophet, John the Baptist, in that it is one of the first tragedies known to have been written in England, and antedated by fifteen years *Ferrex and Porrex* (*Gorboduc*), the first tragedy in the vernacular, makes it worthy of consideration.

The fact that Grimald's play has received so little consideration is, no doubt, due to the fact that there are but three copies of this work known to be in existence in England, two in the library of the British Museum, and the other in the Library of Jesus College, Oxford.

Although published in Cologne, only two copies are known to be extant in Germany. One of these is to be found in the National Library of Wolfenbüttel, and the other in the Council School Library of Zwickau. The Royal Library of Copenhagen and the National Library of Paris each possesses a copy also.

Of the two copies in the British Museum one is MS. No. 12. A. XLVI. This valuable manuscript became the property of George II in 1757. Within the cover the royal arms and the inscription *G.R. II, 1757* are stamped in gold. This volume was presented by George IV to the British Museum. The manuscript, which is in a perfect state of preservation, is eight by five inches in size. A comparison of the handwriting with that of Grimald's letter[1] to Sir William Cecil, which is also in the manuscript collection of the British Museum, shows such similarity that it seems certain that this copy of the play is by the same hand. This fact, together with the great neatness of the manuscript and the absence of stage-directions, leads one to think that this was perhaps

[1] British Museum, MS. Lansdowne 2.

the copy that Grimald submitted to Dr. Richard Cox,[2] Dean of Christ Church, as evidence of his scholastic and literary ability, as did many other students upon their application for membership in the college founded anew in November, 1546, by King Henry VIII, and about to be opened under the name of Christ Church.

The manuscript bears two water-marks: one that of a hand and star, and the other that of a jar, with the letters *C B* on the neck. Both these water-marks are to be found on the paper on which Grimald's letter to Sir William Cecil

[2] Richard Cox was born at Whaddon, Buckinghamshire, of low parentage, in the year 1499. From Eton school he obtained a scholarship in King's College, in Cambridge, of which he became a fellow in 1519; he was thence invited to Oxford by Cardinal Wolsey and was there made one of the junior canons of Cardinal College. In this situation he became remarkable for his learning and his poetical abilities; but his attachment to the opinions of Luther rendered him hateful to his superiors, who threw him into prison on suspicion of heresy. Being however soon released, he left Oxford, and was chosen master of Eton school, which flourished remarkably under his care. In 1537 he commenced doctor of divinity at Cambridge; in 1540 was made archdeacon of Ely, and the following year prebendary of the cathedral, on its being new founded by Henry VIII. In 1546 he was made dean of Christ Church, Oxford. By the recommendation of Archbishop Cranmer and Bishop Goodrich, to the latter of whom he had been chaplain, he not only obtained the above preferments, but was chosen preceptor to Prince Edward, on whose accession to the throne he became a favorite at court, was sworn of the privy council and was made king's almoner. In 1547 he was elected chancellor of Oxford, in 1548 canon of Windsor, and the next year dean of Westminster. On the accession of Queen Mary he was stripped of all his preferments and committed to the Marshalsea. He was however soon released, and immediately left the kingdom. Having resided some time at Strasburg with his intimate friend, Peter Martyr, on the death of Queen Mary he returned to England, and with other divines was appointed to revise the Liturgy. He often preached before the queen, and in 1559 was preferred to the see of Ely, which he continued to enjoy upwards of twenty-one years. He died July 22, 1581, aged eighty-one.

—John Berkenhout, *Biographia Literaria,* ed. London, 1777, p. 159.

is written. Moreover, these marks are to be found on the paper on which the edition of 1568 of Grimald's translation of Cicero's *De Officiis* was printed by Tottel, whose sign, as the colophon of this book and other of his publications show, was that of the hand and star, and from whom Grimald very likely got his paper.

The preface of the manuscript and that of the printed copy show interesting variants, which give some information in regard to the date of the composition of the piece. On page two of the manuscript copy the following lines appear: 'Amor autem ille tuus erga præclaras & ingenuas artes nullo evidentiore declarari potuit argumento, quam quod *Regii* nuper apud nos constituendi in optimamq; formam redigendi magnus author exstitisti: quæ sane cum Lyceo, cum Stoa, cum Academia, cum omnibus omnium Philosophorum bibliothecis non splendore solum ædificij, sed liberalium etiam doctrinarum eximiis professoribus æquiparanda esse videatur'; whereas the printed copy reads: 'Amor autem ille tuus erga præclaras & ingenuas artes nullo evidentiore declarari potuit argumento, quam quod *Aedis Dictatæ Christo* nuper apud nos *constituendæ* in optimamq; formam redigendæ magnus author exstitisti: etc.' In 1545 Henry VIII took over the college known as King Henry the Eighth's College, with all its possessions; and on November 4, 1546, he combined the lately created Cathedral of Oxford and the college just dissolved into one foundation styled 'Ecclesia Christi Cathedralis Oxon. ex fundatione Regis Henrici Octavi.' This foundation began its corporate existence January 14, 1546-7. Hence the composition of the play took place during the year 1546, or previous to that time.

The source of the plot of the play is not, as one would suppose, the Bible, but rather Josephus' *Antiquities of the Jews.* Although the story of John's clash with Herodias is one of the best known of all Bible stories, the account of it to be found in the Bible is surprisingly short. More surprising still is the fact that the well known name of Herodias' daughter, Salome, is not mentioned in the Bible, but is to be found in Josephus. The story is told in Matthew 14. 3-12; Mark 6. 17-29; and Luke 3. 19-20.

On reading the play, it will be readily seen that Grimald found his sources in the following passage from Josephus[3] rather than in the Bible.

About this time, Aretas, the king of Arabia Petrea, and Herod, had a quarrel on the account following: Herod the tetrarch had married the daughter of Aretas, and had lived with her a great while, but when he was once at Rome, he lodged with Herod,[4] who was his brother indeed, but not by the same mother; for this Herod was the son of the high-priest Simon's daughter. However, he fell in love with Herodias, this last Herod's wife, who was the daughter of Aristobulus their brother, and the sister of Agrippa the Great; this man ventured to talk to her about a marriage between them, which address when he admitted, an agreement was made for her to change her habitation, and come to him as soon as he should return from Rome; one article of this marriage also was this, that he should divorce Aretas's daughter. So Antipas, when he had made this agreement, sailed to Rome; but when he had done there the business he went about, and was returned again, his wife having discovered the agreement he had made with Herodias, and having learned it before he had notice of her knowledge of the whole design, she desired him to send her to Macherus, which is a place on the borders of the

[3] Josephus, *Antiquities of the Jews,* London, 1806, 5.18.

[4] (Note by Joseph Whiston, the translator of Josephus.) This Herod seems to have had the additional name of Philip, as Antipas was named Herod-Antipas, and as Antipas and Antipater seem to be in a manner the very same name, yet were the names of two sons of Herod the Great; so might Philip the tetrarch and this Herod-Philip be two different sons of the same father, all which Grotius observed in Matt. xiv. 3. Nor was it, as I agree with Grotius and others of the learned, Philip the tetrarch, but this Herod-Philip, whose wife Herod the tetrarch had married, and that in her first husband's lifetime, and when her first husband had issue by her; for which adulterous and incestuous marriage, John the Baptist justly reproved Herod the tetrarch, and for which reproof Salome, the daughter of Herodias, by her first husband Herod-Philip, who was still alive, occasioned him to be unjustly beheaded.

Op. cit. 3.71.

dominions of Aretas and Herod, and without informing him of any of her intentions. Accordingly Herod sent her thither, as thinking his wife had not perceived anything; now, she had sent a good while before to Macherus, which was subject to her father, and so all things necessary for her journey were made ready for her by the general of Aretas's army; and by that means she soon came into Arabia, under the conduct of the several generals, who carried her from one to another successively, and she soon came to her father and told him of Herod's intentions. So Aretas made this the first occasion of his enmity between him and Herod, who had also some quarrel with him about their limits at the country of Gemalitis. So they raised armies on both sides, and prepared for war, and sent their generals to fight instead of themselves; and, when they had joined battle, all Herod's army was destroyed by the treachery of some fugitives, who, though they were of the tetrarchy of Philip, joined with Herod's army. So Herod wrote about these affairs to Tiberius, who being very angry at the attempt made by Aretas, wrote to Vitellius, to make war upon him, and either to take him alive, and bring him in bonds, or to kill him, and send him his head. This was the charge that Tiberius gave to the president of Syria.

Now, some of the Jews thought that the destruction of Herod's army came from God, and that very justly, as a punishment of what he did against John, that was called the Baptist, for Herod slew him, who was a good man, and commanded the Jews to exercise virtue both as to righteousness towards one another, and piety towards God, and so to come to Baptism; for that the washing (with water) would be acceptable to him, if they made use of it, not in order to the putting away (or the remission) of some sins (only), but for the purification of the body; supposing still that the soul was thoroughly purified beforehand by righteousness. Now, when (many) others came in crowds about him, for they were greatly moved (or pleased) by hearing his words, Herod, who feared lest the great influence John had over the people might put it into his power and inclination to raise rebellion, (for they seemed to do anything he should advise), thought it best, by putting him to death, to prevent any mischief he might cause, and not bring himself into difficulties, by sparing a man who might make him repent of it when it should be too late. Accordingly he was sent a prisoner, out of Herod's suspicious temper, to Macherus, the castle I before mentioned, and was there put to death. Now, the Jews had an opinion that the destruction of this army was sent as a punishment by Herod, and a mark of God's displeasure to him.

The name of Herodias' daughter, Salome, does not appear in this account, but is to be found some pages further on in the same chapter, in the following passage:

> Herodias was married to Herod (Philip), the son of Herod the Great, who was born of Mariamne, the daughter of Simon, the high-priest, who had a daughter, Salome; after whose birth Herodias took upon her to confound the laws of our country, and divorced herself from her husband while he was alive, and married Herod (Antipas), her husband's brother by her father's side; he was tetrarch of Galilee.

Although Grimald must have been familiar with the name of Herodias' daughter, he did not see fit to use it; but instead he has called her Tryphera, a name which he derived from the Greek word τρυφερός—'voluptuous.'

Grimald was by no means the first to make use of the tragic figure of John the Baptist as the central character of a play. His friend, John Bale, had in 1538 made use of him in *John Baptist's Preaching in the Wilderness,* and George Buchanan's *Baptistes,* though not published until 1576, may have been extant in manuscript form before *Archipropheta* was written; but Grimald owed nothing to either of these two plays, nor does he have a thesis, as did Bale, who used his play as a vehicle for the exposition of his anti-papal doctrine; nor as Buchanan, whose theme was human liberty crying out against tyranny and priestcraft. Grimald was certainly indebted to Jacob Schöpper's[5] tragedy based on the life of John the Baptist, and entitled *Ectrachelisitis, sive Johannes decollatus,* which was published in Cologne in 1546.

[5] Jacob Schöpper, Humanist und lateinischer Dramatiker. Er entstammte den Kreisen des Dortmunder Patricierthums, wie aus der Widmung eines seiner Dramen an die Burgermeister Lambert und Nicolaus von Berswordt, seine 'cognati,' hervorgeht, und war von Jugend auf befreundet mit Johann Lambach (Scevastes), der 1543 mit Unterstützung des Rathes das Dortmunder Gymnasium gründete. Ueber seine Lehrer und seinen Studiengang wissen wir

Grimald has followed Schöpper in the introduction of a court fool, who supplies a comic element which Schöpper's fool does not do; in the elaboration of the scenes attending upon the festival occasioned by the celebration of Herod's birthday, at which Salome dances for Herod, and asks for the head of John; in using a great variety of metres; and in making the drama an essentially lyric one; but beyond these points there is no imitation.

The lyric element of the play is most notable. At every opportunity lyric measures are substituted for the regular senarius, or hexameter line. John the Baptist's prayer is lyric in form, and at intervals in it his disciples repeat a refrain like that of a litany; the Syrian's description of Herodias is not a little suggestive of the Song of Solomon; and the banquet scene is full of songs and music.

More unusual that the lyric note of the drama is Grimald's romantic treatment of the passionate love of Herod and

nichts, doch wird er ähnlich wie Lambach in jüngern Jahren den Unterricht der Münsterschen Humanisten genossen, später wenigstens indirect den Einfluss des Joh. Sturm erfahren haben. Seit 1544 ist er in Dortmund als Prediger nachweisbar, zunächst an S. Petri, dann an S. Marien, wo er anfangs Ecclesiast, später Presbyter war, und als Prediger das aristokratische Publicum der Reichstadt zu seinen Zuhören zählte. . . . Von den lateinischen Dramen ist sein Erstlingwerk, der *Ectrachelisitis sive Johannes decollatus* (geschrieben 1544, gedruckt 1546) durch geschickte Anlage, lebhaften Dialog und gute Charakteristik von allen ausgezeichnet.

—*Allgemeine Deutsche Biographie.*

The following list of Schöpper's works is given in Goedeke's *Grundriss zur Geschichte der Deutschen Sprache,* Hanover, 1859, I. 135: Jac. Schöpper, Presbyter zu Dortmund:

(a) *Johannes decollatus,* Colon. 1546, *Ectrachelisitis sive J. decoll.,* Argent. 1565.

(b) *Monomachia Davidis et Goliæ,* Tremon. 1550, Antw. 1551.

(c) *Euphemus,* Bas. f. a.; Antw. 1553.

(d) *Ovis perdita,* Bas. f. a. Antw. 1553.

(e) *Abrahamus tentatus,* Colon. 1546.

(f) *Voluptatis et virtutis pugna,* Colon. 1536; Norib. 1590.

Herodias, a treatment which seems quite modern, and which did not come from classic drama, but which stamps this play as superior to any known drama previously produced in England.

The soliloquy of Jehovah at the beginning of Act V is noteworthy. In this He points out that heavenly wisdom is revealed by earthly folly, that the Abels are made known by means of the Cains, that glory comes by means of the cross, that all is well with John though it does not seem so to men, and that a hidden victory has come to him who has been overcome by violence. He points out, too, the inconceivable joys of those who attain Paradise through suffering. In contrast with the seeming failure of John's life and his inglorious death, there is presented his spiritual triumph, and the promised happiness awaiting him in the life beyond. It is notable that, in this treatment of life, Grimald seems to have anticipated one of the root-ideas in the moral system of Shakespeare—the contrast of the outer life and the life within; the life into which each person enters with others and the life of the soul; the antithesis of being and doing —an idea which Shakespeare worked out in all its fulness in *Macbeth, Hamlet,* and *King Lear.*

ARCHIPRO
PHETA, TRA
GOEDIA

Iam recēns in lucem ēdita.

*Autore Nicolao Grimo-
aldo.*

*Coloniae Marti. Gymnicus excude
bat, Anno M.D. XLVIII.*

The Archprophet,

A Tragedy,

Now first published

by the
Author,

Nicholas Grimald.

Printed by Martin Gymnicus,
Cologne, 1548.

ORNATIS

SIMO, VIRO D. RI- CHARDO COXO NICOLAVS *Grimoaldus* S. P. D.

Posteaquàm hoc à me Poëma Tragicum, Clarissime uir, con fectum fuisset & absolutū, de libroq; nuncupando mecū ipse iam consultarem: habui tandē cum animo statutum ac deliberatum, eius uelut in clientelam fidemq́; tradere, qui ut rei literariæ gnarus ac peritus, sic etiam literato rum hominum studiosus atq; fautor existeret. Quē admodum enim neq; in patrocinio indoctorum dig nitas ulla, neq; in fastitiosorum supercilio ulla gra tia reponitur: ita & ex eruditi patroni iudicio mag na operi accedit autoritas, & ex recipientis benig nitate multa scriptori adfertur alacritas. Ac mihi quidem in ista cogitatione aliquam diu defixo primùm communis hominum uox confirmauit: deinde morum tuorum obseruatio persuasit, esse te unum præter cæteros, qui tum ea doctrina floreas, ut faci lè possis huiusmodi rerum defensionem suscipere: tum ea humanitate abūdes, ut uehementer uelis ho nestorum studiorū rationem attēdere. Fama nimirū & auditione accepi, quomodo in utraq; principiò nostratū Academia moribus atq; disciplinis imbutus fueris: pòst, quæ didiceras, docēdi prouinciā na ctus, recolueris, cōfirmaueris, auxeris: demum eos ex literata pietate fructus perceperis: ut ob egregias uirtutes ingenijq́; dotes, apud optimū illustris simumq́; Regem & gratia plurimùm ualeas, & au

To the Most Excellent Man,
Dr. Richard Cox,
Nicholas Grimald sends
best greetings.

After I had finished writing this tragic poem, most illustrious sir, I considered to whom I should dedicate it, and resolved at last to commit it to the protection and patronage of one who was scholarly, and who was a zealous patron of literary men—for in the patronage of the ignorant there is nothing of dignity, nor in the superciliousness of the fastidious any pleasure; whereas the judgment of a learned patron gives great authority to a work, and the kindness of him to whom a book is dedicated inspires great enthusiasm in the writer. After weighing for some time, first, the common opinion of men, and, secondly, my observation of your character, I was persuaded that you alone, beyond all other writers, were of such excellent learning that you would be able to defend a work of this sort, and that you were a man of such great kindness as earnestly to desire consideration for honorable studies. I have learned from report how, at the outset, you were imbued with sound morals and discipline at both our universities; how, after having entered upon the province of teaching, you reviewed, confirmed, and increased the knowledge that you had already acquired; and how at length you reaped the fruits of your learned piety in the great authority and favor that you enjoy with the best and most illustrious of kings,[1] through the great virtues

[1] Edward VI.

toritate. Nam quid ego de sacris cŏcionibus dică? Quarum mirabilem te artificem omnes, quibus auditus es, uno ore prædicant. Amor autĕ ille tuus erga præclaras & ingenuas artes nullo euidentiore declarari potuit argumento, quàm quòd Aedis dicatæ Christo nuper apud nos constituendæ, in op timamq́; formă redigendæ magnus autor extitisti: quæ sané cum Lyceo, cum Stoa, cum Academia, cŭ omnibus omnium Philosophorum bibliothecis non splendore solùm ædificij, sed liberalium etiă doctri narŭ eximijs professoribus æquiparăda esse uidea tur. Nec uerò sum nescius qua facilitate nonnullorŭ epistolas acceperis, carmina legeris, orationes ad te factas audieris, ita ut admoti sint haud mediocres iuuentuti nostræ stimuli: quantaq́; diligentia de illorum omnium facultate periculum feceris, qui essent in tam illustre sodalitium cooptandi, ita ut non ex domo illi, sed illis domus ornata sit. Historiam igitur ea accipe, quæ est de Iohanne Baptista, uate primario & maximo, tibi sanè satis perspectă, sed eo tamen more modoq́; pertractatam: qui tam doctiores delectare in recognoscendo, q̆ prodesse rudioribus ad intelligendum poterit. Permagni si qui dem (quod ipse tu optimè nosti) ad alicuius rei scientiă atq;explanationĕ nosti interest idpræstare, quod in Poëmatis maximè cernitur, à quo & Poëtis ipsis nomen dederŭt Græci: nempè cùm res gesta uer bis æquatur, cum personæ tăquam rediuiuæ ac spi rantes introducuntur, cùm locus, tempus, dicta, fa-

and gifts of your genius. Why should I speak of your sermons—since all who have heard you with one voice declare that you are an admirable workman? Your love, moreover, for excellent and noble arts cannot be more clearly shown that it has been by your appearance as the great man who recently founded among us, and brought to its present excellent form, the college dedicated to Christ, which seems, indeed, to be comparable to the Lyceum, the Stoa, the Academy, and all the libraries of all philosophers, not only in the splendor of the building, but also in its excellent faculty of liberal arts. Nor am I ignorant of the courtesy with which you have received the letters of certain students, read their poems, and heard their speeches addressed to you, so that no slight incentive has been given to our young men; nor am I less conscious of the trouble you took in making trial of the attainments of all those who were to be elected to so famous a society, so that they might lend distinction to the college, rather than receive distinction from it. Receive, therefore, this history of John the Baptist, a great prophet of the first rank, the theme of which is thoroughly understood by you, and has, moreover, been treated in such a manner as not only to delight the learned, but also to profit those of cruder intelligence. As you best know, it is of the greatest consequence to the understanding and appreciation of any subject that that quality, from which the Greeks gave the name of poet[2] to the writers themselves, be especially noted in poems. Such a thing happens when a deed is portrayed in adequate language, and characters are introduced as though living and breathing; when time, place,

[2] A poet is that which by the Greeks is called a maker, or a feigner: his art, an art of imitation or feigning; expressing the life of man in fit measures, numbers, and harmony, according to Aristotle; from ποιεῖν, which signifies to make or feign. Hence he is called a poet, not he which writeth in measure only, but that feigneth and formeth a fable, and writes things like truth. For the fable and fiction is, as it were, the form and soul of any poetical work, or poem.

—Ben Jonson, *Works,* London, 1875, 9. 212.

cta illustrantur: cùm omne negotium ita sub aspectum auditumq́; subijcitur, ut non tantùm dici aut commemorari, sed fieri iă de geri uideatur. Huius ego generis exercitationibus prӕterquàm quod stylum excolo, & inhӕrentem naturӕ peruersitatem (quóad concessum est) frango, & Christo prӕ terea meo frui assuesco, dum sermonis tractatione & meditatione sacri animus alioqui demissus & afflictus erigitur atq; reficitur. Nec mihi solùm, meísue unius commodis hic inseruisse me sentio: sed & illis omnibus, qui uel in eodem operis ac studij genere uersari contendent, uel hanc priorem Euan gelij partem sibi quasi ob oculos proponi cupient. Cognoscet hic, siue lector, siue spectator uerǎ, soli dam, & infucatam pœnitudinem: qua uia incedendum sit, ut ad Christum ueniatur: quid primus Euǎ gelicӕ disciplinӕ concionator tantoperè hominum auribus, ac mĕtibus inculcauerit. Sciet insuper eiusdem mirificum ortum, incorruptos mores, tinctio nis uirtutem, ardorem in propaganda religione, lo quendi libertatem, pium precandi ritum, acres admonitiones, mortem deniq; Christiano homine dig nam. Videbit & illud, hypocritӕ quàm sibi placeant, quàm cӕci sint amore sui, quàm studeant proprijs commoditatibus: puram autem & synceram sanctimoniam quàm uel dissolutè negligant, uel ini micè insectentur. Considerabit quoq; impium à Deo repudiatum tale monstrum esse, qualis Herodes extitit. Nec abs re fuerit, animaduertere mulie brem petulantiam, luxus regios, aulicorum assentationem: contrà plebeiam simplicitatem, modestiam discipulorum, Baptistӕ constantiam ac fidem, & alia quӕdam scitu fortasse cognituq́; non iniucunda. Quӕ si tu (honoratissime uir) humanè & comiter exceperis, meq́; in aliqua parte apud te hӕ rere, interq́; tuos numerari permiseris, profectò & ingentes mihi animos dabis ad maiora molienda,

words, and deeds are vividly depicted; when the whole action is brought before your eyes and ears, so that it seems not so much to be told, to be narrated, as to be done, to be enacted. Because I cultivate style by exercises of this nature, I both break the inherent perversity of my nature—which is granted—and I accustom myself to delight in my Christ; while, through the consideration and treatment of sacred dialogue, my soul, otherwise downcast and greatly afflicted, is uplifted and refreshed. Nor do I think this concerns me alone, but all those who desire to be engaged in the same sort of labor and study, or who desire this first part of the Gospel to be placed before their eyes. Here the reader or the spectator will learn true, genuine, unfeigned repentance, the way to approach Christ, and the lesson the first preacher of the Gospel so strongly impressed upon the ears and minds of men. He will learn, also, of this same man's wonderful birth, of his stainless life, of the power of baptism, of his zeal in propagating religion, his freedom of speech, devotion in prayer, earnest admonitions, and of his death at last, worthy of a Christian. He will also see how hypocrites delight in themselves, how blind they are in self-love, how eager for their own advantage, and how they either dissolutely neglect pure religion or attack it hostilely. He will observe, too, how so impious a monster as Herod is rejected of God. Nor will he be without an opportunity for noting the wantonness of women, regal luxury, the flattery of courtiers, and, on the other side, the constancy and fidelity of John the Baptist, and other things not unpleasing to learn and to know. Now, most honored sir, if you will kindly and courteously receive this play, and allow me to be connected with you in some way, and to be counted among the number of your friends, you will surely inspire me with tremendous zeal for greater labors, and cause me to

& efficies tantă tuă ut benignitatĕ studio colam sempiterno. Vale. Det Deus propitius te diu nobis reiq; publicæ incolumem, uir, doctissime & integer rime. Oxoniæ, Ex Aede Christi. Anno D. 1547.

PERSONÆ.

Iehoua, Pater cœlestis.
Iohannes Baptista.
Discipuli Iohannis.
Chorus plebeiorum.
Philautus, } Pharisæi.
Typhlus, } Pharisæi.
Gelasimus, morio Herodis.
Syrus seruus.
Herodes Rex.
Chorus Herodianorum.
Syra ancilla.
Herodias regina.
Tryphera, filia Herodiadis.
Chorus coëpulonum.
Chorus Idumæorum.

regard your great kindness with everlasting gratitude.

Farewell. May gracious God preserve you to us and to the state, most learned and most upright man. From Christ Church, Oxford, A.D. 1547.

Dramatis Personæ

Jehovah, the Heavenly Father.
John the Baptist.
The disciples of John.
Chorus of common people.
Philautus, Typhlus } Pharisees.
Gelasimus, Herod's fool.
A Syrian man, a slave.
King Herod.
Chorus of the followers of Herod.
A Syrian girl, a slave.
Herodias, the queen.
Tryphera, the daughter of Herodias.
Chorus of banqueters.
Chorus of Idumæans.

ACTVS I. SCENA I.

Iambici Trimetri. Iehoua.

Ex largitatis fonte abundantissimo
Depromi amicam in gratiam mortalium
Quid amplius potest, quàm prolem ut unicam
Impartiamur, unicum ad cœlos ducem?
Nec parua nos huiusce facti gratia
Manere debet: intereritq́; sedulò
Amplecti, & eximijs dignari honoribus.
Quod ipsum perfici pacto haud alio potest
Prauos rectissimo impios integerrimo
Visente, quàm ut se filios iræ sciant.
Suas abhorreantq́; turpitudines.
Monendum id unum, unumq́; præter cætera
Et omnibus seclis, et hoc quò erraticis
Honora lux affulgeat mortalibus,
Quam nunc adesse commonebatur satis
A Patriarcha, quandò morti cederet:
Tum protinus nostri adfuturum uindicem,
Iudæ cùm sceptrum propago amitteret,
Ecce tibi, nun quid Herodes homo nouus
Rerum potitus est, pastusq́; sanguine?
Sobolemq́; liquit hæredem tyrannidis?
Quò sit tamen testatior, quò plus ualeat
Is, qui iam adest, autoritas pondere:
Baptista, legatum placet decernere
Te, nube qui humana tecto pares uiam
Monstranda cuiq; primùm errata sunt sua, ut
Intelligat, quàm opus sit pœnitentia.
Mox exhibendus assertor salutis est
Is eximet fidentium piacula,
Gratisq́; conferet sedes Olympicas.
Tu perge, quæq́; Iordanis sonum dedit
In littore, ipsis deinde ciuitatibus

ACT I, SCENE I.

Jehovah.

Jeh. From the most bountiful source of my liberality, what greater gift could be bestowed in loving kindness upon man than that I should grant him my only-begotten Son as the one guide to heaven? Nor ought I to have small thanks for this, for it will be of the greatest consequence much to cherish this gift, and to regard it with the greatest honor. For it could hardly be brought about in any other manner than by a visit of the most righteous to the evil, and of the most holy to the impious, that the sons of wrath should know and abhor their infamy. This gift, and this alone above all else, is to be remembered in every succeeding age as well as in this, that there may shine forth for erring mortals that glorious light fully declared to be at hand by the patriarch,[3] as he bowed before death: 'Then straightway shall our Deliverer come[4] when Judah's people have lost dominion.' Behold, has not Herod, the upstart, seized the power, and glutted himself with blood, and has he not left an offspring to be an heir to his tyranny? Yet that He who is now at hand may have more testimony and a greater weight of authority, it pleases me to appoint thee, John the Baptist, as ambassador, to prepare a way for Him who is veiled in human form. First of all, every one must be shown his sins, that he may understand the need of repentance. Then the Author of our salvation is to be revealed, who shall take away the sins of the faithful, and freely bring them to their heavenly home. Go thou and proclaim, then, to all the nations, far and wide, the tidings that have come from

Hoc usq; et usq; clamitet: Dimeter.
Rectam fieri Deo debere semitam:
Spem humani acuminis, cultus nefarios,
Operumq; nitelas: breuiter mala omnia
Exterminanda, & audiendum uocibus
Nostris, & in Deum esse figendam fidem.
Turbare perge montes, & retundere
Ferocientes spiritus: extollere
Conare ualles et demissa pectora.
Christo quod aduentanti obstare uidebitur
Incommodóue possit esse, rescindito.
Nec te tyrannus Idumæus pauidum faciat.
Audientiùs contrà ito, nobis præside.
Vincesq; maximè, quom te uictum autumat.
Nusquàm abero, te tutis fouebo uiribus.

ACTVS I. SCENA II.

Iambici, partim Dimetri, partim Senarij.
Ioannes. Discipuli. Chorus plebiorũ.

Veni ter summe spiritus,
Veni, tuorum repleas
Fidelium pectuscula,
Amore ut ignescant tui.
Quem mihi lapsum ab æthere
Columbæ induto corpore
Regem super descendere.
Fac noscamus patrem deum
Christo docente filio.
Nec hunc recuses mittere,
Parens, per orbem Spiritum:
Et innouabis omnia.
O conseruator unice,
Tuorum qui sacra soles
Aura benigni numinis

Jordan's banks: 'The way should be made straight for the Lord: hope in human wisdom, evil worship, vain-glory in works, in short, all wicked things, must be put aside; our voice must be harkened to, and in God must trust be placed.' Go thou, strive to lay low the mountains, to exalt the valleys, to overthrow the fierce in spirit, and to raise the lowly of heart. Cast down whatever seems to oppose the coming of Christ, or whatever may be of hindrance to Him. Let not the Idumæan tyrant make thee fearful. On the contrary, go thou boldly, for we will be thy guard. Thou shalt conquer most when the tyrant thinks thee overcome. Never will I forsake thee; with my power will I cherish thee.

ACT I, SCENE II.

John, the Disciples of John, Chorus of the People.

John. Come, Thou Almighty Spirit, come, fill the hearts of Thy faithful, that they may burn with love for Thee, whom I saw descending from heaven, in bodily shape like a dove, upon the King. Grant that we may know God, the Father, through Christ, the Son. Nor refuse, O Father, to send this Spirit throughout all the world; for Thou wilt make all things new. O sole Preserver, who with the sacred breath of benignant divinity art accustomed to inspire the

Afflare corda liberûm:
Supero da solamine
Viuamus, amoto metu:
Da præpotens, ut gratia
Quae nos creauit, recreet.
Hac nemora tenùs, et deuia occupans loca,
Sua populum passim fatenten crimina
Iordanis irrigante lustraui freto:
Recepiq; in fidem atq; Christiadum gregem. Id
Iordane Naëmanus lepram abstersit Syrus.
Iordanem Hebræa gens olim Deo duce
Tranauit, optatam cùm adiret patriam.
Iordanem ad ipsum, quem tam sæpè iam adfore
Dixi, deum ostendi coactis gentibus.
Mouetur nunc (viri) mens nostra, saltibus ut
Relictis, deinde gressus per medias feram
Vrbes; & ut nullo retardatus metu
Scelestis liberè dicam mortalibus,
Nefandi eos quamprimùm pœniteat status:
Faustumq; iam diem captent, quo uocibus
Promissa tot uatum uenêre numina.
DISC. Haud parua nos tenebat admiratio,
Interrogantibus responsa cúm dares:
Te non Deum esse, aut Helian, uatem ue. Sed
Tamen dic seriò: non tu horum quispiam es?
IOH. Ned sum soter mundi uenenati salus,[1]
Nec unquàm prædicabor illo nomine.
Quàm sæpè testificatum sciscitantibus
Dedi, esse prorsus indignum me homunculum,
Huic Regi ut uel calciamenta detraham?
Propheta nec sum Tesbius, trans aëra
Qui ardente curru in ipsum uectus est polum.
Quanquam (fatebor) idem agit me spiritus,
Eademq; uis mouet supremi numinis.

[1] Emendation:
IOH. Nec sum soter mundi *uenenanti* salus,

hearts of Thy children, grant that we may live in heavenly peace, all fear being cast out. Grant, omnipotent Father, that that grace which created us may recreate us. Living until now in woods and in lonely places, I have baptized here and there in the flowing waters of the Jordan those who confessed their sins, and I have received them into the faith and the congregation of Christ. In the Jordan, Naaman the Syrian washed away his leprosy. The Hebrew people of old under the leadership of God crossed over the river Jordan when they came to the Promised Land. On the banks of this very Jordan I revealed to the assembled people God Himself, whom I had often declared to be at hand. Now, men, my soul prompts me to leave the wilderness, and to make my way into the midst of cities; and, hindered by no fear, to speak freely to wicked mortals that they may straightway repent them of their state of iniquity, and seek the glad day when the divinity promised by the mouths of so many prophets has come.

Disc. We wondered not a little when to our inquiries you made answer that you were not the Christ, nor Elias, nor a prophet. Tell us now, truly, are you not one of these?

John. I am not the Saviour, the Healing of the envenomed world, nor will I ever preach under that name. How often have I testified to them that questioned me that I am but a weak man, unworthy to unloose the latchet of the sandals of that King. Nor am I that Tishbite prophet who was taken across the sky in a chariot of fire up into heaven. Nevertheless, I confess that the same spirit moves me, and the same power of the supreme Deity instructs me. I am

Vates nec inter præscios poni queo.
Turbas docebant, atq; ducebant uagas
Illi: quibus nouum ipse demonstro ducem.
Illi: futura prædixêre numina:
Digitum sed ipse præsentem intendo ad Deum.
Illi suboscura edidêre oracula.
Sub aspectu sunt ipse quæ pronuncio.
DISC. Amâbo, idcircò nunc qui sis, doce tuos,
Animi nec ambiguos diutiùs tene.
IOH. Amoides ille uates apud seclum prius
Cecinet uocem per atra clamantem auia:
Sternatur ampla Regi uenturo uia.
Ea ipsa uox ego, atq; ille ipse præco sum.
DISC. Modo sed quo uia ista Regi sternitur!
IOH. Tanq̃; sui sunt serui honoratis uiris,
Qui saxa, qui scrobes, qui heri quicquid uiam
Possit salebrosam horridam̃ ue reddere,
Auferre cum summa solent industria:
Ita mortalium ingressuro animos Deo
Eximere pectorum decet me obstacula,
Id est, peccato plurima *&* grauissima,
Eorum maximè, qui Pharisaicam
Præ se ferunt iactantq́; sanctimoniam.
Huc nostra spectat functio potissimùm,
Vt quisq́; in agnitionem adducatur sui:
Vt quilibet sciat quàm possiet parum.
Tetroq́; sit totus coopertus crimine.
Ita planum fuerit, cuiuis uel optimo,
Dei peropus esse lenitate *&* gratia.
DISC. Quo pacto habebitur nostrimet agnitio?
IOH. Præ oculis habete primus quo statu parens
Patratum post scelus fuerit, de quo sumus
Creati *&* nos, patri proles, simillima.
Habitabat ille hortum quidem pulcherrimum,
Et in creata erat præfectus omnia.
Habebat mentis optionem liberam,

not to be accounted among the prophets who taught the multitudes, and led them in their wanderings; I point out a leader. They foretold the divinity to come, but I point out God Himself. They made obscure prophecies, but the things that I declare are in view.

Disc. We pray thee now to tell us, thy disciples, who thou art, and not to hold us longer in suspense.

John. The son of Amos, a prophet of the olden days, foretold a voice crying in the wilderness, saying, 'Make straight a highway for the coming king.' That voice am I; I myself am that herald.

Disc. But how shall this highway be made for the king?

John. As men of rank have servants who with the greatest care are wont to remove stones, pitfalls, whatever may render the way rough and uneven, so it is my duty to remove from the hearts of men whatever obstacles impede the entrance of God to their hearts; that is, their many and most grievous sins, especially the sin of those who vaunt themselves, and who boast of Pharisaic righteousness. To this end my duty particularly points, that every one may be led to a knowledge of himself, and realize how little he of himself can do, and how buried in vile sin he is. Thus it will be made manifest to every one, even to the best, how great is the need of the mercy and grace of God.

Disc. How is this knowledge of ourselves to be had?

John. First hold before your eyes the state in which our first parent was after he had sinned. From him we were created, and we, his offspring, are like unto him. He dwelt, indeed, in a beautiful garden, and had dominion over all that was created. He had free will, that he might follow

Mallet' ne fas sequi, an nefas incurrere.
Hoc summus autor in mandatis ei dedit,
Quoquo modo ne adduceretur, ut semel
De tentatrice usceretur arbore,
Pœnas daturus ausis dignas talibus.
Adamo hunc inuidens Orcus impauidus locum,
Velut iuratus hostis, è solio uirum
Studet turbare. Fœminam per flexilem
Attentat, inducit. Mox illa proruit
In mâlum idemq́; persuadet coniugi.
Labascit fœmineis uir uictus uoculis,
Auidoq́; morsu poma captat improba.
Hinc illæ lachrymæ, nostra hinc calamitas,
Hinc sempiterna turpitudinis nota.
Caducus est fractus ex indissolubili,
Ex integro sentina corruptissima,
Ex libero suæq́; spontis habens malo
Voluntatem, & naturam deditissimam,
Ex unicè charo uas est iræ Dei,
Cœlestis ex hærede beatitudinis ab-
Dicatus, & deuotus ad ima tartara.
Potiores esse uos parente creditis?
Malam arborem fœtus bonos dare quis putet?
Is impius fuit, nos impij sumus.
Is uanus extitit, nos uani existimus.
In insito subiectus est reatui,
Seruimus inhærenti nos turpitudini.
Nam liberum seruus progignere qui potest?
E carne quod natum est, caro est; quæ spiritu
Cum destituatur, ecquis uirtute locus?
DISC. Quid ergo? quid? Legiś ne præscripti exequi
Conabimur salus indè ut speranda sit?
IOH. Mutare si Aethiops potest pellem suam,
Suos aut colores Pardus: & penes uos erit
Malum natura ab ipsa haustum relinquere.
Potestis nil cupere? Potestis proximos

either what was right or what was wrong. The great Creator gave to him this command, that he should in no wise be led to eat of the tempting tree, since, should he do so, punishment worthy of such disobedience would be meted out. Satan, undaunted, envying Adam this place, and as his sworn enemy, sought to cast man down from his seat. Through yielding woman, Satan assailed him and led him on. Soon she seized an apple, and persuaded her husband to do the same. Overcome by the woman's words, man yielded, and eagerly took of the forbidden fruit and did eat. Hence these tears, hence our loss, and the everlasting brand of shame. From being immortal, man became subject to death; from being pure, the vilest dregs; from being a creature of free will, one desiring evil, and having a nature most given to it; from being the only-beloved of God, the vessel of His wrath. Having forfeited his inheritance of eternal happiness, man gave himself over to the depths of hell. Think ye that we are more worthy than our parent? Who can believe that an evil tree will bring forth good fruit? He was wicked; we are wicked also. He lived a vain existence; we too are vain. He fell under the charge of ingrafted guilt; we, too, serve inherent wickedness. What slave can beget a free child? That which is born of the flesh is flesh; when that is forsaken of the spirit, what place is there for virtue?

Disc. What then? Shall we not try to keep the commandments of the law, so that we may thus hope for salvation?

John. If the Ethiopian can change his skin, or the leopard his spots, it will be within your power to abandon the evil that comes from your very nature. Can you covet nothing?

Amare ut altros ipsos? Potestis cætera
Edicta Legis ultró, *&* ex animo sequi?
Cursuq; uestrùm appello conscientiam.
DISC. Tam uera prædicas, quàm quæ certissima.
Deo si nos intercedente iudice
Ignes manent, ignes gehennæ perpetes:
Quid tandem agemus omnium miserrimi?
Pronunciat execrabilem, legalia
Præcepta qui uiuendo non expresserit.
Quò nos feremus? huic quid responsabimus?
Nostræ imbecillitati quis medebitur?
IOH. Facitote nunc, ut Legis ex præstantia,
Vestra explorata fiat impotentia.
Lux ista nil uobiś met arrogare, sed
Reuera indignatĕ ac turpitudinĕ faciat sentire, deplorare,
(*&* habere odio.
Vostrum iam si quis hæc bene perpenderit;
Quàm se reprendet! quàm nihil dabit sibi?
Alienum quàm lubenter subsidium petet?
Sed inuenire non est, præter quem cano
Summum Deum, qui ferre suppetias queat.
His æquitas nostra est, his nostra sanctitas.
Vos hunc magistrum, uos ducem hunc optabitis,
Cuius quidem erga uos immensa munera,
Quæ nunc daturus in terras delapsus est.
Ratione posteaquàm lustraueritis intima:
Nil, siue iucundum *&* uoluptarium,
Diue insuaue ac plenum doloribus fuerit,
Valebit unquàm ab eius amore auellere.
Corde infimo iam uos in genua prouoluite,
Palmas *&* lumina in cœlum iam tollite,
Mecumq; numen implorate supplicies:
Sis tu benignus ac bonus Dime.
Nobis, Pater precantibus.
DISC. Sis tu benignus. *&* c.
IOH. Propensionem agnoscimus
Mentis, Deus, deterrimam,

Can you love your neighbor as yourself? Can you with all your heart obey the other commands of the law? I appeal to the conscience of each one of you.

Disc. The truths that you declare are indisputable. If God judges us sternly, fire remains for us, the everlasting fires of hell. What shall we, most miserable wretches, do? He is pronounced accursed who has not conformed in his life to the precepts of the law. Whither shall we go? What shall we answer? Who shall heal our infirmities?

John. See that, according to the righteousness of the law, your helplessness be made manifest to you, that this knowledge do not make you become arrogant, but cause you indeed to see your own unworthiness and shame, and to bewail them, and to hate them. If any one of you ponder these things well, how he will censure himself! How little he will value himself! How readily he will seek aid from another! But it is not to be found except in Him whom I declare to be the most high God, from whom cometh our help. He is our peace[5] and our righteousness. You will now choose this Master, this Leader, who has descended to earth to give you great gifts indeed. After you have been inwardly purified, nothing pleasant or unpleasant, nothing however joyous or full of grief it may be, will ever avail to root out your love of Him. Now with contrite heart kneel down and raise your hands to heaven, and with me humbly pray to God: 'Be merciful and kind to us, O Father, we beseech Thee!'

Disc. Be merciful and kind to us, we beseech Thee!

John. O God, we know the bent of our mind, and that our

[5] Eph. 2. 14.

Naturam in quæq; pessima
Nostram rebellem proijci,
Hanc elargire gratiam,
Indigna quàm sit pondera
Vt sentiamus criminum
Tui nos cura urgeat.
DISC. Sis tu benignus. *&* c.
IOH. O ipsa qui es benignitas,
Vestuti Adami moribus
Ablatis, inseras nouos,
Tuo *&* refinge spiritu.
Si nos fouens hoc flamine
Pacabis nostra pectora,
Clamabimus, Pater, Pater,
Te corde adorantes pio.
DISC. Sis tu benignus. *&* c.
IOH. Fiemus hinc certissimi
De amore nos erga tuo,
Nobis beandis unicum
Mori quòd natum iusseris.
Qui ob id cùm iam demittitur
Cœlo, terrisq; inambulat:
Fac mente syncera, Pater,
Possimus hunc admittere.
DISC. Sis tu benignus ac bonus
Nobis, Pater, precantibus.
IOH. Agite hoc frequentiùs, atq; inconcussa fide
Supremum sic uocate uos uotis Deum.
Tamen quia is vult uerè, *&* exanimo coli,
Quò haud uestra pertinebit imbecillitas:
A Patre per Natum Piè contendite,
In uos abundé sacrum ut efflet Spiritum.
Ferat qui opem uestris infirmitatibus,
Et optima precandi formula instruat.
  Iam iter emensi turres Herodis arduas
Propè cernimus, iam ostentare ædificia sua

rebel nature is inclined to whatever is most evil. Bestow Thy grace, that we may perceive how shameful is the burden of our sins, and that our love for Thee may urge us on.

Disc. Be merciful and kind to us, we beseech Thee.

John. O Thou who art grace itself, instil in us new ways of life, now that we have put away those of old Adam, and recreate us with Thy spirit. If, cherishing us with Thy Spirit, Thou wilt give our hearts peace, we will cry, 'Father, Father,' and will adore Thee with devout hearts.

Disc. Be merciful and kind to us, we beseech Thee.

John. Let us be most assured of Thy love towards us from this, that Thou, in order to bless us, hast decreed Thy only-begotten Son to die; who for this is even now sent from heaven, and walks on earth. Grant, O Father, that we may receive Him with sincere hearts.

Disc. Be merciful and kind to us, we beseech Thee.

John. Do this often, and with unshaken faith call thus with vows upon the most high God. Moreover, since He wishes to be worshiped sincerely and from the heart, a worship to which your weakness cannot attain, devoutly entreat the Father through the Son that He may breathe into you His Holy Spirit abundantly, to strengthen your infirmities, and teach you the best manner of prayer. Now that our journey is done, we see the lofty towers of Herod at hand, and the

Urbs incipit. DIS. Subibis an Regis domum?
IOH. Subibo, haud absq; spe lucrandi Principis,
Populus quem præmium statim sectabitur.
Ergò auspicite Deo nunc, uiri charissimi,
Vicinam in urbem, qua uia ducit, pergite.
Ponè ego facta præcatiuncula sequar.
O qui tuos amplecteris Dimeter.
Paterno amore filios.
Per omnes terrarum plagas
Celebretur nomen tuum.
O qui polo demissus es,
Pro plebe facturus satis,
Oblatum fac ut ne uiri
Salutem negligant suam.
O qui uitam inspiras nouam
Omnemq́; cursum dirigis,
Mortalium tu pectora
Haustu repleto numinis.
Numen triplex & unicum
Iunctum perenni fœdere,
Da uiuidas uires mihi,
Tuam straturo semitam.
Rex cum suis rectè audiat
Quem tu dedisti nuncium.
Ego fidenter expleam
Mearum quæ sunt partium.

CHORVS.

Versus Anapestici, seu Pindarici.

Lex prisca locis data desertis
Per inhospita erat antra ferarum.
Itidem syluas inter opacas
Cœpit noua lex notior esse.
Hic læticiæ plena crepat uox

buildings of the city begin to appear.

Disc. Will you go to the palace of the king?

John. I shall go, and not without hope of winning the prince, whom the people will at once follow as a leader before others. Therefore, my dear men, depart with the guidance of God, unto the near-by city, whither the road leads. After I have offered a short prayer, I will follow you.

O Thou who dost embrace Thy sons with a Father's love, may Thy name be praised throughout all the world. O Thou who hast been sent from heaven to make a sacrifice meet for the people, grant that they may not despise their salvation. O Thou who inspirest new life, and dost direct every course, fill the hearts of men with desire for God. O threefold Divinity, yet united in one by eternal bonds, grant strength and vigor to me, who am about to prepare a way for Thee. Grant that the king and his people may rightly hear him whom Thou hast sent as a herald, and that I may faithfully do my duty.

Chorus. The law of old time was given in desert places amid the unfriendly caverns of wild beasts; the new law likewise is beginning to be made known amid the forest shades. Here a voice full of gladness resounds which clearly

Quæ nos nobis graphicè ostendens
Linquere nostra docet, atq; monet
Ad gratuitam ire salutem.
Vastos per agros ille, ille sonat
Fuco alienus, pius, intrepidus
Præco, & ab omni parte probandus.
Hic hic procerum laudibus amplis
Nihil intumuit. Non hunc Mystæ,
Non Pharisæi, non instructi
Fraude Leuitæ mulcere nouis
Titulis poterant: siue supremi
Seu Tesbiaci, seu popularis
Vocitaretur nomine uatis.
Laudem unius amplificare
O Christe tuam concupiebat.
Sed & ipsorum iurgia spreuit,
Qui noua cœpta reprehendebat:
Vostros animos inspicite (inquit)
Deprauatos, turpes, miseros,
Et genuina labe nefandos.
Non modò facta, quin dicta etiam
Ac meditata uestra trahent uos
In auarum Orcum, ni Deus insit
Pectore uostro. Hunc hunc precibus
Ergo uocate, hunc supplicibus
Quærite uotis: Quærite, ut ille
Vobiscum habitet: quærite, ut eius
Vestram foueat gratia mentem.

ACTVS II. SCENA I

Philautus. Typhlus.

Supreme Iehoua, quorum ista pertint — Senarij.
Noua religio, quam hic introducit aduena?
Pharisæis ita dedit responsa Solymis?
Ita usus est inaudito baptismate?

reveals us to ourselves, and teaches us to put aside our worldly affairs, and to seek free salvation. A foe to deceit, pious, a bold preacher, wholly acceptable, he calls out through the broad land. He has not been puffed up by the ample praises of the chief men. Neither the priests, nor the Pharisees, nor the Levites, skilled in deceit, were able to flatter him with new titles, whether he were hailed with that of the Most High, or as the Tishbite, or as a prophet of the people. He has sought to magnify the glory of Thee alone, O Christ. He has spurned thus the contentions of those who found fault with new beginnings. 'Look into your hearts,' he has said, 'O ye who are depraved, base, wretched, and stained with innate sin. Not only your deeds, but even your thoughts, will betray you to yawning hell, unless God be in your hearts. Therefore call upon Him in your prayers and supplications; seek Him in your vows, that He may abide with you, and that He may increase your understanding.'

ACT II, SCENE I.

Philautus, Typhlus.

Phi. Great Jehovah! Whither will this new religion lead, which this stranger is introducing? Has he thus answered the Pharisees of Jerusalem? Has he used an un-

Quasi lotionibus nostris absit puritas.
Manibus edulia lotis cuncta tangimus.
Lauamus è foro reuersi corpora.
Mundamus aquis sellas, patellas, pocula,
Cubilia picta, & omnem suppelectilem.
TY. Docuit peccata item faterier sua
Rudem popellum: nil nos tale docuerit.
Nos plures quàm ille fundimus preces Deo.
Heddomade nos uno bis abstinentia
Feram domamus carnis impotentiam.
Decimam nos elargimur indigis partem Scazon.
Nostrarum opum omnium. Nos infra sunt alij
Plæriq; mortales. PHI. Et is tamen (sua
Quæ est impudentia) omnia hæc uertit uicio,
Nihiliq́; pendit, auditis modò credimus.
Pessum profectò, si pergit, nostrum ordinem
Dabit. Reprendit cuncta, laudat neminem.
TY. Quandò igitur in isthanc asserunt eũ
Venisse, de adventu Regem monebimus,
Arcere qui & vult, & potest, si errauerit.
PHI. Rectissimè putas. Nam illum si carpserit,
Aequa nequaquàm (opinor) mente perferet
Apud plebem tamen quia gratiosus est,
Eum contra coràm nihil profabimur.
Sat est, si cogatur cum Herode colloqui.
De religione, & de sacris ceremonijs.
Contrarijs non congruent contraria.

ACTVS II. SCENA II.

Gelasimus. Pharisæi. Syrus. Herodes.
Chorus Herodianorum.

Quis (hem) pultando nostras effringit fores? Senarius.
Hem, adsunt sancti sancti, adsunt (hem) patres mei
Auete, auete. Hui q̃d tot preculæ uolũt?

heard-of baptism, just as if our bathing were lacking in thoroughness? We touch no food except with washed hands. On coming from the market-place we bathe our bodies. We cleanse with water the seats, plates, cups, painted couches, and all the furniture.

Ty. He has also taught the common people to confess their sins, but let him teach us nothing of the sort. We utter more prayers to God than he does. Twice every week we subdue the fierce lust of the flesh by fasting. A tenth part of all our wealth we bestow upon the poor. Others, for the most part, are inferior to us.

Phi. Yet, if we may believe what we hear, such is his impudence that he disparages all this, and counts it as nothing. Certainly, if he continues, he will put an end to our order. He censures everything, and praises no one.

Ty. Since they say that he has come into the city, we will warn the king of his arrival, who is both willing and able to check him if he err.

Phi. You judge most rightly. For if he were to find fault with Herod, I think that Herod would in no wise endure it calmly. Nevertheless, since this man is in favor with the people, we will say nothing against him openly. It will be enough if he be brought to talk with Herod. Contraries will not agree with contraries.

ACT II, SCENE II.

Gelasimus, Pharisees, a Syrian, Herod, Chorus of Herod's Men.

Gel. Well, who is breaking in our doors with knocking? Ah, there are pious people here, pious people! Ah, my fathers are here! Hail, hail! Oh, what do all these prayers

Sic sæpè labra motat nostra simia.
PHI. Dic sodes, ubi Rex est? GE. Ubi Rex? hic ego
Sum rex morionis. PHI. Non: morio tu Regis es.
Benè si conuertas. GE. Au morio tu Regis es.
Benè pater doces, morio tu Regis es.
TY. Syrum nobis amâbo, è tectis euoca.
GE. Exi Syra, procu' adest: amâbo (inquit) Syram.
TY. Ha per Deos omitte plura dicere.
Vah nec te conuenire auemus, nec Syram.
GE. Facilè credo, ne aselli sitis ad lyram.
PH. Nihil iste aget. Pulsandum Typhle rursum est.
GE. Magistelli mei quàm in multa mussitant?
Num, num: ba, ba, be: annon bellu' ego quoq;
Pharisæus essem, sed labra terit labor.
SY. Quis ad fores? Hui uos eratis hic patres?
Quid statur? quare non tulisti' intro pedem?
TY. Nec pensa nostrarum precum persoluimus,
Molestos interuenire nec decet Regi. Scazon.
SY. Habetis ergò, quod Rex ipsus audiat?
TY. Habemus, tu modò parare uiam uelis.
SY. Faxo lubens. TY. Eum nos hic morabimur.
GE. Pulchrè iuuat nos cum morione morarier.
Ohe, nummus distribuunt. Date, hæc aliquid caua
Capiat manus. Ohe, factum liberaliter.
Hijs ego pecunijs emam ex Syra osculum.
SY. Pharisæi te, Rex, præstolantur ad fores.
HER. Nec hos introduxisti? SY. Recusant ingredi,
Precibus quia non adhuc est cuncta posita suis.

mean? Our ape often moves his lips just as they do.

Phi. Tell us, if you please, where is the king?

Gel. Where is the king? Here. I am king of the fools.

Phi. No, you are the fool of the king, if you turn the words aright.

Gel. Ah, you are the king's fool. You teach me well, father. You are the king's fool.

Ty. Call the Syrian from his quarters, I pray you.

Gel. Come out, please, you Syrian girl; here is some one for you, he says.

Ty. Oh, for God's sake, say no more. Bah! We wish to see neither you nor a Syrian girl.

Gel. I can easily believe that you would be asses at the lute.

Phar. This fellow will do nothing. We must knock again, Typhlus.

Gel. What a lot my masters mumble! Mum, mum, ba, ba, be, be! Wouldn't I make a fine Pharisee? But such work wears out one's lips.

Syr. Who is at the door? Ah, is it you, fathers? Why do you stand there? Why did you not come in?

Ty. We had not yet completed the number of our prayers, and it is not fitting to disturb the king.

Syr. Have you anything which the king should hear from you yourselves?

Ty. We have, if you will only provide a way.

Syr. I will do so gladly.

Ty. We will wait for him here.

Gel. It gives us great pleasure to wait with a fool. Oh, they are giving money! Give me some! Let this empty hand have some! Ah, generously done! With these coins I will buy a kiss from the Syrian girl.

Syr. The Pharisees, O king, are waiting at the door.

He. Why did you not bring them in?

Syr. They refused to enter, because not all their prayers were yet finished.

HER. Quid ô Mystæ nunc principes, rei quid est?
PHI. Iamdudum fama nostras ad aures pertulit.
Rumorq́; uerus & constans percrebuit,
Venisse in urbem hanc, sacra qui doceat noua:
Opaca inter ferarum lustra qui hactenus
Valde asperam uitam traxisse dicitur.
Eó confluit proximarum gentium
Numerosa multitudo, inter quas uel bona
Pars tinctionem, & doctrinam eius arripuit:
Ibiq́; nactus est multos comites, manus
Nec parua plebis hunc quaqua sequitur uia.
Tuae maiestate hæc monstranda duximus,
Ne te ignorante ritu' irreperent noui.
HER. Vadite, lustrate ciuitatem omnem citò.
Aut hunc adducite, aut exeius asseclis.
Gustare, & horum, & sermonem ipsius uolo.
GEL. Abijt Rex intrò ad uxorem, & cũ eo Syrus
Togati ad templa Pharisæi: domestici
In urbem: ego iam rectà in promptuarium:
Manete, dum apporto potum sitientibus.

ACTVS II. SCENA III.

Syrus. Syra. Gelasimus.

Mirum cuiquam erit, q̆ Rex Heriodadem — Senarius.
Sic ardeat? sic in mente atq; oculis ferat?
Cui formæ fulgor ac decu' est eiusmodi, ut
Videntur esse diuinum naturæ opus.
In oculis ipse amor locum elegit sibi,
Petis, proterius, claris, ludubundulis.
Ebori' instar candidi dentes. Labellula
Suffusa natiuo quodam uelut minio.
Nasus elegans uenusto libratur spatio,
Eöæ pulchra par est aurôræ coma.
Genas formosas grata tingit purpura.

He. Now, chief priests of the mysteries, what is it?

Phi. Some time ago a report reached our ears; a true and oft-repeated rumor was noised about, that a man has come into this city who teaches new doctrines, one who is said hitherto to have led a hard life amid the dark haunts of wild beasts. To him a great multitude of neighboring people have gone out, of whom a goodly number have accepted his doctrine, and baptism at his hands. There he has gathered together many disciples; the band of common people which accompanies him wherever he goes is not a small one. We thought that these things should be made known to your Majesty, lest, when you were unaware, they should inaugurate new rites.

He. Go, search all the city quickly. Either bring hither the man or some of his followers. I wish to talk with him and with them.

Gel. The king has gone in to his wife, and the Syrian after him; the gowned Pharisees have gone to the temple, and the servants to the city. I will straightway hie me to the wine-cellar. Stay here while I bring drink to the dry.

ACT II, SCENE III.

Syrian, Syrian girl, Gelasimus.

Syr. Does any one wonder that the king burns so with love for Herodias, and that she haunts his eyes and his mind? The beauty and the splendor of her form is such that it seems to be some divine work of nature. Love has chosen a place for himself in her eyes, which are alluring, wanton, clear, merry. Her teeth are white as ivory, and her dainty lips, delicately colored, are parted a little. Her fine nose is well poised amid lovely surroundings. Her hair is as beautiful as the dawn. A pretty red suffuses her well-

Serena frons, & tanquam stella, lucida est.
Ab ore roseo dulcis ambrosia fluit.
Collum tenellulum, succi plenum, uiueum.[2]
Papilla laxum haud prominens implet sinŭ,
Sed circumcisa, mollis, blanda, eburnea, ac
Tenero æqualis botro sedet rotundula.
Totius membra corporis scitissimè
Compacta, Regi' amore sunt dignissima.
Sed digniora sunt morum suauitas,
Et linguæ gratia, quêis priori coniugi,
Et cæteris multùm antecellit fœminis.
SY. Etiam, Syre, hæc ad tanta naturæ bona
Accessit optimæ fortunæ flatus, &
Vitæ mirabilis quædam iocunditas.
Quàm animi ex sententia toto' exigit dies!
Comando insumit matutina tempora.
Vir ad mensă accipit post lautè & splendidè.
A cibo, amœnis confabulationibus,
Collusionibus, ambulationibus,
Iocis, osculis, risuq́; tempus fallitur.
Tum cœna sumptuosa cantionibus
Sequitur condita lætis, quam excipiunt choreæ,
Tali, alea, tesseræ, ac potatiunculæ.
Soporam feruido dat noctem coniugi,
Et somno. Easdem cum sole ad uices redit.
GE. Solus cum sola? hui. Syrus cum Syra? ohe.
Heus, heus, fugitis? heus, heus, Syra, est quod te uelim
Nam (quod quidem inter nos licebit dicere)
Habeo tibi denarium, sed ita tamen
Mihi ut redda' osculum. Ah, ne fuge, obolum quoq;
Adijicam, si geres morem: mane, mane.

[2] Emendation:
Collum tenellulum, succi plenum, *niueum.*

shaped cheeks. Her forehead is serene, and shines star-like. Her lips distil sweet ambrosia. Her snowy neck, full and round, is most delicately shaped. Her breasts do not swell to fill a flabby bosom, but stand there trim, soft, charming, white as ivory, rounded like tender grapes. All the parts of her body, most elegantly joined together, are most worthy of a king's love. But more worthy still is the sweetness of her manners and the grace of her speech, in which she far excels his former wife and the rest of the women.

Syr. Girl. And also, Syrian, to these great gifts of nature is added the favor of great fortune, and a certain wonderful joy of living. How she passes her days quite according to her inclination! The morning hours she passes at her toilet. After that, her husband entertains her at the table in elegant and splendid fashion. The time is whiled away by food, with pleasant talk, in playing together, with short walks, with jests, with kisses, and with laughter. Then follows a sumptuous dinner, spiced with joyful songs, followed by dances, games of chance, dicing, and drinking. The drowsy night she gives to her ardent spouse, and to sleep. With the sun she returns to a like round of amusement.

Gel. Alone together! Ah, Syrian man with Syrian maid! Hah! Hi! Are you running off? Ho there! Syrian girl, I want you, for I have something to tell you in private. I have a denarius for you if you will give me a kiss. Oh, do not run away. I will give you an obolus too, if you will give me one. Stay, stay!

ACTVS II. SCENA IIII.

Herodes. Herodias. Gelasimus.

Quĕadmodŭ agitur delicolŭ meŭ? HE. Hercule,
Si lætus es tu, ego læta, liliolum meŭ.
HE. Quis ô quis talem non amet faciem lubens?
Quis non exosculetur hanc lubentius?
Da, da roganti basium mihi, cor meum.
HER. Sic sic suauissimum caput. Sanè nihil
Mutuum ad amorem iam posse adijici puto
Regit mens una nostra amborum corpora.
Idem est uelle, est idem nolle, ijdem ambo sumus.
Ego quidem (apertè ut proferam, quod sentio)
Ex te uno maximam uoluptatem capio.
Tu (quod palàm in dictis, factisq; cernitur)
Ex me una maximam uoluptatem capis.
Quæ non mihi nego, nec negare soleo tibi.
Quæ non tibi negas, nec negare soles mihi.
Ego Herodem dies, noctesq; cogito.
Tu Herodianem dies noctesq; cogitas.
Reuelli à te, non si maritum Cæsarem
Sperare ausim, uellem, amicŭ ô decus meŭ? HE. Vt
Veneres fundis Venus mea melletissima,
Nunc progrediamur. Iunge te lateri meo.
Est compellandus aduena hic nobis. Scazon.
GEL. Talem ô si coniugem ducere,
Perpetua cantilena isthæc foret mea.
Quă pulchra amicula mea? q̃ pulchra amicula es?
Vt interim taceam quod est intrinsecùs.
HER. At qui hic erit peregrinus, cuiusmodi est?
HE. Rerum esse sacrarum autorem aiunt nouum.
Comitatum plebe, & assuetum saltibus.
HER. Me si audis, ne manum cuius porrige.
HE. Hominis iuuabit ex sermone scire, qua
Vagum popellum instruxerit fiducia.
Nisi fortè in ipsius natura eluceat

ACT II, SCENE IV.

Herod, Herodias, Gelasimus.

He. How is my beloved?

Her. By Hercules, if you are joyful, I too am so, my darling.

He. Who, who would not love such a face? Who would not gladly kiss it? Sweetheart, give me a kiss, I beg you.

Her. There, there, my dearest! Truly I judge no addition could be made to our mutual love. One mind animates the bodies of us both. Our likes and dislikes are both the same. We are both of one mind. Indeed—to speak freely what I think—you alone give me the greatest pleasure, and I alone give you the greatest, as is evident from deeds and words. What I do not deny to myself I do not deny to you; what you do not deny to yourself you do not deny to me. Day and night I think of Herod. Of Herodias you think day and night. Not if I might hope for Cæsar as a husband would I desire to be separated from you, my beloved sweetheart.

He. Like Venus you radiate loveliness, my sweetest. Now let us go on. Come by my side. A stranger is to be summoned before us here.

Gel. Oh, if it were granted me to take such a wife, this would be my song everlasting: 'How beautiful is my little love! How beautiful is my little love!' Meanwhile I will keep quiet as to what is in my heart.

Her. But who is the stranger that will be here, and what sort of man is he?

He. They say that he is a new preacher of religion, who dwells in the wilderness, after whom the people flock.

Her. If you listen to me, do not extend your favor to any one.

He. I should like to learn from the man's own lips by what assurance he teaches the wandering crowd. Unless, perchance, something excellent appears in his nature, he shall

Excellens quippiam, illicò amandabitur.
HER. Rectè statuis, mihi hæc sedet sententia.
HE. Adsunt: Deserte sellulas, mora sine.
Nobi' alteram sodali ponite alteram.
Hic scistantibus sub die sedebimus.

ACTVS II. SCENA V.

Chorus Herodianorum. Herodes.
Herodias. Chorus Plebeiorum.
Discipuli Iohannis.

Quod imperasti Rex, quos apprehendere
Licebat, rusticos, comitesq́; adduximus.
Haud occurebat ipsemet quærentibus.
HER. Ruricolæ, amâbo qua spe consectamini
Peregrinum istum? aut ei quæ uita uiuitur?
CHO. Ple. Scelerũ si conscia mens internũ uulnu' habet,
Nociua ponere, & salubria sumere
Docet. Trenquilitatem conscientiae
Per hunc nos posse consequi confidimus.
Vixit uerò integerrimê. Nempe à puero
Se subducens frequenti à multitudine
Commercioq́; uulgi, eremum intrauit. Hic
Vestitus hirsutis cameli pellibus
Syluestres melle misto captabat cibos,
Similiśq; uictu erat lucos colentibus,
Turbam & multam sordes fatentibus suas
Superfusis tingebat in Iordane aquis.
HER. Quid ais ad hæc, nostra? HE. Nunq̃ audita ꝑferũt
HE. Inusitata, si hæc ita se habẽt, canũt.
CHO. Ple. Et plura, & mira de huius ortu dicere
Comites sciunt, ad summa natum quæ qrguunt.
HE. Memorate quæso, nos intenti ora tenebimus.
DIS. Sacerdos fortè Zacharias unu' optimus

be sent away at once.

Her. You are right in your decision. That, too, is my opinion.

He. They have come. Arrange the seats without delay. Place one for us, and another for my consort. Here, under the open sky, we will sit during the inquiry.

ACT II, SCENE V.

Chorus of Herod's Men, Herod, Herodias, Chorus of the People, Disciples of John.

Cho. of Her. As you commanded, O king, we have brought here the country folk and such of his companions as we could seize. The man himself did not fall into our hands, though we searched for him.

He. Country people, pray wherefore do you so eagerly follow this stranger, and what manner of life does he lead?

Cho. of Peo. If the soul, conscious of its sins, has an inward wound, he teaches it how to lay aside harmful things, and to accept what is wholesome. We believe that through him we can arrive at peace of conscience. He has lived most uprightly. Indeed, from boyhood he withdrew from the multitude and from vulgar traffic, and went into the wilderness. There his raiment was of camel's hair, his meat was locusts and wild honey, and his manner of life was like that of those who dwell in the forests; and he washed in Jordan's overflowing waters a great multitude of people who confessed their sins.

He. What think you of this, wife?

Her. They tell us unheard-of things.

He. If these things be true, they do indeed tell strange matters.

Cho. of Peo. His followers tell further of many wonderful things that they know of his birth, which argue that he was born to do great things.

He. Tell me of them, I pray you. We will listen attentively.

Disc. By chance, a certain excellent priest named Zacha-

Abiada' inter, delectus est opera ad sacra.
Coniuncta cui coniunx animo Elisabeta erat.
Vnum torquebat hos malè, quòd pessumè
Audirent, nullos cùm tulissent liberos.
Adeoq́; canam ad ætatem peruenerant.
Omnisq́; spes prærepta erat propaginis:
Quom unice fungens suo maritus munere
Sacræ ædis intima solus loca
Tota expetebat illic mente præmia
Coniugij, hominum & salutem ab imo pectore
Rogabat expectatam multa secula,
  Ecce tibi, de cœlo ipso lapsus Angelus
Dextera stetit miroq́; fulsit lumine, Scazon.
Tremuli quod huius oculi ferre uix possĕt
Cui Nuncius, Collige teipsum, inquit: Supplicies
Aethereus, audiuit preces Rex. Nam breui
Veniet Seruator, & coniunx edens tibi
Ante ambulonem magnum maximi Dei
Pensabit hunc miro merorem gaudio.
Ioannem natum uocabis nomine:
Et dotibus præstabit hic, & munere
Neq́; uolaptatibus luxúue diffluet:
Contentus at lympha tenui, nec uina, nec
Siceram hauriet, nec quod uim mentis arduam
Tardare, lædere, aut penitus adimere queat.
Nimirum materno latentis utero
Pectus replebit totum Spiritus sacer.
Multo' olim uertet ad surgentia lumina.
Nam Heliæ instinctus numine ac potentia
Summa loquendi libertate, perficiet,
Suis mortales ut sceleribus agnitis
Teneantur uenturi desiderio Dei.
Hæc nuntius, Zacharius positu metu:
Quónam, inquit, argumento huiusce gaudij
Futuri nobi' hærentibus facies fidem?
Nunc & mihi planè, & pudicæ conijugi

rias, one of the course of Abia,[6] was chosen to perform the sacred rites. His wife, Elizabeth, was greatly attached to him. One thing, which gave them ill repute, troubled them greatly. They had no children, and had arrived at hoary old age when all hope of offspring was taken from them. When the husband in turn was performing his office alone in the Holy of Holies, there with all his soul he asked for pledges of wedlock, and for the salvation of men, awaited for so many years. Behold, an angel, descending from heaven itself, stood at his right hand, shining with marvelous light, upon which his fearful eye could scarcely look. The messenger, however, said to him: 'Be of good cheer. The heavenly King has heard thy prayers and supplications, for the Saviour will shortly come, and thy wife, begetting the great herald of the most high God, shall lay aside her sorrow for joy and gladness. Thou shalt call thy son John, and he shall be endowed with great talent and ability. His life shall not be spent in pleasure or in excess, but he shall drink water; neither wine nor strong drink shall he taste, nor what can make a vigorous mind become sluggish, do it injury, or take it away entirely. He shall be filled with the Holy Ghost even from his mother's womb. He shall turn many in days to come to the rising light, for, endowed with the spirit and the power of Elias, with the greatest eloquence, he shall bring it about that men, realizing their own sinfulness, shall be filled with a longing for the coming God.' Thus the messenger spoke. Zacharias laid aside his fear, and said: 'What token will you grant to us, perplexed as we are, as an assurance of this coming joy? Surely weary old age now

[6] The order of Abia, or Abijah, was the eighth of the twenty-four courses of priests, the arrangement of which is ascribed to David (I Chron. 24. 3). To this course Zacharias, the father of John the Baptist, belonged (Luke 1. 5).

Senectus effœta seculis prolem negat.
Solitus naturæ cursus an mutabitur?
Quo continget modo uigore, & sanguine
Vacuis, quod annis haud accidit florentibus?
Tum ille: Gabriel, ait, sum ego interpres Dei:
Cuius uerum esse nuncium quò intelligas,
Cùm signa prolis adfuturæ clara, tum
Capies inanis pœnam diffidentiæ.
Fugiet uox, nec licebit sensa promere
Dicendo, donec in lucem tuus êditus
Filiolus dicta comprobauerit mea.
Dum aguntur hæc ædi' in sacræ penetralibus
Senĕ inter & Angelon, turba omni' ad ostia
Expectat insuetas trahentem illic moras.
Tandem progressus est foras, uoltu quidem
Mirabilem præ se ferente læticiam:
At cogitata prorsus conantem eloqui
Menti' index sermo, linguæ & usus deserit.
Hinc colligunt eum, solo cùm esset loco,
Cœleste quippiam, mortali lumine
Haussisse. At ille, quo saltem poterat modo,
Signis nutuq; uocis exæquat uices.
Iam functionis absoluto tempore,
Domum ad uxorem statim se contulit suam.
Quæ simul ac senserat moueri uiscera,
Sese abdit in conclaue rem totam tegens
Quinto usq; dum orbe luna recrêrat menstrua.
Et secum: Nunc uideo Deum, inquit maximo
Cumulasse me beneficio, quòd pignore
Inexpectato connubium decorat meum.
Ità ut iam haud infœcunda dicar ampliùs,
Sed facta mater eiu' unius munere.
Ergò promissa lux aderat, & tempora
Complêrat uxor iusta, cùm auras sentiens
Vitales anili infans è uentre prodijt.
Tum confluentes agminatim plurimi

denies to me and my virtuous wife a child. Shall the usual course of nature be changed? How shall this, which was denied to youthful years, happen to those who are without vigor and without blood?' Then the angel answered: 'I am Gabriel, the messenger of God. That thou mayst understand that I am His true messenger, thou shalt receive a sure sign of the coming child, and also a punishment for thy vain doubts. Thy voice shall fail thee; thou shalt not be able to express thy thoughts in speech until thy little son, born into the light, shall attest my words.' While these things between the old man and the angel took place within the Holy of Holies, all the multitude waiting at the doors marveled that the old man tarried beyond his wont in the temple. At length he came out, his face shining with great joy; but language, the discloser of mind, and the power of speech, left him, as he strove to utter his thoughts. They gathered from this that when he was alone in the holy place he had seen with mortal eye some heavenly vision. However, as far as he was able, by signs and nods he made up for his lack of voice. When the days of his ministration were accomplished, he straightway departed to his own house to his wife, who, as soon as she saw that she had conceived, hid herself in her chamber, concealing the whole matter till the moon waxed in its fifth monthly revolution. 'Now I perceive,' she said to herself, 'that God hath rewarded me with the greatest of blessings, for He graces my marriage with an unexpected pledge, so that I shall no longer be called barren, but be made a mother by His favor alone.' Thus the promised day came, when the mother fulfilled her proper time, and the child, breathing the breath of life, issued from her aged womb. Then very many of those who were united

Cognatione quidam propinqui, & amicitia
Gratulantur mirandum in modum puerperæ,
Deus quam pulchra prole matrem fecerat.
Et octauam cùm uidisset lucem puer,
Et more cognatiq; eò conuenerant,
Vt pellem inscinderent, ac nomen inderent,
Putantes uelle mutum, & elinguem patrem
Id ipsum quod uulgò, est ferè gratissimum,
Genitoris nomine hunc puellum insigniunt.
Mater contrà secreto edocta flamine: haud
Zachariam, ast Iohannem palàm asserit
Vocari oportere. Illi uoce incognita
Conturbati negant sua quenquam in tribu
Id nomini' obtinere. Consulitur pater,
Vt signa, quo modo esset affectus, daret.
Resignatis tabellis tum scriptorijs
Animi concepta pandit interpres manus.
Loquuntur uoce pro uiua mutæ notæ
Iohannes nomen summo editum è polo,
  Stupefacti sunt omnes, & attoniti nimis,
Quia noua illis placebat appellatio,
Matriq; surdus assentitus est pater,
Qui protinùs quôm scripserat, factu' eloquens
Bonitatem, & æquitatem prædicat Dei.
Tremefecit horridus uicinos tum stupor,
Et corda per gentes humilis strauit pauor.
Nam nuncia extemplò harum rerum fama, per
Iudeæ sinu' & regiones proximas
Volans, replebat his aures sermonibus:
Perperisse anum, demissa nomina æthere,
Diuinitùs promissum filium, patrem
Mutum, è mutoq; redditum facundum. Ita ut
Stupescentes plæriq; apud se dicerent:
Quis hic tam prodigiosè prognatus puer
Futurus est? Nam tot rerum miracula
Testantur ortum haud diuino sine numine.

to her by ties of kinship or of acquaintance came to congratulate her, whom God in so wonderful a child-bearing had made the mother of so beautiful a child. When the boy had seen the eighth day, the relatives, according to custom, came to circumcise him, and to give him a name. Thinking the dumb and speechless father would desire it, they called the child after the name of his father, which is commonly most pleasing to people. The mother, however, taught by secret inspiration, openly declared that the child ought not to be called Zacharias, but John. Astonished by this unexpected speech, they reminded her that none of her kindred was called by that name. The father was consulted, that he might signify what his wish was. Then, when a writing-table was opened, his hand, acting as an interpreter, made known the thoughts of his mind, and mute signs spoke for the living voice, saying that John was the name given of high heaven. All marveled and were greatly astonished that this strange name pleased the parents, and that the deaf father agreed with the mother. But as soon as he had written he regained his speech, and declared the goodness and righteousness of God. Then dread amazement made those that dwelt round about them shudder, and fear made the hearts of the people humble. The fame of these things being carried forthwith throughout all Judea and the neighboring regions, the ears of the people were filled with these reports: that an old woman had conceived; a name for the child had been given from heaven; the son had been promised by God; the father had been made dumb, and had again been given the power of speech. Very many, therefore, in amazement said to one another: 'What manner of child shall this boy, so wonderfully born, be? For so many miraculous things testify that he is not born without divine purpose.'

HE. O mi uir, hæc quidem nobis oratio
Clarè depingit hospitem minimè malum.
HE. Sic mihi uidentur prorsus, suauium meum.
Quæ tam miranda narrauistis, ô uiri,
Faciunt ut optimè de ignoto sentiam.
Maturate, & duci reperto dicite
Apud nos magno in expectatione eum
Esse, & patêre ingressuro nostros lares.

ACTVS II. SCENA VI.

Philautus. Typhlus.

Quàm uariũ uolgus est, & quàm uolaticũ? Senarius.
Quàm citò desciscunt à uetustis ad noua?
Videś ne plebiûm quanta hunc stipet manus?
Periculum est, ne nostrum obscuret ordinem,
Paulò plus si inualeat. TY. Nemo hactenus potuit,
Tametsi id moliebatur quàm plurimi.
Nam explosa iam pridem Essenorum opinio est:
Fata fieri quoniam putabat omnia.
Qui pendier censum uetabant Cæsari,
Coörtis erant extincti seditionibus.
Saducæi supersunt, qui tum moribus,
Nobis quidem cedunt, tum opinionibus.
PHI. Quid si, ne forsan hic impostor impudens
Popellũ ad quintam sectam à nobis auocet.
Aduersùs hunc Saducæos acumanus quoq;?
TY. Herclè, uti dicis licèt sint aduersarij,
Nec animo coniuncti uitæ ue formula:
Amici erunt in hoc tamen negocio,
Quòd & ad eorum æstimationem pertinet.
PHI. Agè, persequamur institutum haud segniter.

Her. This speech, my husband, clearly described to us a guest not at all evil.

He. So it certainly seems to me, my sweet. The wonderful things you have told us, men, give me the highest opinion of this stranger. Hasten, find your leader, and say that we are eagerly awaiting him, and that our doors are open to him whenever he shall come.

ACT II, SCENE VI.

Philautus, Typhlus.

Phi. How changeable the common people are, and how inconstant! How quickly they turn from the old to the new! Do you not see what a crowd surrounds this low fellow? There is danger that if he become a little more powerful, he will weaken our order.

Ty. No one so far has been able to do so, although many have tried. The opinion of the Essenes, that all things happen by fate, has long since been exploded. Those who forbade that tribute should be paid to Cæsar were put to death when sedition arose. The Sadducees remain, who are as inferior to us in character as they are in their views.

Phi. But lest, perchance, this impudent impostor should lead the people away from us to form a fifth sect, should we not also incite the Sadducees against him?

Ty. By Hercules! As you say: although the Sadducees are our enemies, and have nothing in common with us in their manner of life, in this business they shall be our friends, for it concerns their reputation.

Phi. Come. We must not execute lazily what we have decided upon.

ACTVS II. SCENA VII.

Iambici, partim Dimetri, partim Senarij.
Ioannes. Discipuli. Chorus Plebeiorum. Syrus.

Summa ô Patris potentia,
Iesu clementissimè,
Aspirans, ut fauonius,
Meos conatus præueni.
Et adiuuans, ut dux bonus,
Bonos progressus annue.
Verè tu uerbum Patris es,
Verè tu mens, tu dextera.
Verbum iam uerba suppetat,
Mens autem mentem dirigat,
Ducatq́; dextram dextera.
SY. Extrarium istum in conspectu dari cupio,
Apud nos tanta cuiuis expectatio est.
DIS. Vagantes huc illuc te quæritauimus,
Magister, quare tam diu moram creas?
CHO. Ple. Rex cognito uitæ modo, ac origine
Tua, miro affectu' est desiderio tui,
Requirens congressu' atq; sermones tuos.
IOH. Hæc ipsa non me ut spero, sed Deum efferĕt.
Petrosa, comites, conscendamus limina.
SY. Quid? hiccine est? ita. non. imô ita, ipsus est.
Similes habent lactucas labra. Quàm pares
Ruditate sunt! Herus procedit obuiam.
Aggredere quicunq; es. Rex conuenire uult.

ACTVS II. SCENA VIII.

Iohannes. Herodes. Syrus. Discipuli.
Chorus Plebiorum.

Pax Tetrarcha tibi. HE. Tibi simul, uir bone. Senarius.

ACT II, SCENE VII.

John, Disciples, Chorus of People, a Syrian.

John. Most merciful Jesus, who art endowed with the supreme power of the Father, breathing like a soft wind upon me, and approving of my good progress, aid me like a good leader. Verily, Thou art the word of the Father, verily Thou art His mind, His right hand. Let now Thy word supply me with words, Thy mind direct my mind, and Thy right hand guide mine.

Syr. I wish that this stranger might be brought into view. There is a great deal of curiosity among us in regard to him.

Disc. Wandering here and there, we have sought you, master. Why did you delay so long?

Cho. of Peo. The king, having learned of the manner of your life and of your birth, has a great desire to see you, and asks for a meeting and a talk with you.

John. This, I hope, will be to God's glory, and not to mine, comrades. Let us ascend the stone threshold.

Syr. What! Is this he? Yes? No. Yes, it is he himself. His lips are like lettuce. How like it they are in roughness! The master comes your way. Approach, whoever you are, the king desires to meet you.

ACT II, SCENE VIII.

John, Herod, a Syrian, Disciples, Chorus of People.

John. Peace to you, tetrarch!

He. And to you also, my good man. Marvelous reports

Tuarum fama rerum incredibili' occupat
Nostras ô frequenter aure', ex quo fit ut ardeam
Dicentem audire te ad ea quæ rogauero.
Quid est, quo de pergis monere hominum greges?
IOH. Propinquam ut ad salutem se parent. Quia
Tanquàm frugi colonus herba' inutiles
Tribulos, lolium, lappas, auenas, carduos,
Runcare ac demetere priùs ferè solet,
Quàm spem anni totiu', & selecta semina
Inepto conetur solo committere:
Sic animo' infectos oportet sorde criminum
Purgare ne priu' atq; tretra flagitia
(Quòad mortalibus liceat) euellere.
Quàm diuina inferi queat persuasio, aut
Salutis mens firma spe sustentarier.
Scelerumq; urticas auferens si effecero,
Vt pullulans uiciorum sylua ne imperet,[3]
Meis hinc uiribus ascribi nihil potest.
Deo uni dona debemus omnes omnia.
HER. Sed ad salutem quo modo parabimur?
IOH. Suum mens ægra debet morbum agnoscere,
Talemq; flere ac lamentarier statum,
Vitamq; scelerum consciam deponere: &
Com honore maximo excipere medicum Deum,
Salutaribus eam qui moribus imbuet.
Mens iam secura fit beatæ uitæ, ubi
Pax est, bonorumq; omnium affluentia.
HER. Haud facilè sentietur morbus eius modi.
Quid autem, si quis hunc minùs medicum petat?
IOH. Eum scito ipsum olim adfuturum iudicem,
Fandi memor, & nefandi contemptum sui
Qui Erebi multabit æternis cruciatibus.
HER. Perorasti sermonis haud sine pondere.
Gratus ades assectis unà tuis. Dato

[3] Emendation:
Vt pullulans *uiciarum* sylua ne imperet,

of your doings have come often to my ears, so that I much desire to hear you answer my question, which is: What are you striving to teach the multitudes of people?

John. To prepare themselves for the salvation that is at hand. As the cultivator of fruit is accustomed in the first place to root up and cut out useless weeds, thorns, tares, burrs, wild oats, and thistles, before he ventures to commit to the unfit earth his chosen seeds, the hope of the whole year, so it is necessary for me first to purge souls stained with sin, and, as far as a mortal may, to pluck out foul deeds of shame, that heavenly persuasion may find an entrance, and the soul be sustained by a firm hope of salvation. If I, taking away the stinging nettles of sin, bring it about that the sprouting seed is not choked by a forest of tares, nothing of this is to be ascribed to my power, for to the one God we all owe all gifts.

He. But in what manner shall we prepare for salvation?

John. The sick soul ought to know its own disease, straightway to lament and bewail it, to lay aside the recognized life of sin, and with the greatest gratitude to receive God, the Physician, who will imbue it with healthful modes of living. Thus the soul becomes assured of a blessed life, in which there is peace, and which abounds in all that is good.

He. A disease of such sort is not easily recognized. What if one does not seek this physician?

John. Know that He will surely come as a judge, and, mindful of right and wrong, will punish with the eternal torments of hell all those who have despised Him.

He. Your words have not been without weight. You and your followers are welcome here. Give me your hand,

Dextram, et succede nostris hospes penatibus.[4]

ACTVS II. SCENA IX.

Gelasimus. Syra. Chorus Herodianorum.

In principio creat cœlum et terram Deus. Senarius.
SY. Ha, ha, he: quorsū, obsecro, ibit hæc oratio?
GE. Auete, honorandi uiri. Date ueniam
Antequam de re, pauca de me dicere.
Morionem me uocat ulgus. Quid si uocet?
Nolite quoslibet metiri nomine.
Pro me responsum habet materna fabula:
In illo tempore admirata ficus erat,
Cur quæ sapiens arbor putaretur morus
A stulticia tamen caperet nomen suum.
Morus mox ista rettulit: Dimeter.
Nomen neq; confert, neq; adimit sapientiam,
Quid me uetat igitur prudentem existere?
Sed nos pergamus, auditiores, ad cætera.
Terra autem inanis, & uacua penitus extitit.
SY. Ha, ha, he: CHO. HERO. Ha, ha, he.
Habitat in uobis ipse diabolus, uiri
Fratres, ita exundatis sceleribus omnibus,
Nugis abundant mimi, scorta blanditijs,
Alea rixis, aula fabellis, fora litibus,
Crebris susurris cæna, fastu fœminæ.
Profectò hic mundus est res immundissima
Atq; ne tenebræ super abyssi conuexa erant.
CHO. Ha, ha, he. SY. Ha, ha, he.
Seu potiùs acuta quadam quæstiuncula.
Quid cuiq́; nostrum scire difficillimum est?
Tu quid putas? quid tute? quid tu deniq́;?
Certè ego puto, ut suum quis agnoscat patrem.
Quid est Patriarches? Patriarches? Et quid est

[4] Quis novis hic nostris successit sedibus hospes,
Aeneid 4. 10.

my guest, and enter our abode.

ACT II, SCENE IX.

Gelasimus, a Syrian girl, Chorus of Herod's Men.

Gel. In the beginning God created the heaven and the earth.

Syr. Girl. Ha, ha, ha! Whither, prithee, will this speech lead?

Gel. Hail, worthy men! Pardon me if I speak a few words about myself before touching upon my subject. The vulgar herd call me a fool. What if they do? Do not measure any one by a name. An old wives' tale has an answer for me. Once upon a time a fig-tree had wondered why a mulberry, which might be considered a wise tree, nevertheless received its name from folly.[7] Then the mulberry replied, 'A name can neither confer nor take away wisdom. What forbids me, then, a wise existence?' But let us proceed, my hearers, to other matters. The earth without form and utterly void has appeared.

Syr. Girl. Ha, ha, ha!

Cho. of Hero. Ha, ha, ha!

Gel. The devil himself dwells in you, men and brothers, so overwhelmed with sin. Players abound in jokes, harlots in blandishments, games of chance in quarrels, the court in gossip, the market-places in lawsuits, feasts in whispering, and women in pride. This world is certainly most foul. Was there not darkness upon the face of the deep?

Cho. of Hero. Ha, ha, ha!

Syr. Girl. Ha, ha, ha!

Gel. Lest I should be too long-winded, I shall conclude with a story, or, rather, with a sharply pointed little question: What seems to each one of you to be the most difficult thing to know? What do you think, what do you, and lastly, what do you? I certainly think it is, how one is to know his own father. What is a patriarch, a patriarch? And what

[7] The mulberry tree is called in Latin 'morus,' a word which also means 'foolish' or 'silly.'

Morio? Morio? Quid fœmina? quid? nisi fatua.
Et spiritus domini motus per aquas fuit.
SY. Ha, ha, he. CHO. Ha, ha, he.

ACTVS II. SCENA X.

Herodes. Herodias. Iohannes.

Dum uoluo mente suspensus quæ protulit
Iohannes iste, quem Baptistam nominant,
Animumq́; dum verso (coniunx) per omnia, in
Summum profectò me stuporem conijcit,
Quinam tantus loquendi honos, quæ pectoris
Vis illa præsens, quod numen lateat in eo.
Fortassis (ô coniunx mihi optatissima)
Deus uel quispiam, uel ex Deo status est.
Quàm fronte se gerit bona imperterritum?
Vox quàm sonat suauis corda ore commouens
Quibus animis præcellit, atq; audacia?
Intrepido enim uoltu quæ, & quanta protulit?
E multis sunt tamen quædam haud adhuc satis
A me intellecta. Qua propter rogabitur
Eandem denuò telam retexere.
Syre, fac ut prodeat Zachariæ proles. Scazon.
HER. Quis credat hũc, mi uir, uastum atq; rusticũ
Pectore, tam miras habere res reconditas,
Nisi qui audiat loquentem? HE. Vera prædicas.
Mihi hospes dic, tu cur aqua tingas, alius
Verò igne ueniat lustraturus: & tamen,
Te autore, labem omnem eximat numen Dei.
IOH. Per summam rerum harunce similitudinem,
Quæ sub oculos cadunt, quod mente solum modò
Et una cogitatione cernitur,
Id in conspectu animi uolebam ponere.
Vndam uides labeculas abstergere, &
Anhelam præterèa sitim restinguere.

is a fool, a fool? What is a woman? What, indeed, save a vain thing? And the spirit of the Lord moved upon the face of the waters!

Syr. Girl. Ha, ha, ha!

Cho. of Hero. Ha, ha, ha!

ACT II, SCENE X.

Herod, Herodias, John.

He. Wife, when I, perplexed in mind, consider what he whom they call John the Baptist has said, and when I review everything, I am greatly astonished at the grace of speech, strength of courage, and divine authority there is in him. Perchance, my dearest wife, he is some god, or some one sent by a god. With what noble bearing he fearlessly conducts himself! How sweetly sounds the voice that moves our hearts! How he surpasses in courage and boldness! What subjects, and how many of them, he has fearlessly presented! There are some among them, however, that I do not sufficiently understand. Therefore he shall be asked to repeat the thread of his discourse again. Syrian, bring the son of Zacharias before us.

Her. My husband, who would believe that this crude country fellow had such wonderful things hidden away in his heart, if they had not heard him speak?

He. You are right. Tell me, my guest, why you baptize with water, since another is coming who will baptize with fire; yet through your agency the divine power will take away all stains of sin?

John. This matter, which can only be perceived by the intellect and with thought, I wish to place before the eye of the mind, by means of the great likeness to those things which are visible to the eyes. You see that water removes stains, and also quenches panting thirst. The same power is

Eadem uis cernitur supero in flamine.
Namq; abluit fœdatam conscientiam
Nefario scelere, cor instillans nouum.
Orbis iste cùm primum tener concreuit, ac
Statua discors est rerum concordia:
Tellus haud antè gramina, herbas, arbores,
Seminaq́; produxit quouis in genere, quàm
Cœlestis aura sacrosanctusq́; Spiritus
Semel se motasset ponti per æquora.
Ita prorsus in hac forma suorum sit noua.
Quos inter nullos egregios frustus feret.
Nisi terra cordis (sic uti loquar) sui
Diuino, tanquam aqua, irrigetur Spiritu.
A me igitur undis erant abluti corpora
Pertæsi crimina, & ueniam orantes Deum,
Vt indicium certum atq; testificatio
Foret piati animi terrenis sordibus.
Item ignis ille, quo deleturus aio
Peccata Principem venturum, idem ualet.
Quippè obijectum simul materiem ut occupat,[5]
Lumen mittit lateq́; dispargit suum:
Sic quoq́; Dei summi potentia unica,
Et uiua, & efficax uirtus atq; motio
In pectora irrepens suorum hic Spiritus
Quæ abhorrent à sui natura exurit, &
Perfundit luce mentes, qua suos benè
Cœlestis hæredes regni regant gradus.
HE. Profectò splendidè dixisti & optimè.
Tu ad ista quid sentis thalami consors mei?
HER. Per mihi uidentur mira, quæ attulit, omnia.
IOH. Iam animum grauis subit res, dudŭ quæ mihi
Proposita. Quod bona Rex fiat cum uenia,
Multa monendus mihi es: sed unum præ omnibus
Habeo, quod te scire tua plurimum interest.
HER. Iohannes, ipse te lubens audiuero,

[5] Emendation:
Quippe *obijectam* simul materiem ut occupat,

seen in the Spirit from above, for it cleanses the defiled conscience of its foul sin, and renews the heart. When this new world was first formed, and the discordant concord of things was established, the earth did not produce grass, herbs, trees, and seed, each after its own kind, until the most holy breath of heaven, the Spirit of God, had moved upon the face of the waters. Just so in this new creation of His people; none of them will bear good fruit unless the soil of his heart, so to speak, is bedewed by the Holy Spirit, as by water. The bodies of the people who were weary of their sins, and asked pardon of God, were therefore washed by me, that there might be a sure sign and testimony of the soul's purification from the sins of the world. So, too, that fire, with which I say the Prince will come to take away the sins of the world, has the same power. For as soon as it seizes on what is exposed to it, it sends forth and scatters its light afar. So, also, this Spirit, this wonderful power of God, enduring, mighty, and stimulating to virtue, entering the hearts of His people, burns up what is repellent to its nature, and fills the soul with a light by which the heirs of the heavenly kingdom may direct their steps aright.

He. You have spoken most nobly indeed. What do you, my consort, think in regard to this?

Her. All that he has said seems wonderful to me.

John. Now there comes to mind a grave matter of which I have long purposed to speak. By your favor, O king, I have many counsels to give you, but there is one thing above all which greatly concerns your welfare to know.

He. I will listen gladly to you, John, whatever you may

Mihi quæcunq; de me prædicaueris
Agè, intùs liberum sermonem habebimus.

CHORVS.

Popellum uates inclytus
Dum lucis attentum nouæ
Amore incendit sedulò
Vitamq́; surgentem canit
Beatam stulti intelligunt,
Sed eruditi eam negant
Vocem se posse perpeti.
Habet narranti plebis fidem
Rudis, reiecta, ignobilis.
Adesse regni existimans
Diuini fausta tempora.
At almi Legum interpretes
Et artium ampla gloria
Et florentes honoribus,
Quæ Iohannes palàm edidit
Salutis de scientia
Nulli putabant usui.
Quis tam impudenter nos iubet
Nouam ingredi uiam? inquiunt:
Quid? nonne uatum oracula
Callemus? & Legis sacras
Tenemus consuetudines?
Vana est doctrina scilicet
Nostra & patrum persuasio?
Videte. Nolunt discere
Opinione qui sua
Periti sunt, nec fidere
Deo, qui præsidunt sibi.
Oblatrant pertinaciter,
Ita sunt cùm præcones probi

say concerning me. Come, we shall have an uninterrupted talk within.

Cho. While the famous prophet inspires the attentive people who are stirred with a constant longing for the new light, and he foretells the blessed life coming, the simple understand, but the learned cannot endure his words. The people—crude, despised, low-born—have faith in his story, and think that the blessed time of the kingdom of God is nigh at hand. But the interpreters, who cherish the law, who flourish in the dignity and the ample honors of their profession, think that what John has openly declared is of no avail toward a knowledge of salvation. 'Who is it,' they ask, 'that so boldly commands us to enter upon a new path? What! Know we not the sayings of the prophets, and do we not observe the sacred customs of the law? Is vain then our teaching, and the belief of our fathers?' See, they who are wise in their own conceit do not wish to learn; nor do those who rely on themselves wish to trust in God. They rail continually; such criers of virtue as they cannot be led

A uero abduci non queunt:
Ab ijs expugnatoribus
Tradantur horridæ neci.

ACTVS III. SCENA I.

Typhlus. Philautus.

Philaute precibus perductis iam ad exitium, Senarius.
In regia feramus pedes palatia.
Vt quemadmodum ab Essenis in urbe uellitur
Autoritas huiusce, ità hic uerti queat.
Si enim perrexerit nihil abfore suspicor,
Quin omnem Iudæam statim peruertat: &
Nos cum professione nostra exterminet.
PHI. Facilé hominem uel argumentis uicero.
Fac te Baptistam ea siue in re disputem.
Quid demŭ ait? TY. Quid? Dirigite Domino uias.
PHI. Domino uias dirigite? Nondum ergò uiam
Tenemus. Ergo èrramus, ille unus sapit.
Deo uias parate? Nondum ergò Deus
Cognoscitur. Dæmon colitur ergo malus.
TY. Nec ista occultè ait, sed publicè intonat.
PHI. Quis hunc intollerabilem hæreticum neget?
TY. Doctê concludis: Hùc precante' intrabimus.

ACTVS III. SCENA II.

Herodias. Syra.

Animi infelix in somnos nulla soluier,[6]

[6] At non infelix animi Phœnissa, nec umquam
Solvitur in somnos, oculisve aut pectore noctem
Accipit: ingeminant curæ, rursusque resurgens
Sævit amor, magnoque irarum fluctuat æstu.
Aeneid 4. 529-533.

from the path of truth; let them be given over by these stormers to a horrible death.

ACT III, SCENE I.

Typhlus, Philautus.

Ty. Philautus, now that our prayers are finished, let us betake our steps to the king's palace, so that while the influence of this man is being destroyed in the city by the Essenes, it may also be subverted here. If he should go on, I think that nothing would prevent him from perverting all Judea, and from destroying us and all our class.

Phi. I will easily overcome this man in argument. Pretend that you are the Baptist, if you will, so that I may argue the subject. What is it that he says?

Ty. What? Make straight the way for the Lord.

Phi. Make straight the way for the Lord! Therefore we do not yet have the way. So we are wandering. He alone knows. Make straight the way for the Lord. So then God is not yet known. Therefore it must be an evil spirit that is being worshiped.

Ty. He does not say these things secretly, but loudly cries them in public.

Phi. Who can deny that the man is an intolerable heretic?

Ty. You come to a wise conclusion. Let us enter here praying.

ACT III, SCENE II.

Herodias, a Syrian girl.

Her. So unhappy of mind am I that I can neither lose

Oculisne, aut pectore accipere noctĕ queo
Ingeminans curæ, rursus & redivivu' amor
Sæuit furore non ferendo exæstuans.
SY. Irarum campo idoneum adde terminum,
Quem præter nemo potest impunè currere.
HE. Quid agam? Iterum priorem irrisa coniugem
Experiar, & Philippi connubia repetam?
Quem ego sum tanto dedignata opere uirum?
Excludar hisce tam beatis nuptijs.
Deus perdat nefarium istum, talia
Qui suadet: At uerò haud diu data hæc dabit.
Nec inulta me, nec longùm enim lætabitur,
Solitam modò præstet coniunx mihi gratiam.

ACTVS III. SCENA III.

Syrus solus.

Per caput iuro, iamdudum tragœdiæ
Acerbæ apud nos excitantur & graues
Quôm enim coniunx herodiana senserat
Iugalé Iohannem tædas incessere
Tanquàm nefarias, odijs acerrimis
In huc exarsit, omnes neruos ingenij
Eò intendens, se isthoc ut exoluat metu,
Magnoperè, opinor, Herodem mouebit in
Baptistam, ad eius colloquia cùm uentum erit.
Nam uersat in animo dolo' ac dirum nefas.
Malè habet hoc, mentem quòd subinde Rex
Ei aduertit, rebusq; in agendis consulit.
Atq; ecce, ut incedunt loquentes inuicem.

myself in sleep, nor, groaning with care, can I take the night upon my eyes or upon my breast, while love returns to madden me, and rages with a fury not to be borne.

Syr. Girl. Place that bound to the field of your passions, beyond which no one can pass unpunished.

Her. What shall I do? Shall I make a laughing-stock of myself by trying to seek a union with Philip, my first husband, the man whom I so much despised? Shall I be kept out of this happy marriage? May heaven destroy that abominable man who advises such a thing! Indeed, he shall not long proclaim such things, nor shall I be unavenged, for he shall not long exult if my husband only shows me his accustomed favor.

ACT III, SCENE III.

A Syrian girl.

Syr. Girl. On my life, I swear that tragic circumstances, grave and painful, are coming upon us, for when the wife of Herod perceived that John was attacking her marriage as being impious, she was inflamed with the greatest hatred of him, and set to work with all the power of her mind to free herself from this fear. When Herod comes to speak to her, I expect that she will warn him very insistently against the Baptist, for she is revolving dreadful plots and dire wickedness in her mind. She takes it ill that the king heeds him, and consults him in the things that he is doing. Lo, here they come talking together.

ACTVS III. SCENA IIII.

Herodes. Iohannes.

Si has nuptias uel damnas, uel redarguis,
Nobi' unicam uitæ uolaptatem inuides.
Cætera quæreprehendis, sanè perpetiar:
In hoc ut à nobis nihil dissentias.
Qua liberalitate tum domum tibi,
Tum animum patefecimu' ipsum, e minimè fugit.
IOH. Non sunt, Antippa, non sunt sacra fœdera
Soluenda, nec thalami iugalis uincula,
Nisi si in decreta uis Dei committere.
Tu pacta fraterni lecti, & uiolans fidem
Potitus coniuge
Viuente adhuc à fratre rapta, quæ ex eo
Natam suscepit, atq; illam superstitem:
Facis contra fa' & iura, quæ Mosi Pater
Summus dedit, nobis Moses contradidit,
Ego tibi fero supremi præco iudicis
Quóusq́; temnes magnum ultorem criminum?
Quóusq́; iram lacesses tanti uindicis?
Resipisce, quæso, turpem amorem respue.
Per tibi opus est iam facti pœnitudine.
HER. Sanè pudet (fatebor) pigetq́; is pœnitet:
Et agnosco me iam intulisse iniurias
Thalamo germani. At hoc coniŭx mea qui feres?
Quam ego, quæ item me plus ocellis diligit.
Variæ uocant curæ scissa hùc, illùc meæ
Ancipiti cogitatione pectora.

ACTVS III. SCENA V.

Syra. Syrus. Gelasimus.

Ades dum, amâbo te Syre. Canentem audias Senarius.

ACT III, SCENE IV.

Herod, John.

He. If you condemn or disapprove of this marriage, you begrudge us our only happiness in life. I will, indeed, suffer the rest of your reproof, if only you do not differ from us in this. With what freedom our palace and our heart itself has been laid open to you, that you well know.

John. Antipas, holy vows or the bonds of marriage are not to be dissolved, unless you wish to transgress the decrees of God. You, violating honor and your brother's marriage vows, have seized upon his wife, and taken her away while he is still living, though she has a daughter by him who is also living. You are acting contrary to the laws and statutes which the Father almighty gave to Moses, and Moses delivered to us, which I, the herald of the supreme Judge, make known to you. How long will you scorn the mighty Avenger of sin? How long will you provoke the wrath of such an Avenger? Come to your senses, I beseech you! Reject this base love. You have much need of repentance for such a deed.

He. Truly, I confess that I am ashamed. I am sorry, and I repent. Now I see that I have wronged my brother's marriage-bed. But, O my wife, whom I love, and who loves me more than her very eyes, how will you bear this? My heart is rent by various cares, which call me now this way, now that, in my indecision.

ACT III, SCENE V.

A Syrian, a Syrian girl, Gelasimus.

Syr. Girl. Syrian, come here, I beg you! You should

Morionem nostrū, ut rusticam uocē uariat?
Vt occinit? insuetos ut effundit sonos?
Si interfuisses concioni huius, Syre,
Risum edisses, sat scio, supra modum.
SY. Iocabor paulùm. Heus tu, explica digitos tuos
Primus, secundus, tertius, Dimeter.
Quartus, quintus, Quot hic numero sunt?
GE. Quindecim.
SY. Ha, he Gelasime. SY. Ha, he. tetigisti rem acu.
GELA. Rides? Dabis igitur osculum. SY. Ah necquis-
SY. Tacete nam hùc Tyrannus intendit gradum. (sime.

ACTVS III. SCENA VI.

Herodes. Herodias.

Est, ô sodalis candidissima, quemadmodum Senarius.
Rebare. Connubium hoc nostrum nefas putat
Nouu' hospes. It contrà inuictis rationibus.
HER. Est hostis, haud hospes, uir acceptissime.
HER. Imo illud unum protestatur, aiens
Se mihi, tibiq; uelle consultum optimè.
He. Quid uiris ægram, coniunx ô pulcherrime?
Quid dicta me terres timentem tristia?
Si mihi quæ quondā erat, quā & esse nunc decet,
In amore uis foret: non hunc diutiùs
Ferres, canere uel cogeres Palinodiam.
Her. Ab eo permulta dicta sunt diuinitùs
Quæ cogitata (nescio quo pacta) mea
Tulere ad aspectus rerum cœlestium:
Postquàm autem uerba fecit his de nuptijs.
Reuerentia noua, & sancto ueluti metu
Vehemens quieta uox perculsit pectora.
Sed eccum nostris prodeuntem ex ædibus
Huccine puta', uxor, à gradu constantiæ
Posse unquam deijci? Modestiam audiciam

hear our fool singing. How he changes his clownish voice! How he croaks! How he pours out queer sounds! Had you been at the assembly, I know that you would have learnt to laugh beyond measure.

Syr. Now I will jest a little. Hark! Stick out your fingers; one, two, three, four, five. How many is that?

Gel. Fifteen.

Syr. Ha, ha, Gelasimus!

Syr. Girl. Ha, ha! You hit it off that time.

Gel. You laugh? Give me a kiss then?

Syr. Girl. O you bad, bad man!

Syr. Silence! For the tyrant is coming this way.

ACT III, SCENE VI.

Herod, Herodias.

He. It is just as you thought, my beautiful wife. Our new guest considers that this marriage of ours is unlawful. He opposes it with invincible arguments.

Her. He is an enemy, not a friend, dearest husband.

He. On the contrary, he declares that he wishes only the best for you and for me.

Her. Why worry me till I am ill, my noble husband? Why do you terrify me? I am afraid of these harsh words. If your love were as strong as it once was, and as it still ought to be, you would endure this man no longer, but would force him to recant.

He. Many things were admirably said by him which, I know not how, have led my thoughts to the consideration of heavenly things: and when he afterwards spoke of our marriage, a still voice filled my breast as it were with new reverence and holy fear. Did you imagine, wife, that he, going forth from our palace, can ever be turned from the path of constancy? I seem to recognize his modesty as

Videor agnoscere audacem & modestiam.
O quanto in illo maius est, quàm se refert?
Adibo. Scicitabor, Vt hominem audias.
HER. Nisi cum uiro nunc res agatur acerrimè,
Citò causam cadam, euadamq́; miserrima.
Nebulo iste nobilis tantum (heu scelus) ualet
Quem ego: Sed interim mihimet non deero.[7]

ACTVS III. SCENA VII.

Iohannes. Herodes. Chorus Plebeiorum.
Herodias. Chorus Herodianorum.

Ave Rex. HE. Et tu Iohãnes. Sed quidnam ais?
Nũ pertinax te adhuc uertet sentẽtia?
An potius coniugem mihi abreptam cupis?
IO. Sanctit lex, quod priùs monebam, Mosica:
Non posse fratris uxorem unum ducere
Alterius, & uiui, & gaudente prole. Tu
Superstite fratre, filia superstite,
Ipsius irato sponsam retines Deo.
HE. Quàm animũ perturbat hæc mẽ responsio?
Nec habeo quo defendam, & hanc amo unicè.
CH. Pleb. Cũmotus est. Amâbo res quorsum accidat,
Aduortamus. Nam & iras illa concipit.
HER. Vincor ueris Herodias. Quis hæc neget?
HERO. Ergóne dissipatio,.mi uir, fœdere
Subeunda erunt nunc fata tam crudelia?
Ergóne te propter spretæ pudiciciæ
Non ulla habetur cura aut ratio? Hæccine
Sacra illa est confirmata coniugio fides?
Data hæc est dextera? Hæ nostræ spes? hæccine
Promissa quæ nobis tam pulchra feceras?
Certè ego famæ, pudori, patriæ, uiro,
Ac omnibus te rebus unum prætuli,

[7] Quos ego—sed motos præstat componere fluctus.
Aeneid I. 135.

audacity, and his audacity as modesty. How much more there is in that man than appears! I will go to him. I will question him so that you may hear.

Her. Unless the affair with the man is now most shrewdly managed, I shall quickly lose my case, and go forth most wretched. This idle rascal has such power! Alas, the disgrace! And him I'll—but meanwhile I shall not neglect my cause.

ACT III, SCENE VII.

John, Herod, Chorus of People, Herodias, Chorus of Herod's Men.

John. Hail, O King!

He. And you, John, what say you? Has your headstrong way of thinking changed yet, or do you still wish to have my wife torn from me?

John. The Mosaic law,[8] as I told you before, decrees that a man may not take in marriage the wife of a brother, while that brother still lives, and there is a child living. You, while your brother and his daughter still live, are keeping his wife from him, thus stirring the wrath of God.

He. How this answer troubles my mind! I have no defense, and I love her exceedingly.

Cho. of Peo. He is troubled. Pray, let us see how the affair will turn out. She is growing angry.

He. I am overcome by the truth, Herodias. Who can deny these things?

Her. Then, my husband, if our union be dissolved, what a cruel fate we must endure! Shall there be no thought or care for her who spurned modesty for your sake? Is this, then, a husband's sacred vow of fidelity? Is this the pledge that was given? Is this the end of our hopes, and of the promises so fair that you made? Truly, I chose you alone in preference to good repute, to modesty, to my native land,

[8] Lev. 20. 21.

Et hanc amori tanto mercedem dabis,
Vt uerear ne cuiusquam iniqua oratio
Tam citò tædas queat pactas disiungere?
O utinam aut occupares haec præcordia
Leuior igni', aut amori par esses meo.
Quin par eris, ni fallar, an tua non sum ego
Herodias? Non es tu item Herodias meus?
At non iocos, risus, amœna, gaudia
Tecum solebam tractare arbitrio tuo?
Furtiuus haud amor noster, sed coniugium
Verum est, Iohannes quodcunq; garriat.
Palàm dextras coniunximu' idq; nemine
Redarguente præter istum Barbarum.
Agè ô marite mi, ô marite perfice,
Iunctos ut affectus tam amico uinculo[8]
Ne inepti, obscuri, agrestis atq; ignobilis
Homuncionis uerba uana distrahant.
IOH. In me loqui ferro: Tu rem perpende Rex.
Dei præ amore sperne amorem fœminæ.
Dubitabis huic mundo cœlum anteponere?
Mirum in modum te quæso Rex, quid agas uide.
HER. Sceleste orationem interpellas meam?
Quid? hunc si audi' omnium quos terra sustinet
Nequissimum, quid nobis fiet obsecro?
Odijs quem incensum dereliqui magni' ego
Philippum ad coniugem captiua deferar.
Ibi seruitutem seruitura miserriman,
Fugientem tu sequêre sponte Aretiadem.
Quæ te (si dijs placet) tam pulchrè charam habet
Acies paternas ut contra conducere
Parata sit, sitiens tuorum sanguinem
Potes hunc adhuc uultu remisso cernere?
Potes præbere aures illi? potes pati, ut
Et uiuat saluus, & domo liber tua

[8] Emendation:
Iunctos ut *affectos* tam amico uinculo.

to my husband before all things; and this you give me in return for so great a love, the fear that the wicked speech of any one may so quickly dissolve these marriage bonds! Oh that you had fired this heart with a less fervid flame, or that you loved with a passion like mine! But you will so love me, if I be not deceived. Am I not your Herodias? Are not you my Herod? Have I not been wont to supply you with jests, laughter, pleasure, and delight, according to your desire? Our love is not secret, and our marriage is a true one, let John rail as he will. We openly plighted our vows. No one has objected save this barbarian. O my husband, my husband, see that the vain words of this ignorant, low-born, boorish, worthless fellow do not separate those united by such bonds of love.

John. I desire to speak. Consider, O King. Reject the love of woman for the love of God. Do you hesitate to prefer heaven to this world? I beseech you most earnestly, O King, look to what you do.

Her. Wretch, do you interrupt my pleading? If you listen to this man, the vilest in all the world, pray, what will become of us? I shall be carried a captive to my husband, Philip, whom I have inflamed with the greatest hatred by my desertion, there to spend my life in most wretched bondage. You will willingly follow the modest daughter of Aretas,[9] who, Heaven help us! holds you so dear that, thirsting for the blood of your people, she would be ready to lead her father's army against you. Are you able to look upon this man with patience? Can you give ear to him? Can you allow him to live in safety, to enjoy your palace freely,

[9] Herod's first wife, whom he had divorced in order that he might marry Herodias, and who was now seeking revenge for the treatment she had received from him.

Fruatur, & non punita licentia
Vagetur, qui no' in hasce conijci uelit
Calamitates? Immò multetur potiùs
Vel morte digno. Nobi' enim de industria huc
Deligatu' est ab inuidis, & hostibus.
Obtestor (ô mi uir) te ego ut, si unquàm tibi
Voluptati uel oblectamento fui,
Si forma, si ingenium, si colloquia tibi,
Si amore' incenderunt: neci hunc me meritissimæ
Iam trade, ne nimius me mœror conficiat,
Et hic exanguis te cogente concidam
Questus sed nunc meos si nullos audies,
Nefanda si huius admittes hortamina,
Ac me tuam sines interfici ab hostibus:
Potiùs tu uitam hanc quam̃ absume morte, tu
Hisce manibus (qua' ego lubens exosculor)
His manibus, inquam, me iam occidito: Sic ego
Animam patiar mihi auferri cum sanguine.
O mi uir, mi uir optime, Dimeter.
Profari plura non queo
Præ lachrymis fluentibus.
O mi uir, mi uir optime.
HER. Parce metu, omitte flere. Nolo (per genium
Nostrum, mihi uxor, crede, crede) nolo ego
Reuelli à te donec durabit spiritus.
Tibi quò cessit nostri, obsecro, fiducia?
Immemores haud ita, nec ingrati sumus,
Amoris ut tui no' obliuio cœperit.[9]
IO. Caue Rex dicta ne labantur pectore:
Quae si spernis, grauiora opinione tua
Mala sequentur. Mentem regas tuam, qui aliàs
Regis, nec feminæ regendum mancipes.
HER. Toleras an hæc quae audio, nec ulcisci potes?
Vilissimus maiorem uerna sentiat.
HE. Ite simul, ite serui, quid statis? recens

[9] Emendation:
Amoris ut tui no' obliuio *ceperit.*

and to go about at will with his audacity unpunished, who seeks to plunge us into such misfortunes? Rather, let him be punished, and with the death he merits, for surely he is sent hither purposely by our envious enemies. O my husband, I beg you, if my beauty, my ability, my speech have ever been a source of pleasure to you, and have fired you with love, now give this man over to the death that he merits, that I may not perish from excess of grief, and fall lifeless here at your bidding. But now, if you will hear none of my complaints, if you will listen to the wicked exhortations of this man, if you will permit me, your own, to be slain by my enemies, rather take this life away by death, and with these hands, which I gladly kiss, kill me now. I would thus endure that my life should be taken from me, and my blood be shed. O my husband, my good husband, I cannot speak more because of my flowing tears. O my husband, my good husband!

He. Do not fear; cease your weeping. I do not wish to be parted from you while the breath of life lasts. O my wife, believe me, believe me, I implore you in the name of the guardian spirit of our house. Whither, I beg you, has your confidence in us gone? We are not so unmindful, nor so ungrateful, that forgetfulness of your love should overcome us.

John. Beware, O king, lest my words slip from your mind, for if you despise them, greater evils than you think of will follow. You who rule over the minds of others, rule your own, and do not become a bondsman to be ruled over by a woman.

Her. Can you bear these things which I hear, and not avenge them? Let this vile wretch find that you are more than a bondsman.

He. Go at once, slaves. Why do you stand? While this

Dum pectus hoc nostrum indignatio ferit,
Hunc factiosum in carcerem detrudite
Rabulam, qui nos, nostramq́; turbat animulam.
Huad temere suspicati sunt sacri, Patres
Noua te sparsum in uolgu' & praua dogmata,
Qui nos contra tam liberè audeas loqui:
Properate: ne qua meis esto dictis mora.
IOH. Deum quæcunq; propter ibo ad uincula.
Mentem propugnans cœlestem facilè fero.
Meliora, si tibi caues, sequere monitus.
HER. Sane hic auras anhelitu diuerberet
Inani. Nos curemus intus corpora.
HE. Fiat mea lux. CH. PLE. legamu' ad carcerem
Si discipulis rem dixerimus totam priùs. (gradus

ACTVS III. SCENA VIII.

Syrus solus.

Ha, ha, he. Vafris ut dissimulator à mortalibus? Senarius.
Animo hæc æquo se ferre Iohãnes ait.
Credo quidem, quia non secùs fieri potest.
Ego sic sæpè prauam audiui coniugem,
Quae coniugi quoties pœnas dedit suo,
Hæc diceret secum graui suspirio:
Animo æquo (uti decet) feremus omnia
Præsertim plus (tacitè hoc) cum uiribus ualet.

ACTVS III. SCENA IX.

Discipuli. Chorus Plebeiorum.
Iohannes.

Et oĩa hæc ultro boni accipit? CH.P. Accipit Senarij.
DIS. Cœlestis hic uir est, non morti proxuma

insult newly stirs our breast, take away this seditious fellow, and cast him into prison, this brawler who troubles us and our dear soul. The holy fathers did not without cause suspect you of preaching new heresy to the people, you who dare to speak so boldly against us. Hasten, and let there be no delay in doing our commands.

John. I will endure any chains in God's cause; as a champion of the divine will, I shall easily endure them. Being warned, take heed to yourself that you follow a better course.

Her. Let this fellow split the very air with his vain bellowing, if he likes. Let us go in and enjoy ourselves.

He. Let it be so, my light of day.

Cho. of Peo. As soon as we have told the whole thing to his followers, let us betake our steps to the prison.

ACT III, SCENE VIII.

A Syrian.

Syr. Ha, ha, ha! What pretences cunning mortals make! John says that he bears things undisturbed. I believe he bears them so, because he cannot change them. Thus I have heard a bad wife, as often as she suffered punishment from her husband, say with a heavy sigh, 'We must bear all things patiently, as is fitting, more especially (this to herself) when he is the stronger.'

ACT III, SCENE IX.

Disciples, Chorus of People, John.

Disc. And does he take all this in good part?

Cho. of Peo. He does, indeed.

Disc. This man who does not flee from punishment for

Qui ueritatis ergo supplicia fugit.
An extat inter mortales nostro duce
Præstantior? Sunt ista supra hominem, quæ agit.
Vt ut de Iesu multi magna proferant,
Sine dubio non est cum hoc æquandus tamen.
CHO.PLEB. De Iesu? Quid? Num is inceptat aliquid (noui?
DIS. Ab eo tinctos aquis est fama plurimos.
CH.PL. Hic ipsus est quĕ Iohannes nobis quasi
Potiorem se frequenter extulit uirum.
DIS. Hominis in hoc modestiam est agnoscere.
CH.PL. Ita. Nam & hic noster clari' è parentibus,
At ille à fabro obscuram originem tulit.
Macherontam (si placet) uetamu', ut certior
De rebus his fieri Baptista possiet.
IO. Custos Iesu fidissime Dimeter.
Fidentium, quo preside
Nil est usquàm periculi:
Obfirma sic pectus meum,
Nullis ut hinc terroribus
A lege desciscam tua.
DIS. Licet precantis uocem haurire: Attendite.
IO. Tu noster in cœlis pater
Cöoptasti me in filium.
Tua est Christus potentia,
Cuius cohæres ipse sum.
Sic persuasor me spiritus
Informat imo pectore.
DIS. Pax à Deo tibi sit. IO. Sit uobis item.
A te iam olim magister edocti sumus
Eam uirtutis esse conditionem, ut hoc
In seculo deuoto uanitatibus
Nil sit homines uanos quod offendat magis.
Quamobrem minùs grauatè, quod facis ipse, nunc
Ista ferimus non expectata uincula.
Hoc unum nos tamen magnoperè mouet,
Ingentem multitudinem ità adhærescere

his truthfulness, although death is nigh, is holy. Is there among mortals a nobler man than our leader? The things that he does are beyond human power. Although many have told great things of Jesus, without a doubt He ought not to be compared to this man.

Cho. of Peo. Of Jesus? Is He undertaking anything new?

Disc. There is a report that very many are being baptized by Him.

Cho. of Peo. This is He whom John often declared to us to be greater than himself.

Disc. In this the modesty of the man is to be seen.

Cho. of Peo. It is, for this man of ours comes of renowned parents, but that one had his origin from obscure working people. If it pleases you, let us toward Machærus,[10] so that the Baptist may be informed of these things.

John. O Jesus, most steadfast Guardian of those who believe on Thee, with Thee as a protector, there can be no danger anywhere. Strengthen my heart, so that through fear I depart not from Thy law.

Disc. We can hear his voice in prayer. Listen.

John. O Father in heaven, Thou hast chosen me for Thy son. Christ is the manifestation of Thy power, with whom I am co-heir. So the Spirit persuades me in the very depths of my heart.

Disc. May the peace of God be with you.

John. And with you also.

Disc. We were once taught by you, master, that in this age, given to vain things, it was the condition of virtue that there was nothing that more offends vain men. For this reason we bear these unexpected bonds the less unwillingly, as you yourself do. Nevertheless, this one thing greatly astonishes us, that a great multitude follows the Nazarene,

10 The castle of Macherus, where John was imprisoned and beheaded, was a fortress lying on the southern extremity of Peræa, at the head of the Dead Sea.

Nazaræo illi, quem quidem quondam ipsimet
Lauisti undis, totoq́; testimonium
Præbebas. Namq́; ubi antè tu uersatus es,
Multos instruit, multos tingitq́; aquis uiros.
Palæstinos per urbes nemo clarior.
IO. Magnificis nec pompis oportet, ô uiri,
Nec in, nec ostentatione splendida:[10]
Sed spiritali cum uirtute & gratia
Regnum suum auspicetur iste satrapes.
Attamen ut commonstretur euidentiùs,
Et ante oculos, interq; ponatur manus:
Addite duo, me rogate nomine:
Seruator sit ne, uates quem canunt sacri,
Futurus, expectari an alius debeat.
DIS. Adimus & mandata deferimus tua.

ACTVS III. SCENA X.

Herodias. Herodes.

Herodias infelix, quæ nunc fata impia[11] Senarij.
Te tangunt? Nullus huic dolori finis erit?
Sed spem inter, & metum dubia uitam trahes?
Nunquàm miserrimum beata, ignobilem
Præclara, iunctum libera, uilem houmnculum
Habita summo in precio, regina rusticum
Superare possis, & digna morte perdere?
At aspra uolgi odia nitentem retrahunt.
Si iuuat: uiuet causa funeris mei.
Si exitio tradam: à plebe dicar improba
Irae laxas dedisse habenas horridæ.
Nunc huc dubia, nunc illuc mente fluctus.
Animus curas in omnes hic diducitur.

[10] Emendation:
Nec *ui*, nec ostentatione splendida:

[11] Infelix Dido, nunc te facta impia tangunt.
Aeneid 4. 596.

whom you yourself once baptized with water, and to whom you bore testimony. In the place where you once dwelt he is instructing and baptizing many men with water. Throughout the cities of Palestine no man is more renowned.

John. It is not necessary, men, that this governor should found his kingdom with glittering pomp, or force, or splendid show, but with spiritual grace and virtue. Nevertheless, that it may be the more plainly manifested and be self-evident, let two of you go and ask him in my name whether he is the Saviour who the holy prophets foretold should come, or do we look for another.

Disc. We will go hence, and deliver your message.

ACT III, SCENE X.

Herod, Herodias.

Her. Unhappy Herodias! what accursed fates now come upon you! Will there be no end to this sorrow? Shall you drag on your life, ever wavering between hope and fear? Shall you, who are fortunate, never be able to overcome, and to put to the death he deserves this miserable man; him who is ignoble, while you are renowned; him a prisoner, you free; him a vile wretch, you highly regarded; him a crude country fellow, you a queen? But the bitter hatred of the common people restrains my effort. If he prevails, the author of my death lives. If I deliver him to death, I shall be called a monster by the people for having given free rein to my terrible wrath. Doubtful of mind, I turn now this way, now that. My mind is torn with cares of every sort.

HE. Quid sola sic mœres, uoluptas unica?
HER. Aderaś ne tu, mi uir? meum solatium?
HE. Nil hæsites huius de amore pectoris.
Scis ut sponte prætulerim te cunctis unam ego,
Thori & mei libens in parte locauerim,
Mutata nec loco cedit sententia.
HER. Nil ô nil suspicabar de te huius modi.
HE. Ad osculationibus frontem exporrige.
Collo implica brachium. Pergamus intrò, ubi
Naturæ nostræ iura nouabimus.

CHORVS.

Anapestici.

Ecce, ecce, malum, quo miserè gens
Quæq; laborat. Ecce, ecce malum,
Quod quà terræ, quà mare serpit,
Vt furor iste agit incautos?
Vt blanda sitis bibit ipsam animam?
Sampsons tener amor infractum
Fregit, & fortia rumpens
Molli iacuit lite subactus.
Quin hoc sale sal hominum Solomon
Immoderatè resparsus erat.
Quidnam hoc sibi uult? Meliora quidem
Sæpè uidemus, atq; probamus.
Ruimus tamen in deteriora.
Sacra eloquij maxima uirtus
Trahit innumeros, id ut arripiant:
Sed uix pauci rectè orsa tenent.
Quàm bene Saulus cœperat? Atqui
Rursus redijt suum ad ingenium.
Etiam Herodes quanto studio
Animum appulerat Archiprophetæ?
Sed & ille citò (mobilitatem

He. Why do you grieve thus alone, my sole delight?

Her. Are you come, my husband, my consoler?

He. Do not doubt my heart's love for you. You know that I freely preferred you to all, and that I gladly made you my wife, nor has there been any change in my feelings toward you.

Her. I suspected nothing of that sort in you, nothing whatever.

He. Raise up your brow for a kiss. Put your arms around my neck. Let us go in. There we will renew our vows.

Cho. Lo, behold the evil with which mankind is wretchedly afflicted, the evil which prevails on sea as well as on land! How this madness goads on the heedless! How like pleasant thirst it drinks up the very soul itself! Tender love subdued the invincible Samson; he who broke strong bonds was laid low, and overcome in the soft struggle of the couch. With this salaciousness, Solomon, the salt of the earth, was sprinkled beyond measure. What does this mean? That whereas we often see and approve what is good, nevertheless we rush on to worse things. The wonderful influence of divine power impels innumerable people to lay hold upon what is good and holy, but few persevere in what they had so well begun. How well did Saul commence, but he turned again to his former ways. With what zeal did Herod hearken to the Archprophet! But—mark the change-

Spectate hominum) animi cæcus
Cœpta reliquit. Cauti este uiri:
Inuidius Orcus ex principio
Sæpè decoro finem efficit
Perniciosum. Semina ut ille
Noxia sparsit, humiles curæ
Ad se reuocant, atq; pericli
Ingruit horror. Cauti este uiri,
Ne præsentes uana cupido
Vitæ in peiùs uosmet referat.
Plæraq; turba oblita semel
Dei in antiquum sublapsa ruit.
Cauti este uiri: Aequora scindens,
Et respiciens simul à tergo
Rectos nequeat ducere sulcos.

ACTVS IIII. SCENA I.

Dimetri. Phalecij. Syrus. Chorus Herodianorum.

Aue lux festiuissima,
Diesq́; expectatissima.
Tandem uenisti gaudijs
Tempus dicatum mollibus.
Quicquid libebit hoc die,
Idem licebit hoc die.
Hoc die citharia, lyris, tubisq́;
Cantu mellifluo, nouoq́; plausu
Omnis undiq; perstrepet popellus.
Huc huc ô socij uenite læti,
Vernis tempora floribus ligati.
Nunc ô nunc sacra festa præparemus
Herodi Domino, facetijsq́;
Canticisq́;, epulisq́;, saltibusq́;.
Nunc donis cumuletur arca sancta.

ableness of the man—blind of heart, he abandoned what he had begun. O men, beware; greedy Pluto often makes a terrible end of what had a good beginning. As Pluto scatters his evil seeds, mean cares call us to their side, and fears of danger assail. Be on your guard, O men, lest the vain desire of the present life lead you to a worse thing. The multitude, for the most part, once forgetting God, and slipping into their old way, go on to ruin. Be cautious, O men. In ploughing the field, one who looks back cannot guide the furrow aright.

ACT IV, SCENE I.

A Syrian, Chorus of Herod's Men.

Syr. Hail, festal morn, most looked-for day! At length you have come, the time dedicated to tender joys. On this day one may do whatever one pleases. On this day, with cithern, lyre, and trumpet, with sweet song and new applause, all the people everywhere make much noise. Hither, come hither, glad comrades, your temples bound with the flowers of spring. Now, O now, let us prepare the sacred festival, for Herod, our master, with merrymaking, singing, eating, and dancing; now let the sacred treasury be heaped

Rem diuinam agit ipse Rex, uidete.
CHO. Manibus idem pedibusq́; conamur Syre,
Id enim sacris ab officijs reuertimur,
Feramus hosce odores ut lectissimos,
Galbanum, onycha, stacten, thusq́; lucidum,
Quó ædis uaporentur sacræ penetralia:
Et cætera, quæ ulli erunt ministris usui.
SY. Vos ite. Reginam sequentem ego sequar.

ACTVS IIII. SCENA II.

Herodias. Tryphera. Syra.
Gelasimus. Syrus.

Hodie solennem honorem Rex Deo feret,
Largoq́; luxu conuiuas excepturus est.
Margaritas idcirco sumes: coloribus
Corpusculum fucabis: torques, & aureos
Geres annulos, & armullas: nunc deniq;
Addes artem super natiuam gratiam.
Profer (puella) chirothecas, annulos,
Gemmas, crepidulas, & mundum omnem relliquū.
SY. Vel cuncta ex isthac suppetentur cistula.
HE. Læuum cinget lacertum armilla fulgida.
Ardebit gemma pendula in medio sinu. Hic
Radios fundentem amplos carbunculum cape.
Hic fulgeat uestis unione candido.
Gerenti habe tutamen fidum jaspidem,
In isthoc orbe complicatum argenteo.
Hic Eliotropia est errare nescia.
Clarus hic Berillus est forma sexangula.
Hic uim uerbis addens Smaragdus clauditur.
Tibi ecce Magnetem, qui perficiet labris
In istis ut sedeat Suadela, & Gratia.
E collo baccatum monile pendeat.
Sine laxa uestis ad imos defluat pedes,

with gifts. See, the king himself is now performing the sacred rites.

Cho. of Hero. With hands and feet we are striving, Syrian, for that is our purpose in returning from the sacred ceremonies to bear these choicest of spices—galbanum, ointments, oil of myrrh, and clear frankincense—that the Holy of Holies of the temple may smoke with incense; other things, too, we bring, that may be of use in the sacred service.

Syr. Go. I shall follow the one who follows the queen.

ACT IV, SCENE II.

Herodias, Tryphera, a Syrian girl, Gelasimus, a Syrian.

Her. To-day the king pays solemn honors to God. He is going to receive his guests with great splendor. Therefore put on your pearls. Paint your little body with colors, wear your necklaces, your rings of gold, and your bracelets. Then, too, add art to your natural grace. Quick, girl, my ring-cases, my rings, jewels, sandals, and all the rest of my ornaments.

Syr. Girl. Here they are, all out of this casket.

Her. A shining bracelet shall encircle my left arm. Here, in the midst of my bosom, a pendant shall gleam. Here let there be a carbuncle that pours forth many rays. Here my robe shall shimmer with a large single pearl. Now take the jasper set in this silver circle, a faithful guard to the wearer. Here a striped jasper, which prevents its wearer from wandering. This shining beryl is six-angled in shape. Here is enclosed an emerald, which gives power to one's words. See, here is a loadstone for you, which shall make persuasion and grace sit upon those lips. About your neck let a necklace of pearls be hung. Let your robe hang down

Figuris ut distincta præniteat magis.
TRY. Ha, ha, he, he, uideś ne noster ut morio
Ornamento sedet capitis indutus mei?
HER. Exue homniis monstrum. Reddas, reddas mihi,
Inquam citò. Non me nosti? Colaphum cape.
GE. Noui meliùs, quàm exopto. Philippi uxor es.
HERO. Hem porrige alteram mâlam. Eñ accipe & caue
Ne omninò tale quicquam insanus effutias.
GEL. Hei ueritas odium, atq; uerbera item parit.
Dum uiuo, nunquàm ego posthàc uerum loquar.
HER. Iam eloquere cuia sim. GEL. Herodis.
HER. Sed utrius
Herodis? GEL. Adesdum, in aurem edisseram tibi:
Antippæ nunc es, quæ priùs Philippi eras.
HE. Hoc dicere est in aurĕ? Abi hinc mală in crucĕ.
Malosq; cruciatus, abi trifurcifer.
Sic ô sic nata. Cuncta te apprimè decent.[12]
Accerse fidicinem Syre: experiar equidem
Quo & orbe, quo & gestu ipsa te componere,
Motuq; quo possis uestigia ducere. Haud
Didicisti frustra, opinor, saltus effingere.
Agé dum, percussa plectra dent sonos, uago ut
Gradu uersemus orbem saltatorium.
Varios mecum, certosq; absoluito numeros
Filiola, & hinc atq; hinc procurrito gyros.
Leuibus sic sæpè pulsato pedibus solum,
Celeres sæpè hoc suspende plantas ordine
Semper agilis recto te corpore moueas.
Da nunc, amâbo, industriæ specimen tuæ.
Iam circuitus age spatiosos, collige
Iam angustŭ te in locum, iam eodem pergito
Incessu, iam uarijs ambito flexibus.
Pulchrè, ità uiuit Deus, in numerum pedes agis.

[12] Sic, sic iuvat ire sub umbras.
Aeneid 4. 660.

to your feet, so that the figured cloth may show off the more effectively.

Try. Ha, ha, ha! Do you see how our fool is sitting with my ornaments on his head?

Her. Take them off, you monster of a man. Give them to me, give them to me; quickly, I say! Do you not know me? Take that box on the ear.

Gel. I know you better than I wish. You are Philip's wife.

Her. Ha! Give me the other cheek. There, take that, and beware. Do not be mad enough to blab such things.

Gel. Alas, truth ever begets hatred, and blows as well! As long as I live I will never again speak the truth.

Her. Now tell whose I am.

Gel. The wife of Herod.

Her. But of which?

Gel. Come hither. I will explain, and whisper it in your ear. You, who are the wife of Antipas, were formerly that of Philip.

Her. Do you say this to me? Away to the hangman, and to dreadful torture! Go, you arrant knave. That is the way, my daughter. Everything is wonderfully becoming to you. Syrian, summon the lute-player. Indeed, I wish to see through what figures you can go, with what bearing you carry yourself, and how you arrange your steps. I believe that you have not learned to dance in vain. Come, then, let the lute strike up and give forth its sound, that we may tread the dancers' circle. Dear daughter, go through with me the various standard figures, and here and there do your turns. Lightly beat the ground often with your feet thus; often in this manner check your swift steps. Always, agile, move your body aright. Give me now, I pray you, an example of your art. Now make a wider circle, now withdraw into a narrow space. Now proceed with the same step, now circle with various bendings. As God lives, you mark the

Liba mihi osculum. En fragrantes accipe
Odores. Sic sic ad regem epulantem uenies
Vocata. Nunc ad templa tempus nos uocat.

ACTVS IIII. SCENA III.

Discipuli. Iohannes. Chorus
Plebeiorum.

Baptista saluos sis. IO. O aduenistis benè Senarij.
DIS. Magister, imperata tua peregimus.
Homo ille, nos ad quem legasti nuncios,
Spectantibus nobis (dictu mirabile)
Sola leuabat uoce infirma corpora,
Animis & impuros fugabat spiritus.
Tandem ora soluens: De me nil dicam opus est,
Tantùm ite (ait) hæc uati responsa reddite,
Quæ uestris hausta sunt oculis & auribus:
Fuerant qui cœci, habent per me iam luminis
Vsum. Genua trahebant qui ægra, poplite
Robusto incedunt. Lepra tabuerant quibus
Vrente membra, amara exoluntur lue.
Obstructæ nuper aures iam capiunt sonos,
Immanibus furijs curantur perciti,
Mentemq́; recipiunt ualentem & integram.
Reuiuiscunt, uigentq́; cassi lumine:
Breuiter, Amóides ut quondam prædixerat,
Nunc spiritu demissi facti humillimo,
Salutis sempiternæ optabile nuncium
Magni æstimant: quod contumaces respuunt.
Fœlix (ait) nostri quem nil offenderit,
Sed agnoscens & amplexans persuaserit
Sibi, ueram in me uno uitam consistere.
Hæc dicta ubi dederat, nos dimisit duos.
IO. Videtis ipsi nunc (comites charissimi)
Huiusce Iesu, quem uobis Deum esse tam

rhythm with your feet beautifully. Give me a kiss. Take these fragrant perfumes. So, so, you shall come when summoned to the king at the feast. Now time calls us both to the temple.

ACT IV, SCENE III.

Disciples, John, Chorus of People.

Disc. Hail to thee, John.

John. Welcome.

Disc. We have done your commands, master. Wonderful to say, while we were looking on, the man to whom you sent us with a single word relieved those infirm of body, and from the heart cast out unclean spirits. At length He opened His mouth and said: 'There is no need that I should speak concerning myself.' 'Go,' He said, 'report to the prophet only what things you have drunk in with your eyes and ears; those who were blind have now through me the use of their sight; those who dragged feeble knees now walk with firm joints; those whose members had wasted away through consuming leprosy are delivered of the odious plague; ears that lately were stopped now hear; those troubled with fierce tormenting spirits now recover sound, healthy minds; those that were dead are raised up and made whole.' In brief, as Amos once foretold, the people who were greatly cast down in spirit now highly esteem the longed-for messenger of everlasting salvation, but the perverse reject him. 'Blessed,' He said, 'is he whosoever shall not be offended in me, but who, recognizing and receiving me, is persuaded that in me alone there is eternal life.' When He had spoken these words He sent us two away.

John. Now you yourselves, dearest companions, see such works of this Jesus, whom I have so often declared to you

Crebrò affirmaui, talia opera, qualia
Nec ego, nec abtiqui uates, nec quispiam
Alius omninò perpetrauit hactenùs.
Nec obscurum est sacris rerum miracula
Haec respondêre uaticinationibus.
Et è factis qui sit, cum intelligi licet,
Etiam ad loquelas mentem nunc attendite.
Felix (ait) est, nostri quem nil offenderit.
In eo numirum omnis constat felicitas.
Ille, ille est, quo beati si uoltis fieri,
Carêre haud possitis: me autem nihil est opus.
Debetis hinc ad illum iam decedere.
Animus modò sit ipsam salutem consequi:
Nos quid moramini? nostrum præsagium
Concluditur iam: Euangelion at illius
Fusum per orbem in honore semper habebitur.
Regem inter & preconem, lucernam inter &
Solem, famulam & herum discrimen cernite.
Deinceps Christo queatis ut domino frui,
Pijs ipsum uotis uocare assuescite.
Ego interim precibus idem contendam meis.
DIS. Habemus gratias: Quod uis, uolente eo
Omnia solus qui perficit, præstabitur.

ACTVS IIII. SCENA IIII.

Herodes. Herodias. Syrus. Syra.
Chorus Herodianorum.

Viri domestici, atq; amici singuli — Senarius.
Celebrate nobiscum festa isthæc annua.
HER. O quot quot Regi uoltis & mihi bene,
Votis sacrate almum hunc diem felicibus.
SY. Inoffenso nitens sol currat lumine.
SYR. Cœlo sereno lux hæc fausta fulserit.
CH. HER. Redeat prosper dies natalis, principi
Sua referamus ut quotannis munera.

to be God, as neither I, nor the prophets of old time, nor any one else, has performed to this day. Nor is it doubtful that these miracles conform to the sacred prophecies. As it is permitted us to understand who He is from His deeds, turn your thoughts also to His words. 'Blessed,' He said, 'is he whosoever shall not be offended in me.' Doubtless in Him all our bliss lies. He, He it is whom you cannot be without if you wish to be blessed. Of me you have no need. You ought now to go hence to Him, if your desire be to follow Salvation itself. Why do you delay? Our heraldship is over, but his Gospel, spreading throughout the world, shall be held in honor for ever. See now the difference between the king and the herald, the lamp and the sun, the slave and the master. Now that you may enjoy Christ as your Lord, accustom yourself to call upon Him with holy vows. Meanwhile I will strive in my prayers to do the same.

Disc. We thank you. If He, who alone brings all things to pass, be willing, what you wish shall be done.

ACT IV, SCENE IV.

Herod, Herodias, a Syrian, a Syrian girl, Chorus of Herod's Men.

He. Men of our household, and every friend, celebrate with us this annual festival.

Her. As many as wish the king and me well, hallow this blessed day with auspicious vows.

Syr. May the sun run its shining course without a cloud.

Syr. Girl. Let the blessed light of day shine forth from a clear sky.

Cho. of Hero. O prince, may your birthday return with good fortune again and again, that we may present our gifts yearly.

ACTVS IIII. SCENA V.

Herodias. Syra. Gelasimus.
Iohannes.

Tu hic operire. Ad carcerem me confero, Senarius.
Vt sola solum paucis aggrediar uirum.
SY. Curabitur. Sed quidnă hominis? Bone uir, ubi
Fuisti dudŭ. GEL. Apud inferos. SY. Apud inferos?
Quid obsecro te, illinc uidisti? GEL. Dæmona
Prădentĕ. SY. Quid quæso te, habuit in prandiŭ?
GEL. Pharisæos & fœminas. SY. Dij te pessumè
Disperdant furcifer procax. Dimeter.
HER. Ioannes. IOH. Adsum hera. HER. Perfenestram
Aliquantisper liceat: si me, si teipsum amas, (colloqui
Ea mentem ne tuam capiat dementia,
In isthac ut uelis hæresi persistere.
Faxo, sis uinuersa in aula principis
Honoratus, muta modò sententiam.
IOH. Non est mihi loquendum aduoluntatem tuă,
Dei uoluntas cui repugnat maximè.
HER. In squallido iacebis ergò carcere.
IOH. Quantalibet perferam Deum propter mala.
HER. Siccine ais? an non? hoc mihi crede, acerrimas
Improbe dabis pœnas, ni retractaueris.
Me si lædes in cotem cadet nouacula.
Stolidus accepto non nisi cum malo sapit.
GEL. Caue Iohannes, petis cornutam bestiam.
Si me audies, scenæ seruire discito.
Viuere nequit, uersutus esse qui nequit.

ACTVS IIII. SCENA VI.

Herodes. Herodias.

Euelli ergo insita haud potest persuasio? Senarij.

ACT IV, SCENE V.

Herodias, a Syrian girl, Gelasimus, John.

Her. Close the doors here. I am going to the prison to speak a few words with this man alone.

Syr. Girl. It shall be done. But what of the man? My good sir, where have you been?

Gel. In hell.

Syr. Girl. In hell? What, pray, did you see there?

Gel. A devil having his breakfast.

Syr. Girl. What, pray, did he have for breakfast?

Gel. Pharisees and women.

Syr. Girl. May the gods completely destroy you, you insolent rogue.

Her. John!

John. Here am I, mistress.

Her. Let us speak together through the window for a while. If you have any regard for me, if you have any regard for yourself, do not be so possessed with madness as to persist in this heresy. I will make you honored throughout the court of the king, if you will but change your opinion.

John. I must not speak as you will, for God's will and yours are greatly at variance.

Her. You will lie in a squalid prison.

John. For God's sake I shall endure evils, however great.

Her. Do you speak thus to me? Believe me, wretch, I will give you the most bitter punishment unless you retract. If you attempt to hurt me, your knife will strike flint. A dolt is not wise until he has suffered evil.

Gel. Beware, John, you are pursuing a horned beast. If you will listen to me, you will learn to play a part. He cannot live who cannot be cunning.

ACT IV, SCENE VI.

Herod, Herodias.

He. Cannot this set opinion be rooted out?

HER. Animo quidĕ perstat confidentissimo.
Precio nec ullo, nec precibus impellitur
Nobiscum ut sentiat. HER. Quid ergò? HERO. Qui bonis
Flecti uerbis negat, frangatur uiribus.
HER. Modus est in promptu, caussæ prætestum haud item
HER. Deliquit, in nos egit. Ratio probabilis.
HER. Et scelerŭ purus, & æqui obseruantissimus
Plærisq; censetur. HER. Sui simillibus.
HER. Populus, quem tinxit, hunc mirum in modum colit.
HER. Rudem adamant rustici. Tu doctos interroga.
HE. Pro Messia multi, pro uate quisq; habet.
HER. In hoc alijs credes, quod se se ipsus negat.
HE. Cuiusdam singularis sit modestiæ.
HER. Illéne modestus, qui nil parcit regibus?
HE. Memorandus ortus, uitaq; inculpabilis
Faciunt audaciorem. HER. Fabula, fabula,
Absume leto, & expleas animum meum,
Iners tacebit uolgus & uariabile,
Rem posteaquam approbarint prudentes patres.
HE. At hij pauci plebis præ multitudine.
HER. Nonne meilores, quàm plures satiùs est sequi?
HE. Quid immoror multis? Obstat uirtus uiri,
Obstat uolgi tumultus & inuidentia:
Hominem cur non iubeam iam nunc interfici:
Tamen in uinculis tua manebit gratia.

Her. He persists in it with great stubbornness. No price and no prayers can move him to agree with us.

He. What then?

Her. He who refuses to yield for fair words should be subdued by force.

He. The way is obvious, but the pretext for it is not so clear.

Her. He has offended, he has acted against us.

He. But by very many he is regarded as innocent of wrongdoing, and as most observant of what is just and right.

Her. By such as are like himself.

He. The people whom he baptized honor him greatly.

Her. The ignorant admire a boor. Ask the learned.

He. Many think him the Messiah; and every one, a prophet.

Her. In this, together with others, you believe what he himself denies.

He. That may be but a mark of his singular modesty.

Her. Do you call him modest who does not spare kings?

He. His memorable birth and his stainless life render him the bolder.

Her. Tales, idle tales! Grant me my desire, and save me from death. The stupid and fickle multitude will be silent, when once the wise fathers have approved the deed.

He. But they are few compared with the multitude of people.

Her. Is it not better to follow the better class of people than mere numbers?

He. Why do I hesitate so much? The worth of the man, and the disquietude and hatred of the people, prevent me from ordering him to be put to death now. Nevertheless, in chains he shall remain for your sake.

ACTVS IIII. SCENA VII.

Herodias. Syra.

Quid nunc agam? Popellum propter scilicet Senarij.
Renuit uernă è medio maritus tollere.
SY. Equidem modis omnibus rogandum existimo,
Ab opinione ut ultrò desciscat sua.
HER. Orabam. At ille nulla cuiusquàm prece[13]
Mouetur, nec uoces audit intractabilis.
Deus (inquit) aures obstruit placidas mihi,
Vt unquàm ne uotis ausculent talibus.
Deo nimirum est hic labor, cura hæc Deum
Quiteum tangit, ipsa quo demum uiro
Fruar? Quid sperem? Immota mens illi manet
Silice durior. Inanes funduntur preces.
Flectere sed quôm nequirem orando, mox minis,
Pòst supplicijs in eum agebam. Volui adeò
Nihil inexpertum & intentum linquere.
Illa una iam sanè mihi restat uia. Huc
Incumbet omnis cura & cogitatio.
Ità qui quæ uolt, agit: quæ non uult, perferet.

ACTVS IIII. SCENA VIII.

Herodes solus.

Anime quid uersas? Cur non cæde pessimi Senarius.
Latronis amplam libertatem uindicas?
Lucrum putabit. Dignum ob hoc uita reor,
Quòd imminentem non exhorrescat necem.
Medullas an tuas uorabit ignis, &
Tamen exultabit interim securitas?
Aude anime, cœpta tanta si uis exequi,
Forsan iugali crimen abscondes face.

13 . . . Sed nullis ille movetur
fletibus, aut voces ullas tractabilis audit;
Aeneid 4. 438-9.

ACT IV, SCENE VII.

Herodias, a Syrian girl.

Her. What shall I do now? On account of the rabble, my husband refuses to do away with this low slave.

Syr. Girl. I think, indeed, that one ought to plead with him in every way, so that he may of his own accord withdraw his decision.

Her. I have begged him, but he is not moved by the entreaties of any one; he is intractable, and will not listen. 'God,' he said, 'has closed my too compliant ears, so that they shall never listen to such a thing.' That, methinks, is a work for a god, that is a subject of anxiety for a god, as to what man I should enjoy! What can I hope for? His mind remains unchanged, and harder than flint. My prayers are poured out in vain; when I could not move him by talking, I worked on him with threats, and then by imploring him upon my knees, for I wished to leave no means untried, no force unexerted. Now, indeed, there remains for me but that one way. To that all my care and thought shall turn. Thus he who does the thing he wishes, in the end brings about what he does not wish.

ACT IV, SCENE VIII.

Herod alone.

He. O mind, on what do you dwell? Why do you not give yourself perfect liberty through the death of this worst of all ranters? He will account it a gain. I deem him worthy of life, because he does not fear the death that threatens him. Shall a fire devour one's very marrow, and peace of mind meanwhile be banished? Be bold, my heart! if you wish to finish the great things that you have begun, you may perchance conceal your offense with the nuptial

Honesta quædam scelera successus efficit
Herodes siste, siste furibundum impetum.
Respice uerendos diuini mores uiri,
Quod metuit, auget, qui scelus obruit.

ACTVS IIII. SCENA IX.

Philautus. Typhlus.

Blando hactenus ultu simulauimus odium, Trimet.
Primoq; inceptu cum popello diximus,
Cautè quidem, magni nos illum pendere.
Iam multa cùm incusantem ferre non potest
Herodes, occultè instigemus ad necem.
TYPH. Et hoc autoritatem ad nostram pertinet,
Et Reginæ quoq; uehementer gratum erit.
Verùm quodnam nos crimen obiectabimus?
PHI. Inuremus rerum nouandarum notam.
TY. Satis hoc: Excogitari nil grauius potest.

ACTVS IIII. SCENA X.

Herodias sola.

Mé ne incepto meo uictam desistere?[14]
Peregrinū nec posse hūc certădo sternere?
Quó referor? quæ' ue mutat mentem insania?[15]
Stat propositum exequi (fremant omnes licèt)
Et cum quo iure, quáue abolere iniuria.
Non mens, non animus: sola deest occasio.
Furere furorem, qua in iuratum hostem queam.

[14] Haec secum: Mene incepto desistere victam,
Aeneid 1. 37.

[15] Quid loquor, aut ubi sum? Quæ mentem insania mutat?
Aeneid 4. 595.

torch. Success makes some evil deeds honest. O Herod, resist thy mad impulse, resist it! Consider how the character of this divine man ought to be reverenced. He who covers over crime with crime only makes the very thing he feared more terrible.

ACT IV, SCENE IX.

Philautus, Typhlus.

Phi. So far, with bland countenances we have concealed our hatred. At first, with the people, we cautiously said that we esteemed him highly. Now that Herod can no longer endure him, since he finds so much fault, let us secretly urge that he should be put to death.

Ty. And this not only affects our standing, but will be most pleasing to the queen. But what complaints shall we lodge against him?

Phi. We will brand him with having tried to stir up a revolution.

Ty. It is enough. No greater offense can be alleged.

ACT IV, SCENE X.

Herodias alone.

Her. Shall I, then, desist from my purpose, baffled, powerless to overthrow this stranger in the struggle? Whither am I borne? What madness turns my brain? Though all cry out against it, I shall follow my resolve to destroy him rightly or wrongly. Neither the desire nor the intention is lacking, but only the opportunity to wreak my wrath, as I may, on my sworn enemy.

ACTVS IIII. SCENA XI.

Iohannes solus.

Mortalium Rex & pater,
Qui nos habes pro filijs,
Potesq́; solus omnia:
Ago immortales gratias,
Quòd sic in terris egerim
Concessa uitæ tempora.
Nunc ergò inconcussa fide,
Lætaq́; conscientia,
Expecto securus diem
Eam, ad regnum qua transeam
A te promissum (mi pater)
Quo non potest fidelior
Solo uel cœlo existere.
Hoc ille nobis asserit,
Suo & parabit sanguine,
Cuius terrarum per plagas
Præco præcurrens extiti.
Hausit tuum qui spiritum
Materna in aluo spiritus
Membra ista linquens gaudia
Feratur ad cœlestia.

ACTVS IIII. SCENA XII.

Herodias. Herodes. Chorus Idumæorum. Chorus Herodianorum. Gelasimus. Syrus. Chorus Coëpulonum. Tryphera. Syra. Philautus. Typhlus.

Frequentes conneuenêre iam per limina
Idumæi, lucem celebraturi optimam,
Quæ prima te nobis sub auras extulit.

ACT IV, SCENE XI.

John alone.

John. O King and Father of men, who dost look upon us as Thy sons, Thou alone canst do all things. I give Thee eternal thanks that I have thus spent my allotted time of life upon the earth. Now, therefore, with unshaken faith and with untroubled conscience, I confidently await that day when I shall enter into the kingdom promised by Thee, O Father, than whom there can be none in heaven or on earth more to be trusted. He, whose herald I have been, going on before Him through the regions of the world, declares that He will purchase this with His own blood, that my spirit, which in my mother's womb drank in Thy Spirit, may, on leaving this body, be borne to heavenly joys.

ACT IV, SCENE XII.

Herodias, Herod, Chorus of Idumæans, Chorus of Herod's Men, Gelasimus, Chorus of Banqueters, Tryphera, a Syrian girl, Philautus, Typhlus.

Her. Now the Idumæans in throngs press through the gates to celebrate that day of days which first gave thee to

Et aim multi mensis accubuêre splendidis.
Famuli nec intùs desunt, qui dapibus eas
Onerent & ardentia qui ponant pocula.
Superest, aduenantes excipiamus comiter
Proceres. Nihil morati aderunt certò scio.
Agite, mensa interea sternatur orbibus
Argenteis, globato tritico, & sale.
Non cochlearia, non desint mantilia.
HE. Meritissimò quidem te, Herodias, amo,
Cui nostra tantæ sunt curæ natalica.
Tota operis hæc tuis superbit regia.
Ità lautè, splendidè, atq; liberaliter
Epulas instruxisti: aula ut omnis iam sonet
Iuuenibusq́; senibusq́;, simul plaudentibus.
Hilares audin' sonos? Tectis succedere
Libeat, & applausus dare: Atqui tu Syre
Venientes quôm primates uideris, euoca,
Eugè, eugè, euax, euax. CHO. IDV. Iò, iò, iò,
Iò, uiuat, Herodes: iò, iò, iò,
Iò, uiuat Herodes: iò, iò, iò.
GEL. Iò, iò, iò, iò, iò, iò.
CHO. HER. Ornata mensa hæc est, hera quemadmodum
Visamus iam quo struxerint modo penum, (iubet.
Quibus in manu eius extat procuratio.
GEL. Isti penum quærant, pœna hic superest mihi
Et regis & reginæ, & (si superis placet)
Puerorum huic malæ cohæret dextera.
Vtinam essem Sampson, omnes traderem neci.
CH. HE. Suo ponuntur quæq́; lances ordine:
Phasiana, cycuns, phoenicopteros, pauo,
Meleagrides, Perdices, atagênes, capo,
Anates, ficedulæ, anseres, passerculi,
Pinguis ferîna, agnina, uitulina, bubula,
Aprugna, ueruecina, & ouilla caro ad manum est.
Stant & maris rapinæ: murices, lupi,
Et ampla quam patella Rhombum sustinet.

us. Many have already reclined at the splendid tables. Nor are there servants lacking within to load those tables with the viands, and to place the glowing cups. It is left for us only to receive the coming nobles courteously. I know well that they will come with no delay. Come; in the meantime, let the table be laid with silver plates, wheaten cakes, and salt; let the spoons and napkins be ready.

He. That I should love you, Herodias, is indeed most fitting, for you have taken such great pains over our birthday feast. All the royal palace is resplendent with your work. So elegantly, splendidly, and bountifully have you ordered the feast that all the palace resounds with the applause of both old and young. Do you not hear the joyous sounds? I should like to go and bestow my applause too. And, Syrian, when you see the nobles entering, do you cry out: 'Well done! well done! bravo! bravo!'

Cho. of Idu. Hurrah! hurrah! hurrah! Long live Herod! Hurrah! hurrah! hurrah!

Gel. Hurrah! hurrah! hurrah!

Cho. of Hero. This table is set as our mistress commanded. Let us see now how they who have charge of the food have provided it.

Gel. They look for bread, but only dread awaits me; the right hand of the king and of the queen, and, if it so please the gods, of their children, too, will strike this cheek. Oh, that I were Samson, I would hand them over to slaughter.

Cho. of Hero. The dishes are now placed in order—pheasants, swans, and flamingoes. A peacock, guinea-hens, partridges, woodcock, capon, ducks, fig-peckers, geese, sparrows, fat game, lamb, veal, beef, wild boar, wether, and sheep's flesh are at hand. Here are the spoils of the sea—purple-fish, pike, and a large platter holding turbot. Here

Liba hiç adorea, hic pultes sunt candidæ:
Hic offulæ, minutal, oxygorum: hic auium
Cerebella, & odora iusculis iecuscula.
Regifico demum luxu abundant omnia
Reuolat Syrus. Mensa obseruetur. Ecce iam
In lumine est totus coëpulonem chorus.[16]
SYR. Adsunt Idumæi, & Galileides tibi:
Tuam uidere maiestatem gestiunt.
HE. Grati omnes adestis, grati adestis herculè.
GEL. Omnes aduenistis, aduenistis herculè.
Me uos incolumen uidere posse gaudeo.
HER. Saluete heroës, heroinæq; optimæ.
Diem hunc dum uestra condecorat præsentia,
Mens profectò uir ueluti renascitur.
Vultiś ne introspicere? Vulgus promiscuum
Quàm hilariter appositis uescantur ferculis?
CHO. COE. Eià, eià: plaudite, plaudite. CH. IDV. Iò,
Iò uiuat Herodes: iò, iò, iò, (iò, iò,
Iò uiuat Herodes: iò, iò, iò.
GEL. Bo, bo, bo, bo: bibat Herodes; bo, bo, bo, bo.
HER. Strepitu dum̃ turbæ personant intus atria,
Atq; uario miscentur tecta murmure:
Nos in hoc quasi recessu genio indulgebimus.
Lætiq; læta conuiuua curabimus.
HER. Niueo planè lapello hæc signtur dies.
Qua uos omens unius ergò principis.
Galiliæ totius coijstis principes.
Iam iam uos lymphas fundite
Vasis, ministri, argenteis.
Adeste, nunc clarissimi
Viri, digitis ut seruuli
Aquas odoras præbeant:
Tu subministra sedulò
Nympha, hinc & hinc mantilia.
Tu uerò, aselle, quid taces?

[16] Emendation:
In *limine* est totus coëpulonem chorus.

are cakes of spelt, here is white pottage; here are tidbits, minced meat and sauce; here are the brains of birds, and sweet-smelling little livers with broth. Truly everything is set out with regal lavishness. The Syrian hurries back. Let the table be served. See, the whole crowd of banqueters is already appearing in the doorway.

Syr. Man. The Idumæans and Galilæns have come to see your Majesty.

He. By Hercules, you are all welcome, you are all welcome!

Gel. By Hercules, you have all come, you have all come; I am glad that I am hale and hearty, and able to see you.

Her. All hail, most worthy lords and ladies. When you grace this day with your presence, my husband is born again. Do you wish to look within, and see how gayly the common people fill themselves with the food set before them?

Cho. of Banq. Ah! Well done! well done!

Cho. of Idu. Hurrah! hurrah! hurrah! Long live Herod! Hurrah! hurrah! hurrah!

Gel. Bah! bah! bah! Long drink Herod! Bah! bah! bah!

He. While the inner court resounds with the noise of the crowd, and the house is disturbed with the mingled din, we will enjoy ourselves in this nook for a time, and then, happy as we are, we will look after our happy guests.

Her. This day on which all you chiefs of Galilee assemble in honor of our prince is indeed marked with a white stone. Now, servants, pour out water in the silver basins. Come, now, most noble men, so that the servants may give you scented water for your hands. Maid, put napkins carefully here and there. You, fool, why are you silent? Are you

Nihil dices tantis uiris?
Nobis uel nomen da tuum.
GEL. Quicunq́; percupit sibi
Nomen meum dono dari,
Morio Herodis uocabitur.
CHO. COE. Ha, ha, ha, he, he, he.
HER. Dic nomen, mater quod tibi
Adhùc infantulo dedit.
GEL. Solebat mater me quidem
Prolem pulchram, formosulam, &
Scitum puellum dicere:
Amabat me mirum in modum.
Negabat nec mamas mihi
Unquàm uel octonario.
CHO. COE. Ha, he. Profectò bellulum.
Habes, ô Rex, homunculum:
Mouebit qui risus tibi,
Quandò lubebit affatim.
HE. Discumbe uita mea; nam te propter locum Senarij.
Ipse occupabo. Sis tu proxima, obsecro,
Cultissima heroina: Vosq́; proximæ.
Tribune sede: Sedete primores ordine.
Benè est. Iam prima ferunt ministri fercula.

CARMEN HERODIANORUM

Sapphicum

Splendida Herodis recolamus omnes
Festa nascentis, celebremus omnes
Hunc diem faustum, ueneremur omnes
Tempora lætè.
Ite florentes iuuenes, caputq;
Vestrum Idumaeis redimite plamis.
Plaudite huic claro niueoq́; festo
Tota corona.
HER. Ad iussa state, & epulas distribuite nunc
Famuli, passimq́; mensis uini ponite

going to say nothing to such men? Tell us at least what your name is.

Gel. Whoever longs for my name as a gift shall be called Herod's fool.

Cho. of Ban. Ha, ha, he, he, he!

Her. Tell me the name that your mother gave you when you were a baby.

Gel. My mother was wont to call me a beautiful child, a well-formed and knowing boy. She loved me wondrous well, and she never denied me her breast, even when I was eight years old.

Cho. of Ban. Ha, ha! You have a wonderful fool, O king, who will inspire you with abundant laughter whenever you are so disposed.

He. Recline, my dear, and I myself will take the place next to you. Recline next to us, most gentle lady; and you, tribune, be seated. Gentlemen, take your places according to your rank. It is well. Now the servants are bringing on the first course.

Song of Herod's Men.

Splendor of Herod, let us delight in it;
Feast of his birth, praise ye the might of it;
Day of all days, hail ye the light of it;
Happy the day!
Joyous, ye youths, scatter the flowers for it;
Palm trees of Edom, wreathe ye the bowers for it;
Praise ye the feast, shining the hours of it;
Crown it to-day.

Her. Attend to the orders; now pass the dishes, servants; and all about the tables place cups of old wine. See that

Antiqui plena pocula. Dimeter.
Curate nil desit. Vos promptas ad pinguia
Iam fercla dexteras omnes extendite.
GEL. Dictum puta, A nobis nihil fiet citiùs.
HE. Agè dum comeditur atq; libitur, musice
Suaui os oblectes cantiuncula, &
Pariter cum uoce spargat læticam lyra.
Audite lætas huc mentes aduortite.

CANTILENA MIMICA.

Hexameter.

O vigor è uino ueniens, ô succo benigne,
Tu timidos audêre iubes, leporiq; leonem
Inferis, imbelles in bella & prœlia trudis.
Tu solidum neruis robur, mentemq; ministrat.[17]
Tu Ponto lectis medicina potentior herbis
Languores languêre, sensumq; doloris
Cogis ut ipse dolor ponat. Facundia surgit
Fœcundo fœcunda mero, uerbisq; redundat.
Ergò uaganter scypho geminet lætissima turba.[18]
Guttere distincto, repetaq; Propino, propino.
HE. Bellissimè. Hem cape hoc, tuaq; labra prolue.
HER. Ama me, puer, hos minutiores Trimetri.
Irrora calices bono falerno. Phalecij.
Hæc sunt pocula fœminis bibenda
Istis egregijs, meo & marito.
Quin audi reliqua imperata, fac ut
Mox cellarius eligat ministros,
Bacchi munera læta qui propinent.
SY. Equidem sine mora præcepta exequar tua. Senarij.
HER. Nunc audiamus organicam symphoniam.

[17] Emendation:
Tu solidum neruis robur, mentemq; *ministras.*
[18] Emendation:
Ergo *uagante* scypho geminet lætissima turba.

nothing is wanting. All hold your hands ready now for the rich dishes.

Gel. Think of the old saying, 'No sooner said than done.'

He. Now, while we eat and drink, let music and sweet song delight us. Let the lyre and the voice increase our pleasure. Listen, hither turn your joyful minds.

Cho. Song of the Mimes.

O strength which comes of wine, O blessed juice,
You who command the fearful to be bold,
The timid hare to be like unto the lion,
You who impel the weak to war and battle,
And to our sinews strength and vigor bring,
More potent than the chosen herbs of Pontus,
You make our weariness become aweary,
And bitter grief to lay aside its grief.
Great eloquence arises from much wine,
And from it glorious words abundant spring.
The gladdest gathering is thrice joyful made
By this, the cup, which, passing, cries from out
Its silver throat, 'Here's health, here's health to you!'

He. Very pretty! Here, take this, and wet your lips.

Her. Boy, pray fill those smaller goblets with good Falernian. These are the cups for those noble women and my husband. But listen to the rest of my commands. See that the steward soon chooses servants to perform the glad rites of Bacchus.

Syr. Man. Indeed I will do your bidding without delay.

Her. Now let us hear the symphony. Let not the cithern,

Non cithara, non tuba, non obtumescat lyra.
Agitote dum simul sonos edant omnia.

Symphonia.

SY. Ventriculas inter frequens uersatur quæstio,
Pisce optimo qui maximè incolitur lacus:
Quis aër alitibus abundant: terra quæ
Præ cæteris edules effundit feras.
Quæ fercla molli iure natare debeant.
Quæ sicca gulæ in auernum trudi oporteat.
Nouitate quare potes adiecta cibis,
Acutiùs mandent sepulchra corporis.
Quantum intersit uariam mensam facere dapibus.
Ferunt secunda iam conserui fercula.

CARMEN HERODIANORUM

Elegiacum

Si quid habent terræ, si uasta quid æquora lautum,
  Ponitur hospitibus, Rex uenerande, tuis.
Animus adduxit mensam natalis ad istam
  Conspicuosq; Deos, conspicuasq; Deas.
Intus regali lapidosa per atria luxu
  Turba sedet repetens omina fausta tibi.
Omina fausta tibi magna dum uoce precantur,
  Plebis Idumeæ plausus ad astra uolat.

HER. I, natam accerse, cum conuiuis ut patrem Trime.
Salutet. HE. Rectè ais. Lepida est me herculè.
Iam denuò fiant concentus musici.

Symphonia.

CARMEN PROPINATORUM

Hexametrum

Accipe spumantĕ Bromo, Rex inclyte, trullă.
  Dŭ cadus egregius depromit nobile nectar, Elegiacu.

the trumpet, nor the lyre be silent. Strike up, and let all the instruments resound together.

Music.

Syr. Man. Among the epicures these questions frequently arise: 'What lake produces the very best fish? What place most abounds in birds? What country above all others furnishes the most eatable wild game? What dishes ought to swim in delicate sauce? What ought to go down dry to the depths of one's gullet? By means of what novelty can one whet the appetite to demand food more eagerly, and of how much importance is it to vary the courses at the table?' Now the servants are bringing in the second course.

Cho. of Herod's Men.

If your lands, if the seas have anything choice,
It is served to your guests, mighty king.
Love has brought to this, the feast of your birth,
Godlike women and men. Within
Marble halls and amid regal pomp sit the throng,
Entreating good omens for you—
For good omens for you loudly they pray.
The applause of the people of Edom
Reaches up even unto the glittering stars.

Her. Go, summon hither my daughter, that with the banqueters she may salute her father.

He. You say well. By Hercules, she is a charming girl. Now again let there be music.

Music.

Cho. of Ban.

Most noble king, accept this foaming beaker,
The splendid beaker glows with foaming wine.

Quisq; sua antiquo proluat ora mero.
Hoc cape tu ciantho dulcem, Regina, liquorem,
  Dum cadus egregius, &c.
Ista, Tribune, bonum dabit amphora plena falernŭ.
  Dum cadus egregius, &c.
En Baccho, Proceres, plenum cratêra beato,
  Dum cadus egregius, &c.
Splendide Rex, uino sapit hæc metreta uetusto.
  Cœlesti ambrosia patera hæc, Regina, repletur.
Incundo iste calix humore, Tribune, redundat.
Hic scyphus, Heroës, mulsum prædulce recondit.
  Dum cadus egregius, &c.
TRY. Salue mi Rex. Viri saluete amplissimi,
Epulumq; istud uobis benè uortat omnibus.
HE. Per hoc tuum capitulum in tempore aduenis,
Quid enim uobis esse potius in præsentia
Chorearum debeat iucunditatibus?
Qua in arte te puto nunc posse plurimum.
Epulis remotis, Herodias delitiæ meæ,
Placidos cum filiola lusus agas tua,
Tibi has iungens heroinas comptissimas:
Iam agite, choros iam curua indicat tibia.
Sic sic mensis addentur plena gaudia.
Incipite: Nos adsidentes intuebimur.

Saltatio.

HE. Vt insignis arte nata, Herodias, tua
Ingreditur? Vt alias longè supereminet?
Vt oris habitum fingit? Vt format sibi
Motum? Vt totius deinde gestum corporis
Cŏponit? CH. COE. O mediusfidius, Rex, nil suprà.
HE. Non sat uidisse semel, morari sed iuuat
Vsq; & iterum atq; iterum saltantem cernere.
HER. Vt omnia facis magnificè ac regaliter?
Duc tu mea orbem filiola, quæ sic places.
Regi. Hoc ipse, hoc ego, hoc omnes ualdè uolunt.

Let each one drink of this most royal liquor,
And thou, O queen, receive the fragrant beaker,
  The splendid beaker glows with ancient wine.
O tribune, taste, O taste this drink divine,
  The splendid beaker glows with ancient wine.
Most noble king, may good wine e'er befriend you!
Most lovely queen, may sweetness e'er attend you!
  The splendid beaker glows with ancient wine.
Most gallant youths, great courage this will lend you!
  The splendid beaker glows with ancient wine.

Try. All hail, my king. All hail, most noble men. May this banquet please you all!

He. By your head, you come at the right time, for what could be preferable to the delights of the dance? And in that art I think you now excel all others. Now that the feast has been removed, Herodias, my delight, with your daughter lead the figures of the dance, joining with you these most elegant ladies. Begin. Let the curved pipes sound the dance. Thus, thus, great pleasure will be given to the banqueters. Begin, we will sit and look on.

Dance.

He. With what wonderful grace, Herodias, your daughter moves! How far she surpasses all others! How she changes her expression! What telling gestures she uses! How the movements of her whole body are ordered!

Cho. of Ban. By the god of truth, O king, nothing could be better!

He. It is not enough to have seen her dance once, but it pleases us to stop to see her again and again.

Her. You do everything magnificently, regally. You, my daughter, who thus please the king, lead the circle. This, indeed, he, I, all of us keenly wish.

HER. Nouam nobis harmoniam excitate musici,
Nostra ut nouo lusu teneantur lumina.

SALTVS:

HE. Papè ore ab agregio quantum decus enitet?
Quàm grata uirtus exit uenusto è corpore?
Quos hæc dedit motus? Ità mouit spiritus,
Vti uix apud me sim præ immensa læticia.
CH. COE. Ingentes, Rex habemus omnes gratias,
Tua dignatos mensa, & hoc spectaculo
Qui expleuisti. HE. Huc ades ô puella splendida.
Posce à me quid uoles, haud frustrà poposceris.
Per supremum Iehoua, perq; regium hoc
Diadema iuro, dabitur quicquid postules,
Mediam licèt imperij partem rogaueris.

CARMEN HERODIANORUM

de secundæ mensæ bellarijs.

En portamus, Rex optime, Dimeter.
Tibi poma electissima.
En quæ mâla inter cætera.
Melimella primas obtinent
En græcula, & uoconia,
Volema, & ampullacea,
Et orbiculata, cum pyris:
Iuglandes, atq; amygdali,
Auellanæq; & castaneæ,
Hic sunt nuces, hic arborum
Scatent fœtus primarij.
TRY. Se Rex daturum quicquid exoptauero. Senarij.
Iurat. Ego, tibi (mater) quod uisum erit, petam.
HERO. Reperisti nata uiam, qua me ulciscar probè.
Ac liberasti summa solicitudine. I,
Tradi tibi protinùs in patella postules
Ioannis à ceruice diuulsum caput.
Præibo ego, ut sim in re præsente. En ocyùs

He. Musicians, awake fresh harmony, that our sight may enjoy the dance anew.

Dance.

He. Wonderful! From her fair face what glorious beauty shines! How much grace and skill there is displayed in her lovely body! What movements she makes! I am so stirred that I can scarce contain myself for my joy and pleasure.

Cho. of Ban. We, whom you have honored by your banquet, and entertained by this spectacle, all thank you greatly, O king.

He. Come here, beautiful maid. Ask of me what you will, you shall not ask in vain. By the great Jehovah, and by this kingly crown, I swear that whatever you desire shall be granted you, even unto the half of my kingdom.

Song of Herod's Men,
(sung during the dessert)

Cho. of Hero.

Most worthy King, behold the choicest fruits we bring.
See the honey-apples that excel all others;
Behold the pears of Greece, and of Voconia too;
Warden pears, pears big-bellied and round.
See here the walnuts, almonds, filberts, chestnuts,
The first fruits of our trees, in great abundance.

Try. The king swears that he will give me whatever I desire. So I come to you, mother, to know what will be best.

Her. You have found a way, my child, to avenge me well, and to free me from my greatest trouble. Go, ask that the head of John, severed from the neck, be given to you at once in a charger. I will lead the way, so that I may be there.

Properato, pectoris priusquàm ille regij
Refrigerat feruor. TRY. Mecum iste erit labor.[19]
HERO. Prosit, marite, quod edis. At saltatricula
Qualis uidebatur tibi? Dimeter.
HERO. O luce magis coniunx dilecta coniugi, an
Feres unquàm tanti partus digna præmia?
Quos lusus quanto cun decôre præbuit
Nata hic tua? Quocirca hisce testibus
Iuraui me daturum quod rogauerit.
HER. Regaliter, ut soles, dixisti decus meum.
TRY. Scio iam petituræ factum hoc silentium.
Tradi mihi protinus in patella postulo
Iohannis à ceruice diulsum caput.
HE. Dabo quodcunq; obuenerit, ne uel leuis
Vel periurus uidear. I lictor, amputa
Baptistæ caput, & in quadra positum feras.
Nihil hic non succedat uolo ex sententia.
Edite, bibite, ridete, plectra tangite.

Symphonia.

CH. HER. Ecce caput (eximia uirgo) adfertur tibi.
TRY. Genitrix ego tibi reddo charissima.
HER. Accipio quàm lubens. Quid obstupescitis?
Non periurus maritus esse uult meus,
Oditq; uel cane peiùs & angue perfidos.
TRY. Non est quod admiremur, principes uiri.
Rerum nouarum, & seditionis autor fuit.
HER. Dapibus expleti iam subite palatia.
Idumen in totam patebit hac iter.[20]
SYRA. Deum immortalem. Quod peractum nunc scelus
Non ista poscit hoc tempus spectacula.[21] (est?

[19] Mecum erit late labor: nunc qua ratione, quod instat.
Aeneid 4. 115.

[20] Emendation:
Idumen in totam patebit *hoc* iter.

[21] Non hoc ista sibi tempus spectacula poscit.
Aeneid 6. 37.

Oh, hasten quickly, quickly, before the warmth of the king's feeling cools.

Try. That shall be my work.

Her. May what you eat benefit you, my husband. But how did the little dancer please you?

He. O wife, dearer than the light of day, how can you ever be fitly rewarded for such a child? Such grace did your daughter display in her dances that I have sworn before these witnesses to give her whatsoever she desires.

Her. You have spoken royally, as is your wont, my treasure.

Try. I know that all are now silent that I may make my request. I ask that the head of John, cut off from his neck, be given me in a charger.

He. I will give it, come what may, lest I should be thought either fickle or perjured. Go, lictor, cut off the head of the Baptist, and bring it here in a charger. I desire that everything here should be as is wished. Eat, drink, laugh, strike the lyre.

Music.

Cho. of Hero. Behold the head is brought to you, most excellent maid.

Try. Dearest mother, I give it to you.

Her. I receive it gladly. Why are you silent? My husband does not wish to be forsworn, and hates those who break their word worse than a dog or a snake.

Try. There is nothing for us to be amazed at, my lords. He was the author of rebellion and sedition.

Her. Now you who have feasted, enter into the palace. All Idumæa will be free to come hither.

Syr. Girl. Immortal God! what crime has been committed now? The time demands no such sight as this.

CHORVS.

Anapestici.

Sancti ora uiri mersa cruore,
Ense nefando caput ablatum,
Medios inter gerit Heroäs
Regia mensa. Quò me uortam?
Voltis rabiem cernere Bacchis?
Voltis furias discere amoris?
Deniq; uoltis aut epulandi,
Aut saltandi noscere fructus?
Huc huc oculos uertite uestros.
Hæc hæc tacita ponite mente.
Primi ac summi fœderis omne
Cupidus cùm Rex ius uiolaret:
Facilè frangit fasq́; fidemq́;,
Tot delitijs extimulatus.
De conuiuiis quid memoretur?
Qui ad uentosi nutum domini
Nutant: quiq́; ad Nolo, parati
Referunt Nolo: Qui ad quodq́; Volo,
Reddunt etiam Volo: qui si Non
Dicitur, esse ingeminant Non.
Sin Ita dictum est, & Ita ingeminant.
Conuictorum tanto è numero
Regis amicus haud erat ullus
Qui flagitium non tolerandum
Admonitrice uoce uetaret,
Aut metuebant scilicet omnes,
Aut dira ipsi facta probabant.

ACTVS V. SCENA I.

Iehova.

Secùs tecum est Iohannes, quàm homines putăt. Senarij.

Cho. The head of the holy man, stained with blood, the head cut off by impious sword, is displayed on the king's table in the midst of great men! Whither shall I turn? Would you as a Bacchante behold madness, would you learn of the frenzy of love, in short, would you see the fruits of feasting and dancing, hither turn your eyes. Look at these things with calm mind. Since the lustful king violated all the law of the foremost and greatest compact, under the spur of so many pleasures, he readily sets at naught divine law and human rights. What shall be said of the banqueters? They, changeable as the wind, nod to their master's nod. When he says, 'I do not wish it,' they are all ready with: 'I do not wish it.' When he says, 'I wish it,' they echo: 'I wish it.' If 'No' be said, at once they reiterate 'No.' But if 'Yes' be said, they repeat 'Yes.' Out of so many guests, there was no friend of the king to advise him against committing so intolerable a crime. All, indeed, were either afraid, or else approved of the dreadful deed.

ACT V, SCENE I.

Jehovah.

Jeh. O John, it is otherwise with thee than men think.

Occulta ui uictum sequitur uictoria.
Modus extat definitus, ordoq́; stabilis,
Qui nostris continuatur in actionibus:
Per stulta terrea cœlestem sapientiam
Prodere, & Abelos per Caïnos ostendere,
Mundum per infirmum monstrare potentiam,
Per crucis ignominiam donare gloriam.
Ità nostri uarijs exagitationibus
Assuefacti, posita sui fiducia,
Nihil hæsitantes ad nos unos confugiunt.
Gaudia quibus ipsis perpetua parauimus,
Animis inæstimabilia mortalium.

ACTVS V. SCENA II.

Herodis sola.

Heu quàm ingens æstuat in corde intimo pudor?[22]
Furens ut amor? Mens ut facinoris conscia?
Me turbat ut misto dolore insania? Vt
Insultat accusatrix cogitatio?
Scio, acerba me multorum circumstant odia.[23]
Quid deinde? Oderint me herclè, dū metuāt modo,
Regina si maneo, mea quid interest?

22 . . . Aestuat ingens
Uno in corde pudor, mixtoque insania luctu,
Et Furiis agitatur amor, et conscia virtus.
Aeneid 12. 666-8.

23 . . . Scio acerba meorum
Circumstare odis: hunc, oro, defende furorem.
Aeneid 10. 905-6.

A hidden victory falls to him who is overcome by violence. There is a definite method and a fixed order which is continued in all our actions—to reveal heavenly wisdom by worldly folly, to make the Abels known by means of the Cains, to demonstrate our power by earthly weakness, to grant glory by means of the shame of the cross. Thus our people, accustomed to various persecutions, lay aside confidence in themselves, and, without hesitation, flee to us alone, for whom we have prepared everlasting joys, such as have not been conceived by the minds of men.

ACT V, SCENE II.

Herodias alone.

Her. Alas! what great shame wells up from the depths of my heart! How love rages! How conscious the soul is of guilt! How madness mingled with grief confounds me! How accusing thought reviles me! I know that the fierce hatred of many surrounds me! What then? By Hercules, let them hate me so long as they fear me! If I remain queen, what care I?

ACTVS V. SCENA III.

Chorus Plebeiorum. Syra.
Discipuli. Herodes. Syrus.

Eamus: Propter hæc epularum gaudia Trimetri.
E neruo forsitan poterit nunc eximi.
SY. Atrocem ô regem: flebile ô spectculum:
O dirum, ô horrendum, ô tyrannicum scelus.
Ferro ablatum insontis est nefario caput.
DIS. Quid est, q̆ sic gemitus das post conuiuium
Syra? Adeamus, atq; rem uocemus, obsecro,
In quæstionĕ: Omnem (Syra) quid lachrymis faciĕ
Fœdasti? Alacrem epulæ debeant reddere.
SY. Non istæ epulæ, non istæ, quas intuerier
Vix potui: mente quas, & corpore fugio.
DIS. Quid? Ecqd' obtigit damnum tibi? SY. Haud meŭ.
Sed publicum est. Referre præ lachrymis nequeo.
DIS. Siste Syra, fœmineos luctus, & rem explica.
SY. Est, est humeris abscissum Baptistæ caput,
Caput humeris abscissum, heu, quàm crudeliter?
DIS. Itáne uero? Dic, dic, Syra, facta prædicas?
SY. Hei facta, facta, & nimium uera prædico,
Rex quæ iussit, fera suadente coniuge.
DID. Tyranne uecordissime ad nutum improbæ, &
Arbitrium fœminæ, mortí ne tradis eum.
Qui uoluit atra mortis è caligine
Te ferre ad ipsa ueræ uitæ lumina? An
Virum immerito absumpsisti leto, qui tibi
Pereunti opem & salutem adferre nisus est?
Capiebat hic somnos inter securus feras.
Tu quauis tigride truculentior, haud satis
Habebas in carcerem dare, nisi dederes
Etiam neci. Sed qui fiebat obsecro?
Sceleris tanti esse quæ potuit occasio?

ACT V, SCENE III.

Chorus of the people, a Syrian girl, Disciples, Herod.

Cho. of Peo. Let us go. Perhaps because of these joys of the banquet he may now perchance be freed from prison.

Syr. Girl. O cruel king! O doleful spectacle! O dire, terrible, and tyrannical crime! The head of the innocent man has been cut off by a wicked sword.

Disc. Why is it that she thus laments after the banquet? Let us come with you, and call the thing into question, I beg of you. Why have you stained your face with weeping, Syrian? Feasts should make one joyful.

Syr. Girl. Not such feasts as these, which I could scarce bear to look upon, that I flee from body and soul.

Disc. What! Has any evil befallen you?

Syr. Girl. The injury has been done not to me alone, but to the people. I am not able to tell it for tears.

Disc. O Syrian, cease your womanly lamentations, and explain the matter.

Syr. Girl. The head of the Baptist has been cut from his shoulders! How cruelly, alas, has his head been cut from his shoulders!

Disc. Can this be true? Tell us, tell us, Syrian girl, do you speak truly?

Syr. Girl. Alas, it is true, it is true. I say what is all too true. The king commanded it, his ferocious wife urging him to it.

Disc. O mad, mad tyrant, at the beck and wish of a wicked woman, do you deliver to death him who would have brought you out of the darkness of death to the full light of true life? Have you, with unmerited death, slain him who strove to bring help and deliverance to you who were perishing? This man slept untroubled amid wild beasts, but you, more bloodthirsty than the tiger, did not judge it enough to put him in prison, but delivered him over to death. How, I beseech you, did it occur? What could be the occasion for so great a crime?

SY. Fortè Herodiadis puella saltans Phalecij.
Herodi placuit nimis nimisq́;,
Sic ut coniugis ille delicatæ
Affectusq́; meroq́; consepultus,
Ac motu salientis obstupescens,
Claram laudibus omnium intuentium
Quiduis poscere uirginem iubêret.
Matris filia persuasa uerbis
Baptistæ caput ergo postulabat
Rex tristis (simulabat ille quandam)
Ni tum (tristiciam) uolensq́; nolens
Concessit, uelut ante iure fœdus
Iurando dederat. Ferox ligatum,
Iam iam lictor eum petit: rotatq́;
Ensem fulmineum: rapitq́; ab armis
Et ceruice caput. Tremit per antra
Hic corpus, caput hic. Rubente tabo
Tota exundat humus. Ruunt repenté
Tantorum scelerum feri ministri
Conuiuisq́; gerunt caput cruentum
Discumbentibus, ac truci tyranno.
Tum lictor cupidæ dedit puellæ,
Quæ matri cupidissimæ offerebat,
Illi cùm stupuêre cæde facta:
Ridens regia. Quid stupetis? inquit,
Coniunx, Quippè meus maritus odit
Tum periura, tum negata pacta.
DIS. Fidum regem, at fidum tantummodò, fidem
Præstare cùm grauius multo est, quàm fallere.
CH. PLE. Hæccine oculis æquis alme aspectans pater?
Vatem innocentĕ, perq́; doctum, & integrŭ
Ità cadere incestæ? Quo uoltu cernere
Poterant tam dira conuiuæ spectacula?
Hijś ne auspiciis natalis est actus dies?
Datur hoc tandem uocanti ad recta premium? In

Syr. Girl. It chanced that the daughter of Herodias pleased the king beyond measure with her dancing, so that, overcome by affection for his lovely wife and by wine, and captivated by the movements of the dancer, he desired the girl, distinguished by the applause of all those looking on, to ask for what she would. The girl, persuaded by the words of her mother, therefore demanded the head of John the Baptist. The king sadly, or else pretending something of sorrow, both willing and unwilling, granted the request, since he had given his oath upon it. Now a fierce lictor seeks the fettered man. He waves his gleaming sword. He severs the head from the shoulders and trunk. A shudder runs through the cavern. Here lies the trunk, there the head. All the ground is wet with ruddy gore. The savage performers of this dreadful deed suddenly rush forth, bear the bloody head to the diners reclining at the table, and to the grim tyrant. Then the lictor gave it to the girl who desired it, and she presented it to her most eager mother. When all were stricken dumb at the murder that had been done, the queen, laughing, said, 'Why are you astonished? My husband and consort hates alike both false oaths and promises denied.'

Disc. The king keeps faith, but such faith alone as it is far worse to keep than it is to break.

Cho. of Peo. O mighty Father, canst thou see with eyes unmoved an innocent, learned, and most upright prophet fall before an incestuous woman? With what countenance could the guests behold such a dreadful sight? Was the natal day celebrated under these auspices? Is this the reward given to him who invokes what is right? Do they not

Mentem haud uenit Deum sperare iudicem?[24]
DIS. Querelas, ô socij, quid prodest fundere?
Attamen utinam fieret potestas corporis,
Humi ut possemus nunc honestè condere.
CHO. PLE. Rex prodit: Ex ipso iam postulabitur.
HE. Hui quã irrequietũ animũ gero? furijs quibus
Incensus agitor? Inire somnos dum uolo,
Qui me tremores? quæ auferunt insomnia?
Nunc usq́; & usq́; recursat promissum improbum.
Nunc sanctimonia Iohannis, & cæsi caput.
Videor mihi interdum patrijs è finibus
Exul, inops, cuiq́; contemptus mortalium,
Etiam charissima comitante Herodiade
Quercu famen in nemore concussa uincere.
Quod utinam non fuissem pollicitus mala
Tanta puellæ petaci, aut nefario
Stetissem promisso. O me atrocem, & impium.
DIS. Aue rex. Factum quôm infectum fieri nequit.
Truncum tamen nobis, & cadauer cedito:
Vt quam necessitudo nostra postulat,
Beneuolentia præstetur iusta mortuo.
HE. Abite, capite, præstate: ô dolor, dolor.
Vade Syre, reclude carcerem: ô dolor, dolor.
Quàm tædat cœli conuexa tuerier?[25]
DIS. Tumulus effodatur isthic, quo demortuus
Humetur. Ianuæ gurgustij patent.

ACTVS V. SCENA IIII.

Chorus Plebeiorum. Discipuli Iohannis.

O ploranda nimis tempora, tempora. Asclepia.

[24] Nec venit in mentem quorum consederis arvis?
Aeneid 4. 39.

[25] Mortem orat; tædet cæli convexa tueri.
Aeneid 4. 451.

expect the justice of God?

Disc. O friends, what profits it to pour forth laments? Oh, that we had the disposal of his body, so that we could commit it with honor to the earth!

Cho. of Peo. The king is coming this way. Now we will ask him himself.

He. Alas, what a troubled mind I bear with me! What furies madden and drive me! When I would sleep, what trembling seizes upon me, and what restlessness! Now, again and again, my wicked promise recurs to me, now the thought of the holiness of John and of his severed head. Sometimes I seem to see myself exiled from my fatherland, needy and despised of all men, and with my dearest companion, Herodias, striving to overcome my hunger with acorns in the forest. Would that I had not promised such evil things to the girl who besought them, or that I had not stood by my wicked promise! Woe is me, cruel and impious that I am!

Disc. Hail, king. That which is done cannot be undone. Nevertheless, give us the trunk and the dead body, so that, as our intimacy with him demands, the friendly rites may be bestowed upon the dead.

He. Go, take it. Do your office. O grief, grief! Go, Syrian, open the prison. O grief, grief! How it wearies me to live!

Disc. Here let a mound be heaped up, where the dead is to be buried. The doors of this lowly dwelling-house are open.

ACT V, SCENE IV.

Chorus of People, Disciples of John.

Cho. of Peo. O times, times much to be deplored! O

O deflenda nimis funera, funera.
DIS. Hunc nos ô sancte te aspicimus uates? Hui
Iam fœda truncus in arena relinquitur? Senarij.
Ecce, ecce cruore rubens humus madet. Quis hanc
Speciem cernendo à lachrymis sibi temperet?
CHO. PLE. O ploranda nimis, *&* c.
DIS. Reditus hij nostri, *&* expectata gaudia?[26]
Huius tua modi sunt, Herodes, hospitia?
Quantum, hei Iudæa, præsidium tibi abstulit[27]
Atra hæc dies, mersitq. acerbo funere?
CHO. PLE. O ploranda nimis, *&* c.
DIS. Nostræ lux uitæ, ità nos potuisti linquere?
Quid ô quid Christus de te iam, quid audiet?
An uerò tectum humo corpus miserabile? Et
Caput, hei, caput meretricem habere coniugem?
CHO. PLE. O ploranda nimis, *&* c.
DIS. Sepulchrum sic possum, sic actum funus est.
Voce supremum ciemus iam: Vale, uale.
CHO. PLE. Baptista Iohannes uale, uale, uale.

Τέλος

Πᾶσα ἐνί τῷ θεῷ χάρις καὶ δόξα.

[26] Hi nostri reditus, expectatique triumphi?
Aeneid II. 54.

[27] Præsidium, Ausonia, et quantum tu perdis, Iule!
Aeneid II. 58.

death much to be lamented!

Disc. Is this you that we look upon, O holy prophet? Ah, is your body thus left on the unclean sand? See, see the ground is red and wet with blood! Who, looking on such a sight, can refrain from tears?

Cho. of Peo. O times, times much to be deplored! O death most grievous!

Disc. Is this our return, and our looked-for joy? Is your hospitality of this sort, O Herod? What a helper, O Judea, has this dark day taken from you, and overwhelmed with bitter death!

Cho. of Peo. O times, times much to be deplored! O death much to be lamented!

Disc. O light of life to us, could you thus leave us? What oh what, shall Christ now hear of you? Shall He, indeed, hear of your piteous body covered with earth, and of your head possessed by that harlot-wife?

Cho. of Peo. O times, times much to be deplored! O death much to be lamented!

Disc. Thus his grave is made, thus his burial is finished. Now let us raise our last cry, Farewell! Farewell!

Cho. of Peo. John the Baptist, farewell, farewell, farewell!

The End.

To the one God be all thanks and glory.

THE SHORTER POEMS OF NICHOLAS GRIMALD

PREFACE

HENRY THE EIGHTH'S reign was comparatively peaceful. England, having settled her internal troubles, became a power to be reckoned with in European politics; this brought the country into touch with other European countries, and its intellectual life under the influence of the Renaissance. The feeling of security, which had come to the people through the establishment of a strong dynasty, made possible again the social and intellectual life which the Wars of the Roses had destroyed, and this intellectual life was quickened by relations with France and Italy. Every one was eager to know something of the 'new learning,' education spread, and men of culture and of literary attainments were no longer rare.

The Wars of the Roses had stopped literary production; in the meantime the language had changed notably, and the new writers who now sprang up had to bridge the gap. They could get little inspiration from the work of their predecessors; instead, they found it in that of foreign poets, especially those of Italy.

As education in those days was almost entirely humanistic, every educated man was familiar with versification, and the ability to write verses was not an unusual accomplishment. The poets of the time did not write for the public, but only for their own pleasure and that of their friends, among whom their compositions circulated in manuscript, for they seem to have had an aversion to allowing their works to appear in print. George Puttenham, in his *Arte of Englishe Poesie,* says of their attitude: 'Now also of such among the Nobilitie or gentrie as may be very well seene in many laudable sciences and especially in making of Poesie it is so come to passe that they have no courage to write, and if they have, yet are they loath to be known of their skill, so

I know very many notable gentlemen in the court that have written commendably and suppressed it agayne, or else suffered it to be publisht without their owne names to it: as if it were a discredit for a gentleman to seem learned, or to shew himself amorous of any good Art.'[1] The cause of this attitude might be ascribed to bashfulness, fear of criticism, or to dislike of coming before the public.

It was the custom in those days for those who were fond of poetry to keep commonplace books, poetical notebooks, in which they copied such compositions as were being circulated in manuscript and pleased them. Such a notebook as this probably served as the original for the anthology, *Songes and Sonettes*. That the idea of publishing one's poems was a new one, and probably had not occurred to many a writer's mind, may be seen from the fact that the best-known contributors, Henry Howard, Earl of Surrey, and Sir Thomas Wyatt, had been dead ten and fourteen years respectively; and two of the minor contributors, Sir Francis Bryan, and George, Lord Rochford, the ill-fated brother of Anne Bullen, were no longer living. Tottel, in presenting the book to the public, says in a half-apologetic manner: 'It resteth nowe (gentle reder) that thou think it not evill doon, to publish, to the honor of the Englishe tong, and for the profit of the studious of Englishe eloquence, those works which the ungentle horders of such treasure have heretofore envied thee.'[2]

The publication of this anthology was, as far as known, the first appearance of anything of its kind in England. Its advent on the eve of Elizabeth's accession may well be regarded as one of the notable events in the history of English letters, and marks as distinct an epoch as did the *Lyrical Ballads* of Coleridge and Wordsworth in 1798. The abandonment of worn-out epithets, the adoption of the language of the day, and the introduction of new verse-forms is due

[1] George Puttenham, *The Arte of Englishe Poesie,* Arber. London, 1869, p. 37.

[2] *Tottel's Miscellany,* London, 1870, p. 2.

to the contributors to this volume. Modern verse may be said to date from it. Henry Morley, in writing of the first years of Elizabeth's reign, says: 'The sweet spirit of song rises in the early years of Elizabeth's reign like the first chirping of birds after a thunderstorm. *Tottel's Miscellany* . . . was as a brake from which there arose immediately before the reign a pleasant carolling.'[3]

The immediate popularity of this work, and its widespread influence on literary taste and on poetry, are shown by the number of editions through which it passed, and by the many collections of poetry which were put forth in the latter part of the sixteenth century under various titles, such as: *A Paradise of Dainty Devices, A Gorgeous Gallery of Gallant Inventions, The Phœnix Nest, England's Helicon,* and *A Poetical Rhapsody.* A second edition of *Songes and Sonettes* appeared during the same year, a third appeared in 1559, and others in 1565, 1567, 1574, 1587; in all, eight editions within a period of thirty years.

That Shakespeare, who lived in the next generation, was familiar with this anthology, we know from the fact that the First Gravedigger sings four stanzas of Lord Vaux's poem contained in it, entitled *The Aged Lover Renounceth Love;* and in the *Merry Wives of Windsor,* Act I, Scene I, Master Slender says: 'I had rather than forty shillings I had my booke of *Songes and Sonettes.*'

The first edition of the anthology was an unpretentious-looking octavo, which gave little hint as to the unusual quality of its content; Tottel, however, drew attention to that in his preface, and pointed out that the verse included in the volume showed that Englishmen could write quite as good poetry as Italians. This edition, which appeared June 5, 1557, contains a short prose preface by him, entitled *The Printer to the Reder,* thirty-six poems by Surrey, ninety by Wyatt, forty by Grimald, and ninety-five by 'uncertain authors.'

[3] Henry Morley, *English Writers,* London, 1892, 8.212.

Following these are four additional poems by Surrey, and six by Wyatt. The first position in the book was accorded to the poems of Surrey, probably because of his rank.

On July 31 of the same year, less than two months after the first edition, a second was printed. In this edition Tottel's preface again appears. Then come the poems of Wyatt and Surrey, to which are added the four additional poems of the former, and the six of the latter, which appeared at the end of the first edition. Following these there are but nine of the forty poems of Grimald in the first edition. Next come the poems by uncertain authors, to which thirty-six poems are added, and last of all comes an alphabetical index of the first lines of the poems, which did not appear in the first edition.

It is notable that not only have a great part of Grimald's compositions been omitted, but also that it is those of a personal nature that have been dropped: *A funerall song, upon the deceas of Annes his moother,* his elegies on the death of his friends, William Chambers and Chambers' brother Nicholas, and verses to various women. Furthermore, his name is deleted, and the poems remaining are presented as *Songes written by N. G.* In the subsequent reprints from Tottel's press no further alterations were made.

Several theories have been advanced in regard to the cause of the editor's treatment of Grimald's work in the second edition. Arber, in the introduction of his edition of the *Miscellany,* says[4] in regard to the editorship of it: 'Of its contributors living: there were Lord Vaux, who was about 46, Grimald 39, Heywood 50, and Churchyard, 37 years of age. If to any of these four, we might assign as a guess, first the existence of the work, in conjunction with the printer; then its chief editing and supervision through the press; it would be to Grimald.' This was a reasonable

[4] *Op. cit.*, p. xv.

assumption, since Grimald as an instructor in rhetoric was doubtless a better judge of poetry than were the other three.

Secondly, Arber says:[5] 'We know that he (Grimald) was previously in business relations with the Printer of this work: for Tottel had printed in 1556 Grimald's translation of Cicero's *De Officiis,* dedicated by him, as his humble 'Oratour,' to Thirleby, Bishop of Ely; and on the 23 of April, 1558, Tottel finished a second edition of the same work.'

As his third argument, Arber adds:[6] 'Furthermore, the only poems suppressed in the revision, are Grimald's own. It may, therefore, be fairly guessed that Grimald, if not the originator, was the chief editor of this collection of poetry upon a plan then new to English literature.' If Grimald was the editor, he showed unusual modesty in regard to his work, and small appreciation of its merits, for the poems retained—*Of the IX Muses, Musonius the Philosopher's saying, Description of Vertue, Praise of Measure-keeping, Man's life after Possidonius of Crates, Metrodorus' minde to the contrarie, Of friendship, The death of Zoroas, Marcus Tullius Ciceroes death,* and *Of M. T. Cicero*—are those which for the most part have the least poetical merit.

Herman Fehse, in his dissertation on Henry Howard, Earl of Surrey,[7] gives as a probable reason for the fact that the greater part of the poems were printed anonymously, that the publisher was led to name no living authors, since they were people of rank, who avoided appearing before the public; that both the named writers were dead, and that therefore he had no reason to conceal their names; and that in order to heighten the anonymity, he changed the name of Nicholas Grimald to *N. G.* Fehse seems to have overlooked the fact that Sir Francis Bryan and George, Lord Rochford, were also dead, and that their names could have been made

[5] *Op. cit.,* p. xv.

[6] *Op. cit.,* p. xv.

[7] *Henry Howard, Earl of Surrey, ein Beitrag zur Geschichte der Petrarchismus in England,* Chemnitz, 1883.

public, too, and have added to the interest in the book and increased its sale, though it is possible that the editor did not know that they were among 'the uncertain authors.'

Heinrich Kolbe has advanced the theory[8] that the editor intended a sort of lyric-erotic anthology, in which the person of the poet retired quite into the background; that the editor, however, in order to procure the book a good reception upon its appearance in public, gave the names of the two best-known poets of that time, Surrey and Wyatt.

The anthology, however, shows no notable marks of any editorship other than those alterations mentioned. It seems more probable, since Grimald had become *persona non grata* because of his recantation during the Reformation, and because of his having betrayed his friends, the Protestant martyrs, Cranmer, Latimer, and Ridley, to the Roman Catholic prelates, that Tottel, fearing Grimald's name would injure the sale of the book, removed all of his poems with any personal allusions, and for his name substituted his initials.

In Tottel's preface, he calls the attention of the reader to the fact that the poets, whose work 'the ungentle horders up of such treasure have envied thee,' and which he now for the first time presented to the public, excelled in the art of writing in 'small parcelles,' that is, in the art of writing short lyrics, as contrasted with the cumbrous form the lyric had hitherto taken.

Notable among these short lyrics is the sonnet. No sonnet is known to have been in print in England before the coming of this book; therefore to Wyatt, Surrey, and Grimald must be given the honor of having introduced to their countrymen this form of composition, which for a time occupied every literary man's attention.

In his high service to poetry Grimald took a part that has

[8] *Metrische Untersuchungen über die Gedichte der 'Uncertain Authors' in Tottel's Miscellany,* Marburg, 1902.

not received due attention; his contribution was not alone in the field of the sonnet, but he was a pioneer in other fields. First, Grimald was a student of Greek and Latin, and a teacher of rhetoric, which in his time dealt largely with Latin versification, rather than with English prose. In consequence, his efforts are often devoted to making poetry a medium of terse and sententious expression of ideas, by applying his knowledge of classical versification to English poetry. That Grimald had composed epigrams we know from the fact that Bale records that he published a volume entitled *Carmina et Epigrammata,* which was probably a translation of poems and epigrams that he had made from the Latin or the Greek. His use of the heroic couplet for the purposes of epigram is a marked feature of his work; and that he was something of a forerunner of the classicists of the eighteenth century may be seen from the following from *Prayse of measurekepyng:*

> The auncient Time commended not for nought
> The Mean. What better thyng can there be sought?
> In meane is vertue placed: on either side,
> Both right and left, a misse a man shall slide. . . .
> Too slender building bad, as bad too grosse
> One an eye sore, the other falls to losse.
> As medicines help in measure, so (God wot)
> By overmuch the sick their bane have got.

Warton says[9] of him that he 'yields to none of his contemporaries for a choice of chaste expression and the concise elegancies of didactic versification. Some of the couplets in his poem *In Praise of Moderation* have all the smartness which marks the modern style of sententious poetry, and would have done honor to Pope's ethic epistles.'

Grimald is particularly fond of another sort of rhymed couplet, possibly in imitation of the French Alexandrine,

[9] *A History of English Poetry,* 1840, 3. 69. This comment appears only in early editions of the work.

with lines alternately twelve and fourteen syllables in length, and called 'poulter's measure.' In his *Certain rules of instruction in English verse,* George Gascoigne[10] says of it: 'It is the commonest sort of verse that we use nowadays. I know not how to name it, unless I should say that it doth consist of Poulter's measure which giveth XII for one dozen and XIV for another.' This form of versification Grimald by his skill kept from falling into a mere jingle, which it later in other hands became, and was eventually discarded. The following poems are in poulter's measure: *A True Love, Of Mirth, Man's Life after Possidonius or Crates, Metrodorus Minde to the contrarie, Of Friendship, The Garden, An Epitaphe of the ladye Margaret Lee.*

But Grimald was something more than a mere epigrammatist. In the following lines from *The Garden* and *A True Love,* he shows a feeling for nature very much akin to that of some of the poets of the seventeenth century:

Trees spred, the coverts wyde, with shadows fresh and gaye:
Full well their branched bowz defend the fervent sonne awaye.
Birds chatter, and some chirp, and some sweet tunes doo yeld:
All mirthfull, with their songs so blithe, they make both ayre and
  feeld.
The garden, it allures, it feeds, it glads the sprite:
From heavy hartes all doolful dumps the garden chaseth quite.
Strenth it restores to lims, draws, and fulfils the sight:
With chere revives the senses all, and maketh labor light.
O, what delites to us the garden ground dothe bring?
Seed, leaf, flowr, frute, herb, bee, and tree, and more, then I may sing.

—*The Garden.*

What sweet releef the showers to thirstie plants we see:
What dere delite, the blooms to beez: my true love is to me.
As fresh, as lusty vere foule winter doth exceed:
As morning bright, with scarlet sky doth passe the evenings weed.
As mellow pears above the crabs esteemed be:
So dothe my love surmount them all, whom I yet hap to se.

—*A True Love.*

10 Ed. Arber, London, 1868, p. 39.

In direct contrast to the expression of a sincere love of nature is his new treatment of the love of woman, characterized by all that pedantry and allusion which marked the writers of the later school whom Dr. Johnson called the 'metaphysical poets.' This may be seen in *The Lover to his dear, of his exceding love, The lover asketh pardon of his dere,* and *To L. I. S. A funerall song, upon the deceas of Annes his moother,* is also marked by an excess of classical allusion, but nevertheless it has much real feeling, tender regard, and genuine sorrow.

But the most important service of Grimald in the cause of poetry was his exploit in the field of blank verse—the unrhymed pentameter line. In the address of *The Printer to the Reder* of the *Miscellany,* Tottel says: 'If parhappes some misslike the statelinesse of stile removed from the rude skill of common eares: I aske help of the learned to defend their learned frendes, the authors of this work.' Evidently the 'common eares' were unused to such regular cadence as that of some of the poems included in the *Miscellany,* and especially to that of the two poems of Grimald, *The Death of Zoroas* and *On the Death of Marcus Tullius Cicero.* These poems were possibly the first published poems in blank verse in the English language. On June 21, sixteen days after the appearance of the first edition of *Songes and Sonettes,* Tottel published Surrey's translation of the second and fourth books of Virgil. This was the second appearance of blank verse in English.

There is in existence, however, another edition of Surrey's translation of Virgil which contains but one book, the fourth. The volume, which was printed by John Day for William Owen, is undated. It is thought by Gladys D. Willcock,[11] who has been interested in determining the date of its publication, to have been printed about 1554, three years previous to the appearance of Tottel's *Songes and Sonettes.*

[11] *Mod. Lang. Rev.* 14. 163-172; 15. 113-123; 17. 131-149.

The title-page of Day's edition speaks of the author as 'the late Earle of Surreye.' This places the date of publication after January 19, 1547, when Surrey was beheaded on Tower Hill. The volume was dedicated to Thomas, Duke of Norfolk, the son of Surrey, which advances the date of publication to one later than August 25, 1554, when the son of Surrey, on the death of his grandfather, became Thomas, fourth Duke of Norfolk. If the volume was printed in 1554, it must have been printed between August 25, when Surrey's son became Duke of Norfolk, and October 26; for on the latter date John Day was sent to the Tower for printing 'noyty books' (*Machyn's Diary,* p. 72). John Strype's *Ecclesiastical Memorials* (Oxford, 1822, 3. 1-320) also bears record of his commitment, and states that the books that offended were 'unsuitable to the present government,' the Roman Catholic sway of Queen Mary.

How Day came to be released is not known, but, according to Strype (*Annals of the Reformation* I. 1. 266-7), he fled over the sea. It seems strange that he should return to England before the end of Mary's reign, yet when the charter was granted to the Company of Stationers on May 4, 1556, his name appeared fifty-sixth on the list. Of the Company of Stationers, Richard Tottel was also a charter member. If his edition of Surrey's translation of the second and fourth books of Virgil, published June 21, 1557, had been registered by the Company of Stationers, Day could not without a penalty have afterward published Surrey's translation of the fourth book. But no such registration appears on the books of the Stationers' Company, the first registration of any book being on July 19, 1557. As Tottel was unprotected, Day could have printed his edition without penalty, and the more freely since he was not using Tottel's text, as Miss Willcock's collation shows.

Miss Willcock also shows that Day's edition of the fourth book was from what seems to be an earlier MS. than Tottel's, but this does not argue that it was printed earlier, but merely that an earlier MS., or rather MSS., came to Owen's hand, and Day, being ignorant that Tottel had already printed such a translation, or not caring if he had, printed this MS. That he could have been ignorant of Tottel's edition is quite possible and not improbable, since Roger Ascham in his *Scholemaster,*[12] in writing of Surrey's translation, seems to know only Day's edition.

The title-page of Day's edition calls particular attention to the fact that the translation is 'drawne into a straunge meter.' Its form is stressed; evidently it was considered that this would add to the attractiveness of the volume, and increase its sale. Previous to 1557, the English people knew nothing of the 'straunge meter' which came to them from Italy, and with which they became acquainted through the medium of *Songes and Sonettes.* It is doubtful if the advertisement of a 'straunge meter' would have appeared before that date.

Miss Willcock states that Day's career as a printer falls into two well-marked halves: in his early period, 1553-4, his work was very ordinary journeyman printing, not remarkable for finish or for workmanship; after the accession of Elizabeth (1559), he became one of the most outstanding of English printers, while the quality of his product underwent a marked improvement, due to his employment of foreign refugees. Because of the quality of the workmanship displayed in the printing of Surrey's translation of the fourth book of the *Aeneid,* she assigns the work to the earlier period. But she has overlooked the fact that this period extends to 1559, which is two years after the appearance of *Songes and Sonettes.*

In the dedicatory epistle, William Owen, for whom John Day printed the translation of the fourth book of the *Aeneid,* acknowledges the imperfections of his manuscript, and speaks of others better than his own, whose owners 'were

[12] Ed. Arber, p. 66.

more wylling that the same should be kept as a private treasure'; but he managed to borrow two other manuscripts from owners who were not so loth to have their literary treasures brought before the common gaze, and by these he corrected his manuscript. It is evident from Miss Willcock's collation that the two borrowed manuscripts which he employed were by no means perfect. Much that may seem poor typography may have been but the result of the poor quality of the manuscripts that Owen had at hand.

The statement which Miss Willcock makes in regard to the employment of refugees is an assumption. It is founded on that of E. Gordon Duff in his *Century of English Book Trade* (London, 1905, p. 58), for which he gives no authority, and which seems nothing but a surmise. As a matter of fact, Day fled from England during Mary's reign and went to the Continent, where he may or may not have acquired new ideas in regard to printing. But if he did, he does not appear to have shown them immediately upon his return to England, for not until 1566, nine years after the appearance of *Songes and Sonettes,* when Archbishop Parker became Day's patron, through whose generosity Day was able to cut new fonts, did the quality of his work notably improve.

Little reliance can be placed upon arguments in regard to workmanship in questions of the typography of this period, which is a most uncertain quantity. Furthermore, the mere necessity of a change of workmen, from any cause whatever, and the employment of workers none too skilled, might result in a radical change in output, a change which might come in a day's time. Since Day's edition is undated, it would seem that Grimald's blank verse may have claim to being the first published, until further proof can be adduced as to the priority of Surrey's. As to Grimald's verse being the more widely circulated, there can be no doubt, as the number of editions of *Songes and Sonettes* bears witness; nor can there be any doubt that Grimald, as a contributor of two specimens of blank verse to that volume, and as a teacher of rhetoric in Christ Church, must have diffused a knowledge of this new verse-form throughout England, more than did any other writer of his time.

Warton says[13] of Grimald's compositions: 'I have a suspicion that these two pieces in blank verse, if not fragments of larger works, were finished in their present state, as prolusions, or illustrative practical specimens, for our author's course of lectures in rhetoric'—a course which Grimald began at Christ Church in 1547, the year that Surrey died. But there is no reason for thinking that they could not have been written very much earlier than that, for Grimald's *Christus Redivivus,* which was written as early as 1541-2, shows him as a poet of no mean order, and a master of a variety of verse-forms, to which he calls attention in his marginal notes.

Warton, in writing further of Grimald's blank verse, says: 'To the style of blank-verse exhibited by Surrey, he added new strength, elegance, and modulation. In the disposition and conduct of his cadences, he often approaches to the legitimate structure of improved blank-verse, but we cannot suppose that he is entirely free from those dissonances and asperities, which still adhered to the general character and state of our diction.'

B. A. P. Van Dam, who made a study of Grimald's blank verse, makes the following comment:[14] 'We have thus in all no more than 203 lines of blank verse written by Grimald. There is no occasion for textual criticism, except in so far as we again, as everywhere, find a few words printed in full which the poet had intended to be shortened. . . . All the lines that show inversion of accent are of the harmonious type. In fact, unharmonious lines, i.e., such as have inversion of accent without a verse-pause preceding, are met with

[13] *Op. cit.* 3. 69.

[14] *William Shakespeare, Prosody and Text,* London, 1900, pp. 239-240.

exclusively in Surrey's blank verse, and completely disappear from all blank verse written after him, so that we shall not have to refer to them in the sequel. Grimald, who is thus found to have first rejected for English blank verse the structure of Italian or French lines, is as justly as Surrey, nay perhaps with greater right than the latter, entitled to being dignified with the name of the father of English blank verse.'

SONGES WRITTEN BY NICOLAS GRIMALD.

(from *Songes and Sonettes*)

I

A true love.

What sweet releef the showers to thirstie plants we see:
What dere delite, the blooms to beez: my true love is to mee.
As fresh, and lusty vere[1] foule winter doth exceed:
As morning bright, with scarlet sky, doth passe the evenings weed:
As melow peares above the crabs esteemed be:
So doth my love surmount them all, whom yet I hap to se.
The oke shall olives bear: the lamb, the lion fray:
The owle shall match the nightingale, in tuning of her lay:[2]
Or I let my love let slip out of mine entiere hert:
So deep reposed in my brest is she, for her desert.
For many blessed giftes, O happy, happy land:
Where Mars, and Pallas strive to make their glory most to stand
Yet, land, more is thy blisse: that, in this cruell age,
A Venus ymp,[3] thou hast brought forth, so stedfast, and so sage.
Among the muses nyne, a tenth yf Jove would make:
And to the Graces three, a fourth: her would Apollo take.
Let some for honour hoont, and hourd the massy golde:
With her so I may live, and dye, my weal cannot be tolde.

2

The lover to his dear, of his exceding love.

Phebe twise took her horns, twise layd them by,
I, all the while, on thee could set no yie.
Yet doo I live: if life you may it call,
Which onely holds my heavy hert, as thrall.

Certesse for death doo I ful often pray,
To rid my wo, and pull these pangs away.
So plaines Prometh, his womb no time to faile:
And, ayelife[1] left, had leefer, he might quaile.
I erre, orels who this devise first found,
By that gripes[2] name he cleped love unsound.
In all the town, what streat have I not seen?
In all the town, yet hath not Carie been.
Eyther thy sier restraines thy free outgate,
O woman, worthy of farre better state:
Or peeplepestered London lykes thee nought,
But pleasant ayr, in quiet countrie sought.
Perchaunce, in olds our love thou doest repeat,
And in sure place woldst every thing retreat.
Forth shall I go, ne will I stay for none,
Untyll I may fromwhere finde thee alone.
Therwhile, keep you of hands, and neck the heew:
Let not your cheeks becoom or black, or bleew.
Go with wélcoverd hed, for you incase
Apollo spied, burn wold he on your face.
Daphne, in grove, clad with bark of baytree:
Ay mee, if such a tale should ryse of thee,
Calisto found, in woods, Joves force to fell:
I pray you, let him not like you so well.
Eigh, how much dreed: Here lurks of theevs a haunt:
Whoso thou beest, preyseeker prowd, avaunt,
Acteon may teach thee Dictynnaes ire:
Of trouth, this goddesse hath as fiers a fire.
What doo I speak? O chief part of my minde.
Unto your eares these woords no way doo finde.
Wold god, when you read this, observe I might
Your voyce, and of your countinaunce have sight,
Then, for our love, good hope were not to seek:
I mought say with myself, she will be meek.
Doutlesse I coom, what ever town you keep,
Or where you woon,[3] in woods, or mountanes steep:

I coom, and if all pear not in my face,
Myself will messenger be of my case.
If to my prayer all deaf, you dare saye, no:
Streight of my death agilted shall you go.
Yet in mid death, this same shall eate my hart:
That Carie, thou wert cause of all the smart.

3

The lover asketh pardon of his dere, for fleeyng from her.

Lovers men warn the corps[1] beloved to flee,
From the blind fire in case they would live free.
Ay mee, how oft have I fledd thee, my Day?
I flee, but love bides in my brest alway.
Lo yet agayn, I graunt, I gan remove:
But both I could, and can say still, I love.
If woods I seek, cooms to my thought Adone:
And well the woods do know my heavy mone.
In gardens if I walk: Narcissus there
I spy, and Hyacints with weepyng chere:
If meads I tred, O what a fyre I feel?
In flames of love I burn from hed to heel.
Here I behold dame Ceres ymp[2] in flight:
Here bee, methynk, black Plutoes steeds in sight.
Stronds if I look upon you, the Nymphs I mynde:
And, in mid sea, oft fervent powrs I fynde.
The hyer that I clyme, in mountanes wylde,
The nearer mee approcheth Venus chylde.
Towns yf I haunt: in short, shall I all say?
There soondry fourms I view, none to my pay.
Her favour now I note, and now her yies:
Her head, amisse: her foot, her cheeks, her guyse.
In fyne, where mater wants, defauts I fayn:
Whom other, fayr: I deem, she hath soom stayn.
What boots it then to flee, sythe in nightyde,
And daytyme to, my Day is at my side?

A shade therfore mayst thou be calld, by ryght:
But shadowes, derk, thou, Day, art ever bright.
Nay rather, worldly name is not for thee:
Sithe thou at once canst in twoo places bee,
Forgive me, goddesse, and becoom my sheeld:
Even Venus to Anchise herself dyd yeeld.
Lo, I confesse my flight: bee good therfore:
Jove, oftentimes, hath pardond mee for more.
Next day, my Day, to you I coom my way:
And, yf you suffer mee, due payns wyll pay.

4

N. Vincent to G. Blackwood,
agaynst wedding.

Sythe, Blackwood, you have mynde to wed a wife:
I pray you, tell wherfore you like that life.
What? that henceforth you may live more in blisse?
I am beguylde, but you take mark amisse.
Either your fere[1] shall be defourmd: (and can
You blisful be, with flower of frying pan?)
Orels, of face indifferent: (they say
Face but indifferent will soon decay.)
Or faire: who, then, for many men semes fine.
Ne can you say, she is all holly mine.
And be she chaste (if noman chaunce to sew)
A sort of brats she bringes, and troubles new:
Or frutelesse will so passe long yeres with thee,
That scant one day shall voyd of brawlyng bee.
Hereto heap up undaunted hed, stif hart,
And all the rest: eche spouse can tell a part.
Leave then, this way, to hope for happy life:
Rather be your bed sole, and free from strife.
Or blessed state if any path be here:
It lurketh not, where women wonne so nere.

5

G. Blackwood to N. Vincent,
with weddyng.

Sythe, Vincent, I have minde to wed a wife:
You bid me tell, wherfore I like that life.
Foule will I not, faire I desire: content,
If faire me fayle, with one indifferent.
Fair, you alledge, a thousand will applie:
But, nere so oft requirde, she will denie.
Meane beautie doth soone fade: therof playn hee,
Who nothing loves in woman, but her blee.[1]
Frute if she bring, of frute is joyfull sight:
If none, what then? our burden is but light.
The rest, you ming,[2] certesse, we graunt, be great,
Stif hert, undaunted hed cause soom to freat.
But, in all thinges, inborne displeasures be:
Yea pleasure we, full of displeasure, se.
And marvail you, I looke for good estate,
Hereafter if a woman be my mate?
Oh straight is vertues path, if sooth men say
And likewise, that I seek, straight is the way.

6

The Muses.

Imps of King Jove, and quene Remembrance[1] lo,
The sisters nyne, the poets pleasant feres.
Calliope doth stately style bestow,
And worthy prayses payntes of princely peres.
Clio in solem songes, reneweth old day,
With present yeres conjoynyng age bypast.
Delitefull talke loves Comicall Thaley:
In fresh green youth, who doth like laurell last.
With voyces Tragicall sowndes Melpomen,
And, as with cheyns, thallured earr shee bindes,
Her stringes when Terpsichor dothe touche, even then

Shee toucheth hartes, and raigneth in mens mindes.
Fine Erato, whose look a lively chere
Presents, in dauncyng keeps a comely grace.
With semely gesture doth Polymnie stere:
Whose wordes holle routes of renkes[2] doo rule in place,
Uranie, her globes to view all bent,
The ninefolde heaven observes with fixed face.
The blastes Euterpe tunes of instrument,
With solace sweet hence heavie dumps to chase
Lord Phebus in the mids (whose heavenly sprite
These ladies doth inspire) embraceth all.
The graces in the Muses weed, delite
To lead them forth, that men in maze they fall.

7

Musonius the Philosophers saiyng.

In workyng well, if travell you sustaine:
Into the winde shall lightly passe the payne:
But of the deed the glory shall remaine,
And cause your name with worthy wightes to raigne.
In workyng wrong, if pleasure you attaine:
The pleasure soon shall vade,[1] and voide,[2] as vaine:
But of the deed, throughout the life, the shame
Endures, defacyng you with fowl defame:
And still torments the minde, bothe night and daye:
Scant length of time the spot can wash awaye.
Flee then ylfwading pleasures baits untreew:
And noble vertues fayr renown purseew.

8

Marcus Catoes camparison of mans life with yron.

Who wold beleeve mans life like yron to bee,
Byt proof had been, great Cato, made by thee?

For if, long time, one put this yron in ure,[1]
Folowing ech day his woork, with bysye cure:
With dayly use, hee may the metall wear,
And bothe the strength, and hardnesse eke impaire.
Again, in case his yron hee cast aside,
And carelesse long it untoucht abide:
Sythe, cankered rust invades the mettall sore,
And her fowl teeth there fastneth more and more.
So man, in case his corps hee tyre, and faint
With labor long: his strength it shall attaint.
But if in sluggard slothe the same doth lye:
That manly might will fall away, and dye:
That bodies strength, that force of wit remoove:
Hee shall, for man, a weaklyng woman proove.
Wherfore, my childe, holde twene these twaine the waye:
Nother with to much toyl thy lyms decaye,
In idle ease nor give to vices place:
In bothe who measures keeps, hee hath good grace.

9

Cleobulus the Lydians riddle.

One is my sire: my soons, twise six they bee:
Of daughters ech of them begets, you see,
Thrise ten: wherof one sort be fayr of face,
The oother doth unseemly black disgrace.
Nor this holl rout is thrall unto deathdaye,
Now worn with wastful time, but live alwaye:
And yet the same alwaies (straunge case) doth dye.
The fire, the daughters, and the soons distry.
Incase you can so hard a knot unknit:
You shall I count an Edipus in wit.

10

Concerning Virgils Eneids.

By heavens hye gift, incase revived were
Lysip,[1] Apelles, and Homer the great:
The most renowmd, and ech of them sance pere,
In gravyng, paintyng, and the Poets feat:
Yet could they not, for all their vein divine,
In marble, table, paper more, or lesse,
With cheezil, pencil, or with poyntel fyne,
So grave, so paynt, or so by style expresse
(Though they beheld of every age, and land
The fayrest books, in every toung contrived,
To frame a fourm, and to direct their hand)
Of noble prince the lively shape descrived:
As, in the famous woork, that Eneids hight,
The naamkouth[2] Virgil hath set forth in sight.

11

Of mirth.

A heavy hart, with wo encreaseth every smart;
A mirthfull minde in time of need, defendeth sorowes dart.
The sprite of quicnesse seems, by drery sadnesse slayn:
By mirth, a man to lively plight, revived is agayn.
Dolour dryeth up the bones: the sad shall sone be sick:
Mirth can preserve the kyndly helth, mirth makes the body quick.
Depe dumps do nought, but dull, not meet for man but beast.
A mery hert sage Salomon countes his continuall feast.[1]
Sad soll, before thy time, brings thee unto deaths dore:
That fond condicions have bereft, late daye can not restore.
As, when the covered heaven, showes forth a lowryng face,
Fayr Titan, with his beam of light, returns a goodly grace:
So, when our burdened brest is whelmed with clowdy thought,

A pleasant calm throughout the corps, by chereful hart is brought
Enjoye we then our joyes, and in the lorde rejoyce:
Faith makyng fast eternal joye, of joyes while wee have choyce.

12

To L. J. S.

Charis[1] the fourth, Pieris[2] the tenth, the second Cypris,[3] Jane,
One to assemblies thre adjoyned: whom Phebus fere, Diane,
Among the nymphs Oreades, might wel vouchsafe to place:
But you as great a goddesse serve, the quenes most noble grace:
Allhayle, and while, like Terpsichor, much melody you make:
Which if the field, as doth the court, enjoyd, the trees wold shake:
While latine you, and french frequent: while English tales you tel:
Italian whiles, and Spanish you do hear, and know full well:
Amid such peares, and solemne sightes, in case convenient tyme
You can (good Lady) spare, to read a rurall poets ryme:
Take here his simple sawes, in briefe; wherin no need to move
Your Ladishyp, but thus lo speakes thabundance of his love.
The worthy feates that now so much set forth your noble name,
So have in ure,[4] they still encreast, may more encrease your fame.
For though divine your doings be, yet thews with yeres may grow:
And if you stay, streight now adayes fresh wits will overgo.

Wherfore the glory got maintayne, maintayne the honour
great.
So shal the world my doom approve, and set you in that seat,
Where Graces, Muses, and Joves ymp, the joyful Venus,
raigne:
So shall the bacheler blessed bee, can such a Nymph obtaine.

13

To maistres D. A.

What cause, what reason moveth me: what fancy fils my
brains
That you I minde of virgins al, whom Britain soile sustains
Both when to lady Mnemosynes dere daughters[1] I resort,
And eke when I ye season slow deceave, with glad disport?
What force, what power have you so great, what charms
have you late found,
To pluck, to draw, to ravish hartes, and stirre out of their
stownd?[2]
To you, I trow, Joves daughter hath the lovely gyrdle lent,
That Cestos hight: wherin there bee all maner graces blent,
Allurements of conceits, of wordes the pleasurable taste:
That same, I gesse, hath she given you, and girt about your
waste
Beset with sute of precious pearl, as bright as sunny day.
But what? I am beguilde, and gone (I wene) out of the way.
These causes do not so much present your image prest,
That will I, will I, night and day, you lodge within this
brest:
Those gifts of your right worthy minde, those golden gifts
of mind
Of my fast fixed fancie fourm first mooving cause I finde:
Love of the one, and threefold powr: faith sacred, sound,
sincere:
A modest maydens mood: an hert, from clowd of envy
clere:

Wit, fed with Pallas food divine: will, led with lovely lore:
Memorie, conteining lessons great of ladies five, and fowr:
Woords, sweeter, than the sugar sweet, with heavenly nectar
dreast:
Nothing but coomly can they carp, and wonders well exprest.
Such damsels did the auncient world, for Poets penns, suf-
fise:
Which, now a dayes, welnye as rare, as Poets fyne, aryse.
Wherfore, by gracious gifts of god, you more than thrise
yblest,
And I welblest myself suppose: whom chastefull love im-
prest,
In friendships lace, with such a lasse, doth knit, and fast
combine:
Which lace no threatening fortune shall, no length of time
untwine:
And I that daye, with gem snowwhite,[3] will marke, and eke
depaynt,
With pricely pen: which Awdley, first gan mee with you
acquaint.

14

Of m. D. A.

D eserts[1] of Nymphs, that auncient Poets showe,
A r not so kouth,[2] as hers: whose present face,
M ore, than my Muse, may cause the world to knowe
A nature nobly given: of woorthy race:
S o trayned up, as honour did bestowe.
C yllene,[3] in sugerd speech, gave her a grace.
E xcell in song Apollo made his dere,
N o fingerfeat[4] Minerve hid from her sight.
E xprest in look, she hath so soverain chere,
A s Cyprian[5] once breathed on the Spartan[6] bright.
W it, wisdom, will, woord, woork, and all, I ween,
D are nomans pen presume to paint outright,
L o luyster and light: which if old time had seen,

E ntroned, shyne she should, with goddesse Fame.
Y eeld Envie, these due prayses to this dame.

15

A neew yeres gift, to the l. M. S.

Now flaming Phebus, passing through his heavenly region hye,
The uttrest Ethiopian folk with fervent beams doth frye:
And with the soon, the yere also his secret race doth roon:
And Janus, with his double face, hath it again begoon.
O thou, that art the hed of all, whom mooneths, and yeres obey:
At whose commaund bee bothe the sterres, and surges of the sea:
By powr divine, now prosper us this yere with good successe:
This well to lead, and many mo, us with thy favour blesse.
Graunt, with sound soll in body found that here we dayly go:
And after, in that countrey lyve, whence bannisht is all wo:
Where hoonger, thirst, and sory age, and sicknesse may not mell:[1]
No sense perceivs, no hert bethinks the joyes, that there do dwel.

16

An other to l. M. S.

So happy bee the course of your long life:
So roon the yere intoo his circle ryte:
That nothyng hynder your welmeanyng minde:
Sharp wit may you, remembrans redy fynde,
Perfect intelligence, all help at hand:
Styll stayd your thought in frutefull studies stand.
Hed framed thus may thother parts well frame,
Divine demeanour wyn a noble name:
By payzed[1] doom with leasure, and good heed:

By upright dole, and much avayling deed:
By hert unthirld,[2] by undiscoomfite chere,
And brest discharged quite of coward fere:
By sobermood, and orders coomly rate:
In weal, and wo, by holdyng one estate.
And to that beauties grace, kynde hath you lent,
Of bodies helth a perfite plight bee blent.
Dame fortunes gifts may so stand you in sted,
And hee, who gives these graces not in vayn,
Direct your deeds, his honour to maintain.

17

To l. K. S.

To you, madame, I wish, bothe nowe, and eke from yere to yere
Strength with Debore, with Judith faith, with Maudlen zeal, Anns chere
With blessed Mary modest moode: like Sibill, life full long:
A mynde with sacred sprite enspired, with fresh, and body strong:
And, when of your forepointed fate you have outroon the race:
Emong all these, in Joves hye raygn of blisses full, a place.

18

To l. E. S.

As this first daye of Janus youthe restores unto the yere:
So bee your minde in coorage good revived, and herty chere.
And as dame Tellus labreth now her frutes conceived to breed:
Right so of your most forward wit may great avail proceed.
So lucky bee the yere, the mooneths, ye dayes, ye howrs,
That them, with long recours, you may enjoy in blisful bowrs.

19

To m. D. A.

Gorgeous attire, by art made trym, and clene,
Cheyn, bracelet, perl, or gem of Indian river,
To you I nil, ne can (good Damascene)
This time of Janus Calends, here deliver.
But, what, My hert: which, though long sincs certain
Your own it was, aye present at your hest:
Yet here itself doth it resigne agayn,
Within these noombers closde. Where, think you best
This to repose? There, I suppose where free
Minerve you place. For it hath you embraste,
As thHeliconian Nymphs: with whom, even hee,
That burn for soom, Apollo liveth chaste.
Presents in case raarnesse you esteem:
O Lord, how great a gift shall this then seem?

20.

To m. S. H.

To you this present yere full fayre, and fortunable fall,
Returning now his prime part: and, good luck therwithall,
May it proceed: and end, and oft return, to glad your hert:
O Susan, whom among my frendes I count, by your desert.
Joy may your heavenly sprite: endure fresh wit, in ye fyne brayn:
Your knowledge of good things encreas: your body, safe remain:
A body, of such shape, as showeth a worthy wight by kynde:
A closet, fit for to contein the vertues of that minde.
What shall I yet moreover add? God graunt, with pleasaunt mate
A pleasaunt life you lead. Well may that man rejoyse his fate.

21

To his familiar frend.

No image carved with coonyng hand, no cloth of purple dye,
No precious weight of metall bright, no silver plate gyve I:
Such gear allures not hevenly herts: such gifts no grace they bring:
I lo, yat know your minde, will send none such, what then? nothing.

22

Description of Vertue.

What one art thou, thus in torn weed yclad?
Vertue, in price,[1] whom auncient sages had.
Why, poorely rayd? For fadyng goodes past care.
Why doublefaced? I marke eche fortunes fare.
This bridle, what? Mindes rages to restrain.
Tooles why beare you: I love to take great pain.
Why, winges? I teach above the starres to flye.
Why tread you death? I onely cannot dye.

23

Prayse of measure-kepyng.

The auncient time commended, not for nought,
The mean, what better thing can ther be sought?
In mean, is vertue placed: on either side,
Bothe right, and left, amisse a man shall slide.
Icar, with fire hadst thou the mid way flown,
Icarian beck[1] by name had no man known.
If middle path kept had proud Phaeton,
No burning brand this erth had falln upon.
Ne cruell powr, ne none to soft can raign:
That keeps a mean, the same shall styll remain.
Thee, Julie, once did too much mercy spill:
Thee, Nero stern, rigor extreem did kill,
How could August so many yeres well passe?

Nor overmeek, nor overferse[2] he was.
Worship not Jove with curious fancies vain.
Nor him despise: hold right atween these twayn.
No wastefull wight, no greedy goom is prayzed.
Stands largesse just, in egall balance payzd.
So Catoes meal surmountes Antonius chere.
And better fame his sober fare hath here,
To slender buildyng, bad: as bad, to grosse:
One, an eyesore, the tother falls to losse.
As medicines help, in measure: so (God wot)
By overmuch, the sick their bane have got.
Unmeet mee seems to utter this, mo wayes:
Measure forbids unmeasurable prayse.

24

Mans life after Possidonius or Crates.

What path list you to tred? what trade will you assaye?
The courts of plea, by braul, and bate, drive gentle peace away.
In house, for wife, and childe, there is but cark, and care:
With travail, and with toyl ynough, in feelde wee use to fare.
Upon the seas lieth dreed: the riche in foraine land,
Doo fear the losse: and there, the poore like misers poorly stand.
Strife, with a wife, without, your thrift full hard to see:
Yong brats, a trouble: none at all, a maym it seems to bee:
Youth, fond: age hath no hert, and pincheth all to nye.
Choose then the leefer of these twoo, no life, or soon to dye.

25

Metrodorus minde to the contrarie.

What race of life ronne you? what trade will you assaye?
In courts, is glory gott, and witt encreased daye by daye.
At home, we take our ease, and beak[1] ourselves in rest:

The feelds our nature doo refresh with pleasures of the best.
On seas, is gayn to gett: the straunger, hee shall bee
Esteemed, having much: if not, none knoweth his lack, but hee.
A wife will trym thy house: no wife? then thou art free.
Brood is a lovely thing: without, thy life is loose to thee.
Yong bloods be strong: old fires in double honour dwell.
Doo waye that choys, no life, or soon to dye, for all is well.

26

Of Lawes.

When princes lawes, with reverend right, do keep ye commons under
As meek as babes, thei do their charge, and scatter not asunder.
But if they raise their heads aloft, and lawe her brydle slake:
Then, like a tyger fell, they fare, and lust for law they take.
Where water dothe prevail, and fire, no mercy they expresse:
But yet the rage of that rude rout is much more mercilesse.

27

Of frendship.

Of all the heavenly gifts, that mortall men commend,
What trusty treasure in the world can countervail a frend?
Our helth is soon decayd: goodes, casuall, light, and vain:
Broke have we seen the force of powr, and honour suffer stain.
In bodies lust, man doth resemble but base brute.
True vertue gets, and keeps a frend, good guide of our pursute:
Whose harty zeal with ours accords, in every case:
No terme of time, no space of place, no storme can it deface.
When fickle fortune fayls, this knot endureth still:

Thy kin out of their kinde may swarve, when frends owe thee good wil.
What sweeter solace shall befall, than one to finde,
Upon whose brest thou mayst repose the secrets of thy minde?
Hee wayleth at thy wo, his tears with thine be shed:
With thee doth hee all joyes enjoye: so leef a life is led:
Behold thy frend, and of thy self the pattern see:
One soull, a wonder shall it seem, in bodies twain to bee.
In absence, present, riche in want, in sicknesse sownd,
Yea, after death alive, mayst thou by thy sure frend be found.
Ech house, ech towne, ech realm by stedfast love dothe stand:
Where fowle debate breeds bitter bale, in eche divided land.
O frendship, flowr of flowrs: O lively sprite of life,
O sacred bond of blissful peace, the stalworth staunch of strife:
Scipio with Lelius didst thou conjoyn[1] in care,
At home, in warrs, for weal and wo, with egall faith to fare.
Gesippus eke with Tite,[2] Damon with Pythias,
And with Menclus sonne[3] Achill, by thee combined was.
Euryalus, and Nisus gave Virgil cause to sing:[4]
Of Pylades doo many rymes, and of Orestes ring.
Down Theseus went to hell, Pirith, his frend, to finde:
O yat the wives, in these our dayes, were to their mates so kind.
Cicero, the frendly man, to Atticus,[5] his frend,
Of frendship wrote: such couples lo dothe lott but seeldom lend.
Recount thy race, now ronne: how few shalt thou there see,
Of whome to saye: This same is hee, that never fayled mee.
So rare a jewel then must nedes be holden dere:
And as thou wilt esteem thyself, so take thy chosen fere.
The tyrant, in dispayre, no lack of gold bewayls:

But, Out I am undoon (sayth hee) for all my frendship fayls.
Wherfore sins nothing is more kindely for our kinde:
Next wisdome, thus that teacheth us, love we the frendful minde.

28

The Garden.

The issue of great Jove, draw nere you, Muses nine:
Help us to praise the blisfull plott of garden ground so fine.
The garden gives good food, and ayd for leaches cure:
The garden, full of great delite, his master doth allure.
Sweet sallet[1] herbs bee here, and herbs of every kinde:
The ruddy grapes, the seemly frutes bee here at hand to finde.
Here pleasans wanteth not, to make a man full fayn:
Here marveilous the mixture is of solace, and of gain.
To water sondry seeds, the forowe by the waye
A ronning river, trilling down with liquor, can convay.
Beholde, with lively heew, fayr flowrs that shyne so bright:
With riches, like the orient gems, they paynt the molde in sight.
Beez, humming with soft sound, (their murmur is so small)
Of blooms and blossoms suck the topps, on dewed leaves they fall
The creping vine holds her own bewedded elms:
And, wandering out with branches thick, reeds folded overwhelms.
Trees spred their coverts wyde, with shadows fresh and gaye:
Full well their branched bows defend the fervent sonne awaye.
Birds chatter, and some chirp, and some sweet tunes doo yeld:
Allmirthfull, with their songs so blithe, they make both ayre and feeld.

The garden, it allures, it feeds, it glads the sprite:
From heavy hartes all doolfull dumps the garden chaseth quite.
Strength it restores to lims, draws, and fulfils the sight:
With chere revives the senses all, and maketh labour light.
O, what delites to us the garden ground doth bring?
Seed, leaf, flowr, frute, herb, bee, and tree, and more then I may sing.

29

An epitaph of Sir James Wilford knight.

The worthy Wilfords body, which alyve,
Made both the Scot, and the Frenchman sore adrad:
A body, shapte of stomake stout to strive
With forein foes: a corps, that coorage had
So full of force, the like nowhere was ryfe:
With hert, as free, as ere had gentle knight:
Now here in grave (thus chaungeth ay, this lyfe)
Rests, with unrest to many a wofull wight
Of largesse great, of manhod, of forecast
Can ech good English souldiour bear record.
Speak Laundersey,[1] tell Muttrel[2] maruails past:
Crye Musselborough:[3] prayse Haddington[4] thy lord,
From thee that held both Scots, and frekes of Fraunce:
Farewel, may England say, hard is my chaunce.

30

An other, of the same knightes death.

For Wilford wept first men, then ayr also,
For Wilford felt the wayters wayfull wo.
The men so wept: that bookes abrode which bee,
Of moornyng meeters full a man may see.
So wayld the ayr: that, clowds consumde, remaynd
No dropes, but drouth the parched erth sustaynd.
So greeted[1] floods: that, wher ther rode before
A ship, a car may go safe on the shore.

Left were nomo, but heaven, and erth, to make,
Throughout the world, this greef his rigor take.
But sins the heaven this Wilfords goste dothe keep,
And erth, his corps: saye mee, why shold they weep?

31

An Epitaph of the ladye Margaret Lee.

1555.

Man, by a woman lern, this life is what we may call:
Blod, frendship, beauty, youth, attire, welth, worship, helth and al
Take not for thine: not yet thy self as thine beknow.
For having these, with full great prayse, this lady did but show
Her self unto the world; and in prime yeres (bee ware)
Sleeps doolful sister, who is wont for no respect to spare,
Alas, withdreew her hence: or rather softly led:
For with good will I dare well saye, her waye to him shee sped:
Who claymed, that he bought: and took that erst hee gave:
More meet than any worldly wight, such heavenly gems to have.
Now wold shee not return, in earth a queen to dwell.
As shee hathe doon to you, good frend, bid lady Lee, farewell.

32

Upon the tomb of A. W.

Myrrour of matrones, flowr of spouslike love,
Of fayr brood frutefull norsse, poor peoples stay,
Neybors delite, true hert to him above,
In yeeldig worlds encreas took her decaye:
Who printed lives yet in our hertes alway:
Whose closet of good thews, layd here a space,
Shall shortly with the soull in heaven have place.

33

Upon the deceas of W. Ch.

Now, blythe Thaley, thy feastfull layes lay by
And to resound these doolful tunes apply.
Cause of great greef the tyrant death imports:
Whose ugsoom idoll to my brayns resorts.
A gracefull ymp, a flowr of youth, away
Hath she bereft (alas) before his daye.
Chambers, this lyfe to leave, and thy dear mates,
So soon doo thee constrayn envyous fates?
Oh, with what wit, those maners, that good hert,
Woorthy to lyve olde Nestors yeres thou wert.
You wanted outward yies: and yet aryght
In stories, Poets, oratours had sight.
Whatso you herd, by lively voyce, exprest,
Was soon reposde within that mindefull brest.
To mee more pleasant Plautus never was,
Than those conceits, that from your mouth did passe.
Our studiemates great hope did hold alway,
You wold be our schooles ornament, one day.
Your parents then, that thus have you forgone,
Your brethren eke must make theyr heavy mone:
Your lovyng feres cannot theyr teares restrayn:
But I, before them all, have cause to playn:
Who in pure love was conjoyned with thee,
An other Grimald didst thou seem to bee.
Ha lord, how oft wisht you, with all your hart,
That us no chaunce a sonder might depart?
Happy were I, if this your prayer tooke place:
Ay mee, that it dothe cruell death deface.
Ah lord, how oft your sweet woords I repeat,
And in my mynde your woonted lyfe retreat?
O Chambers, O thy Grimalds mate moste dere?
Why hath fell fate tane thee, and left him here?
But wherto these companions in vain make wee?[1]

Such woords in wyndes to waste, what mooveth mee?
Thou holdst the haven of helth, with blisfull Jove:
Through many waves, and seas, yet must I rove.
Not woorthy I, so soon with thee to go:
Mee styll my fates reteyn, bewrapt in wo.
Live, our companion once, now lyve for aye:
Heavens joyes enjoy, whyle wee dye day by daye.
You, that of faith so sure signes here exprest,
Do triumph now, nodout, among the blest:
Have changed sea for porte, darknesse for light,
An inn for home, exile for countrey right,
Travail for rest, straunge way for citie glad,
Battail for peas, free raign for bondage bad.
These wretched erthly stounds who can compare
To heavenly seats, and those delites moste rare?
We frayl, you firm: we with great trouble tost,
You bathe in blisse, that never shall bee lost,
Wherfore, Thaley, renew thy featfull layes:
Her doolfull tunes my chered Muse now stayes.

34

Of N. Ch.

Why, Nicolas, why doest thou make such haste
After thy brother? Why goest thou so? To taste
Of changed lyfe with hym the better state?
Better? yea best of all, that thought can rate.
Or, did the dreed of wretched world drive thee
Lest thou this afterall should hap to see:
Mavortian[1] moods, Saturniam furies fell,
Of tragicall turmoyls the haynous hell?
O, whose good thews in brief cannot be told,
The hartiest mate, that ever trod the mold:
If our farewell, that here live in distresse,
Avayl, farewell, the rest teares do suppresse.

35

A funerall song, upon the deceas of
Annes his moother.

Yea, and a good cause why thus should I playn.
For what is hee, can quietly sustayn
So great a grief, with mouth as styll, as stone?
My love, my lyfe, of joye my jeewell is gone.
This harty zeale if any wight disproove,
As womans work, whom feeble minde doth moove:
Hee neither knowes the mighty natures laws.
Nor touching elders deeds hath seen old saws.
Martius,[1] to vanquish Rome, was set on fire:
But vanquisht fell, at moothers boon, his ire.
Into Hesperian land Sertorius[2] fled,
Of parent aye cheef care had in his hed.
Dear weight on shoulders Sicil brethren bore,[3]
While Etnaes gyant spouted flames full sore.
Not more of Tyndars ymps[4] hath Sparta spoke,
Than Arge[5] of charged necks with parents yoke.[6]
Nor onely them thus dyd foretyme entreat:
Then, was the noorsse[7] also in honour great.
Caiet the Phyrgian from amid fireflame
Rescued, who gave to Latine stronds the name.
Acca,[8] in double sense Lupa ycleaped,
To Romane Calendars a feast hath heaped.
His Capra Jove among the sterres hath pight:
In welkin clere yet lo she shineth bryght.
Hyades as gratefully Lyai[9] did place
Whom, in primetide,[10] supports the Bulls fayr face
And should not I expresse my inward wo,
When you, most lovyng dam, so soon hence go.
I, in your frutefull woomb conceyved, born was,
Whyle wanderyng moon ten moonths did overpasse.
Mee, brought to light, your tender arms sustaynd:
And, with my lips, your milky paps I straynd.

You mee embraced, in bosom soft you mee
Cherished, as I your onely chylde had bee.
Of yssue fayr with noombers were you blest:
Yet I, the bestbeloved of all the rest.
Good luck, certayn forereadyng moothers have,
And you of mee a speciall judgement gave.
Then, when firm pase I fixed on the ground:
When toung can cease to break the lispyng sound:
You mee streightway did too the Muses send,
Ne suffered long a loyteryng lyfe to spend,
What gayn the wooll, what gayn the wed had braught,
It was his meed, that me there dayly taught.
When with Minerve I had acquaintance woon:
And Phebus seemed to love mee, as his soon:
Browns hold I bad at parents hest, farewell:
And gladly there in schoold I gan to dwell:
Where Granta[11] gives the ladies nyne[12] such place,
That they rejoyce to see theyr blisfull case.
With joyes at hert, in this pernasse I bode,
Whyle, through his signes, five tymes great Titan glode:
And twyse as long, by that fayr foord,[13] whereas
Swanfeeder Temms, no furder course can passe.
O what desire had you, therwhile, of mee?
Mid doutfull dreeds, what joyes were wont to bee?
Now linnen clothes, wrought with those fyngers fyne,
Now other thynges of yours dyd you make myne:
Tyll your last thredes gan Clotho to untwyne,
And of your dayes the date extreem assygne.
Hearyng the chaunce, your neybours made much mone:
A dearworth[14] dame, they thought theyr comfort gone.
Kinswoomen wept: your charge, the maydens wept:
Your daughters wept, whom you so well had kept.
But my good syre gave, with soft woords, releef:
And clokes, with outward chere, his inward greef:
Lest, by his care, your sicknes should augment,
And on his case your thoughtfull hert be bent.

You, not forgetting yet a moothers mood,
When at the dore dartthirling death there stood,
Did saye: Adeew, dear spouse, my race is roon:
Wher so he bee, I have left you a soon,
And Nicholas you naamd, and naamd agayn:
With other speech, aspiring heavenly raign:
When into ayre your sprite departed fled,
And left the corps a cold in lukewarm bed.
Ah, could you thus, deare mother, leave us all?
Now, should you live: that yet, before your fall,
My songs you might have soong, have heard my voyce,
And in commodities of your own rejoyce,
My sisters yet unwedded who shall guide?
With whose good lessons shall they bee applyed?
Have, mother, monumentes of our sore smart:
No costly tomb, areard with curious art:
Nor Mausolean masse, hoong in the ayre:
Nor loftie steeples, that will once appayre:
By waylful verse, and doolful song accept.
By verse, the names of auncient peres be kept:
By verse, lives Hercules: by verse Achil:
Hector, Ene,[15] by verse, be famous still
Such former yeres, such death hath chaunced thee:
Closde, with good end, good life is woont to bee.
But now, my sacred parent, fare you well:
God shall cause us agayn togither dwell.
What time this universall globe shall hear
Of the last troomp the rynging voyce: great fear
To soom, to such as you a heavenly chear.
Til then, reposde rest you in gentle sleep:
While hee, whom to you are bequeathd, you keep.

36

Upon the death of lord Mautravers,
out of doctor Haddons latine.

The noble Henry, he, that was lord Mautravers named:
Heyr to the house of thArundels, so long a time now famed:
Who from Fitzalens doth recount discent of worthy race.
Fitzalens, earls of hye estate, men of a goodly grace:
Whom his renowmed father had seen florish, and excell,
In armes, in arts, in witt, in skill, in speaking wonders well:
Whose yeres, to timely vertue had, and manly gravenesse
caught:
With soden ruine is downfalln, and into ashes braught:
While glory his coragious hert enflames to travail great:
And, in his youthly brest ther raigns an overfervent heat.
The perelesse princesse, Mary quene, her message to present,
This Britan lord, as one moste meet, to Cesars broother sent.[1]
On coursing steeds hee rids the waye: in ship hee fleeteth
fast:
To royall Cesars court he comes, the payns, and perils past:
His charge enjoynd perfourmeth hee, attaind exceeding
prayse:
His name, and fame so fully spred, it dures for afterdayes.
But lo, a fervent feever doth, amid his triumphs, fall:
And, with hertgripyng greef, consumes his tender lyms and
all.
O rufull youth, thy helth toofar forgot, and toomuch heed
To countrie, and too parent yeven: why makest thou such
speed?
O, staye your self: your country so to serve dothe right
require,
That often serve you may: and then, at length, succeed you
sire,
But thee perchaunce it likes, thy life the price of praise to
paye:

Nor deth doest dreed, where honor shines, as bright as sonny day.
Certesse no greater glory could, than this, to thee betide:
Though Jove, six hundred yeres, had made thy fatall thread abide.
Of journeys, and of travails huge the cause thy country was:
Thy funerall to honour, forth great Caesars court gan passe.
And, thus, O thus (good lord) this ymp, of heven most worthy wight
His happy life with blisfull death concluded hath aright:
When, in fourt yere quene Maries raign proceeded: and what day,
Was last of Julie moneth, the same his last took him awaye.
From yeres twise ten if you in count wil but one yere abate:
The very age then shall you finde of lord Mautravers fate.
Likewise, was Titus Cesar[2] hence withdrawn, in his prime yeres:
Likewise, the yong prince Edward[3] went: and divers other peres.
Father, forbear thy wofull tears, cease, England, too lament:
Fates favour none, the enmie death to all alike is bent:
The onely mean, that now remains, with eloquence full fine.
Hath Shelly[4] used, in setting forth this barons name divine.
Your Haddon eke, who erst in your life time, bore you good hart,
Presenteth you this monument, of woonted zeal some part.
And now farewell: of English youth most chosen gem, farewell:
A worthyer wight, save Edward, did in England never dwell.

37

Upon the sayd lord Mautravers death.

Mee thought, of late when lord Mautravers dyed,
Our common weal, thus, by her self shee cryed:
Oft have I wept for mine, so layd a sleep,
Yet never had I juster cause to weep.

38

The death of Zoroas, an Egiptian Astronomer, in the first fight, that Alexander had with the Persians.

Now clattering arms, now ragyng broyls of warr
Gan passe the noyes of taratantars[1] clang:
Shrowded with shafts, the heven: with clowd of darts,
Covered, the ayre: against fulfatted bulls,
As forceth kindled ire the Lions keen:
Whose greedy gutts the gnawing hoonger pricks:
So Macedoins against the Persians fare,
Now corpses hide the purpurde soyl with blood:
Large slaughter, on ech side: but Perses more
Moyst feelds bebledd:[2] their herts, and noombers bate.
Fainted while they give back, and fall to flight:
The lightning Macedon, by swoords, by gleavs,
By bands, and trowps, of fotemen with his garde,
Speeds to Darie:[3] but him, his nearest kyn,
Oxate preserves, with horsemen on a plump
Before his carr: that none the charge could give.
Here grunts, here grones, echwhere strong youth is spent:
Shaking her bloody hands, Bellone, among
The Perses, soweth all kindes of cruel death.
With throte ycutt, hee roores: hee lyeth along,
His entrails with a launce through girded quite:
Him down[4] the club, him beats farstryking bowe,
And him the slyng, and him the shinand swoord:
Hee dieth, he is all dedd, hee pants, he rests.
Right over stood, in snowwhite armour brave,
The Memphite[5] Zoroas, a cooning clerk:
To whom the heaven lay open, as his book:
And in celestiall bodyes hee could tell
The moovyng, mettyng, light, aspect, eclyps,
And influence, and constellations all:
What earthly chaunces wold betide: what yere

Of plenty storde, what signe forwarned derth:
How winter gendreth snow: what temperature
In the primetide dothe season well the soyl:
Why soomer burns: why autumn hath ripe grapes:
Whether the circle, quadrate[6] may becoom:
Whether our tunes heavens harmony can yeeld:
Of fowr begynns, among them selves how great
Proportion is: what swaye the erring lightes
Dothe send in course gayn that first mooving heaven,
What grees,[7] one from an other distant bee:
What sterr dothe lett the hurtfull fire to rage,
Or him more mylde what opposition markes:
What fire doth qualifie Mavorses fire:
What house echone doth seek: what planet raigns
Within this hemisphere, or that: small things
I speak: holl heaven hee closeth in his brest.
This sage then, in the starrs had spied: the fates
Threatned him death, without delaye: and sithe
Hee saw, hee could not fatall order change:
Forward hee preast, in battayl that hee might
Meet with the ruler of the Macedoins:
Of his right hand desirous to be slayn,
The boldest beurn,[8] and worthiest in the feeld:
And, as a wight now weary of his life,
And seeking death, in first front of his rage,
Cooms desperatly to Alisanders face:
At him, with darts, one after other, throwes:
With reckles woords, and clamour him provokes:
And sayth, Nectanabs bastard,[9] shameful stain
Of mothers bed: why losest thou thy strokes,
Cowards emong? Turn thee to mee, in case
Manhod ther bee so much left in thy hert:
Coom fight with mee: that on my helmet wear
Apolloes laurel, both for learnings laude,
And eke for Martiall prayse: that, in my shield,
The sevenfold[10] sophie[11] of Minerve contein:

A match, more meet, sir king, than any here.
The noble prince amoved, takes ruthe upon
The wilfull wight: and, with soft woords, ayen,
O monstrous man (quoth he) whatso thou art,
I praye thee lyve: ne do not, with thy death
This lodge of lore, the Muses mansion marr.
That treasure house this hand shall never spoyl:
My swoord shall never bruze that skylfull brayn,
Longgatherd heapes of science soon to spyll.
O, how faire frutes may you to mortall men
From wisdoms garden, give? How many may,
By you, the wyser, and the better prove?
What error, what mad moode, what phrenzey thee
Persuades to bee downsent to deep Avern:
Where no artes florish, nor no knowledge vails?
For all these sawes, when thus the soverain sayde,
Alighted Zoroas: with swoord unsheathed,
The carelesse king there smote, above the greave,
At thopening of his quishes:[12] wounded him
So, that the blood down reyled on the ground.
The Macedon, perceyving hurt, gan gnash:
But yet his minde he bent, in any wyse,
Hym to forbear: set spurrs unto his steed,
And turnd away: lest anger of the smart
Should cause revenger hand deal balefull blowes,
But of the Macedonian chieftanes knights
One, Meleager,[13] could not bear this sight:
But ran upon the sayd Egyptian renk:[14]
And cut him in both kneez: hee fell to ground:
Wherwith a hole route came of souldiours stern,
And all in peeces hewed the silly seg[15]
But happyly the soll fled to the sterres:
Where, under him, he hath full sight of all,
Wherat hee gazed here, with reaching looke.
The Persians wayld such sapience to forgo:
The very fone,[16] the Macedonians wisht,

Hee wold have lyved: kyng Alisander self
Deemd him a man, unmeet to dye at all:
Who woon lyke prase, for conquest of his ire,
As for stout men in feeld that daye subdeewd:
Who princes taught, how to discern a man,
That in his hed so rare a jewell beares.
But over all, those same Camenes,[17] those same
Divine Camenes, whose honor he procurde.
As tender parent dothe his daughters weal:
Lamented: and for thanks, all that they can,
Do cherish him deceast, and set hym free
From derk oblivion of devouryng death.

39

Marcus Tullius Ciceroes death.

Therefore, when restless rage of wynde, and wave
Hee saw: By fates, alas calld for (quod hee)
Is haplesse Cicero: sayl on, shape course
To the next shore, and bryng me to my death.
Perdie these thanks, reskued from civil swoord,
Wilt thou, my countrey, paye? I see mine end:
So powrs divine, so bid the gods above,
In citie saved that Consul Marcus[1] shend.[2]
Speakyng nomore, but drawyng from deep hert
Great grones, even at the name of Room[3] reherst:
His yies, and cheeks, with showrs of teares, hee washt.
And (though a route in dayly daungers worn)
With forced face, the shipmen held theyr teares:
And, strivyng long the seas rough floods to passe,
In angry wyndes, and stormy stowrs made waye:
And at the last, safe anchord in the rode,
Came heavy Cicero a land: with payn,
His faynted lyms the aged fire dothe draw:

And, round about their master, stood his band:
Nor greatly with theyr own hard hap dismayd,
Nor plighted fayth, prove in sharp time to break:
Soom swoords prepare: soom theyr deare lord assist:
In littour layd, they lead hym unkouth wayes:
If so deceave Antonius cruell gleavs[4]
They might, and threats of folowing routs escape.
Thus lo, that Tullie, went, that Tullius
Of royall robe, and sacred Senate prince:
When hee afar the men approche espyeth,
And of his fone the ensignes dothe aknow:
And, with drawn swoord, Popilius[5] threatnyng death:
Whose life, and holl estate, in hazard once,
Hee had preserved: when Room as yet to free
Herd hym, and at his thundryng voyce amazde.
Herennius[6] eek, more eyger than the rest,
Present enflamde with furie, him purseews.
What might hee doo? Should hee use in defense
Disarmed hands? or pardon ask, for meed?
Should hee with woords attempt to turn the wrath
Of tharmed knyght, whose safeguard hee had wrought?
No, age, forbids, and fixt within deep brest
His countreys love, and falling Rooms image.
The charret turn, sayth hee, let loose the rayns:
Roon to the undeserved death: mee, lo,
Hath Phebus fowl, as messanger, forwarnd:
And Jove desires a neew heavensman to make.
Brutus, and Cassius soulls, live you in blisse:
In case yet all the fates gaynstrive us not,
Neyther shall wee perchaunce dye unrevenged.
Now have I lived, O Room, ynough for mee:
My passed lyfe nought suffreth mee to dout
Noysom oblivion of the lothesom death.
Slea mee: yet all thoffspring to coom shall knowe
And this deceas shall bring eternall lyfe.

Yea and (onlesse I fayl, and all in vain
Room, I soomtyme thy Augur chosen was)
Not evermore shall frendly fortune thee
Favour, Antonius: once the day shall coom:
When her deare wights, by cruell spight, thus slayn,
Victorious Room shall at thy hands require.
Mee likes, therwhyle, go see the hoped heaven.
Speech had he left: and therwith hee, good man
His throte preparde, and held his hed unmoved,
His hastyng too those fates the very knights
Bee lothe to see: and, rage rebated, when
They his bare neck beheld, and his hore heyres:
Scant could they hold the teares, that forth gan burst:
And almost fell from bloody hands the swords.
Onely the stern Herennius with grym look,
Dastards, why stand you styll, he sayth: and streight,
Swaps of the hed, with his presumptuous yron.
Ne with that slaughter yet is hee not fild:
Fowl shame on shame to heap is his delyte.
Wherfore the hands also doth hee of smyte,
Which durst Antonius life so lively paynt:
Him, yeldyng strayned goste, from welkin hye,
With lothly chere, lord Phebus gan behold:
And in black clowd, they saye, long hid his hed.
The latine Muses, and the Grayes,[7] they wept:
And, for his fall eternally shall weep.
And lo, hertpersyng Pitho[8] (straunge to tell)
Who had to him suffisde bothe sense, and woords,
When so he spake: and drest, with nectar soote,
That flowyng toung: when his wyndpype disclosde,
Fled with her fleeyng frend: and (out alas)
Hath left the erth, ne wil nomore return.
Popilius flyeth, therwhyle: and, leavyng there
The sensless flock, a gryzley sight doth bear
Unto Antonius boord, with mischief fed.

40

Of M. T. Cicero.

For Tullie late, a toomb I gan prepare:
When Cynthie, thus, bad mee my labour spare.
Such maner things becoom the ded, quoth hee:
But Tullie lives, and styll alyve shall be.

MISCELLANEOUS POEMS

Edmund Gosse, in his *Life and Letters of John Donne,* says of the poets of the sixteenth century: 'The Elizabethan poets were, as a rule, a sociable and sympathetic body of men. They acted and interacted upon one another with vivacity; they met at frequent intervals to encourage themselves in the art they exercised and to read each other's verses. The habit which sprang up of contributing strings of complimentary effusions to accompany the published efforts of a friend was symptomatic of the gregarious tendency of the age.' As evidences of Grimald's activity in this field of composition there are the following six poems, four of which preface William Turner, Dean of Wells' *A Preservative or Triacle agaynst the Poyson of Pelagius* (1551), entitled *D. Hugoni Latimeri Nicolaus Grimoaldus S., Ad Guilielmum Turnerum, Ad Catabaptistam,* and *To the reder.* In the preface of Thomas Cooper's edition of Sir Thomas Eliot's Latin dictionary entitled *Bibliotheca Eliotæ* (1552) there also appear two poems by Grimald: *Nicolaus Grimoaldus ad Thomam Cooperum,* and *Nicolaus Grimoaldus ad lectorem.*

41

D. HUGONI LATIMERO

Nicolaus Grimoaldus. S.

Optime non pigra florens Latimere senecta:
Quẽ Rex, quẽ regis prudẽs, sapiensq́; Senatus,
Tempore quẽlõgo cupit hæc respublica saluũ:
Eccè tui similis ueteranus hic, alter & ipse,
Ad debellandos in religione rebelles
Millibus è multis te gaudet habere patronum.
Quàm benè spectatũ spectatus, amicus amicũ
Aduocat: ut fractis pariter succurrere rebus
Possitis, domini quas impetit hostis acerbus?
Christiadas Christi sic sic defendere partes.
Cónuenit et iunctis huc huc cõcurrere turmis.
Atq; utinam pugnatorum sic copia crescat,
Crescit ut hostilis numerus. Sed qd querar? aut quos
Incusem? O mores tetros, ô tẽpora dira.
Sunt fuci, pecus ignauum: qui melle fouentes
Corpora, desertis stationibùs, omnia produnt.
Sunt cessatores: quos tu, Latimere, notâsti
Sæpè (Deus faxit, fuerit ne fabula surdis
Dicta) suas qui cum res curent, & sibi uiuant:
Cùm pulchros titulos, & nomen inane bonorũ
Bellatorum habeant: uberrima præmia captãt,
Debita miltibus nauis, strenuæq́; cateruæ.
Armatorũ hominũ loca, sed nõ arma capessunt:
Immò aciem turbant longè turpissima monstra.
Ingruit ampla manus, uis multò maxima sæuit.
En inimica cohors: en Papa, Pelagius adsunt:
Cinctus adest crebro, scelerũ caput, agmine Dæmõ
Nõ facilè inuadãt, fũdãt, uincãtq; regãtq;
Ex qua parte iacent torpentia mẽbra ueterno?

Quid facimus? quæ tanta uiros ignauia perdit?
Arua, facos, pecudes, uillas, armaria, tecta,
Diuitias, et opes fragiles, perituraq́; regna,
Quantis praesidijs ultrò defendimus omnes?
Et tamē (heu mētes stupidas, heu mortua corda
Eripitur cœlū, nobis stertentibus ipsum.
Ve miseræ genti: populum quæ fata Britannū
Vrgent, custodes ubi sunt uulpesq́; lupiq́;?
Nunquàm herclè, nunq uictoria clara redibit:
Ni somno addictos homines, & tempore belli
Castra relinquentes: faciant uel prorsus abire,
Cedentes alijs, proprium uel munus obire,
Qui res humanas æqua ditione gubernant.
Atq; colant summis studijs, & honoribus illos:
Qui rectis imbuti animis, & robore magno,
Lubrica constanti superant mendacia uero:
Hic uti Turnerus fecit, fortissimus heros.

42

Ad D. Guilielmum Turnerum.

Perge, fauēte Deo (Turnere grauissime) perge
  Exornare libris tempora nostra tuis:
Et ui cœlesti portenta nefanda domare,
  Quæ populū mostrū peste nocēte premunt:
Dū gaudēt uentres pingues, magniq́; magistri
  Cum uafra obscuris arte latere locis:
Cōpressisq́; sedēt manibus, gregibusq́; relictis:
  Atq; nouis nummis arca tumescit hians
Prædentur uigiles, concesso tempore fures.
  Sed quis erit finis? quis, rogo, finis erit?
Intoleranda dabit uindex tormenta supremus:
  Et scelera horrebit talia quisq́; pius.
Tu uerò instos reprimens acerrimus hostes,
  Defendensq́; tui uerba colenda Dei:

Captabis nitido lætissima cœlo,
  Munera per nullos interitura dies.
Perge igitur Papas animo contemnere toto,
  Clarûm exẽpla uirum tenẽda memor:
Neu quosuis facilè Christi patiaris in æde
  Quelibet ignaros dogmata praua sequi.
Immortale tibi fauet isto nomine numen,
  Próq; suo genitor pignore summus habet,
Et solidas grates imo de pectore promunt
  Lucis amatores, candida turba tibi.
Est satius placuisse Deo, dum recta tueris:
  Quàm seruire stylo dissimulare, malis.
Est satius, paucis iustis tua scripta probari,
  Quàm cum mille hominŭ laude silere leui.
Ergò, fauẽte Deo (Turnere grauissime) perge
  Illustrare libris tempora nostra tuis.

43

Ad Catabaptistam.

Amice, si sapis, tibi caue: caue,
Bonum ne nomen amittas apud bonos:
Item ne corpus in periculum trahas:
Neu mentes plurimas perdens, perdas tuam.
Duas res, obsecro, quantum potes, fuge.
Est una magna pestis, Ignoratio,
Quæ ueritatis lucem nescit assequi.
Est altera, præter hanc, lues uel maxima,
Doceri uelle se negans Superbia.
Autore me: qui non minùs sanè tibi
Rectè consultum, q mihi uolo, & meis:
Sacrum pia uocabis uoce Spiritum:
Qui pectori tuo talem modestiam
Instillet, ut sibi planè renunciet:
Veriq; noscendi te amore sedulo
Inspiret, abiectis malis affectibus.

Ad hunc modum, si comparare te uoles:
Tunc, tunc, uolumen hoc cùm corde légeris
Attento, candido, benigno, serio:
E doctus, optimam redibis in uiam.

44

To the reder.

Lyke as in tyme of Goddes reuengyng wrath:
When fyry Mars, when Saturn colde, and drye
Wyth Soonne in Scorpion conspyrid hathe,
And from the south unholsoome breathis do flye:
Venoomde vapors, they poyson by and bye
The duskid ayer: infectid is the water:
Corrupt is foode of mennis substance the matter:
The moysture hote then rotteth inwardly:
Then stoppid ar the holes of outer skyn:
Then from the hart the heate to veynes dooth hye:
Then native vice abatieth within,
Drawne fast together, dryed, and dryven full thyns
Then wastlich lyvyng wyghtis, without defence,
The raygyng plage, and cruell pestilence:
Ryghte so the Deuyll out sent to trouble us,
With hellysh hotlynges, with Satyrnians,
With creepyng beastes, the light defaysyng thus,
As in this storme styll stoute Pelagians
Blowes forth the blastes of Antichristians:
The bondeslaues of Satan, sowers of lyes,
Masters of Myschief, trompes of heresyes.
Now fostrid is a maddyng maladye
In heddis newfanglid, and bewitchid thaughtis:
Refusyng all goode leachis remedye:
Goddis trouth to fancies plucking, that be naughtis:
Lewde people drawyng by unskylfull draughtis:
Untyll the simple foules, without redres,

Possest of error, faynteth succourles.
Yet, lo, whan as that murren is so brymme:
To his, God shapith sooverayne sauegarde:
By chaunge of place: by purgyng euery lymme:
By bytter sowle, by thynne diet, and harde:
By mouyng members toward, and frowarde:
By Vipars bodye bet, with herbis not voyde
Of vertue: her hedde, and tayle be stroyde.
Likewise goode helpis God giues against the sore
Disease of mynde, and brayne fantasticall:
To seeke sage companye, to use no more
Unholsome stedis:[1] to clenge,[2] and to let fall
The Proude, and coye conceyte: withdrawyng all
Fat fare, and fyne, straunge disshes to forsake,
For Alexander,[3] Woolfbane[4] lest thou take:
To practise heuenly lore, and wysdome brought
Downe from aboue: this medicine to applye
To rescue folke, that hath contagion cought,
And eeke to saue a man continuallye
From dedly poysen: orels to crye
Which was thou mayest cut of the adders hedde,
Or ease thy frende unto thy ancor fledde.
Whyle thou be sounde, wylt thou be safe, & sure?
Folowe, folowe thys worke, thou haste in hande.
Wylt thou hym kenne, that cause is of cure?
He that abode here, and out of the lande,
He that inwarde, did Antichriste withstande?
Goode Doctor Turner: who by skyll is able
To prove the soothe, and to confounde eche fable.

45

NICOLAUS GRIMOALDUS,

ad lectorem.

Messibus, eccè, nouis iterum sunt horrea plena:
Vsibus vt promas, o philomuse, tuis.

Séd; adeò victos duri fateantur agrestes.
  Rustica res tanti nulla laboris eget.
Quid non expugnat vigilans industria? Quid non
  Mens, ardore, potest? sedulitate, manus?
Scriptores recitant que multa uocabula multi:
  Omnia sunt vno dinumerata libro.
Hic, patrias voces omnes, formasque loquendi:
  Romanosq; omnes vnicus Anglus habet.
Verba, note rerum, sic ordine cuncta notantur:
  Vno vt contuitu, singula nosse queas.
Queis caruere patres, tantoque feruntur honore;
  His operis fretus, tu mihi quantus eris?

46

Nicolaus Grimoaldus, ad Thomam Cooperum.

VT viam longam, peregrè profectus,
Ac iter longum cupit expeditè
Confici: nullas remoras nec optat
    Esse viator:
Sed dari certos petit, atque claros
Iudices: qui se temerè vagantem
Retrahant: dempto scrupulo, monentes,
    Quà sit eundum:
Sic amor si quem tenet: expeditq;:
Ter trium sedes nitidas Dearum
Possit: & factos, aditu recluso,
    Scandere montes:
Te, ducem primum, Coopere, captet:
Te sibi iungat, teneris ab annis:
Te legat, voluat, recolat, reuisat,
    Laudet, ametq;.

NOTES ON THE SHORTER POEMS OF NICHOLAS GRIMALD

1.

A true love.

1. *Vere.*—The season of Spring, spring-time.
2. *'The oke shall olives bear: the lamb, the lion fray: The owle shall match the nightingale, in tuning of her lay:'*—See Virgil, *Ecl.* 8. 52-6.
3. *Ymp.*—Imp, scion, offspring, child.

2.

The lover to his dear, of his exceding love.

The second and third of Grimald's poems, *The lover to his dear* and *The lover asketh pardon of his dere,* are so similar in tone that Arber has conjectured (*Tottel's Miscellany,* ed. Arber, London, 1870, Introduction, Sec. 3) that they were both addressed to the same person, whose given name, Carie, Grimald has introduced into the first poem, and whose surname, Day, he plays upon in the second.

The source of this poem[1] is to be found in *Elegia III* of the *Poemata* of Theodore de Bèze, a French theologian, who was one of the most energetic and influential of the Genevese reformers. He is best known for his edition of the Greek New Testament (1565), and his biography of John Calvin. He presented Cambridge University with the famous New Testament manuscript known as the *Codex Bezæ.* His Latin verse was, for the most part, written during his early life. The first edition of his poems, *Poemata Juvenilia,* which was a collection of elegies, *sylvæ,* and epigrams, appeared in 1548, under the pseudonym of Deodatus Seba. Later editions were entitled, *Theodori Bezæ Vezelii Poemata Varia.*

[1] H. H. Hudson, "Grimald's Translations from Beza," *Modern Language Notes* 39. 7. 388.

Elegia III.

Cornua bis posuit, bis cepit cornua Phœbe,
  Nec tamen es tanto tempore visa mihi.
Vivo tamen, si vita potest tibi, Publia, dici,
  Mœrorem et lachrymas quæ fovet una meas.
Certe dura mihi mors sæpe in vota vocatur:
  Mors finem lachrymis impositura meis.
Non aliter queritur ventrem durare Prometheus,
  Et posito mallet numine posse mori.
Fallor enim, aut quisquis figmenta hæc repperit olim
  Vulturis est illi nomine dictus amor.
Quæ non visa mihi platea est? quid in urbe relictum?
  Urbe tamen tota Publia nulla fuit.
Ergo vel miseram cohibent te conjugis iræ:
  O non tam sævo fœmina digna viro!
Vel populosa tibi sordere Lutetia cœpit,
  Et placidi ruris dulcior aura placet.
Forsitan in sylvis nostros meditaris amores,
  Et tuto velles omnia ferre loco.
Ibo igitur, nec me quicquam retinebit euntem,
  Donec sis aliquo sola reperta loco.
Interea manuun serves, collique colorem,
  Et fieri nigras ne patiare genas.
Tecta incede caput: nam te si cernat Apollo,
  Ardeat in vultus ustus et ipse tuos.
In sylvis lauri vestita est cortice Daphne,
  Hei mihi, si de te fabula talis erit!
Calisto in sylvis summo est compressa Tonanti,
  Ne rogo, ne placeat Juppiter iste tibi.
Heu! quid non timeo? latronum hic regna teguntur:
  Quisquis es, hinc auser, prædo cruente, manus:
Actæon doceat violati numinis iras:
  Dictynna certe non minor ista Dea est.
Quid loquor? o nostræ pars maxima, Publia, mentis,
  Non poterunt aures ista ferire tuas.
O utinam præsens verba observare legentis,
  Et frontis possem signa notare tuæ!
Optima tunc nostro spes addi posset amori,
  Et possem mecum dicere, lenis erit,
Perveniam certe quacunque moreris in urbe
  Sive aliquo potius, Publia, rure lates.

Perveniam, et si non mea per se forma loquatur,
  Fortunæ fiam nuncius ipse meæ.
Quod si surda preces ausis contemnare nostras,
  Nempe meæ subito conscia cædis eris:
Attamen hoc media nobis in morte placebit,
  Quod tu causa meæ, Publia, cædis eris.

1. *Ayelife.*—For ever.
2. *Gripes.*—Distressing.
3. *Woon.*—Won, dwell.

3.

The lover asketh pardon of his dere, for fleeyng from her.

See the introductory note to the previous poem.

The source of these lines is to be found in *Elegia V* of Beza's *Poemata:*

Elegia V.

Quisquis amas (aiunt cuncti) fuge corpus amatum,
  Vivere si cœco liber ab igne cupis.
Hei mihi, te quoties fugi, mea Candida! fugi:
  Semper at in nostro pectore regnat amor.
Ecce iterum fateor, fugi te, Candida: verum
  Et potui et possum dicere semper, amo.
Sive abeo in sylvas, nobis succurrit Adonis,
  Et fit tristitiæ conscia sylva meæ:
Sive placent horti, quot florum hic millia cerno,
  Tot stimulis captum me premit asper amor:
Narcissum hinc croceum video, hinc flentes Hiacynthos,
  Hinc miser ante oculos pulcher Adonis adest:
Magna quidem nostræ fateor medicamina flammæ,
  Sed me qui vincit, vincit et ille Deos.
At si prata juvant, o quantas sentio flammas!
  Ardeo tunc flammis totus amoris ego.
Hic videor Cereris fugientem cernere natam,
  Hic videor furvi cernere Ditis equos,
Littora si specto, vitreas tunc cogito Nymphas,
  Fervidaque in medio numina sæpe mari
Quo magis evado montes sublimis in altos,
  Hoc proprior Veneris fit puer ille mihi,
Si placeant urbes: vis semel omnia dicam?
  Illic quum videam plurima, nulla placent.

Illius nunc carpo oculos, nunc illius ora,
  Hæc capite, hæc pedibus displicet, illa genis
Denique materies si desit, crimina fingo:
  Et quæcunque aliis candida, nigra mihi est.
Quid prodest fugisse igitur, cum Candida præsens,
  Atque adeo lateri sit comes usque meo?
Umbræ igitur merito quadret tibi Candida nomen,
  Tale tamen nomen non decet iste color.
Humanum potius debes deponere nomen,
  Una simul gemino quæ potes esse loco.
Parce, rogo, quæcunque Dea es: subjecit et ipsa
  Anchisi sese, res bene nota, Venus.
Ecce fugam fateor, veniam ne, Diva, negato,
  Sæpe mihi veniam Juppiter ipse dedit.
Ipse quidem prima mox ad te luce revertar,
  Quasque voles pœnas, si patiare, feram.

1. *Corps.*—Person.

2. *Dame Ceres ymp.*—Dionysus, Ceres' child by her brother Zeus. When Dionysus grew up, Hera, who was jealous of Ceres and hated her son, threw him into a state of madness, in which he wandered about through many countries of the earth.

4.

N. Vincent to G. Blackwood, agaynst wedding.

Neither G. Blackwood nor N. Vincent appears upon the lists of students of Cambridge or Oxford, among whom most of Grimald's friends probably were. The names do not sound fictitious.

The original of this poem is to be found among the *Epigrammata* of Beza's volume of poems:

Ponticus Cornelio, de uxore non ducenda.

Quum velis uxorem, Corneli, ducere: quæro
  Conjugium placeat qua ratione tibi?
Scilicet ut deinceps vivas fœlicior: atqui
  Fallor ego, aut non hac lege beatus eris.
Uxor enim aut deformis erit, (tune, obsecro, talis
  Si tibi sit coniunx juncta, beatus eris?)

Aut forma mediocris erit: modus iste, fatemur,
  Optimus, at subito deperit iste modus.
Aut formosa, ideoque viris obnoxia mille,
  Et de qua nequeas dicere, tota mea est.
Ut sit casta tamen, (nemo si forte rogarit)
  Mille feret natos, tædia mille feret.
Aut sterilis tecum tardos sic exiget annos,
  Nullus ut e multis sit sine lite dies.
His addas caput indomitum, mentmeque tenacem,
  Cæteraque a multis quæ didicisse potes.
Desine sic igitur vitam sperare beatam,
  Sit potius cœlebs et sine thorus.
His etenim si qua est fœlicis semita vitæ
  Fœmineas juxta non latet illa nates.

1. *Fere.*—Companion.

5.

G. Blackwood to N. Vincent with weddyng.

This poem, which is in reply to the one preceding, is also drawn from one of Beza's *Epigrammata:*

Cornelius Pontico, de uxore ducenda.

Uxorem cupiam quum ducere, Pontice, quæris
  Conjugium placeat qua ratione mihi?
Deformem nolo, formosam exopto: placebit,
  Si nequeo pulchram, quæ mediocris erit.
Formosam, dices, alii mox mille rogabunt,
  At nulli, quamvis sæpe rogata, dabit.
Forma perit subito mediocris: id ille queratur,
  Qui præter formam nil muliebre probat.
Si dederit natos, natos spectare juvabit:
  Si sterilis, quid tum? sarcina nostra levis.
Cætera, quæ narras, certe sunt magna, fatemur,
  Est animusque tenax, indomitumque caput.
Sed sua sunt cunctis connata incommoda rebus,
  Ipsa etiam damnis commoda plena vides.
Et me miraris vitam sperare beatam,
  Si mihi sit deinceps fœmina facta comes?
Semita virtutis stricta est, si vera loquuntur.
  Hæc quoque quam quæro, Pontice, stricta via est.

See notes on the preceding poem.

1. *Blee.*—Complexion, visage.
2. *Ming.*—Remember.

6.

The Muses.

1. *Imps of King Jove, and quene Remembrance.*—The Muses, the offspring of Zeus and Mnemosyne, the goddess of memory.
2. *Renkes.*—Men.

7.

Musonius the Philosophers Saiyng.

Musonius Rufus, a Roman philosopher of the first century A.D., was born in Etruria about A.D. 20-30. He was banished by Nero in 66 A.D. for his alleged share in Piso's conspiracy. When Galba became emperor, the philosopher returned to Rome, and continued there under Vespasian, whose favor he had secured. His philosophy, which is in most respects identical with that of his pupil, Epictetus, is marked by its strong practical tendency.

Musonius' Saying.

Verba Musoni philosophi Græca digna atque utilia audiri observarique; eiusdem utilitatis sententia a M. Catone.

Adulescenti cum etiam tum in scholis essemus, hoc Græcum, quod aposui, dictum esse a Musonio philosopho audiebamus et, quoniam vere atque luculente dictum verbis est brevibus et rotundis vinctum, perquam libenter memineramus *Ἄν τι πράξῃς καλὸν μετὰ πόνου, ὁ μὲν πόνος οἴχεται, το δὲ καλὸν μένει· ἄ τι ποιήσῃς αἰσχρὸν μετὰ ἡδονῆς, τὸ μὲν ἡδύ οἴχεται, τὸ δὲ αἰσχρὸν μένει.*

Postquam istam sententiam in Catonis oratione, quam dixit Numantiæ apud equites, positam legimus. Quæ etsi laxoribus paulo longioribus verbis comprehensa est præquam illud Græcum, quod diximus, quoniam tamen prior tempore antiquioreque est, venerabilior videri debet. Verba ex oratione hæc sunt: Cogitate cum animis vestris: si quid vos per laborem recte feceritis, labor ille a vobis cito recedet, bene factum a vobis, dum vitiis, non abscedet; sed si qua per voluptatem abibit nequiter feceritis, nequiter factum illud apud vos semper manebit.

—*C. Musonus Rufus Reliquiæ,* edidit O. Hense, Leipsic, 1905.

1. *Vade.*—Fade.
2. *Voide.*—Depart, go.

8.

Marcus Catoes comparison of mans life with yron.

Marcus Cato's comparison of a man's life to iron.

M. Porcii Catonis carmen de moribus

Nam vita humana prope uti ferrum est. si exerceas, conteritur, si non exerceas, tamen rubigo interficit. item homines exercendo videmus conteri; si nihil exerceas, inertia atque torpedo plus detrimenti facit quam exercitio.

—Antonii Riccoboni Rhodogini *De Historia Liber cum Fragmentis Historicum veterum Latinorum summa fide ab eodem collectis et auctis,* Basiliæ, Ex Officina Petri Pernæ, Anno MDLXXIX.

1. *Ure.*—Use.

9.

Cleobulus the Lydians riddle.

Cleobulus, who lived between 628 and 588 B.C., was one of the seven wise men of Greece, and a native and Tyrant of Lindus in Rhodes. He was one of the first to give a literary form to the riddle.

Cleobulus' Riddle.

Est genitor, proles cui sit bissena: sed horum cuivis triginta bis, forma dispare, natæ, hæ niveis totæ, fuscis sed vultibus illæ; atque immortales quum sit moriuntur ad unam.

Est autem annus.

10.

Concerning Virgil's Eneids.

1. *Lysip.*—Lysippus, one of the most famous of the Greek artists, a contemporary of Alexander the Great.

2. *Naamkouth.*—Namecouth, known by name, well known, famous.

11.

Of mirth.

1. *'A mery hert sage Salomon countes his continuall feast.'*—See Prov. 15. 15.

12.

To L. J. S.

L. J. S. may be identified with Lady Jane Seymour. *A neew yere's* gift to *l.M.S.*, No. 15; another to *l.M.S.*, No. 16; To *l.K.S.*, No. 17; and *To l.E.S.*, No. 18, were probably addressed to her sisters, the ladies Margaret, Katherine, and Elizabeth. These were the four younger daughters of Edward Seymour, Duke of Somerset, to whom Grimald addressed his *Carmen Congratulatorium* on the Duke's release from the Tower, and his restoration to his family. Grimald's interest in these young women was probably aroused, not only because of their rank, but because of their literary ability. On the death of Margaret of Valois they published a book of verse entitled *Annæ, Margaritæ, Janæ, Virginum heroidum Anglarum in mortem Margaritæ Valesiæ Navarrorum Reginæ* Hecadistichon, Paris, 1550. A French translation of this volume appeared the following year.

The good Duke of Somerset having been beheaded in January last, the King and Council took care of his four younger daughters, as he had six, viz. Anne, Margaret, Jane, Mary, Katharin, and Elizabeth; all bred up to learning. For I find, by order of the King, they were committed, May 2, 1552, to the Lady Cromwel, who was to have 50 pounds per ann. for each of them: which salary was, November 1, increased to 100 marks a year apiece. One of his daughters, viz. the Lady Elizabeth, was before in the keeping of the Lady Smith, (the wife, I suppose, of Sir Thomas Smith, who had belonged to the Duke; or perhaps rather the wife of Sir Clement Smith, who was her aunt.) And in February there was a warrant to the Exchequer, to pay to that lady an annuity of 100 marks towards the finding of Lady Elizabeth, one of the late Duke of Somerset's daughters, during the said Elizabeth's abode with her. One of these ladies, viz. Jane, the third daughter, the Duke her father secretly laboured to match with the King, and employed the Lord Strange, much about his person, to recommend her to him, and to take his opportunity to move the King that way; as that Lord confessed in the said Duke's last troubles. But she died unmarried, as also did two of her sisters, Margaret and Katharin.

—John Strype, *Ecclesiastical Memorials*, Oxford, 1822, 2. 2. 7-8.

Extracts from the *Diary of Henry Machyn,* Camden Society Publications, 1848, pp. 253, 254, 384:

—The xx day of Marche (1560-1) ded[b] at the cowrt the yonge lade Jane Semer, the duke of Somerset ('s) dowther, on of the quen ('s) mayds.

—The sam day of Marche (1561) at after-none at Westmynster (was brought) from the quen('s) armere[a] my lade Jane Semer, with (all the quire) of the abbay, with ijC. of (the) quen('s) cowrt, the wyche she was (one) of the quen('s) mayd('s) in grett faver, and a iiij[xx] morners of (men and) women, of lorded and lades, and gentylmen and gentyllwomen, all in blake, be-syd odur[b] of the quen('s) preve chambur, and she (had) a grett baner of armes bornne, and master Clarenshux was the harold, and master Skameler the nuw byshope of Peterborow dyd pryche. (She was) bered in the sam chapell wher my lade of Suffoke was.

—Funeral of lady Jane Seymour. Daughter of Edward, duke of Somerset, and supposed to have been destined by him to become the consort of his nephew king Edward. A Latin letter written by her (of course under the dictation of her tutor) to the Reformers Bucer and Fagius, dated at Syon, June 12, 1549, is published in the Third Series of Zurich Letters, printed for the Parker Society. She was one of Queen Elizabeth's maids of honour, and shortly before her death had taken an active part in promoting the clandestine marriage of her brother, the Earl of Hertford, with her companion, the lady Katharine Grey, a line of conduct which would certainly have brought upon her the anger of her royal mistress, had she lived until it was discovered. (See Ellis's Orig. Letters, Second Series, vol. ii, p. 272.) Her age was only nineteen. See an engraving of her monumental tablet, with the inscription, erected by "her deare brother" the Earl, in Dart's Westminster Abbey, vol. i, pl. 12. In the accounts of St.

Margaret's parish, Westminster, is an entry of 10s. received at her funeral.

1. *Charis.*—One of the Charites or Graces, the three goddesses who lend charm and beauty to nature and to human life.

2. *Pieris.*—One of the Pierides, the nine daughters of Pierus, King of Emathia, to whom he gave the names of the nine Muses. They entered into a contest with the Muses, and being defeated, were changed into birds. Ovid, *Met.* 5. 300-678.

3. *Cypris.*—The Cyprian, Venus.

4. *Ure.*—Use.

13.

To maistres D. A.

Three of Grimald's shorter poems, *To maistres D.A.*, (No. 13), *Of m.D.A.* (No. 14), *To m.D.A.* (No. 19), are addressed to Damascene Awdley, as the anagram in the second of these poems shows. According to the first she had 'golden gifts of mind,' the second says that she was of 'woorthy race,' while the third pictures her as a lady of 'gorgeous attire.' It seems not unlikely that she was of the noble house of Awdley (Audley), of Staffordshire, in which Eccles lies, the town in which Grimald was licensed to preach in 1551. As this church was one of the most important in that county, it is probable that Grimald came to know various members of the Awdley family. The records of that family do not show any member with the name of Damascene. The name damascene, or damask, which is that of a rose of pink or light red variety, and also that of a fabric of silky surface and elaborate design, popular in mediæval times, may, however, have been only a nickname.

Among the poems by 'uncertain authors' in *Tottel's Miscellany* (Arber, p. 167) there is the following poem entitled *A praise of Audley,* which was probably written on the death of John Tuchet, Lord Audley, who was son of James Audley, beheaded on Tower Hill for the part he took in the Cornish insurrection. In consequence, his son John, the subject of this poem, was attainted, but was restored in blood and honors, and in 1512 became Lord Audley. The following year he attended the King in the French War. He was summoned to Parliament November 23, 1514, to October 21, 1556. He died before January 30, 1557-8.

A praise of Audley.

When Audley had runne out his race and ended wer his days,
His fame stept forth and bad me write of him some worthy praise.
What life he had, what actes he did: his vertues and good name,
Wherto I calde for true report, as witnes of the same.
Wel born he was wel bent by kinde, whose mind did never swarve
A skilfull head, a valiant hert, a ready hand to serve.
Brought up and trained in feats of war long time beyond the seas
Cald home to serve his prince whom styll he sought to please.
What torney was there he refusde, what service did he shone,
Where he was not nor his advice, what great exploit was done,
In towne a lambe in felde full fierce a lyon at the nede,
In sober wit a Salomon, yet one of Hectors sede.
Then shame it were that any tong shold now defame his dedes
That in his life a mirror was to all that him succedes.
No pore estate nor hie renowne his nature could pervart,
No hard mischance that him befel could move his constant hart.
Thus long he lived loved of all as one mislikt of none,
And where he went who cald him not the gentle Peragon
But course of kinds doth cause eche frute to fall when it is ripe,
And spitefull death will suffer none to scape his grevous gripe.
Yet though the ground received have his corps into her wombe,
Lo here he lies that hateth vice, and vertues life imbrast,
His name in earth his sprite above deserved to be well plast.

1. *Mnemosynes dere daughters.*—The Graces, daughters of Mnemosyne, goddess of Memory, and of Zeus.

2. *Stownd.*—Position.

3. *Gem snowwhite.*—The Romans used a white stone or piece of chalk to mark their lucky days on the calendar. Those that were unlucky they marked with charcoal.

14.

Of m. D. A.

The anagram introduced into this sonnet shows that it was addressed to Mistress Damascene Awdley. (See the introductory note of the previous poem.)

1. *Deserts.*—Good qualities, merits, excellencies.

2. *Kouth.*—Well-known, famous.

3. *Cyllene.*—Cyllenius, an epithet applied to Hermes, from his having been born on Mount Cyllene.

4. *Fingerfeat.*—Handicraft.

5. *Cyprian.*—Aphrodite.

6. *The Spartan bright.*—Helen of Troy.

15.

A neew yeres gift, to the l. M. S.

L.M.S.—Lady Margaret Seymour. See introductory note to *To L.J.S.*, No. 12.

1. *Mell.*—Mingle, combine.

16.

An other to l. M. S.

Another to Lady Margaret Seymour. See prefatory note for *To L.J.S.* (No. 12).

1. *Payzed.*—Weighty.

2. *Hert unthirld.*—Heart unpenetrated.

17.

To l. K. S.

To Lady Katherine Seymour. See prefatory note to *To L.J.S.*, No. 12.

18.

To l. E. S.

L.E.S.—Lady Elizabeth Seymour. See prefatory note to *To L.J.S.*, No. 12.

19.

To m. D. A.

To Mistress Damascene Awdley. See prefatory note to *Of m.D.A.*, No. 13.

These lines are a free rendering of one of Beza's *Epigrammata:*

Xenium Candidæ.

Vestes divitiis graves et arte,
  Aptandumve tuo monile collo,
Aut quos India mittit uniones,
  Jani nec queo, nec volo Calendis
Ad te mittere, Candida, una Bezæ
  Dilectissima Candida. At quid ergo?
Ipsam nempe animam tibi dicatam,
  Amorisque tui ignibus perustam:
Quæ, pridem tua sit licet, suamque
  Te pridem dominam vocetque ametque,
Se rursus tibi datque, dedicatque,
  Inclusa his numeris Phaleuciorum.
Quod si munera raritate censes,
  O Dii! quam tibi grande mitto munus!

20.

To m. S. H.

To Mistress Susan H. It has not been found possible to determine the identity of this friend of Grimald.

22.

Description of Vertue.

1. *In price.*—In high regard, honor.

For this poem Grimald is indebted to the following lines of Beza, which are to be found among his *Epigrammata:*

Descriptio Virtutis

Quænam tam lacero vestita incedis amictu?
  Virtus antiquis nobilitata sophis.

Cur vestis tam vilis? Opes contemno caducas.
  Cur gemina est facies? Tempus utrumque noto.
Quid docet hoc frænum? Mentis cohibere furores.
  Rastros cur gestas? Res mihi grata labor.
Cur volucris? Doceo tandem super astra volare.
  Cur tibi mors premitur? Nescio sola mori.

23.

Prayse of measure-kepyng.

1. *Beck.*—Stream. The sea into which Icarus fell, when his wings melted, bears his name.

2. *Overferse.*—Overfierce.

Beza's *Elegia II* is the source of this poem:

In Mediocritatis Laudem

Non frustra solita est medium laudare vetustas:
  Nam nil laudari dignius orbis habet.
In medio posita est virtus, hinc, indeque fallax
  Tota sinistra via est, totaque dextra via est.
Icare, si patrem esses inter utrumque secutus,
  Icarias nullus nomine nosset aquas.
Si medio Phaëton mansisset calle superbus,
  Non esset sæva terra perusta face
Nec lenis nimium, nec durat sæva potestas:
  Quæ medium servat, sola perdidit olim:
Occidit feritas te, truculente Nero.
  Augustus fœlix cur multos mansit in annos?
Nec facilis nimium, nec truculentus erat.
  Nec nimis ipse coli, nec sperni Juppiter optat,
Sed magis una juvat mens moderata Deos.
  Largus opum nullus, nullus laudatur avarus:
Magnus, in his potuit qui tenuisse modum.
  Antoni mensas sic vicit cœna Catonis,
Et tenuem melior fama secuta larem.
  Nec gracilis structura nimis, nec crassa probatur:
Hæc spectatori displicet, illa ruit.
  Ut moderata juvant, sic ægris pharmaca multis,
Heu nimium multis, sæpe petita nocent,
  Dicere plura nefas credo, nam laude nequaquam
Efferi immodica sustinet ipse modus.

24.

Mans life after Possidonius or Crates.

Possidonius.—A Stoic philosopher who taught with so great success at Rhodes that Pompey on his return from Syria, after the close of the Mithridatic war, stopped there to attend his lectures. Cicero was also his pupil. Besides his philosophical works, he wrote treatises on history, geography, and astronomy.

Crates.—One of the most distinguished Cynic philosophers, who flourished about 320 B.C., and who was a pupil of the cynic, Diogenes.

In the *Epistles of Crates* these sentiments which Grimald has attributed to Possidonius or Crates and to Metrodorus appear as those of Heraclitus and of Democritus, who are commonly known as the 'weeping philosopher' and the 'laughing philosopher':

Heracliti philosophia ad vitam humanam.

Quam viam quisque eligeret in hac vita. In foro
litigia et molesta negocia. In dominus cure.
In agri vero satis laboris. In mari timor.
In externa terra si quid possideas timor.
Si aut eges molestum. Coniugatûs?
es non absque cura eris. Non coniugatus vives
magis solitatie. Liberos habes metus cecitas
est vita sine liberis.
Iuventus temerarie Lanicies aut debiles. Alterutrum
eligendum est vel nunquam nasci vel cito
extingui. Omnia risus.

Democriti philosophi contrarium.

Huius modi sit mihi vivendi via. In foro
quidem gloria et prudentes actiones.
In domibus quies. In agris vero amenitas
In mari lucrum. In hospitali terra
si quid possideas gloria. Sin eges
solus es. Coniugatus es, optima domus.
Eris non coniugatus vives sine dolore.
Liberos habes lumen. Vita enim sine

liberis stulta est. Iuventes fortes.
Lanicies rursus pie. Utrumque
igitur eligendum est et nasci et
nunquam extingui. Omnia
igitur in vita bona.

—*Crates' Epistles*, Nüremberg, A. Huber, 1501.

J. W. Mackail, who has made an elaborate study of the Planudean anthology, says that it is a Byzantine tradition which ascribes these epigrams to Heraclitus and Democritus. In his collection of epigrams, these two are attributed to Posidippus and Metrodorus:

Posidippus.

Ποίην τις βιότοιο τάμῃ τρίβον; εἰν ἀγορῇ μὲν
νείκεα καὶ χαλεπαὶ πρήξιες· ἐν δὲ δόμοις
Φροντίδες· ἐυ δ' ἀγροῖς καμάτων ἅλις· ἐν δὲ θαλάσσῃ
τάρβος· ἐπὶ ξείνης δ', ἢν μὲν ἤχῃς τι, δέος,
ἪΗν δ' ἀπορῇς, ἀνιηρόν· ἔχεις γάμον; οὐκ ἀμέριμνος
ἔσσεαι· οὐ γαμέεις; ζῇς ἔτ' ἐρημότερος·
Τέκνα πόνοι· πήρωσις ἄπαις βίος· αἱ νεότητες
ἄφρονες· αἱ πολιαὶ δ' ἔμπαλιν ἀδρανέες.
Ἦν ἄρα τοῖνδε δυοῖν ἑνὸς αἵρεσις, ἢ τὸ γενέσθαι
μηδέποτ' ἢ τὸ θανεῖν αὐτίκα τικτόμενον.

Metrodorus.

Παντοίην βιότοιο τάμοις τρίβον· εἰν ἀγορῇ μὲν
κύδεα καὶ πινυταὶ πρήξιες· ἐν δὲ δόμοις
Ἄμπαυμ'· ἐν δ' ἀγροῖς φύσιος χάρις· ἐν δὲ θαλάσσῃ
κέρδος· ἐπὶ ξείνης, ἢν μὲν ἔχῃς τι, κλέος,
Ἢν δ' ἀπορῇς, μόνος οἶδας· ἔχεις γάμον; οἶκος ἄριστος
ἔσσεται· οὐ γαμέεις; ζῇς ἔτ' ἐλαφρότερος·
Τέκνα πόθος· ἄφροντις ἄπαις βίος· αἱ νεότητες
ῥωμαλέαι· πολιαὶ δ' ἔμπαλιν εὐσεβέες·
Οὐκ ἄρα τῶν δισσῶν ἑνὸς αἵρεσις, ἢ τὸ γενέσθαι
μηδέποτ' ἢ τὸ θανεῖν· πάντα γὰρ ἐσθλὰ βίῳ.

—J. W. Mackail, *Select Epigrams from the Greek Anthology*, London, 1890, pp. 12, 39-40.

A comparison of Grimald's version with the original Greek inclines one to think that very likely he worked directly from the Greek, rather than from some Latin version of these sentiments, since his poems have the same number of lines as the Greek originals. If he did, Grimald's work marks the first translations, from the Greek anthology into English, of two famous epigrams afterwards translated by many other poets.

25.

Metrodorus minde to the contrarie.

Metrodorus.—The name of several Greek philosophers, the most important of whom was a native of Athens, an Epicurean philosopher, and one of the most distinguished of the disciples of Epicurus.

1. *Beak.*—Expose to the warmth of the fire.

See the notes on the preceding poem.

26.

Of lawes.

It is possible that this poem is a reference to Wyatt's rebellion of 1554. This uprising was instigated by Sir Thomas Wyatt, the son of the poet of the same name. When the marriage between Mary I and Philip II of Spain was under consideration, Wyatt conspired to prevent it, and led the men of Kent to Southwark. In his attack on the city of London, he became separated from his men, and was captured. His execution followed soon after. Without his leadership the insurrection proved a failure.

27.

Of frendship.

1. *Scipio with Lelius didst thou conjoyn.*—C. Lælius was from early manhood the friend and companion of P. Cornelius Scipio Africanus. He first appears in history as

the commander of the Roman fleet in the attack on New Carthage, 210 B.C.

2. *Gesippus eke with Tite.*—Gisippus and Titus Quintus Fulvius, two friends who appear in Boccaccio's *Decameron,* Novel VIII, Tenth Day.

3. *Menclus sonne.*—Menœtius' son, Patroclus.

4. *Euryalus, and Nisus gave Virgil cause to sing.*—Euryalus and Nisus. Virgil has immortalized their friendship, *Aen.* 9. 176 ff.

5. *Cicero, the frendly man, to Atticus.*—See Cicero's letters to Atticus.

28.

The Garden.

1. *Sallet.*—Salad.

29.

An epitaph of Sir James Wilford knight.

James Wylford was knighted between the 18th and the 25th of Sept., 1547. He was among the Knights Bannerets and Bachelor Knights made in the camp beside Roxburgh, in Scotland, in the first year of Edward the Sixth's reign, by the hand of the high and mighty Prince Edward, Duke of Somerset, Lieutenant General of all the king's armies by land and sea, and Governor of his Royal Person, and Protector of all his realms, dominions and subjects.

—Wm. A. Shaw, *Knights of England,* London, 1906.

Ye have heard how the Frenchmen fortified the town of Dundee, where Monsieur de Etauges with his companie of horsemen lieing in garrison chaunced in skirmish to be taken by the Englishmen that day in Broughticrag, to the great rejoicing of them that tooke him, and no lesse greefe of the French and Scots for the tried valiancie that was throughlie knowne to rest in him. Moreover, the Englishmen that kept the towne of Hadington all the while against the enimies could not come by anie vittels, but onlie by a convoie of some convenient power to gard the carriages that brought the same to the borders. And as it fortuned at one time when the convoie came and passed up by Dunbar a skirmish was profferred by the French which laie within that castell in garrison. And as *Sir James Wilford* that was there amongst other upon this occasion (according to his wonted valancie) shewed himselfe verie forward and egre against the enemie, he was inclosed by an ambush, which the Frenchmen had laid on eche side the street within the towne, that he could by no means to escape out of their hands, but having his horse slaine under him, was taken prisoner even by a Gascoigne of the countrie named Pellicque, that woone no small commendation for that his good hap, in taking such a prisoner, whose approved powers was verie famous even among the enimies, who saw well inough a resolutenesse in the man rather by perillous adventures to purchase the perpetuitie of renowne, than by defect of courage or negligent service to loose both life and fame.

—Holinshed, *Chronicles of England, Scotland, and Ireland,* London, 1587, 3. 966.

Among the poems by 'uncertain authors' in *Tottel's Miscellany,* pp. 141, 153, there are the following elegy on Sir James Wilford, entitled, *Upon Sir James Wilfordes death,* and some *Verses written on the picture of Sir James Wilford:*

Upon Sir James Wilfordes death

Lo here the end of man the cruell sisters three
The web of Wilfords life unethe had half ysponne,
When rash upon misdede they all accorded bee
To breke vertues course er half the race were ronne
And trip him on his way that els had won the game
And holden highest place within the house of fame.

But yet though he be gone, though sense with him be past
Which trode the even steppes that leaden to renowne
We that remaine alive ne suffer shall to waste
The fame of his deserts, so shall he lose but sowne.
The thing shall aye remaine, aye kept as freshe in store
As if his eares shold ring of that he wrought before.
Waile not therfore his want sith he so left the stage
Of care and wretched life, with joye and clap of hands
Who plaieth lenger partes may well have greater age
But few so well may passe the gulfe of fortunes sandes
So triedly did he treade ay prest at vertues beck
That fortune found no place to geve him once a check.
The fates have rid him hence, who shall not after go,
Though earthed be his corps, yet florish shall be his fame,
A gladsome thing it is that er he step us fro,
Such mirrours he us left our life therby to frame,
Wherfore his praise shall last aye freshe in Brittons sight,
Till sunne shall cease to shine, and lende the earth his light.

Verses written on the picture of Sir James Wilford.

Alas that ever death such vertues should forlet,
As compast was within his corps, who picture is here set.
Or that it ever laye in any fortunes might,
Through depe disdaine his life to traine yat was so worthy a wight
For sith he first began in armour to be clad,
A worthier champion than he was yet England never had.
And though recure be past, his life to have againe,
Yet would I wish his worthinesse in writyng to remaine.
That men to minde might call how farre he did excell,
At all assayes to wynne the praise, which were to long to tell.
And eke the restlesse race that he full oft hath runne,
In painfull plight from place to place, where service was to doon
Then should men perceive, my tale to be of trouth,
And he to be the worthiest wight that ever nature wrought.

1. *Laundersey.*—Possibly Landrecies, in the province of Nord, France.

2. *Muttrel.*—Probably Muthill, Perthshire, N. E. of Edinburgh.

3. *Musselborough.*—In Midlothian county, east of Edinburgh.

4. *Haddington.*—In Haddington county, east of Edinburgh.

The last two of these towns figured in the Pinkie Campaign, 1547-8, which Edward Seymour, Duke of Somerset, the uncle of Edward VI, and the Lord Protector, undertook against the Scotch. The seizure and occupation of Haddington were regarded as most important, as this made the English masters of the country almost up to the gates of Edinburgh. There is no record of engagements at Laundersey or at Muttrel.

30.

An other, of the same knightes death.

For this epitaph of Sir James Wilford, Grimald is indebted to one by Beza:

Guilelmi Budæi

Budæum flevere homines, ploravit et aër;
  Budæus gelidis est quoque fletus aquis.
Sic flevere homines, ut plena volumnia mœstis
  Carminibus quivis Bibliopola terat.
Sic aër luxit, consumptis undique nimbis,
  Ut jam quas plueret non reperiret aquas,
Flumina sic flerunt, ut qua modo navis abibat,
  Currat in offensis sicca quadriga rotis.
Restabant cœlum et tellus, communis ut omni,
  Quamlibet immenso, mœror in orbe foret:
Sed cum cœlum animam Budæi, terra cadaver
  Possideat, quæso, qua ratione fleant?

1. *Greeted.*—Wept.

31.

An Epitaph of the ladye Margaret Lee. 1555.

Lady Margaret Lee.—Sir Henry Wyatt seems to have married about 1502, at which time he probably was forty-two years old. His wife was the daughter of John Skinner of Reigate, in Surrey (*Collins' Peerage,* 3. 428). By her he had three children: Margaret, who married Sir Anthony Lee, ancestor to the Earls of Lichfield; Henry, who seems to have settled early in Kent, where he constantly resided, leading the life of a retired private gentleman; and Thomas, the elder son, the poet.

—G. F. Nott, *The Works of Howard and Wyatt,* London, 1816, Memoirs of Sir Thomas Wyatt, p. vii.

Wyatt never suffered his literary amusements to interfere with his serious vocations. We find him, therefore, still involved in business of various kinds. He undertook the charge of his nephew Henry, the son of Sir Anthony Lee (and of his sister, Margaret Wyatt), a youth then about ten years old (p. xlviii, as above).

Margaret Wyatt is thought to have been one of the four ladies in attendance on Anne Boleyn when she was imprisoned in the Tower, and who were present at her execution. See Agnes Strickland's *Lives of the Queens of England,* Philadelphia, 1851, 4. 211.

32.

Upon the tomb of A. W.

It seems not unlikely that the A. W. of this poem is Lady Anne Wentworth, upon whose death was written the following elegy entitled *Of the' ladie Wentworthes death,* which appears among the poems by 'uncertain authors' in *Tottel's Miscellany* (p. 175), and which has been attributed to Lord Vaux:

Of the ladie Wentworthes death.

To live to dye, and dye to live againe,
With good renowne of fame well led before
Here lieth she that learned had the lore,
Whom if the perfect vertues wolden daine.
To be set forth with foile of worldly grace,
Was noble borne, and matcht in noble race,

> Lord Wentworthes wife, nor wanted to attain
> In natures giftes her praise among the rest,
> But that gave her praise above the best
> Not fame her wedlocks chastnes durst distain
> Wherein with child deliveryng of her wombe,
> Thuntimely birth hath brought them both in tombe
> So left she life by death to live again.

Lady Wentworth was the daughter of Sir James Tyrrel of Gipping, Suffolk, who is said to have been one of the murderers of the Princes in the Tower. She married Sir Robert Wentworth, of Nettlestead, Suffolk county. The Wentworth family was of high connections, as Robert Wentworth's sister Margaret married Sir John Seymour, and became the mother of the Duke of Somerset, Lord Seymour of Sudeley, and of Jane, who was the wife of Henry VIII, and mother of Edward VI. The son of Lady Anne Wentworth, Thomas, Lord Wentworth (b. 1501), succeeded his father October 17, 1528. He was one of the eighty-three signers of the letter to the Pope in favor of the proposed divorce of Henry VIII, was one of the twenty-seven peers by whom Queen Anne Boleyn was found guilty, and went to Calais to receive Henry VIII's fourth queen, Anne of Cleves. He was also one of the six lords of the council to attend on his cousin Edward VI, to whom he subsequently became Lord Chancellor.

33.

Upon the deceas of W. Ch.

The college records of neither Cambridge nor Oxford have any record of Grimald's intimate friend, the blind student, W. Chambers, to whom this elegy is addressed. It seems from the context of the poem (17-18) that he had not yet completed his college course; in that case an account of him is less likely to be found upon the university records.

1. *Wee.*—Woe, lament.

34.

Of N. Ch.

The surname of the person, Nicholas Chambers, to whom this elegy is addressed, is given in the preceding poem, an elegy on the death of his younger brother, W. Chambers. Joseph Foster's *Alumni Oxonienses* records the degree of B.A. as conferred in 1547-8 upon one Nicholas Chambers of Christ Church.

1. *Mavortian.*—Pertaining to Mavors, Mars, i.e., martial.

35.

A funerall song, upon the deceas of Annes his moother.

The content of this poem is interesting in that it is the only source of information in regard to Grimald's early life. In spite of the fact that the deep feeling in this lyric is somewhat smothered by a display of classical erudition, it has been called by Arber a companion-piece to Cowper's *On the Receipt of my Mother's Picture.*

1. *Martius.*—Gaius Marcius Coriolanus, first known as Gaius Marcius.

2. *Sertorius.*—Quintus Sertorius, a Roman general, a native of Nursia, a Sabine village. Sertorius' father died when Sertorius was but a boy. He owed a good education to his mother, to whom he was affectionately attached (Plutarch, *Sertor.* 2. 22.

3. *Sicil brethren.*—Typhon and Enceladus.

4. *Tyndars ymps.*—Castor and Pollux, the sons of Tyndareus and Leda.

5. *Arge.*—Argos.

6. *Charged necks with parents yoke.*—Celobis and Biton, the sons of Cydippe, a priestess of Hera at Argos, were celebrated for their affection for their mother, whose chariot they once dragged, during a festival, to the temple of Hera, a distance of forty-five stadia. (Herodotus 1. 131.)

7. *Noorsse.*—Caieta, the nurse of Creusa and Ascanius.

The promontory of Caieta (modern Gaieta), as well as both the port and town of the name, were believed to have been called from her.

8. *Acca.*—Acca Laurentia, the wife of the shepherd Faustulus, and the nurse of Romulus and Remus after they had been taken from the she-wolf. According to other accounts, she was not the wife of Faustulus, but a prostitute who from her mode of life was called *lupa* by the shepherds, and who left to the Roman people the property she acquired in this way.

9. *Lyai.*—Lyæus, Bacchus. Grimald attributes the metamorphosis of the Hyades to Bacchus, and not to Zeus.

10. *Primetide.*—Springtime.

11. *Granta.*—The river Cam, upon which Cambridge lies.

12. *The ladies nyne.*—The nine Muses.

13. *That fayr foord.*—Oxford.

14. *Dearworth.*—Dearly beloved, esteemed.

15. *Ene.*—Aeneas.

36.

Upon the death of the lord Mautravers, out of doctor Haddons latine.

Henry Fitz Allan, styled Lord Mautravers, only son and heir apparent by first wife, b. in 1538. Knighted as K. B., being fifth in order of Knights so created at the coronation of Edw. VI, 20 Feb., 1546-7. Matric, Cambridge (Queens Coll.) May, 1549. He married (Lic. 12 Apr. 1555) Ann, widow of Sir Hugh Rich, 3d daughter and co-heir of Sir John Wentworth, of Gosfield, Essex. Being sent ambassador to the King of Bohemia, he caught a fever and died sine prole et vita patris 30 June, 1556, at Brussels and was buried in the Cathedral there aged 18. His widow married, between 1573 and 1580, at Gosfield asfd. as 'Ann, Lady Maltravers uxor William Deane Esq.' In her will dated 26 March, 1573, she styles herself 'late wife of Rt. Hon.

Henry Earl of Arundel' and bequeathes her residue to 'my servant' who proved the said will 15 Feb. 1580-1.

—Wm. A. Shaw, *The Knights of England,* London, 1906.

Walter Haddon (1516-1572) was educated at Eton under Richard Coxe, afterwards Dean of Christ Church, and ultimately Bishop of Ely. In 1533 he was elected from Eton to King's College, Cambridge. He declined an invitation to Cardinal College, newly founded by Wolsey at Oxford, and proceeded B.A. at Cambridge in 1537. Together with Cheke, he labored for the reform of ecclesiastical laws, and in 1571 the result of their work was published under the title, *Reformatio Legum Ecclesiasticarum.* He was appointed master of Trinity Hall in 1551-2, and soon after, in 1552, became president of Magdalen College, Oxford, which position he did not hold long. He was much engaged in religious controversies. During his lifetime he enjoyed a great reputation as a writer of Latin prose; but his writings have not been held in such high esteem by later critics. His sympathies were with the cause of Protestantism. By Strype (*Strype's Life of Parker* 2. 365) he has been termed one of the great lights of the Reformation in Cambridge, under King Edward.

The following Latin poem by Dr. Haddon is the source of Grimald's composition:

In Mortem Domini
Matraversi, Comita.

Nobilis Henricus qui Matraversius heros,
Stirpis Arundeliæ maiorum nomine prosco,
Dictus erat, genus atque suum degente trahebat
Fitzallenorum, comitum virtute potentum,
Quem pater excellens florentem viderat armis,
Artibus, ingenio, dulci sermone fluentem,
Consilio plenum, cuius transcenderrat annos
Ante diem virtus veniens, gravitasquė virilis,
Clade ruit subita, generosam gloria mentem,
Dum subit, et nimium iuvenili pectore fervet.

Cæsaris at fratem, Maria hunc regina Britonum
Legavit, iuvenem clarum, lectissima princeps.
Fertur equis, volitansque via pervenit ad aulam,
Cæsaris, et summa comissum laude peregit
Munus, et ad magnam profluxit gloria famam.
Sed venit in medios febris funesta triumphos,
Tabificaque puer, nimiumque, oblite salutis
Ipse tuæ, nimium patriæ memor, atque parentis,
Cur ita festinas? magnum est, moderare laborem
Sic patriæ servire decet, servire frequenter
Ur liceat, seroque tuo succrescere patri.
Sed tibi forte placet vitam pro laude pacifici,
Nec metuis mortem, tanto quae splendet honori.
Gloria non poterat certe contingere maior,
Si tibi sescentos donasset Jupiter annos.
Primæ causa viæ fuit, et tibi cause laboris.
Funeris atque comes processit cæsaris aula.
Sic, o sic superi, iuvenis dignissimus astris,
Fælicem vitam conclusit morte beata.
Cum Mariæ regnum quarto processerat anno,
Julius extremam lucem quam mensis habebat,
Illa eadem, claro iuveni, lux ultima fulsit.
Quattuor a lustris unum si dempseris annum
Hæc Matraver si morientis habebitur ætas.
Sic Titus est Cæsar primis ereptus in annis,
Sic puer est, princeps Eduardus, morte revulsus
Parce pater lachrymis: o Anglia siste dolorem:
Fata favent nulli, mors imminent omnibus hostis.
Quod licet, hoc unum Shelleius ore diserto
Præstitit, ut grato nomen sermone celebret:
Et tuus Haddonus, magnus viventis amator,
Ista tibi ponit studii monumenta prioris
Iamque vale, pubis nostræ lectissima gemma,
Quo post Eduardum maius nil Anglia vidit.

—*D. Gualteri Haddoni Poemata,* London, apud Guilielmum Seresium, 1567.

1. *To Cesars broother sent.*—Ferdinand I, King of Bohemia, brother of Charles V, the Roman Emperor.

2. *Titus Cesar.*—Titus died at the age of forty-four, after having reigned but a little over two years.

3. *Prince Edward.*—Edward VI, the son of Henry VIII. He succeeded to the throne when he was but ten, and died (1553) six years after his accession.

4. *Shelly.*—The author of the elegy on Lord Mautravers, to which allusion is made, may be Sir Richard Shelly (1513-1589), a diplomat in the service of Henry VIII, Edward VI, and Mary I. Many of his letters are among the Harleian and Lansdowne MSS. in the British Museum. According to his own account, he was the author of a treatise on theological subjects.

37.

This epitaph on Lord Mautravers is drawn from an epitaph of Beza:

D. Io. Valentis, Regia consiliis

Extincto nuper Respublica mœsta Valente,
  Visa mihi secum sic gemebunda queri:
Sæpe alios flevi, dum sic raperentur, alumnos:
  Causa tamen nunquam justior ulla fuit.

38.

The death of Zoroas, an Egiptian Astronomer, in the first fight, that Alexander had with the Persians.

The source of Grimald's poem in blank verse, *The death of Zoroas,* is to be found in the Latin poem, the *Alexandreis* of Gautier de Chatillon, who is also known as Philip Gualtier de Chatillon or de Lille, Philippe Gautier de Castellione, Philippus Gualtherius Insularus, Walther von der Lille, Walther von Chatillon, and Gualtherus Tornacensis.

Gautier de Lille ou de Chatillon, poète latin, né à Ronchin-en-Flandre, qui fleurit vers 1170-1180. Il composa un grand nombre d'ouvrages très intéressants et d'une valeur littéraire sérieuse: en voici les principaux: *Tractatus sive dialogus contra Judæos.* Ce traité a pour but de prouver que le Messie attendu par les Juifs n'est autre que Jésus Christ: il fut publié par Oudin à Leyde en 1692 dans les *Veterum aliquot Galliæ et Belgii scriptorum opuscula sacra numquam edita.* Migne le réédité dans *la Patrologie Latine* (t. CCIX); Rhythmi ou poésies rimées; elles ont été publieés par Muldener sous le titre de *Die Zehn Gedichte des Walter von Lille.* (Hanover, 1859); *Alexandreis,* poeme en dix livres et hexamétres, c'est l'histoire d'Alexandre le Grand depuis sa naissance jusqu'à sa mort, d'après Justin, Quinte Curce et la Bible, avec un singulier mélange d'histoire sacrée et d'histoire profane. Le plus ancien manuscript connu est celui de Zwickau de 1208 (Codex Cygneensis); il á été imprimé à Rouen vers la fin du XVe siècle et souvent réédité.

—*La Grande Encyclopédie, Inventaire Raisonné des Sciences, des Lettres, et des Arts,* Paris.

The sources of *The Death of Zoroas* may be readily seen by comparing Grimald's poem with that of Gautier, which follows. Lines 1 to the middle of 4 of Grimald's are derived from lines 1 to 3 of Gautier's. The lines from the middle of line 4 to 6 inclusive are from lines 30 and 31 of the Latin. 8-11 = 119-125; 12-17 = 126-132; 18-24 = 133-140. From 25-99 Grimald's poem follows Gautier's from 140 to the end. This leaves the source of the remaining sixteen lines of Grimald's poem unaccounted for.

ALEXANDREIDOS LIBER TERTIUS

Iam fragor armorum, iam strages bellica vincit
Clangorem lituum, subtexunt astra sagittæ,
Missiliumque frequens obnubilat æra nimbus.
Primus in oppositos prætenta cuspide Persas,
Ocius emisso tormenti turbine saxo
Torquet equum Macedo, qua confertissima regum
Auro scuta micant, ubi plurima gemma superbis
Scintillat galeis, qua formidabile visu
Aurivomis patulas absorbens faucibus auras
Igniti Dario præfertur forma draconis.
Quæ rentique ducem, quem primo vulnere dignum
Obruat, obiicitur Syriæ præfectus Aretes,
Cuius ab aurata volitans ac pendulus hasta
Vindicat astra leo, galeam carbunculus urit.
Primus Alexandri tremebundo traiicit ictu
Chaldæus clipeum, sed fraxinus asseris artum
Formidans aditum fracto crepat arida ligno.
Gnaviter occurrens ferro Pellæus Aretæ

Dissipat umbonem, qua barbara bulla diescit
Principis in clipeo, nec eo contenta trilicis
Loricæ dissarcit opus, cordisque vagatur
Per latebras animamque bibit letalis arundo.
Occidit occisus, largoque foramine manans
Purpurat arva cruor: regem clamore fatetur
Altisono vicisse suum primumque tulisse
Primitias belli, faustum sibi praedicat omen
Græca phalanx, lætosque ferunt ad sidera plausus.
Densatur cunei, Clitus et Ptolemæus in armis
Conspicui tanta levitate feruntur in hostes,
In tauros quantum geminos rapit ira leones,
Quos stimulat ieiuna fames, causamque furoris
Adiuvat excussæ gravis obliquatio caudæ.
Hic Ptolemæus equo Parthum Dodunta supinat
Tempora transfixum cerebroque fluente gementem.
At conto Clitus Androphilon evertere tentat,
Inque vicem sese feriunt clipeisque retusa
Utraque dissiluit obtuso lancea ferro.
Quadrupedi quadrupes armoque opponitur armus,
Pectora pectorobis, orbisque retunditur orbe,
Thorax thorace, gemit obruta casside cassis.
Nec mora poplitibus ambo cecidere remissis
Vectores vectique simul, similesque peremptis
Exanimes iacuere diu: sed corpora postquam
Convaluere prior reparato robore rectum
Inque pedes sese recipit Clitus Androphiloque
Surgere conanti solo furialiter ictu
Demetit ense caput et terrae mandat humandum.
Præditus eloquio bello specieque sinistro
Fuderat in cornu Græcum Mazæus Iollam.
Ultor adest agilis stricto mucrone Philotas,
Et quia Mazæum sonipes submoverat, Ochum
Cominus aggreditur, cuius latus ense bipartit.
Interea multa sudantem cæde Philotam
Hyrcani cingunt equites, quorum agmina rumpunt
Impiger Antigonus, Cœnus, Craterus, et ipse
Parmenio, sine quo nihil umquam carmine dignum
Gessit Alexander: sed quæ provenerit illi
Talio pro meritis magis arbitror esse silendum.
Antigoni iacet ense Phylax, Mida cuspide Cœni,
Amphilochum Craterus adit, quem casside rupta

Abstrahit examinem curru, iungitque ruenti
Automedonta suum, iam viscera rupta trahentem.
More suo ruit in Persas damnatus iniquo
Sidere Parmenio, cui regibus ortus Hysannes
Et Dimus incutiunt hastas lateri: manet ille
Immotus stabilitque fugam pavitantis Orestæ.
Qui pedes exesæ tendebat in ardua rupis.
Hunc simul intuitus perfossum pectus Hysannem
Sternit equo, profugumque equitem restaurat in arma.
Instantemque Dimum rapto mucrone lacerto
Cornipedis planta terit invalidumque relinquit.
His Agilon, his addit Hylan Arabemque Cherippum.
Parte alia furit Eumenides Persasque lacessit
Nunc gladio, nunc missilibus: mucrone Diaspem
Deiicit, Eudochii telum pulmone cruentat.
Dissipat ossa virum, procerum conculcat acervos.
Nec minus in dextro dum pugnat Marte Nicanor
Sanguine spargit agros, Humectat cædibus æquor.
Cui iuvenis facie dives, sed ditior ortu
Quippe genus claro referens a sanguine Cyri.
Obviat Echinus, clipeumque Nicanoris ictu
Provocat, ut laterem tecti vaga veris in ortu
Grando ferire solet, sed respuit æris iram
Tuta domus: verum durato corde Micanor
Irruit in facinus miserandæ cædis, eumque
Qua candens oculis aperit lorica fenestram
Cuspide percellit, et lumine privat utroque,
Dumque per unius aditum scelus ausa cucurrit
Fraxinus, alterius extinxit luminis usum.
Stabat in adverso discriminis agmine diri
Clara propago Nine princeps Ninivita Negusar,
Doctus in obiectos dubia sævire securi,
Doctus et a tergo iaculis lacessere fata.
Nunc iaculo nunc ense furit, nunc vero bipenni
Excruciat cerebrum: iaculo perfoderat Hylam
Actoriden, Dorilum gladio viduaverat armo,
Fuderat Hermogenem cæsa cervice securi.
Hunc ubi multimoda vastantem cæde Pelasgos
Intuitur, stricto celer advolat ense Philotas,
Quaque super conum lucem vomit igne pyropus,
Pertundit galeam, sed lubrica discutit ictum.
Non impune tamen descendit mucro: sinistram

Quam sibi forte manum frontem prætenderat ante
Amputat. Ecce parat ulcisci dextra sororem
Ictibus exposita, et cædis secura securim
Librat et adstanti casum casura minatur,
Ereptamque sibi gemeret fortasse Philotas
Ante dies animam, sed equo prælatus Amyntas
Opposuit clipeum, quem miro transfodit ictu
Machina terribilis, medioque umbone recepta est.
Retrahere ardenti qua iungitur ulna lacerto
Ense viri instantis a pectore cæsa recessit.
Excitat interdum vires dolor: ille recisis
In bello manibus se corpus inutile cernens
Quod potuit fecit et equo se obiecit Iollæ.
Tresque ruere simul, periit perfossus Iollas
Et sonipes iaculis: sed nec tibi, dure Negusar,
Missilium nimbus nec tanta ruina pepercit.
Iam madet herba latens, terramque cadavera celant.
Arva natant sanie, replentur sanguine valles:
Largus utrimque cruor, sed maior inebriat agros
Persarum strages: rarescit barbarus hostis.
Tabescitque animo licet infinitus, eumque
Pauca manus Macetum non cessat cædere, quorum
Defectum numeri fervens audacia supplet.
His igntur iam terga fugæ spondentibus instat
Fulmineus Macedo, perque invia tela, per hostes.
Perque globos equitum, peditum stipante corona,
Ad Darium molitur iter: sed contrahit agmen
Oxathres, Dario quo nemo propinquior ortu.
Hinc dolor, hinc gemitus: perit acris utrimque iuventus,
Involvitque ducum mors uno turbine turbam.
Seminat in Persas leti genus omne cruentas
Excutiens Bellona manus: gemit ille recluso
Gutture, traiecto iacet ille per ilia ferro:
Hunc sudis excerebrat, hunc fundit vel arcus:
Ille vomit saniem fractis cervicibus, illi
Intestina cadunt, alium sibi vindicat ensis:
Hic obit, ille obiit: hic palpitat, ille quiescit.
Stabat ab opposito niveis pretiosus in armis
Memphites Zoroas, quo nemo peritior astris
Mundanas prænosse vices, quo sidere frugis
Defectum patiatur ager, quis frugifer annus.
Unde nives producat hiems, quæ veris in artu

Temperies impregnet humum, cur ardeat æstas,
Quid dedit autumno maturis cingier uvis:
Circulus an possit quadrari, an musica formet
Cœlestes modulos, vel quanta proportio rerum
Quatuor inter se, novit quis sidera septem
Impetus obliquo rapiat contraria mundo:
Quot distent a se gradibus, quæ stella nocivum
Impediat sævire senem, quo sidere fiat
Obiice propitius: Martem quis temperet ignis,
Quam sibi quisque domum quærat, quod sidus in isto
Regnet hemispherio: motus rimatur et horas
Colligit, eventus hominum perpendit in astris:
Parva loquor, totum claudit sub pectore cœlum.
Hic ergo in stellis mortem sibi fata minari
Contemplatus erat: sed enim, quia vertere fati
Non poterat seriem, penetrare audebat ad ipsum
Rectorem Macetum, toto conamine poscens
A tanto cecidisse viro, vitamque perosus,
Morten parturiens in prima fronte furoris
Occurrebat ei, curruque premebat ab alto
Grandine missilium percussum principis orbem.
Nec solum iaculis, sed voce probisque lacessit,
Atque ita: Nectanabi non infitianda propago,
Dedecus æternum matris, cur vulnera perdis
Ignavos agitans? In me converte furorem,
Si quid adhuc virtutis habes: me contere, cuius
Militiam claudit septemplicis arca sophiæ,
Et caput astriferum sibi vindicat utraque laurus.
    Motus Alexander miseretur obire volentis,
Ac placide subicit: proh monstrum, quisque es, inquit,
Vive precor, moriensque suum ne destrue tantis
Artibus hospitium: numquam mea dextera sudet
Vel rubeat gladius cerebro tam multa scienti.
Utilis es mundo: quis te impulit error ad amnes
Tendere velle Stygos, ubi nulla scientia floret?
Dixit, at ille pedes terræ se mandat, eique,
Qua se dissocians ocream lorica relinquit,
Sauciat ense femur et dedicat arva cruore.
Infremuit Macedo, Zoroæque ut parcere posset,
Admissum procul egit equum. Sic ergo remotus
Continuit bilem: verum Meleager eodem
Irruit, et Zoroæ qua cruri tibia nubit

Cædit utrumque genu: tunc cetera turba iacentem
Comminuunt in frusta virum stellisque reponunt.

—M. Philippi Gualtheri ab insula de Castellione *Alexandreis* ad fidem librorum MSS. et impress. recensuit F. A. W. Muldener. In ædibus B. G. Teubneri, MDCCCLXIII.

1. *Taratantar.*—The sound of a bugle or trumpet.

2. *Bebledd.*—Bebled, blood-sprinkled.

3. *Darie.*—Darius III.

4. *Down.*—Smites down.

5. *Memphite.*—Of Memphis.

6. *Quadrate may becoom.*—May be squared.

7. *Grees.*—Degrees.

8. *Beurn.*—Warrior.

9. *Nectanabs bastard.*—Nectanab, the King of Egypt, is said to have won by magic arts the favor of Olympias, the wife of Philip II, King of Macedonia, and thus become the father of Alexander the Great.

10. *Sevenfold.*—A reference to the trivium and quadrivium. In the schools of the Middle Ages the first three liberal arts, grammar, rhetoric, and logic, were termed the trivium; and the other four, arithmetic, music, geometry, and astronomy, were termed the quadrivium.

11. *Sophie.*—Wisdom.

12. *Quishes.*—Cuisses, armor for protecting the thighs.

13. *Meleager.*—The son of Neoptolemus, a Macedonian officer of great distinction in the service of Alexander the Great.

14. *Renk.*—Rink, man, warrior. 1515, Stewart, *Cron. Scot.* III. 7: "With mony rynk that ryall wes and ryke, in plane battel."

15. *Seg.*—Segge, man. 'Through this and such the silly segge lay plasde in puddle still.'—Drant.

16. *Fone.*—Fool.

17. *Camenes.*—Properly Camenæ, prophetic nymphs, belonging to the religion of ancient Italy. Some accounts identify them with the Muses.

39.

Marcus Tullius Ciceroes death.

This poem in blank verse, like the preceding composition, had its source in a Latin poem, *Mors Ciceronis,* by Beza:

Mors Ciceronis, Ex Lib. Historiarum Livii C.XX.
et Vitis Plutarchi et Valer. Max.

Sylva II

Ergo ut ventorum rabiem, pelagique furorem
Indomitum aspexit, fatis heu poscitur, inquit,
Poscitur infœlix Cicero: convertite vela
Et me vicinæ moriturum reddite ripæ.
Scilicet has grates hladiis erepta tuorum
Patria persolves? moriar, sic numina divum,
Sic voluere dei, servata ut consul in urbe
Tullius intereat, nec plura effatus, ab imo
Corde trahens gemitus memoratæ ad nomina Romæ
Imbre oculos, lachrymis genas implevit ab ortis.
At licet assiduis exercita turba periclis
Inviti lachrymas nautæ tenuere, diuque
Obnixi sævos pelagi transcendere fluctus,
Omnia laxarunt iratis carbasa ventis
Et tandem incolumen statuerunt littore proram.
Descendit mæstus Cicero, multoque labore
Membra trahit confecta senex, simul undique magna
Cir cumstabat herum servorum turba, periclis
Nec nimium stupefacta suis, nec tempore duro
Pollicitam fractura fidem: pars apparat enses,
Pars domino assistit, cæcaque ambage viarum
Leticæ impositum ducunt, si fallere sævos
Antoni possint gladios, turbæ que sequentis
Evitare minas. Sic ibat Tullius ille
Tullius ille togæ princeps, magnique senatus,
Quum procul adventare viros, inimicaque signa
Conspicit et stricto mortem procul ense minantem
Poppilium, cuius quondam servaverat ipse
Fortunas, vitamque rei, quum libera Roma
Olim illum audiret, mirareturque tonantem.
Iam quoque sævus adest, et poscit Herennius hostem.
Quid faciat? num forte manus protendat inermes,
Aut mercede petat veniam? num flectere verbis

Defensi quondam conetur militis iras?
Hæc ætas virtusque vetant et pectore in alto
Fixus amor patriæ, Romæque cadentis imago.
Vertite, ait, currus, plenis curratur habenis
Immeritam in mortem: ne pridem nuncia Phoebi
Poscit avis, cæloque novum coniungere civem
Juppiter exoptat. Bruti Cassique beatæ
Vivite vos animæ. quod si non monia nobis
Fata nocent, forsan nec nos moriemur inulto.
Iam vixi mihi Roma satis, me vita vereri
Acta vetat nigræ damnosa oblivia mortis.
Occidite, at noscent venturi cuncta nepotes,
Æternamque dabunt morienti hæc funera vitam.
Immo (aut fallor ego, et frustra tibi Roma creatus
(Augur eram quondam) non semper amica favebit
Antoni Fortuna tibi, civesque peremptos
Tempus erit victrix a te quo Roma reposcat.
Me iuvet interea speratum invisere cælum
    Desierat. iugulum parans, immota tenebat
Ora senex. Illum properantem in fata nec ipsi
Aspiciunt equites læti, positoque furore
Ut nudum videre caput, canamque senectam,
Vix tandem inviti lachryma tenuere cadentes,
Et pene e manibus gladii cecidere eruentis
Unus torva gerens truculentus Herennius ora,
Degeneres quid statis? ait. simul ense superbo
Colla secat, nec adhuc fatiatur cæde: sceleratum
Adiunxisse scelus sceleri iuvat. ergo desertis
Ausas Antoni vitam signare tabellis
Cædit et ipse manus morientem vidit ab alto
Invitus cælo Phœbus, piceaque que refertur
    Nube caput texisse siu. flevere cadentem
Et flebunt Latiæ æternum Graiæque Camœnæ.
Flexaminis vero Pitho (mirabile dictu)
Sueta illi quondamtum res tum verba loquenti
Suggerere, et suam conspergere nectare linquam,
Ut patuit iugulus, fugiente aufugit amico,
Et terras, eheu nunquam reditura, relinquit.
Poppilius volat interea. truncoque relicto,
Antoni portat sævis spectacula mensis.

—*Theodori Bezæ Vezelii Poemata,* Lutetiæ,
ex officina Conradi Badii, M.D. XLVII.

1. *Consul Marcus.*—Marcus Tullius Cicero.

2. *Shend.*—Destroyed.

3. *Room.*—Rome.

4. *Gleavs.*—Glaives, broadswords.

5. *Popilius.*—C. Popilius Lænas, a native of Picenus, who was successfully defended by Cicero, when brought to trial for some offense before the courts of Rome. As the assistance of advocates was gratuitously given, it was an instance of peculiar atrocity that Popilius offered his services to Antony to murder Cicero, his benefactor, for no other reason than to gain Antony's favor.

6. *Herennius.*—A centurion in charge of the soldiers who captured Cicero, and put him to death.

7. *Grayes.*—Graiæ, the Greeks.

8. *Pitho.*—More properly Pythius, Apollo, whose shrine was at Pytho, the ancient Delphi.

40.

Of M. T. Cicero.

The source of this poem is to be found among Beza's *Icones:*

T. Livii.

Tumulum Tito nuper parabam Livio,
Quum sic Apollo jussit ut desisterem:
Hæc mortuos, inquit, decent: vivit Titus.

41.

D. Hugoni Latimero Nicolaus Grimoaldus. S.

Hugh Latimer, the apostle of the Reformation and illustrious martyr, was born at Thurcaston, Leicestershire, about 1485. He was educated at Cambridge, and became attached to the new learning and the new religious ideas which had begun to be established there. He soon became a zealous preacher of the reformed doctrines, and in consequence involved in many controversies. The dispute about Henry VIII's marriage with Catherine of Aragon brought Latimer into notice. He was one of the divines appointed by the University of Cambridge to examine as to its lawfulness. His decision was in favor of the King, that the marriage was null and void. This secured Henry's favor, and he was appointed one of Henry's chaplains, and received a benefice. In 1535 he was appointed Bishop of Worcester, and at the opening of the convocation on June 9, 1536, preached two powerful sermons urging the necessity of reform. After a time the work of reformation retrograded, and Latimer found himself and his bold opinions in little favor. Toward the end of Henry's reign, when the reactionary party, headed by Gardiner and Bonner, was in the ascendant, Latimer resigned his bishopric (1539), and lived in retirement. He was watched very closely, however, and during a visit to London, whither he had come for medical treatment, he was seized and brought before the Privy Council. As he would not accept the Act of the Six Articles, he was cast into the Tower, but on the accession of Edward VI was released; although he regained favor at court, he did not return to his bishopric. On the accession of Mary, he was again imprisoned in the Tower (Sept. 1553); later he was sent to Oxford, together with Ridley and Cranmer, to defend their doctrines concerning the mass before the divines of Oxford and Cambridge (March 1554). After his examination he was excommunicated, and transferred to a common jail in Oxford, where he remained for over a year, becoming feeble, sick, and worn out with the hardships that he endured. On Sept. 30, 1555, he and Ridley were again summoned for trial before the commissioners, and on Oct. 7 he was condemned to be burned. On Oct. 16, 1555, together with Ridley, he was burned 'at the ditch over against Balliol College.' His dying words are famous: 'Be of good cheer, Master Ridley, and play the man; we shall this day light such a candle, by God's grace, in England, as I trust shall never be put out.'

Only four years before the martyrdom of Latimer, Grimald addressed these verses to him whose principles he had adopted and preached. Yet when the hour of trial came, and Grimald, because of his stand for righteousness, was condemned to be hanged, drawn, and quartered, and was thrown into prison with Latimer, he not only deserted him, secretly recanting before the Roman Catholic prelates, but remained in prison, and, serving as a spy upon him and the other two great martyrs of the Reformation, Cranmer and Ridley, secured whatever documentary evidence he could against them, as the price of his life.

The following is a translation of Grimald's Latin verses addressed to Latimer, to whom William Turner dedicated his *Preservative or triacle agaynst the poyson of Pelagius:*

To Doctor Hugh Latimer Nicholas Grimald Sends Greetings

Most worthy Latimer, flourishing in no idle old age, whom the king, the king's wise and prudent council, and the state for a long time, have wished good health, behold one like you, another veteran, who, in fighting to a finish the rebels against religion, rejoices in having you out of many thousands as his patron; as one who has been well tried encourages another well tried, and a friend, a friend; in order that you may together mend one another's broken fortunes, which the bitter enemy of our Lord assails. Thus it is fit that all Christians should defend the cause of Christ, and here join their forces. May the number of the warriors increase as the number of the enemy! But of what do I complain? Whom do I accuse? O shameful manners! O dreadful times! There are drones, an idle herd, who, having nourished their bodies with honey, leave their posts and betray all. There are idlers whom you, Latimer, have often noted (God grant the account be not spun out for deaf ears), who look out for their own interests and live for themselves, who have fair titles and the empty name of good soldiers. These take the plentiful rewards that are due vigorous soldiers, and a vigorous band of men. These take the places of armed men, but not their arms; nay, they rather, as the basest monsters, make the battle a confusion. A large band is assailing us, and a very great force is furiously fighting. Behold the hostile squadron, behold the Pope and Pelagius are here! The devil, the head of wickedness, girt round about with a great force, is here. Let them not invade, rout, conquer, and rule over us. Where do your bodies, lethargic with sloth, repose? What are we doing? What great sluggishness is destroying us men? How ready are we with great forces to defend fields, groves, cattle, villas, houses, chests, riches, perishable treasures, and kingdoms ready to fall! And yet, stupid minds, dead hearts, Heaven itself is snatched away from us while we snore. Woe, miserable race! Where are thy watchmen? Who directs the fate of the British people? The foxes and the wolves? Never, by Hercules! never will glorious victory return, unless these men, given to sleep and to abandoning their camp in the time of war, are made to depart straightway, or to hand over their duties to those who govern human affairs with impartial rule, and cherish with the greatest zeal and honor those who, possessed of upright minds and great strength of purpose, overcome deceitful falsehood by the constancy of truth, as this Turner, the bravest of heroes, has done.

42.

Ad D. Guilielmum Turnerum.

William Turner (d. 1568), Dean of Wells, physician and botanist, was educated at Pembroke Hall, Cambridge, where he was intimate with Nicholas Ridley, afterwards Bishop of London, who was his instructor in Greek. He often heard Latimer preach, and accepted his teachings. His *Preservative or Triacle agaynst the Poyson of Pelagius* was written in reply to one Robert Cooke, a man of heretical opinions, who held a subordinate office at court, with whom he carried on a religious controversy.

Pelagius, a British monk who flourished during the first quarter of the fifth century, originated a doctrine regarded by the church as heretical, that guilt belongs only to the free action of the will, therefore man is not guilty of Adam's sin, nor is his will corrupted, that children have no original sin, and that they ought not to be baptized. Man chooses by his own power, but God's grace comes in to assist those who choose the right. Augustine, on the contrary, held that man's will was wholly corrupted, and that we could choose the right way only by the power of the grace of God.

The following is a translation of Grimald's Latin verses addressed to William Turner:

To Doctor William Turner.

Continue, most worthy Turner, with God's assistance to adorn our age with your books, and with power from heaven to quash the wicked tales which like a pestilence afflict our people; while fat gluttons and great lords rejoice to lie hid with cunning in concealed places, and to sit with folded hands, while their flocks are deserted, and their gaping treasure-chests swell with new sums of money. The thieves, an opportunity being given them, prey upon the watchmen. "What end will there be of this," I ask, "what end?" The Supreme Judge will give unbearable torments, and every pious man will be horror-stricken at such crimes. But you who are most eager in repressing your rightful enemies, and in defending the precious words of your God, will gain the most joyful rewards in the shining heavens, rewards which will not perish in days to come. Continue, therefore, to despise the Popes with all your soul, splendid example of men, mindful that the illustrious examples of illustrious men should be followed; and do not easily permit any of the ignorant in the Church of Christ to follow whatever base teachings they choose. The immortal Deity favors you with a splendid name, and the Father on high regards you as His own child. And the lovers of light, a shining crowd, give you their heartfelt thanks. It is better to have pleased God while defending the right, than to serve in a hypocritical manner the interests of those who are evil. It is better that your writings should be approved by a few just men, than that they should be praised by a thousand, and be without the praise of the good. Continue, most worthy Turner, continue with God's help to illuminate the darkness of our times.

43.

Ad Catabaptistam.

Catabaptist.—A nickname of the sixteenth and seventeenth centuries for any one who rejected the doctrines of the Church in regard to baptism.

The following is a translation of Grimald's Latin verses addressed *Ad Catabaptistam:*

To the Catabaptist

Friend, if you are wise, look to yourself. Beware lest you lose a good name among those that are good, lest you bring your body into danger, lest you lose your own soul in wrecking many. Two things I beg you to flee from with all your power. One is Ignorance, that great bane which knows not how to follow the light of Truth. The other, worse than that, the greatest plague of all, is Pride, resisting any desire to be taught. With me as your guide—were it as well with you as it is with me and mine!—with pious voice you will call upon the Holy Spirit, who into your heart will instil such humility that it may take counsel freely with itself, and, evil passions being cast aside, may inspire you with eager love for knowledge of the truth. If you will conform to this standard, then, when with mind attentive, unprejudiced, and well-disposed, you have read this book, instructed as you will be, you will return to the right way.

44.

To the reder.

1. *Stedis.*—Substitutes.
2. *Clenge.*—Get rid of.
3. *Alexander.*—An umbelliferous plant, formerly cultivated and eaten like celery. The seeds were used for medicine.
4. *Woolfbane.*—Monkshood or aconite.

46.

Nicolas Grimoaldus, ad Thomam Cooperum.

Thomas Cooper (1519?-1594), Bishop of Winchester and writer, was born at Oxford, where he was educated at Magdalen College. He became Master of Magdalen College School, and afterwards practised as a physician in Oxford. His literary career began in 1548, when he edited a Latin dictionary, *Bibliotheca Eliotæ,* and in 1549 he published a continuation of Thomas Lanquet's *Chronicle of the World,* known as *Cooper's Chronicle.* In 1565 appeared the first edition of his greatest work, *Thesaurus Linguæ Romanæ et Britannicæ,* and this was followed by three other editions.

Queen Elizabeth was so pleased with the *Thesaurus,* generally known as Cooper's Dictionary, that she expressed her determination to promote the author as far as lay in her power. He became subsequently Dean of Christ Church in 1567, Dean of Gloucester in 1569, in 1571 Bishop of Lincoln, and in 1584 Bishop of Winchester.